D0734443

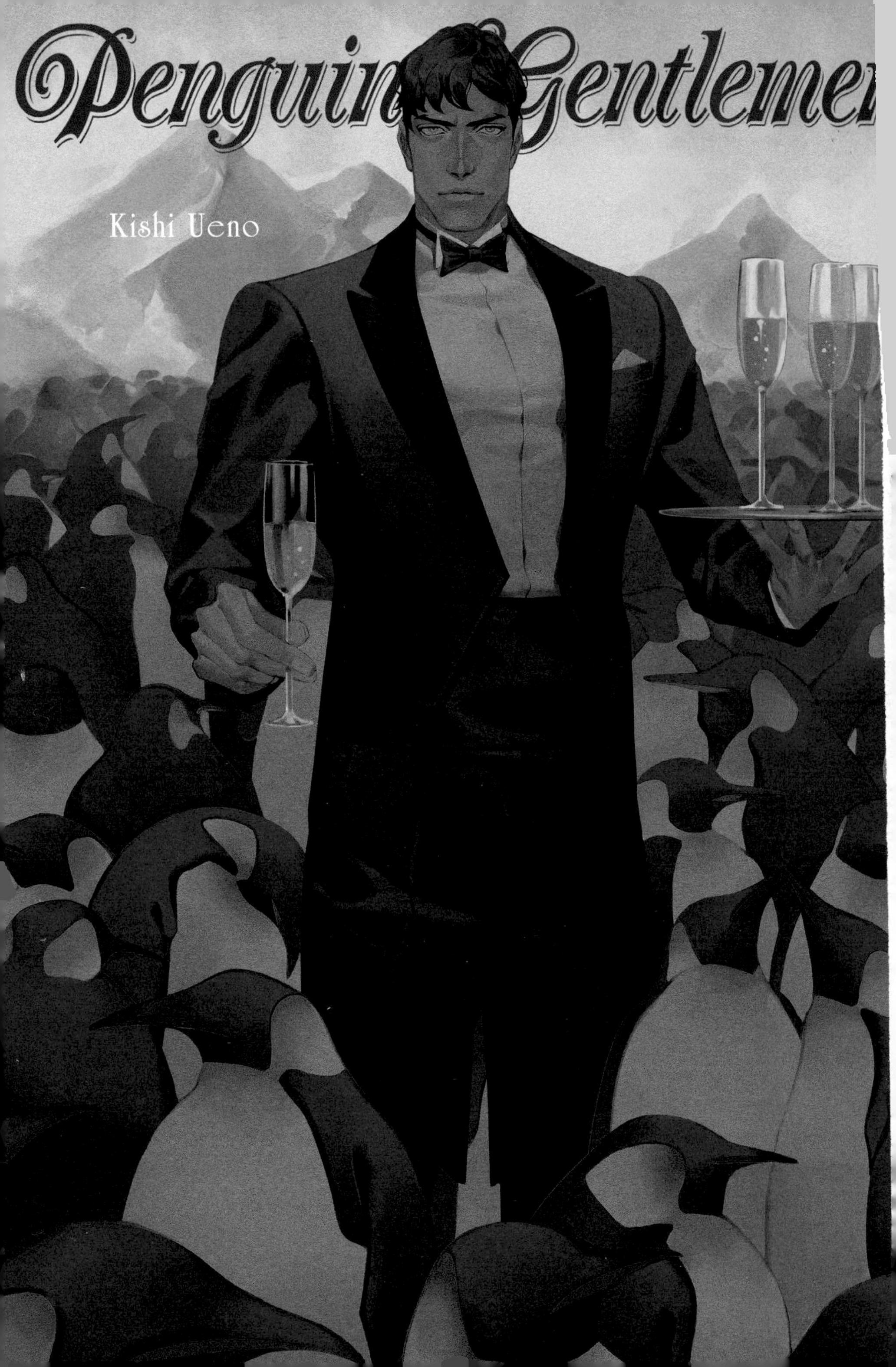
Penguin Gentlemen
Kishi Ueno

◆ Prologue ◆

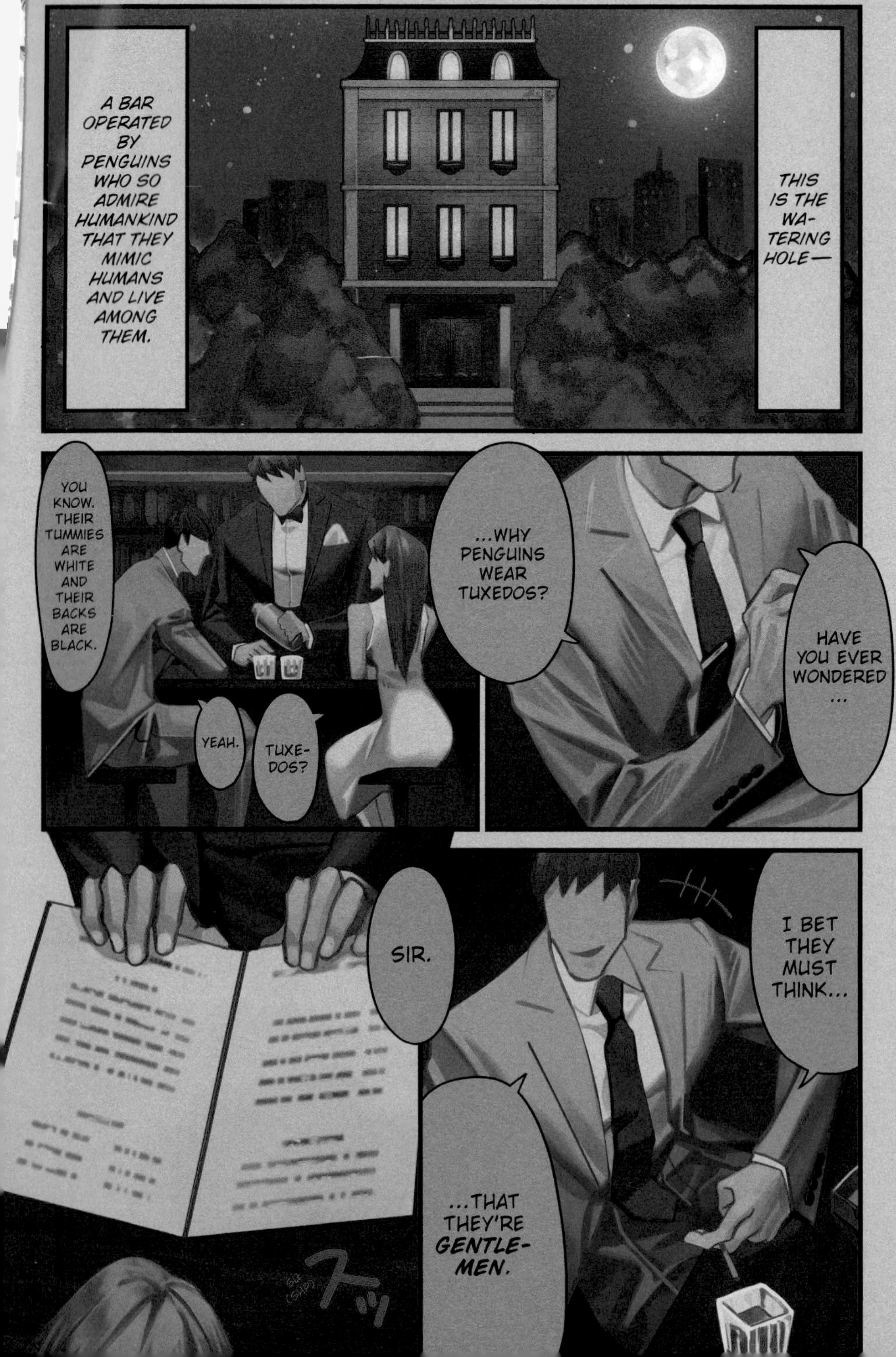

THIS IS THE WA-TERING HOLE—
A BAR OPERATED BY PENGUINS WHO SO ADMIRE HUMANKIND THAT THEY MIMIC HUMANS AND LIVE AMONG THEM.
HAVE YOU EVER WONDERED...
...WHY PENGUINS WEAR TUXEDOS?
TUXE-DOS?
YEAH.
YOU KNOW. THEIR TUMMIES ARE WHITE AND THEIR BACKS ARE BLACK.
I BET THEY MUST THINK...
...THAT THEY'RE *GENTLE-MEN.*
SIR.
スッ

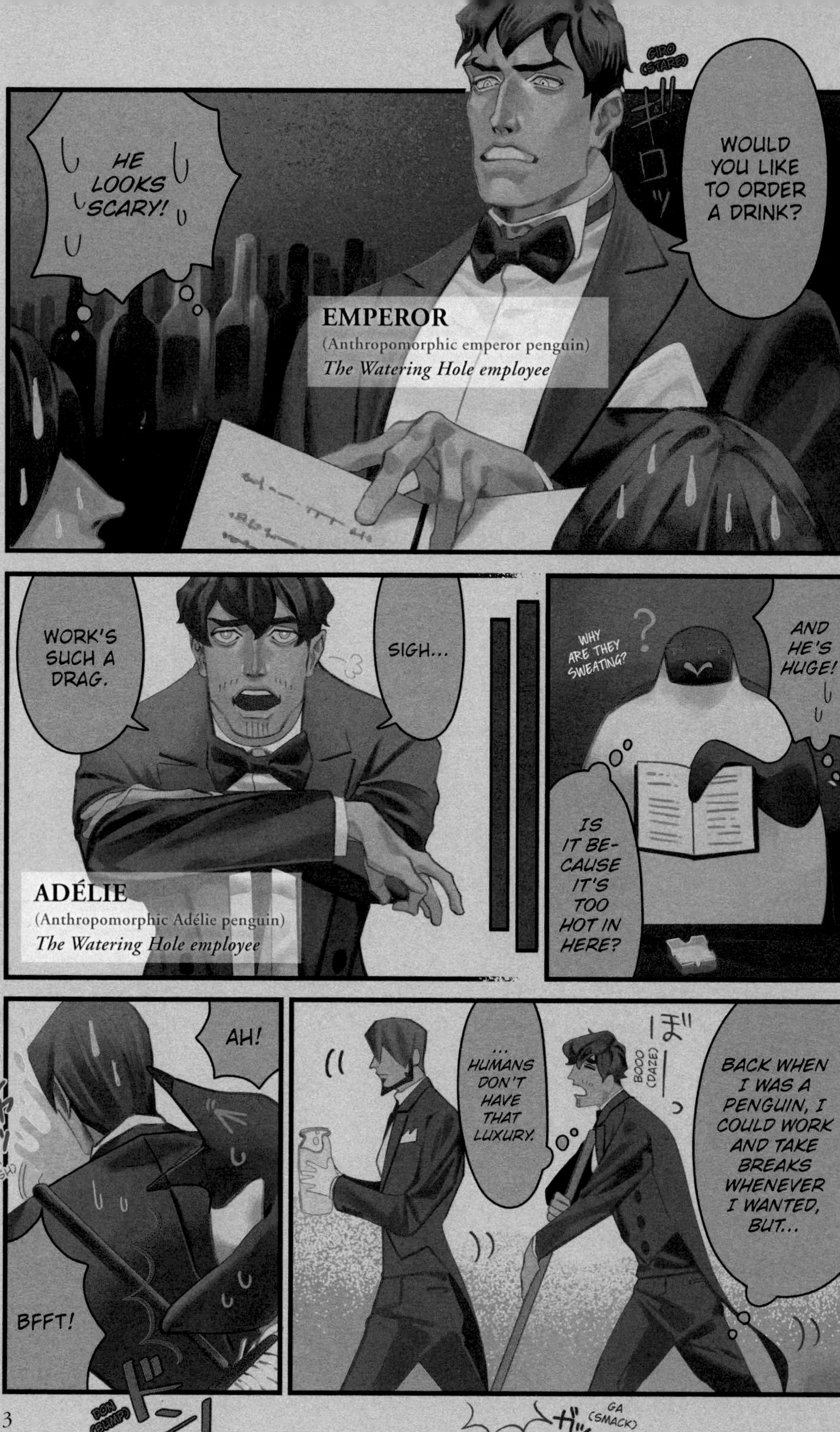
WOULD YOU LIKE TO ORDER A DRINK?
GIRO (STARE)
HE LOOKS SCARY!
EMPEROR
(Anthropomorphic emperor penguin)
The Watering Hole employee
AND HE'S HUGE!
WHY ARE THEY SWEATING?
IS IT BECAUSE IT'S TOO HOT IN HERE?
SIGH...
WORK'S SUCH A DRAG.
ADÉLIE
(Anthropomorphic Adélie penguin)
The Watering Hole employee
BACK WHEN I WAS A PENGUIN, I COULD WORK AND TAKE BREAKS WHENEVER I WANTED, BUT...
BOOO (DAZE)
...HUMANS DON'T HAVE THAT LUXURY.
GA (SMACK)
AH!
BISHA (SPLASH)
BFFT!
DON (BUMP)

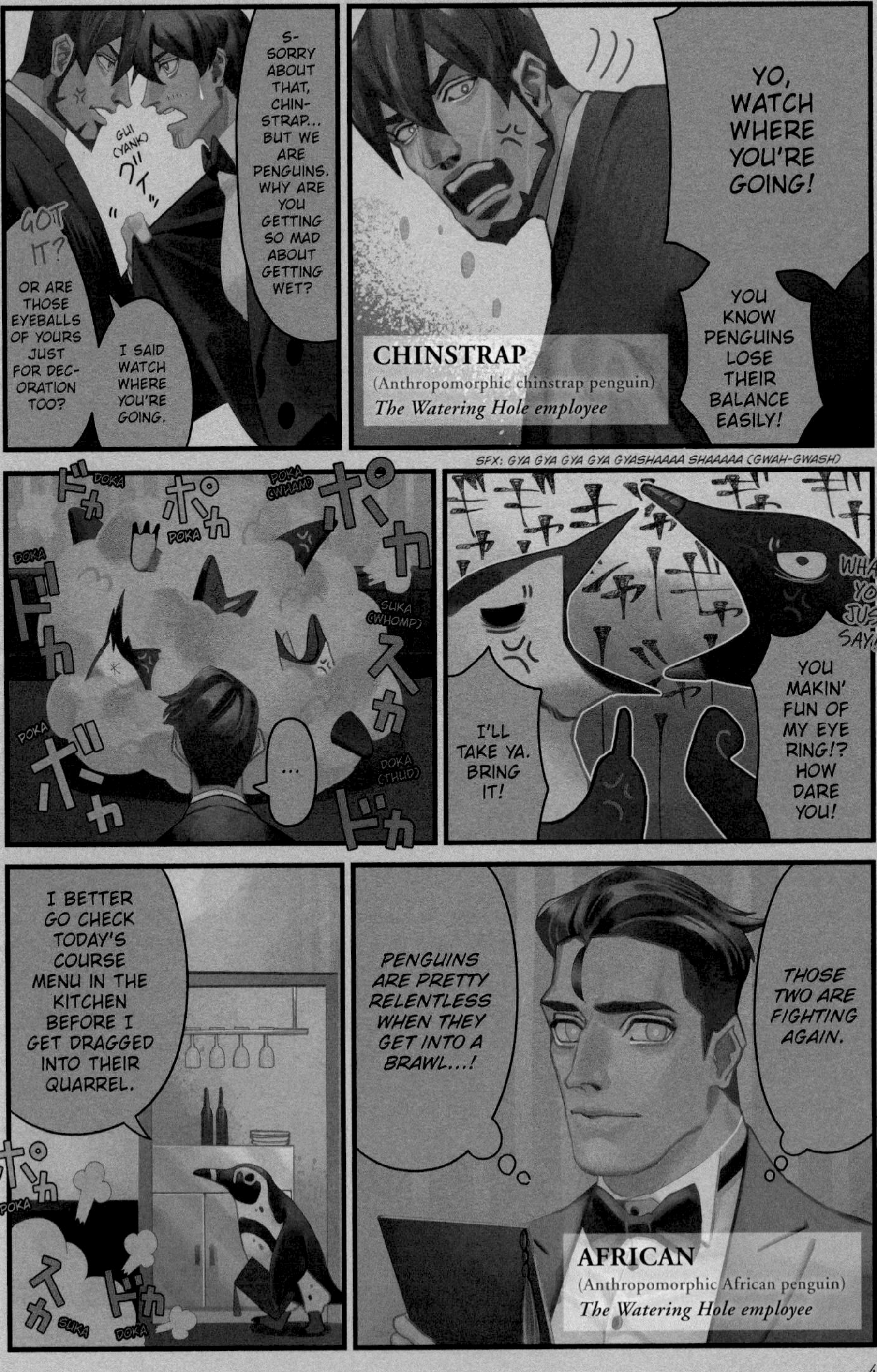
YO, WATCH WHERE YOU'RE GOING!
YOU KNOW PENGUINS LOSE THEIR BALANCE EASILY!
CHINSTRAP
(Anthropomorphic chinstrap penguin)
The Watering Hole employee
S-SORRY ABOUT THAT, CHINSTRAP... BUT WE ARE PENGUINS. WHY ARE YOU GETTING SO MAD ABOUT GETTING WET?
GUI (YANK)
GOT IT?
OR ARE THOSE EYEBALLS OF YOURS JUST FOR DECORATION TOO?
I SAID WATCH WHERE YOU'RE GOING.
SFX: GYA GYA GYA GYA GYASHAAAA SHAAAAA (GWAH-GWASH)
WHAT'D YOU JUST SAY!?
YOU MAKIN' FUN OF MY EYE RING!? HOW DARE YOU!
I'LL TAKE YA. BRING IT!
POKA (WHAM)
DOKA
POKA
DOKA
SUKA (WHOMP)
...
DOKA (THUD)
POKA
THOSE TWO ARE FIGHTING AGAIN.
PENGUINS ARE PRETTY RELENTLESS WHEN THEY GET INTO A BRAWL...!
AFRICAN
(Anthropomorphic African penguin)
The Watering Hole employee
I BETTER GO CHECK TODAY'S COURSE MENU IN THE KITCHEN BEFORE I GET DRAGGED INTO THEIR QUARREL.
POKA
DOKA
SUKA

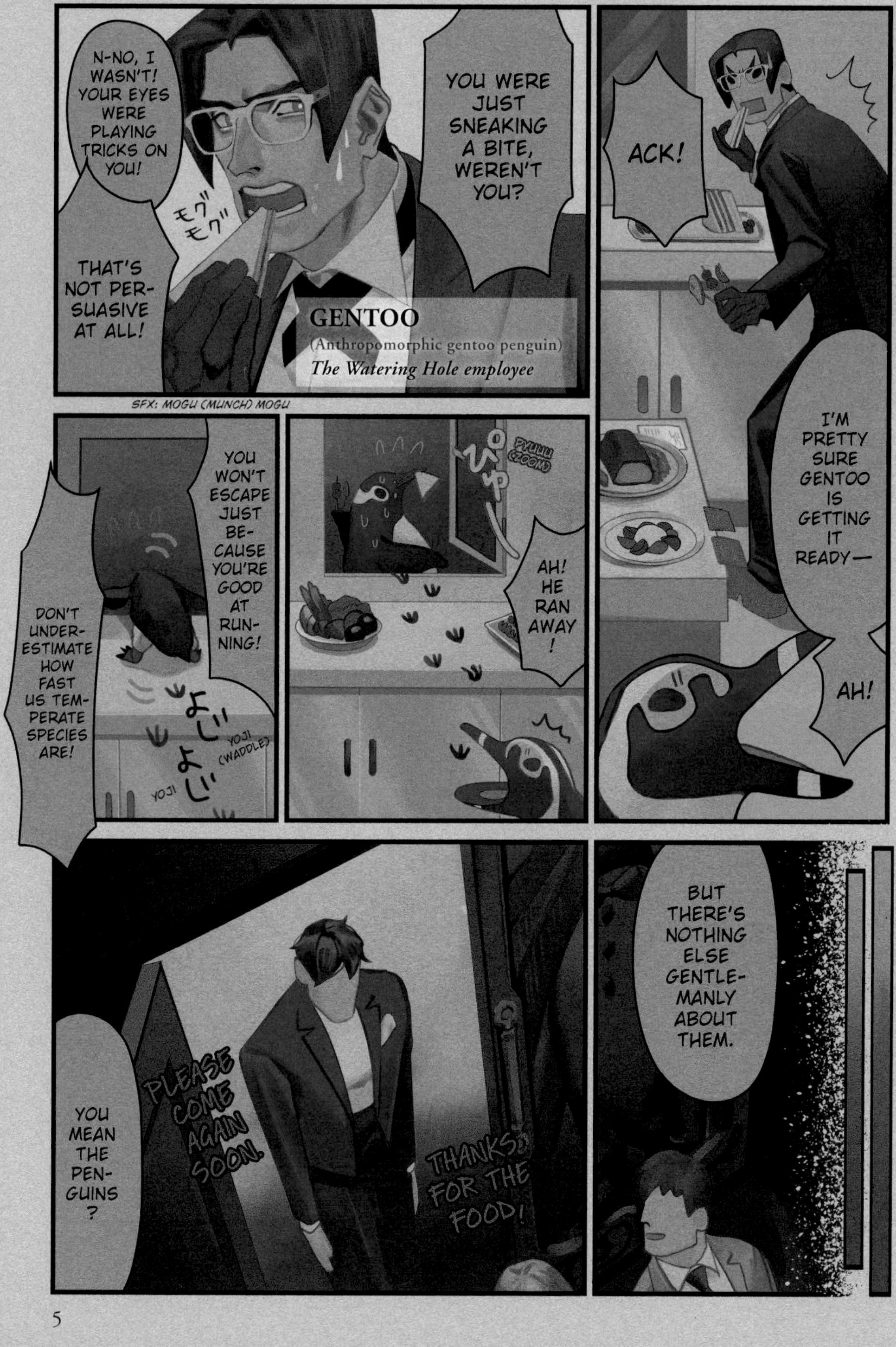

ACK!
I'M PRETTY SURE GENTOO IS GETTING IT READY—
AH!
YOU WERE JUST SNEAKING A BITE, WEREN'T YOU?
N-NO, I WASN'T! YOUR EYES WERE PLAYING TRICKS ON YOU!
モグモグ
THAT'S NOT PERSUASIVE AT ALL!
GENTOO
(Anthropomorphic gentoo penguin)
The Watering Hole employee
SFX: MOGU (MUNCH) MOGU
ぴゅ
PYUUU (ZOOM)
AH! HE RAN AWAY!
YOU WON'T ESCAPE JUST BECAUSE YOU'RE GOOD AT RUNNING!
DON'T UNDERESTIMATE HOW FAST US TEMPERATE SPECIES ARE!
よじよじ
YOJI (WADDLE) YOJI
BUT THERE'S NOTHING ELSE GENTLEMANLY ABOUT THEM.
THANKS FOR THE FOOD!
PLEASE COME AGAIN SOON.
YOU MEAN THE PENGUINS?

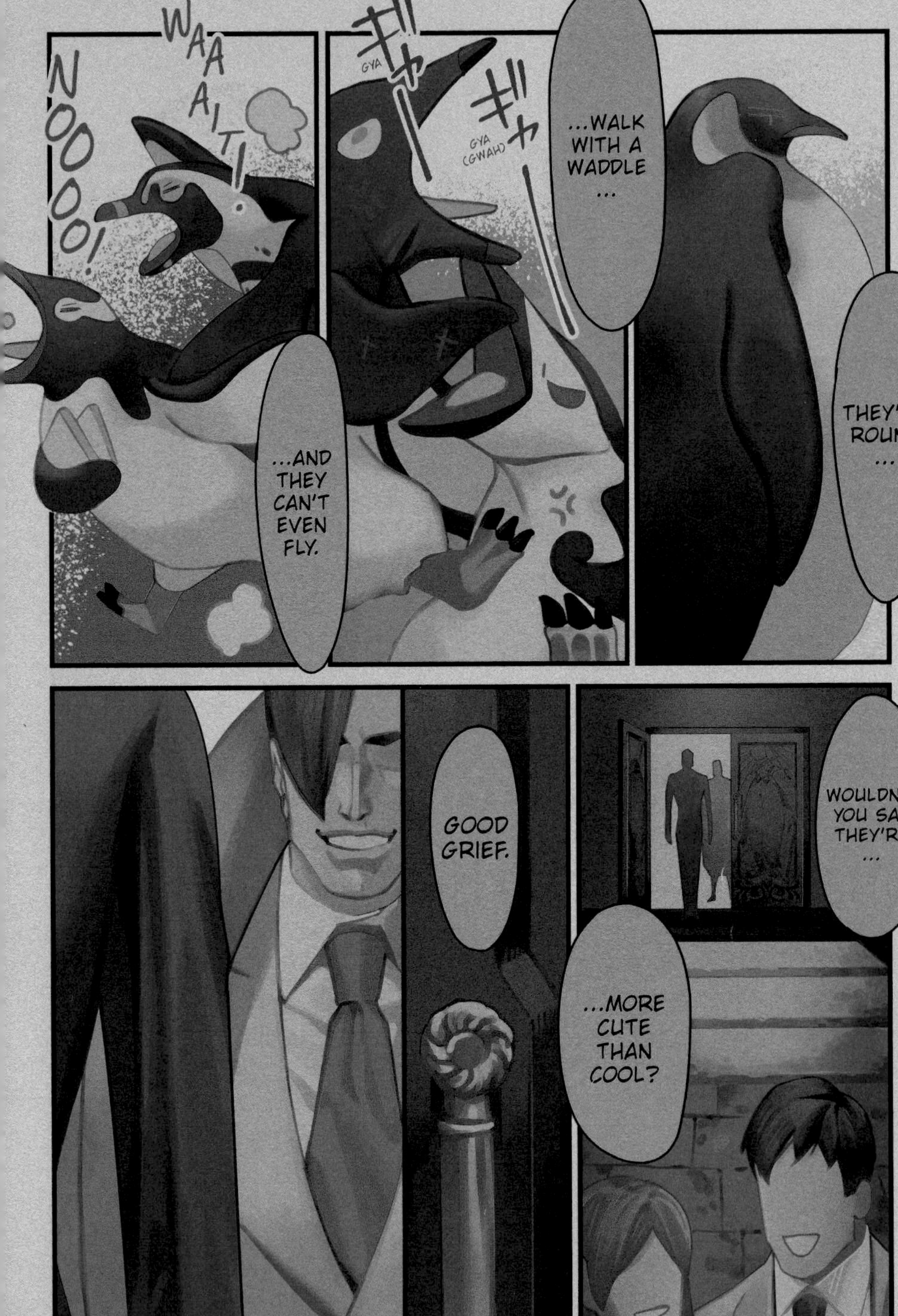

THEY'RE ROUND ...
...WALK WITH A WADDLE ...
GYA
GYA (GWAH)
...AND THEY CAN'T EVEN FLY.
WAAAAIT!
NOOOOO!
WOULDN'T YOU SAY THEY'RE ...
...MORE CUTE THAN COOL?
GOOD GRIEF.

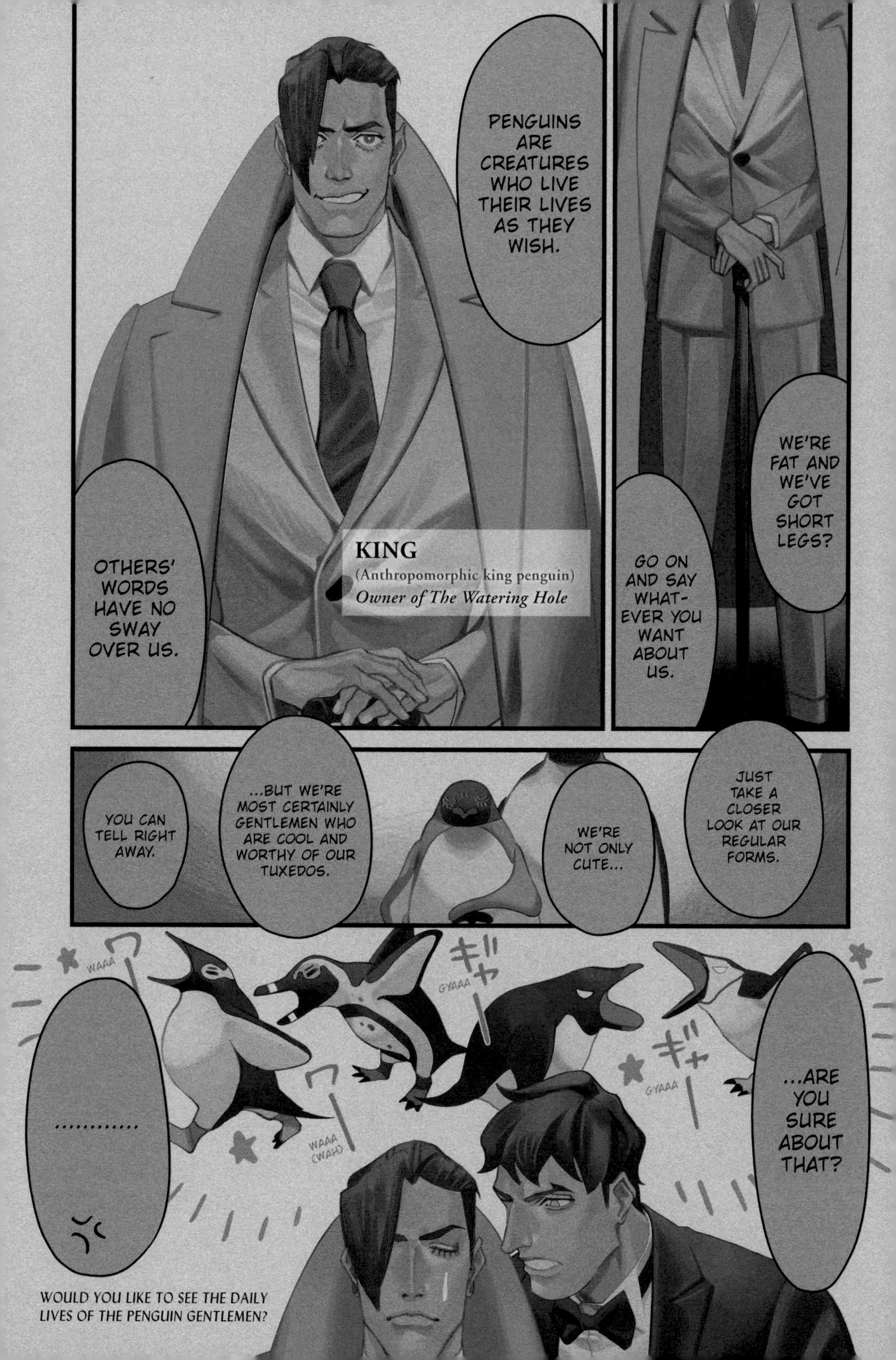
WE'RE FAT AND WE'VE GOT SHORT LEGS?
GO ON AND SAY WHAT-EVER YOU WANT ABOUT US.
PENGUINS ARE CREATURES WHO LIVE THEIR LIVES AS THEY WISH.
KING
(Anthropomorphic king penguin)
Owner of The Watering Hole
OTHERS' WORDS HAVE NO SWAY OVER US.
JUST TAKE A CLOSER LOOK AT OUR REGULAR FORMS.
WE'RE NOT ONLY CUTE...
...BUT WE'RE MOST CERTAINLY GENTLEMEN WHO ARE COOL AND WORTHY OF OUR TUXEDOS.
YOU CAN TELL RIGHT AWAY.
...ARE YOU SURE ABOUT THAT?
GYAAA
GYAAA
WAAA
WAAA (WAH)
....
WOULD YOU LIKE TO SEE THE DAILY LIVES OF THE PENGUIN GENTLEMEN?

CHARACTERS

IN A COUNTRY SIMILAR TO JAPAN, THERE ARE PENGUINS DISGUISED AS HUMANS WORKING AT A BAR.

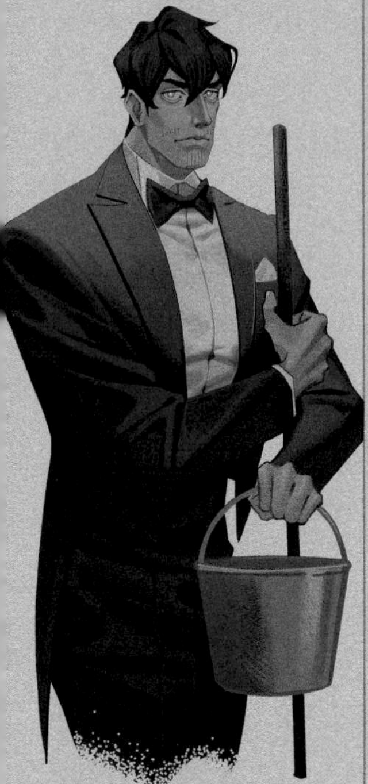

ADÉLIE

EMPLOYEE AT THE WATERING HOLE.
SERIOUS AND ATTENTIVE OF OTHERS BUT RELATIVELY SCATTERBRAINED.

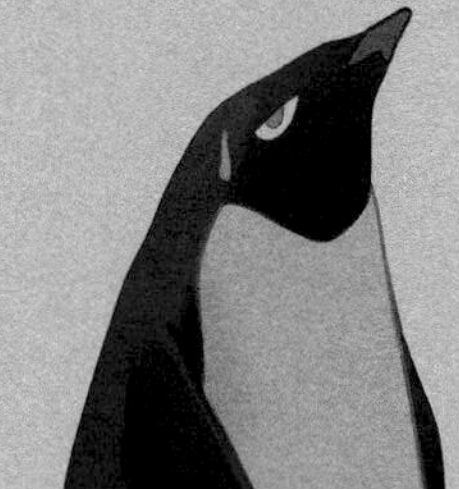

ADÉLIE PENGUIN

GENUS PYGOSCELIS.
DISTINGUISHED BY THE WHITE RINGS THAT ENCIRCLE ITS EYES. OFTEN USED IN BUSINESS LOGOS AND THE LIKE.

EMPEROR PENGUIN

GENUS APTENODYTES.
THE BIGGEST SPECIES AMONG PENGUINS.
RAISES ITS YOUNG DURING THE COLDEST TIMES OF THE YEAR IN ANTARCTICA.

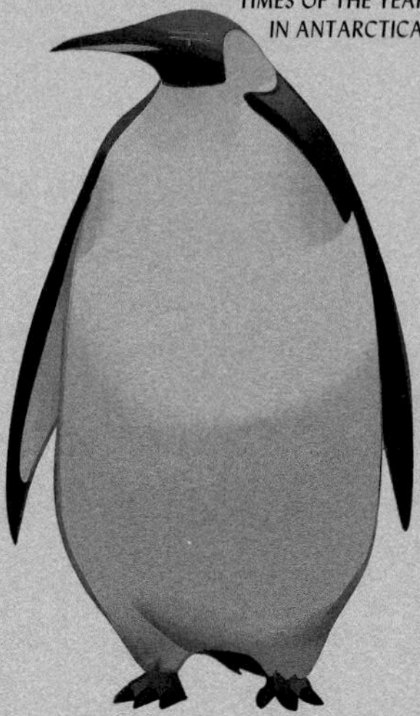

EMPEROR

EMPLOYEE AT THE WATERING HOLE.
HAS A SCARY FACE BUT IS A NATURAL GENTLE GIANT.

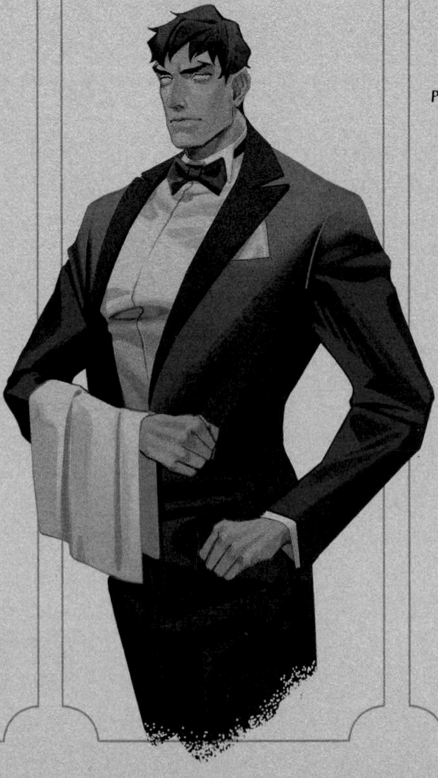

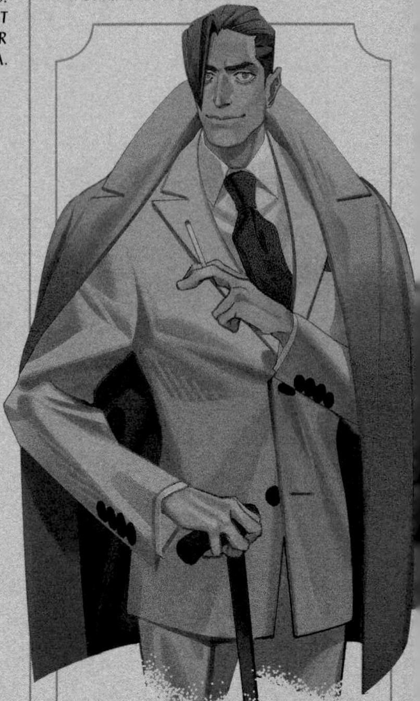

KING

THE OWNER OF THE WATERING HOLE.
PRIDEFUL AND A BIT OF AN EGOTIST BUT GOOD AT TAKING CARE OF OTHERS (ACCORDING TO HIM).

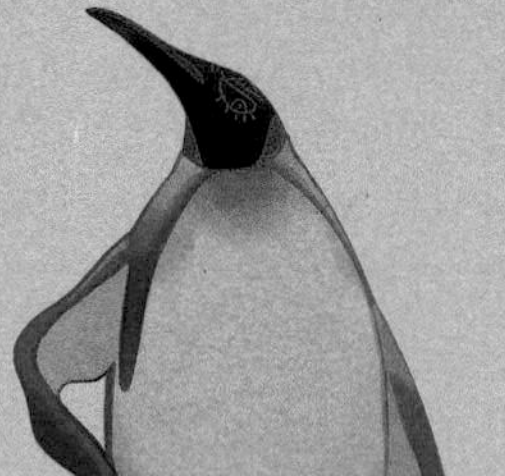

KING PENGUIN

GENUS APTENODYTES.
THE SECOND BIGGEST SPECIES AMONG PENGUINS. DISTINGUISHED BY ITS GRAY BACK AND COLORFUL MARKINGS.

Gentoo Penguin

GENUS PYGOSCELIS.
HAS A WHITE LINE THAT CONNECTS ITS EYES. THE FASTEST SWIMMERS AMONG PENGUINS.

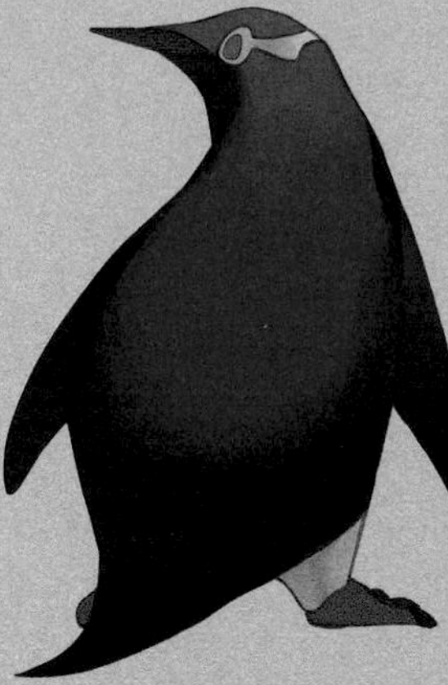

Gentoo

EMPLOYEE AT THE WATERING HOLE.
FRIENDLY AND A GLUTTON BRIMMING WITH CURIOSITY ABOUT ALL FOOD.
A BIT OF A COWARD.

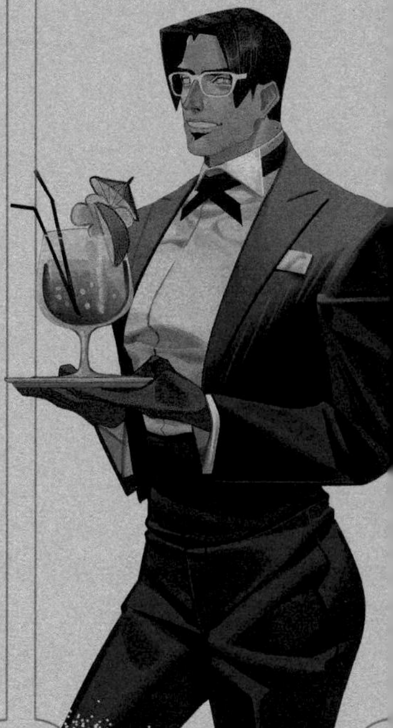

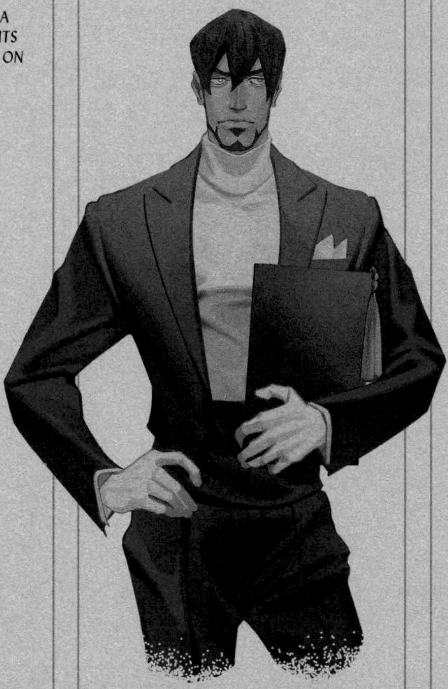

Chinstrap

EMPLOYEE AT THE WATERING HOLE.
TACITURN AND COLD TOWARD EVERYONE. QUICK TO LOSE HIS TEMPER BUT CARES A LOT ABOUT HIS FRIENDS.

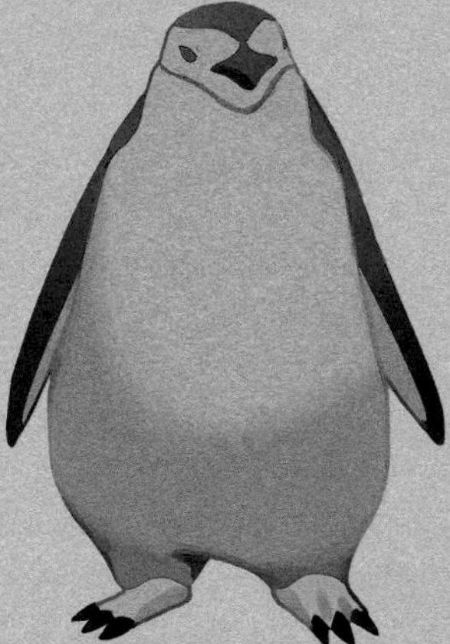

Chinstrap Penguin

GENUS PYGOSCELIS.
HAS A BLACK LINE THAT RUNS UNDER ITS CHIN, WHICH MAKES IT LOOK LIKE IT'S WEARING A HELMET.

African Penguin

GENUS SPHENISCUS.
A TEMPERATE SPECIES THAT HAS A BLACK BELT ENCIRCLING ITS TORSO, WITH SPOTS ON ITS BELLY.

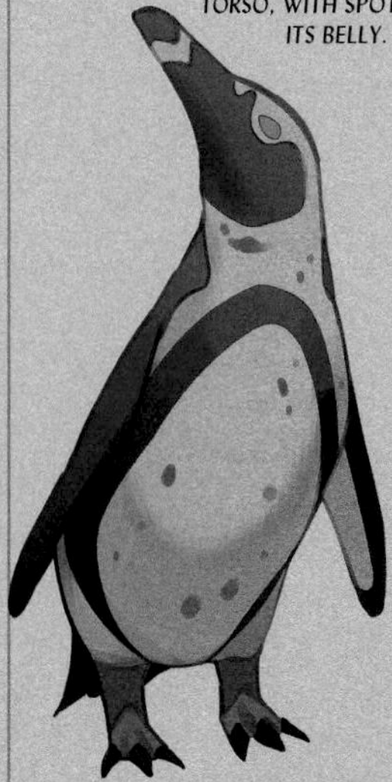

African

EMPLOYEE AT THE WATERING HOLE.
UP FRONT ABOUT HIS FEELINGS AND TACTFUL. A HARD WORKER WHO CAN ALSO BE SHY.

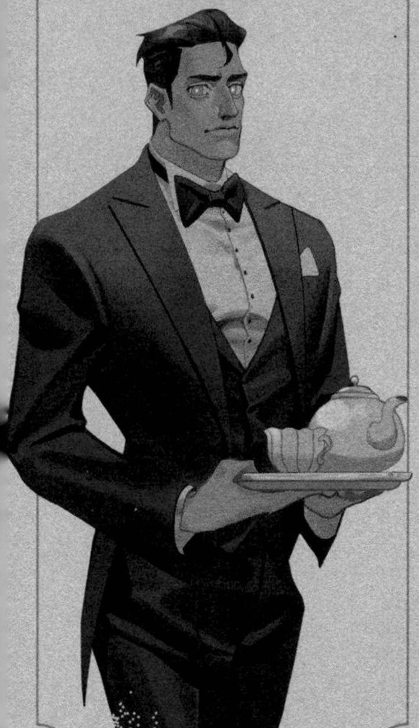

Contents

How to Tell Apart the Aptenodytes Penguins · The Origins of
Their Names · The Dexterous Aptenodytes Penguins · Emperor's
Brooding · Sense of Distance · There Are Different Degrees of
Coldness in Antarctica Too · Earrings · Flipper Slap · Huddling

Do You Know the Pygoscelis Penguins? · About Adélies · About
Gentoos · About Chinstraps · Differences in Pygoscelis Penguin
Personalities · Differences in Nests Among Pygoscelis Species ·
Adélie Heads · Gentoo's Feeding · How to Tell Genus Spheniscus
Penguins Apart · African's Name · African's Vocal Call · The Faces
of Temperate Zone Penguins · How Many Species Are There in All?

Staff

Supervisor: Kazuoki Ueda

Designer: Youko Akuta

DTP: Takuya Ogawa (Kokageya)

Proofreading: Bakushu Art Center

Penguin Gentlemen

Chapter 1

The King and the Emperor

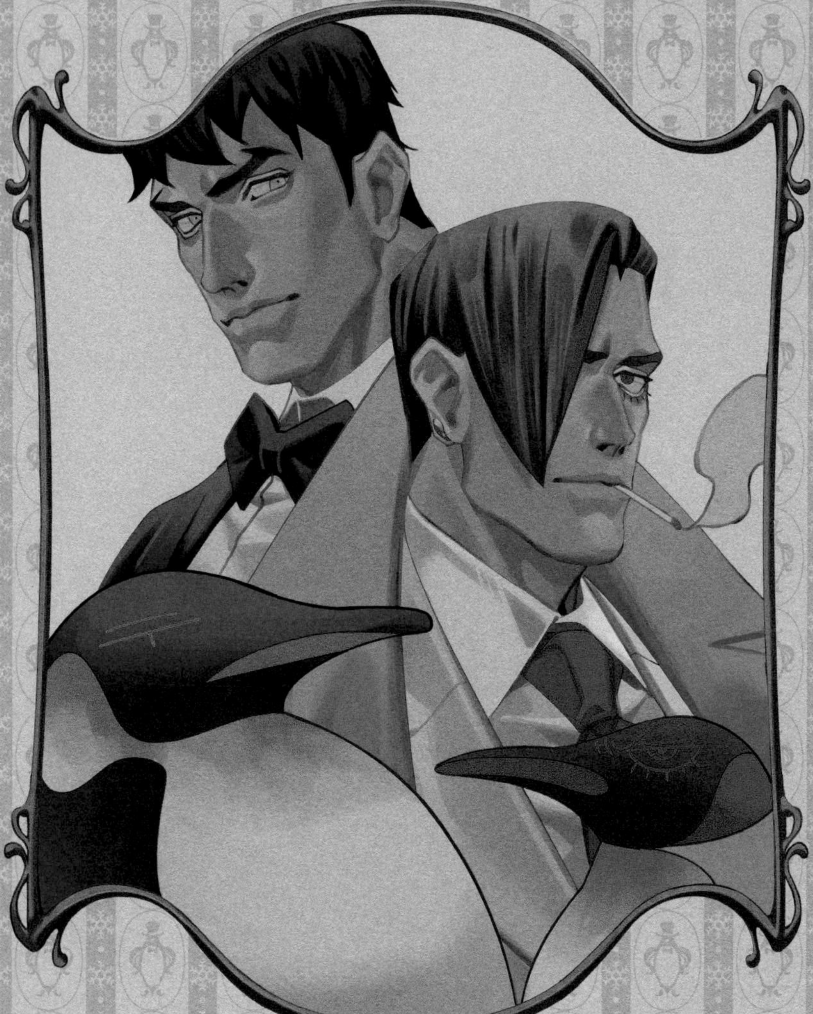

♦ How to Tell Apart the Aptenodytes Penguins ♦

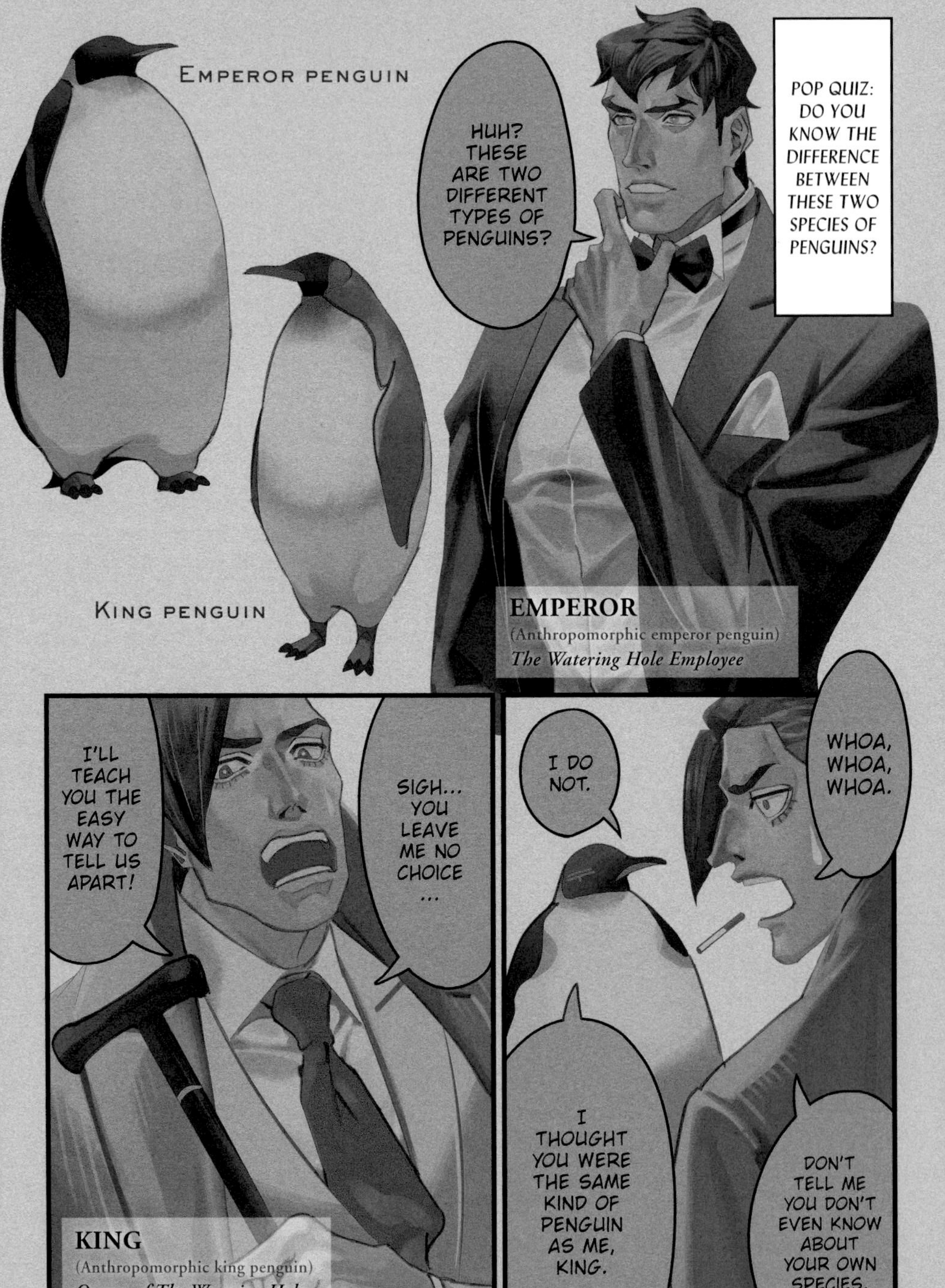
POP QUIZ: DO YOU KNOW THE DIFFERENCE BETWEEN THESE TWO SPECIES OF PENGUINS?
HUH? THESE ARE TWO DIFFERENT TYPES OF PENGUINS?
EMPEROR PENGUIN
KING PENGUIN
EMPEROR
(Anthropomorphic emperor penguin)
The Watering Hole Employee
WHOA, WHOA, WHOA.
I DO NOT.
DON'T TELL ME YOU DON'T EVEN KNOW ABOUT YOUR OWN SPECIES.
I THOUGHT YOU WERE THE SAME KIND OF PENGUIN AS ME, KING.
SIGH... YOU LEAVE ME NO CHOICE...
I'LL TEACH YOU THE EASY WAY TO TELL US APART!
KING
(Anthropomorphic king penguin)
Owner of The Watering Hole

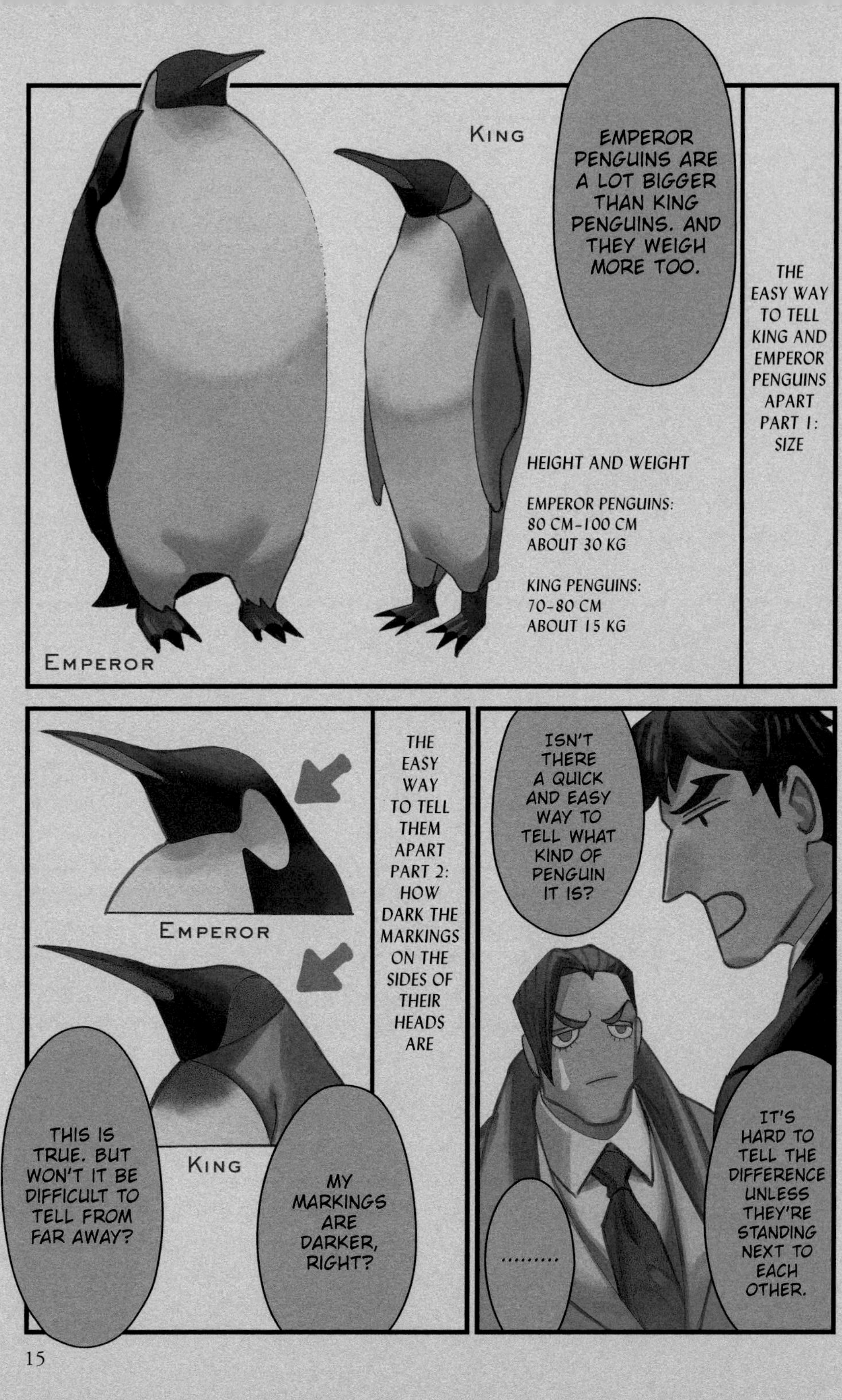
THE EASY WAY TO TELL KING AND EMPEROR PENGUINS APART PART 1: SIZE
EMPEROR PENGUINS ARE A LOT BIGGER THAN KING PENGUINS. AND THEY WEIGH MORE TOO.
KING
HEIGHT AND WEIGHT
EMPEROR PENGUINS: 80 CM-100 CM ABOUT 30 KG
KING PENGUINS: 70-80 CM ABOUT 15 KG
EMPEROR
ISN'T THERE A QUICK AND EASY WAY TO TELL WHAT KIND OF PENGUIN IT IS?
IT'S HARD TO TELL THE DIFFERENCE UNLESS THEY'RE STANDING NEXT TO EACH OTHER.
....
THE EASY WAY TO TELL THEM APART PART 2: HOW DARK THE MARKINGS ON THE SIDES OF THEIR HEADS ARE
EMPEROR
KING
MY MARKINGS ARE DARKER, RIGHT?
THIS IS TRUE. BUT WON'T IT BE DIFFICULT TO TELL FROM FAR AWAY?

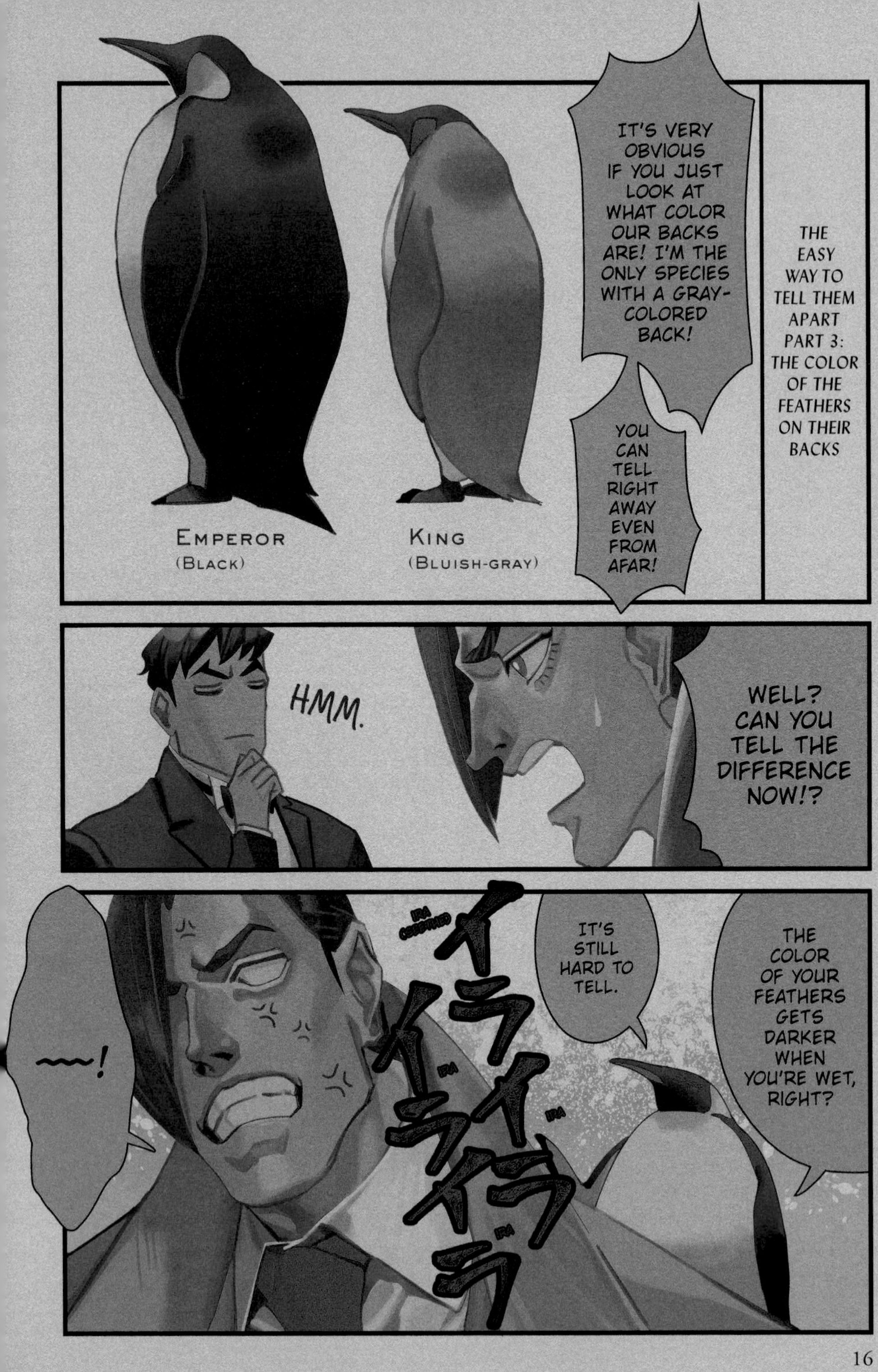
THE EASY WAY TO TELL THEM APART PART 3: THE COLOR OF THE FEATHERS ON THEIR BACKS
IT'S VERY OBVIOUS IF YOU JUST LOOK AT WHAT COLOR OUR BACKS ARE! I'M THE ONLY SPECIES WITH A GRAY-COLORED BACK!
YOU CAN TELL RIGHT AWAY EVEN FROM AFAR!
KING
(BLUISH-GRAY)
EMPEROR
(BLACK)
WELL? CAN YOU TELL THE DIFFERENCE NOW!?
HMM.
THE COLOR OF YOUR FEATHERS GETS DARKER WHEN YOU'RE WET, RIGHT?
IT'S STILL HARD TO TELL.
IRA
IRA
IRA
~~~!
~~~

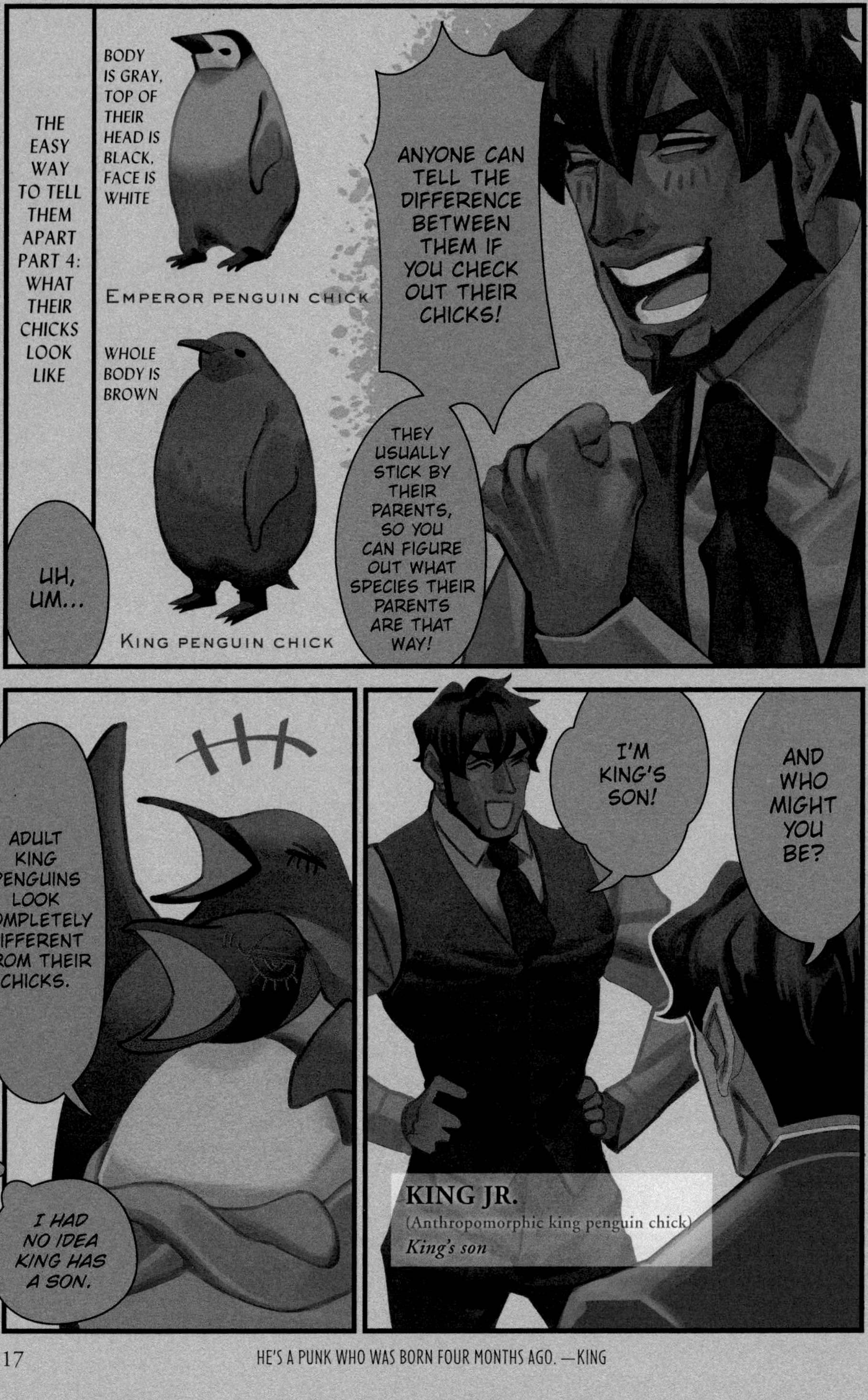
ANYONE CAN TELL THE DIFFERENCE BETWEEN THEM IF YOU CHECK OUT THEIR CHICKS!
THEY USUALLY STICK BY THEIR PARENTS, SO YOU CAN FIGURE OUT WHAT SPECIES THEIR PARENTS ARE THAT WAY!
BODY IS GRAY, TOP OF THEIR HEAD IS BLACK, FACE IS WHITE
EMPEROR PENGUIN CHICK
WHOLE BODY IS BROWN
KING PENGUIN CHICK
THE EASY WAY TO TELL THEM APART PART 4: WHAT THEIR CHICKS LOOK LIKE
UH, UM...
AND WHO MIGHT YOU BE?
I'M KING'S SON!
KING JR.
(Anthropomorphic king penguin chick)
King's son
ADULT KING PENGUINS LOOK COMPLETELY DIFFERENT FROM THEIR CHICKS.
I HAD NO IDEA KING HAS A SON.

HE'S A PUNK WHO WAS BORN FOUR MONTHS AGO. —KING

◆ The Origins of Their Names ◆

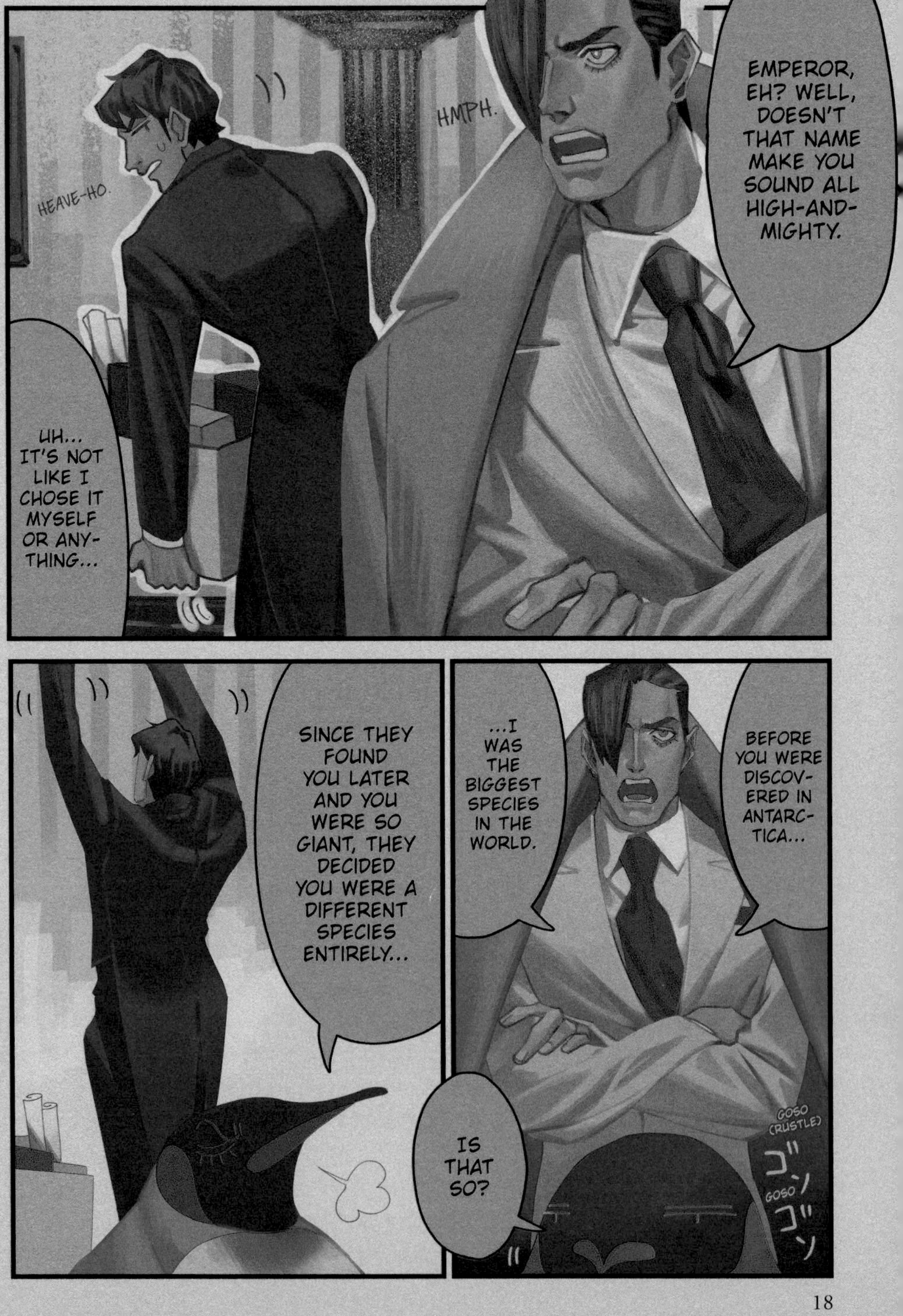
EMPEROR, EH? WELL, DOESN'T THAT NAME MAKE YOU SOUND ALL HIGH-AND-MIGHTY.
HMPH.
HEAVE-HO.
UH... IT'S NOT LIKE I CHOSE IT MYSELF OR ANY-THING...
BEFORE YOU WERE DISCOV-ERED IN ANTARC-TICA...
...I WAS THE BIGGEST SPECIES IN THE WORLD.
IS THAT SO?
GOSO (RUSTLE)
GOSO
SINCE THEY FOUND YOU LATER AND YOU WERE SO GIANT, THEY DECIDED YOU WERE A DIFFERENT SPECIES ENTIRELY...

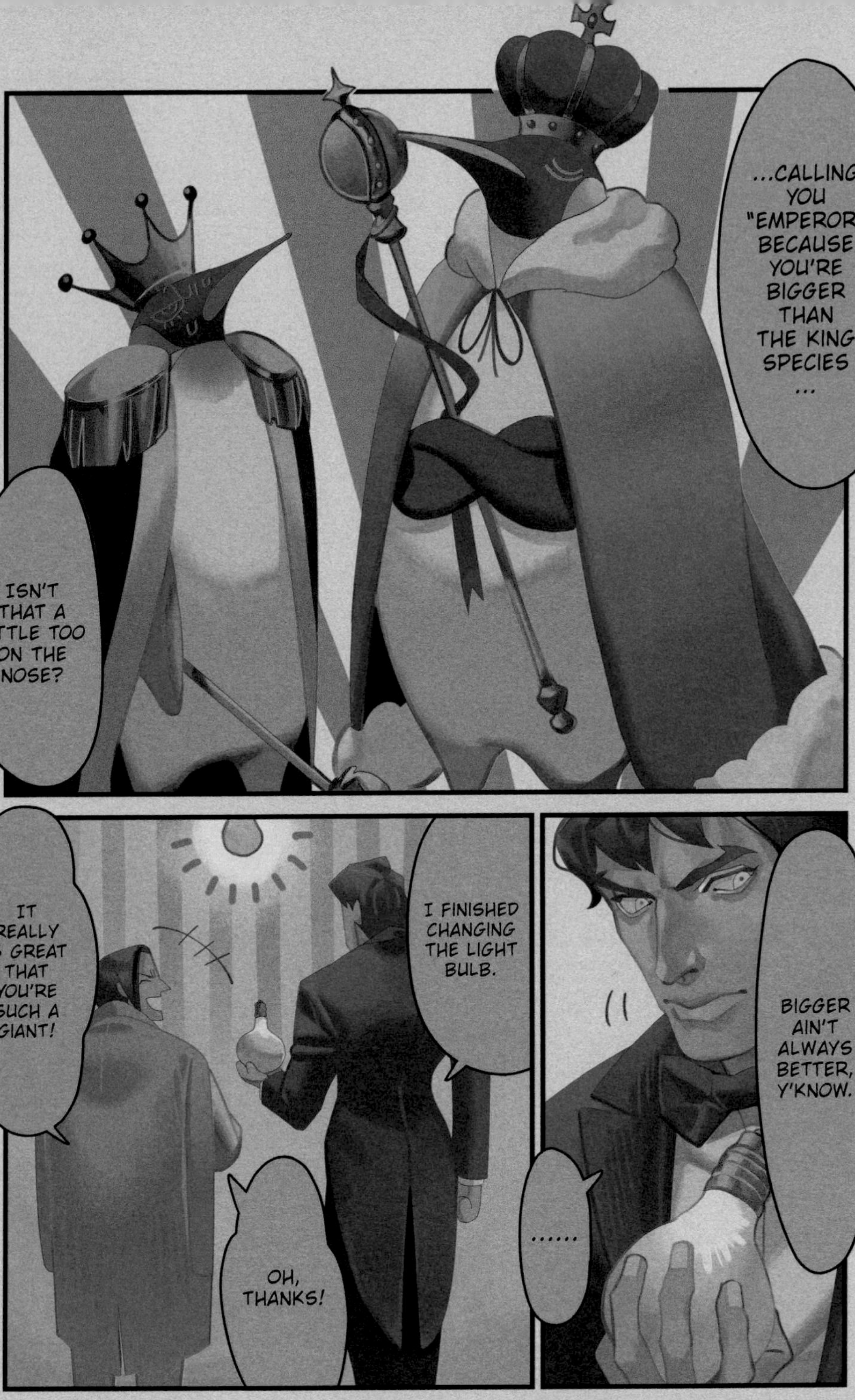
...CALLING YOU "EMPEROR" BECAUSE YOU'RE BIGGER THAN THE KING SPECIES...
ISN'T THAT A LITTLE TOO ON THE NOSE?
BIGGER AIN'T ALWAYS BETTER, Y'KNOW.
......
I FINISHED CHANGING THE LIGHT BULB.
IT REALLY IS GREAT THAT YOU'RE SUCH A GIANT!
OH, THANKS!

CAN'T YOU JUST ASK WITHOUT EXCUSES...? —EMPEROR

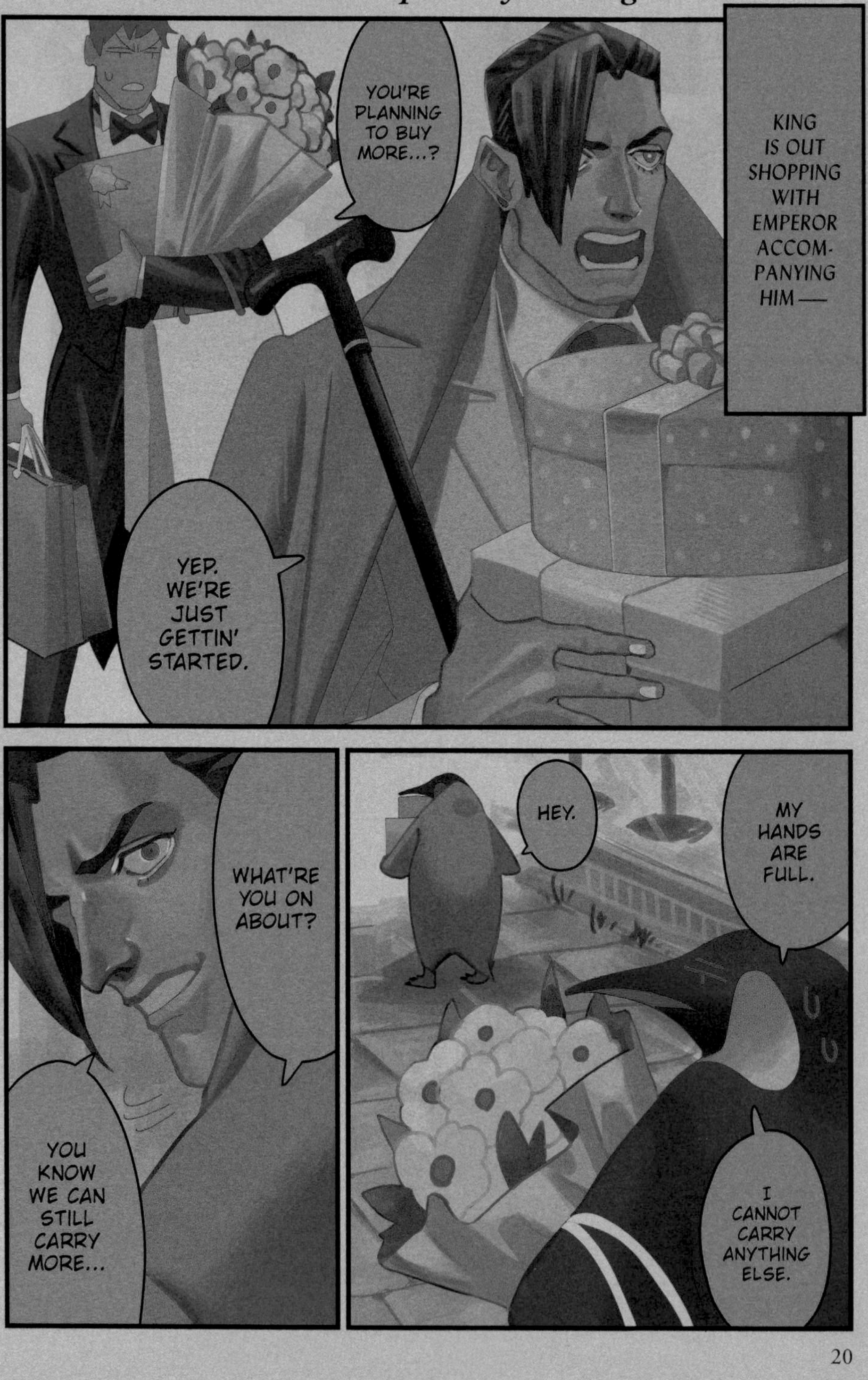
KING IS OUT SHOPPING WITH EMPEROR ACCOMPANYING HIM—
YOU'RE PLANNING TO BUY MORE...?
YEP. WE'RE JUST GETTIN' STARTED.
MY HANDS ARE FULL.
HEY.
I CANNOT CARRY ANYTHING ELSE.
WHAT'RE YOU ON ABOUT?
YOU KNOW WE CAN STILL CARRY MORE...

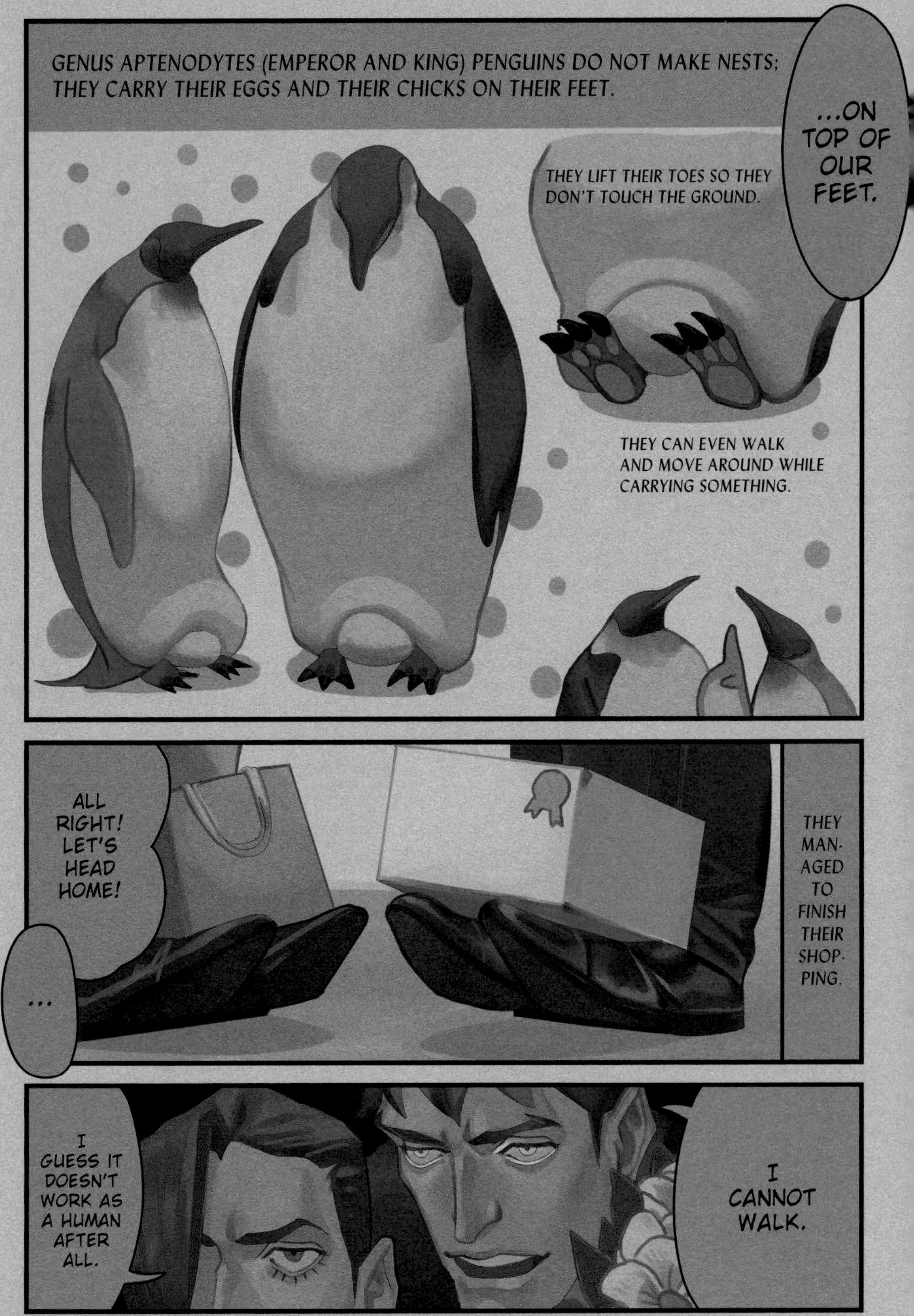
...ON TOP OF OUR FEET.
GENUS APTENODYTES (EMPEROR AND KING) PENGUINS DO NOT MAKE NESTS; THEY CARRY THEIR EGGS AND THEIR CHICKS ON THEIR FEET.
THEY LIFT THEIR TOES SO THEY DON'T TOUCH THE GROUND.
THEY CAN EVEN WALK AND MOVE AROUND WHILE CARRYING SOMETHING.
THEY MANAGED TO FINISH THEIR SHOPPING.
ALL RIGHT! LET'S HEAD HOME!
...
I CANNOT WALK.
I GUESS IT DOESN'T WORK AS A HUMAN AFTER ALL.

I QUIETLY CALLED A TAXI... —EMPEROR

♦ Emperor's Brooding ♦

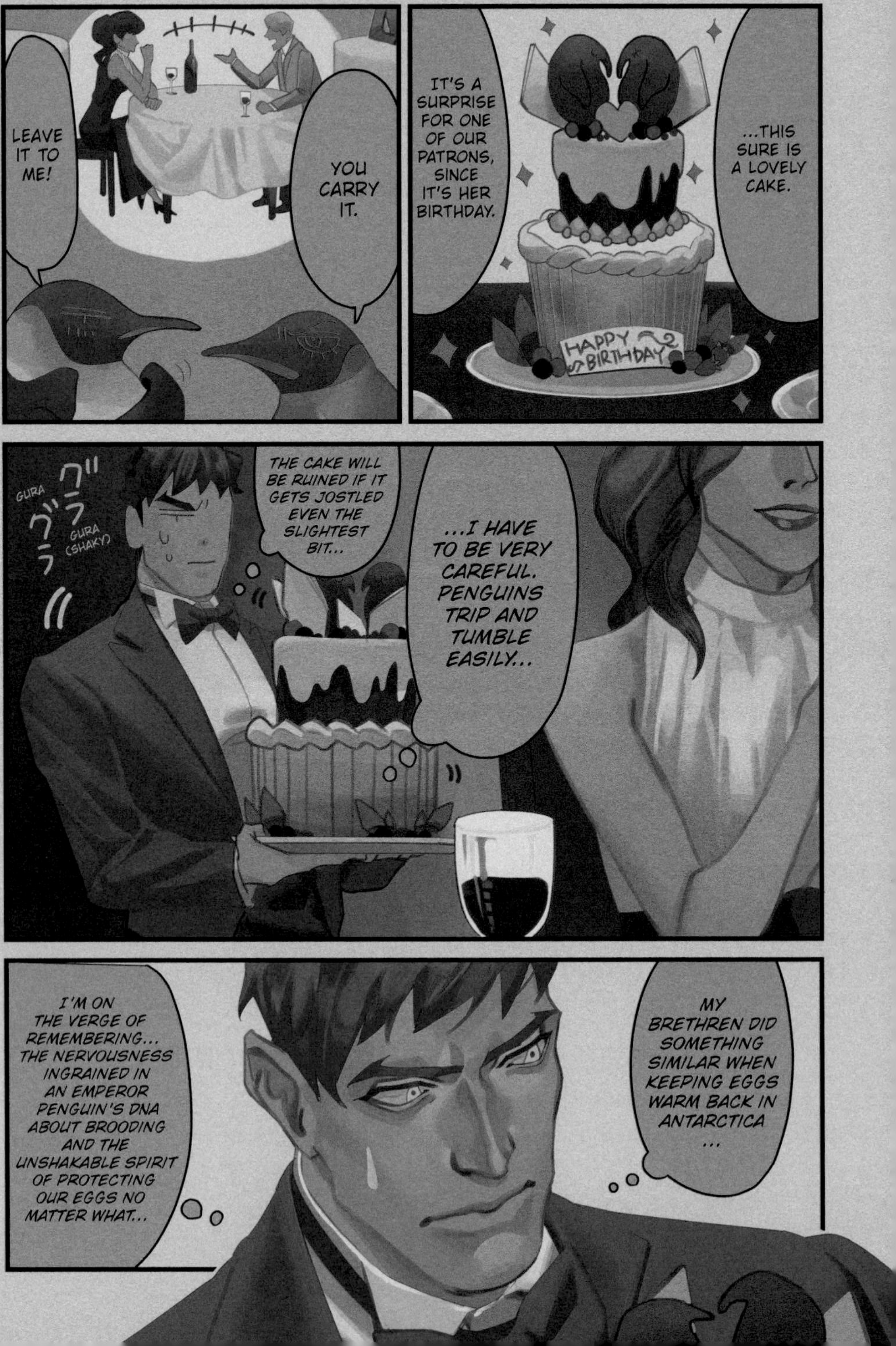
...THIS SURE IS A LOVELY CAKE.
IT'S A SURPRISE FOR ONE OF OUR PATRONS, SINCE IT'S HER BIRTHDAY.
HAPPY BIRTHDAY
YOU CARRY IT.
LEAVE IT TO ME!
...I HAVE TO BE VERY CAREFUL. PENGUINS TRIP AND TUMBLE EASILY...
THE CAKE WILL BE RUINED IF IT GETS JOSTLED EVEN THE SLIGHTEST BIT...
グラ GURA
グラ GURA (SHAKY)
MY BRETHREN DID SOMETHING SIMILAR WHEN KEEPING EGGS WARM BACK IN ANTARCTICA ...
I'M ON THE VERGE OF REMEMBERING... THE NERVOUSNESS INGRAINED IN AN EMPEROR PENGUIN'S DNA ABOUT BROODING AND THE UNSHAKABLE SPIRIT OF PROTECTING OUR EGGS NO MATTER WHAT...

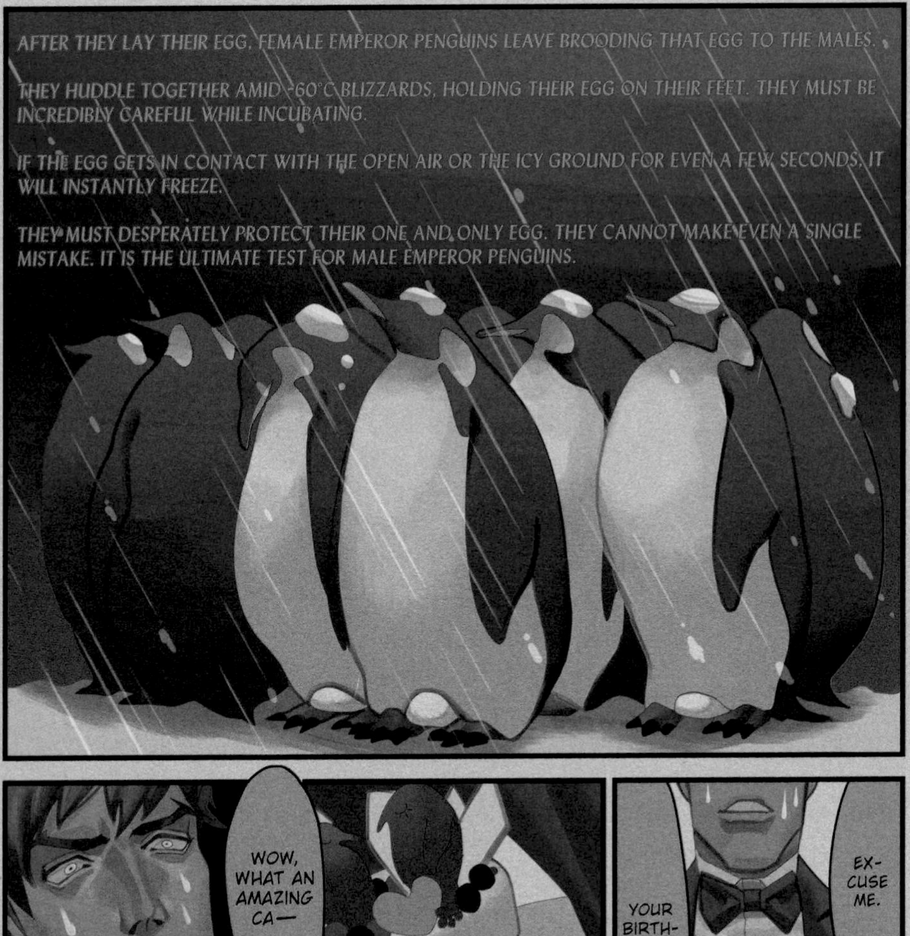
AFTER THEY LAY THEIR EGG, FEMALE EMPEROR PENGUINS LEAVE BROODING THAT EGG TO THE MALES.
THEY HUDDLE TOGETHER AMID -60°C BLIZZARDS, HOLDING THEIR EGG ON THEIR FEET. THEY MUST BE INCREDIBLY CAREFUL WHILE INCUBATING.
IF THE EGG GETS IN CONTACT WITH THE OPEN AIR OR THE ICY GROUND FOR EVEN A FEW SECONDS, IT WILL INSTANTLY FREEZE.
THEY MUST DESPERATELY PROTECT THEIR ONE AND ONLY EGG. THEY CANNOT MAKE EVEN A SINGLE MISTAKE. IT IS THE ULTIMATE TEST FOR MALE EMPEROR PENGUINS.
EX-CUSE ME.
YOUR BIRTH-DAY CAKE ...
OOH!
WOW, WHAT AN AMAZING CA—
HAPPY BIRTHDAY
...IS HERE.
WHY DOES HE HAVE SUCH A FRANTIC LOOK ON HIS FACE!?

I MANAGED TO COMPLETE MY TASK WITHOUT ANY INCIDENT... —EMPEROR (DAZED)

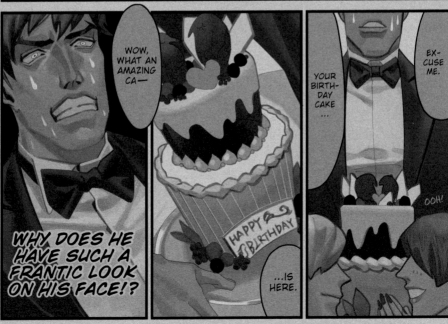

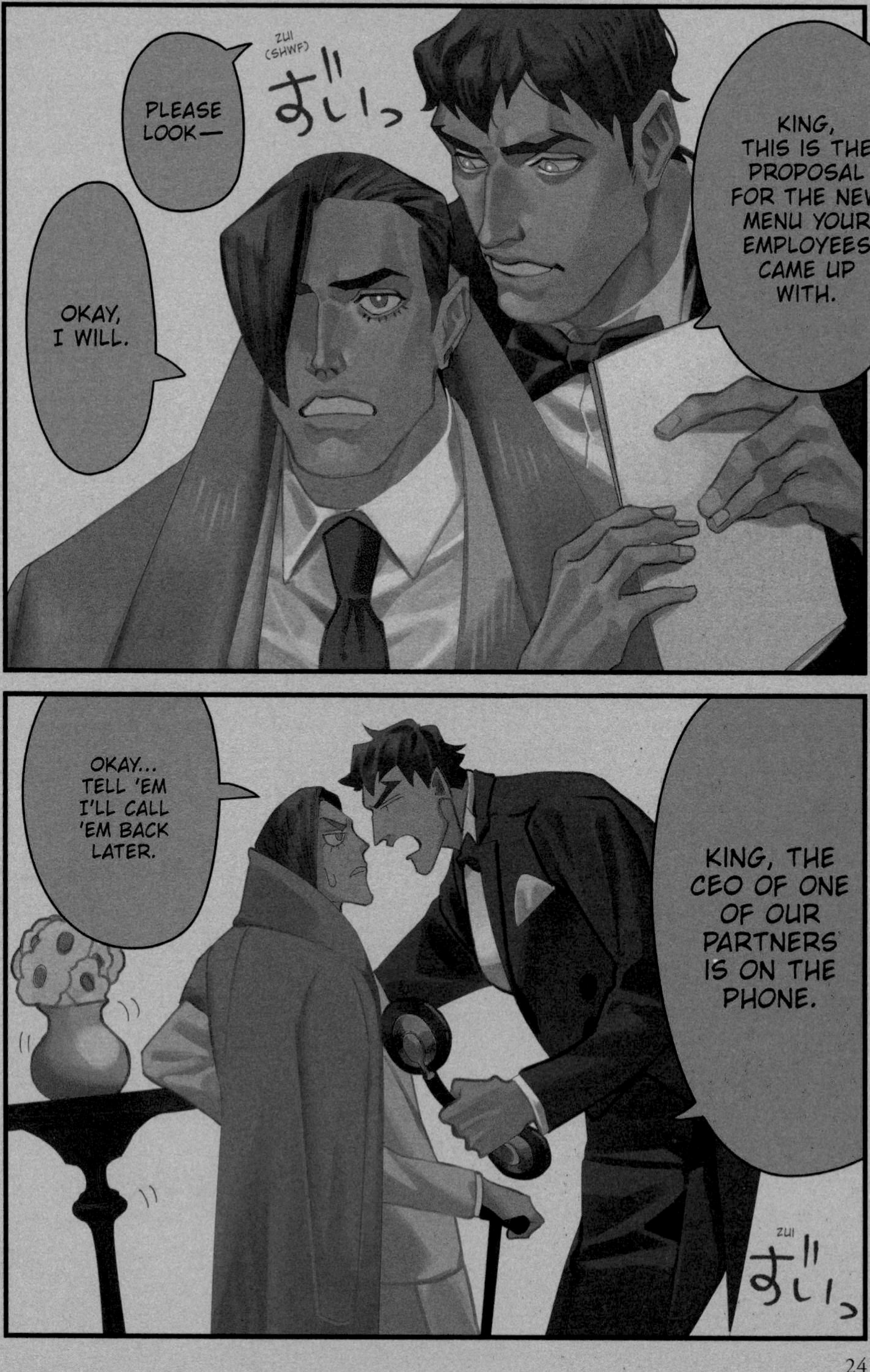
KING, THIS IS THE PROPOSAL FOR THE NEW MENU YOUR EMPLOYEES CAME UP WITH.
ずいっ
ZUI (SHWF)
PLEASE LOOK—
OKAY, I WILL.
KING, THE CEO OF ONE OF OUR PARTNERS IS ON THE PHONE.
ずいっ
ZUI
OKAY... TELL 'EM I'LL CALL 'EM BACK LATER.

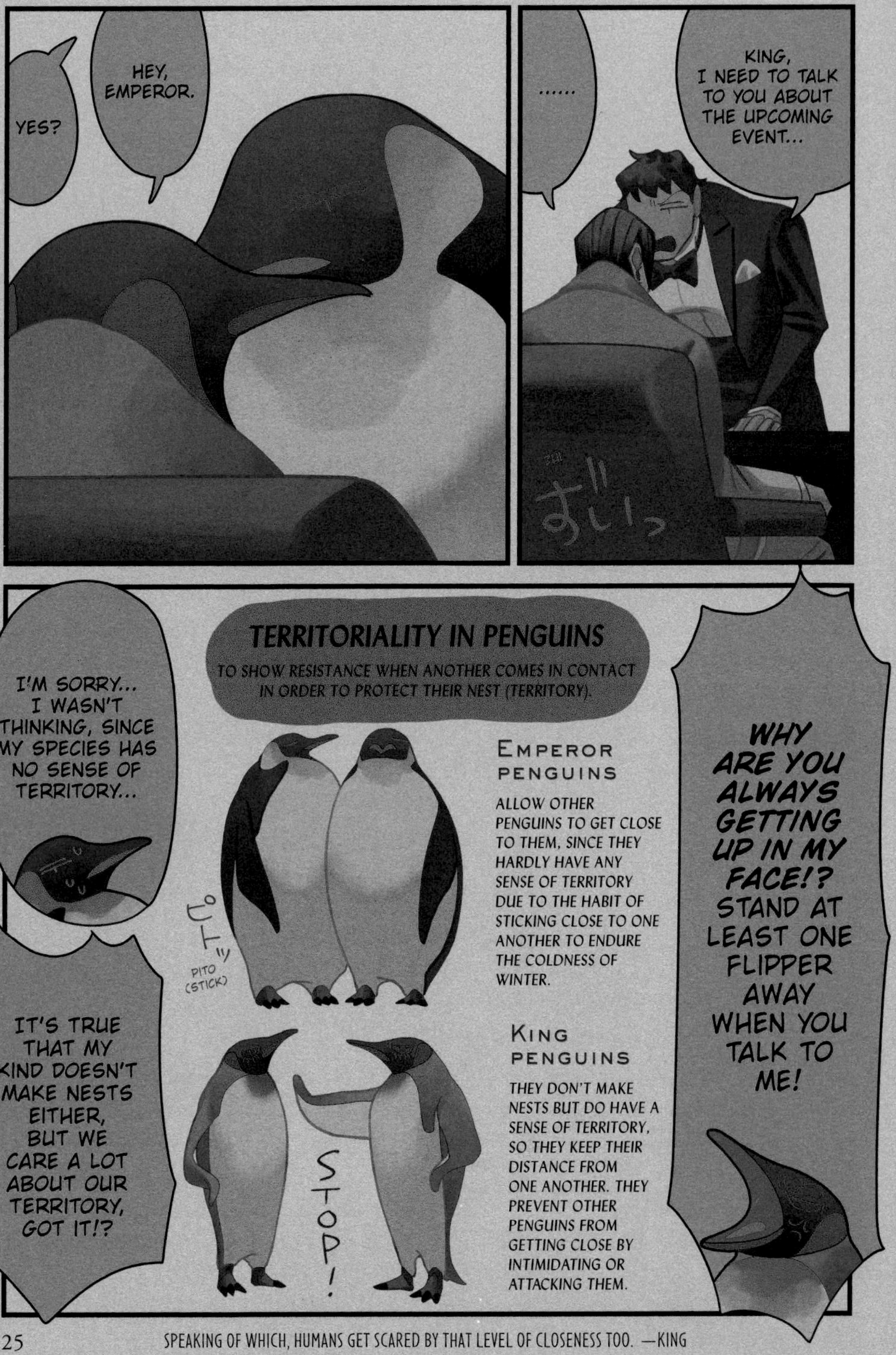
KING, I NEED TO TALK TO YOU ABOUT THE UPCOMING EVENT...
......
ずいっ
HEY, EMPEROR.
YES?
WHY ARE YOU ALWAYS GETTING UP IN MY FACE!? STAND AT LEAST ONE FLIPPER AWAY WHEN YOU TALK TO ME!
TERRITORIALITY IN PENGUINS
TO SHOW RESISTANCE WHEN ANOTHER COMES IN CONTACT IN ORDER TO PROTECT THEIR NEST (TERRITORY).
EMPEROR PENGUINS
ALLOW OTHER PENGUINS TO GET CLOSE TO THEM, SINCE THEY HARDLY HAVE ANY SENSE OF TERRITORY DUE TO THE HABIT OF STICKING CLOSE TO ONE ANOTHER TO ENDURE THE COLDNESS OF WINTER.
ピトッ
PITO (STICK)
KING PENGUINS
THEY DON'T MAKE NESTS BUT DO HAVE A SENSE OF TERRITORY, SO THEY KEEP THEIR DISTANCE FROM ONE ANOTHER. THEY PREVENT OTHER PENGUINS FROM GETTING CLOSE BY INTIMIDATING OR ATTACKING THEM.
STOP!
I'M SORRY... I WASN'T THINKING, SINCE MY SPECIES HAS NO SENSE OF TERRITORY...
IT'S TRUE THAT MY KIND DOESN'T MAKE NESTS EITHER, BUT WE CARE A LOT ABOUT OUR TERRITORY, GOT IT!?

SPEAKING OF WHICH, HUMANS GET SCARED BY THAT LEVEL OF CLOSENESS TOO. —KING

◆ *There Are Different Degrees of Coldness in Antarctica Too* ◆

IT'S COLD.

YEAH, THERE'S NO WAY I'M GOING OUT IN THIS.

BUT WE HAVE A MEETING WE NEED TO GET TO.

ABOUT -30°C OUTSIDE

ONE ESPECIALLY COLD NIGHT DURING A BLIZZARD

ビュオオオオ
BYUOOO (WHOOSH)

BYUOOO

THINK AGAIN, EMPER-OR!

THIS SHOULDN'T BE TOO COLD FOR YOU, RIGHT?

AREN'T YOU A PENGUIN FROM ANTARC-TICA?

MINE WILL AS WELL, THOUGH...

BECAUSE MY SHOES ARE GONNA GET ALL WET.

THEN CARRY ME ON YOUR BACK.

...WHY ARE YOU ON ME? YOU'RE HEAVY.

ひょいっ
HYOI (JUMP)

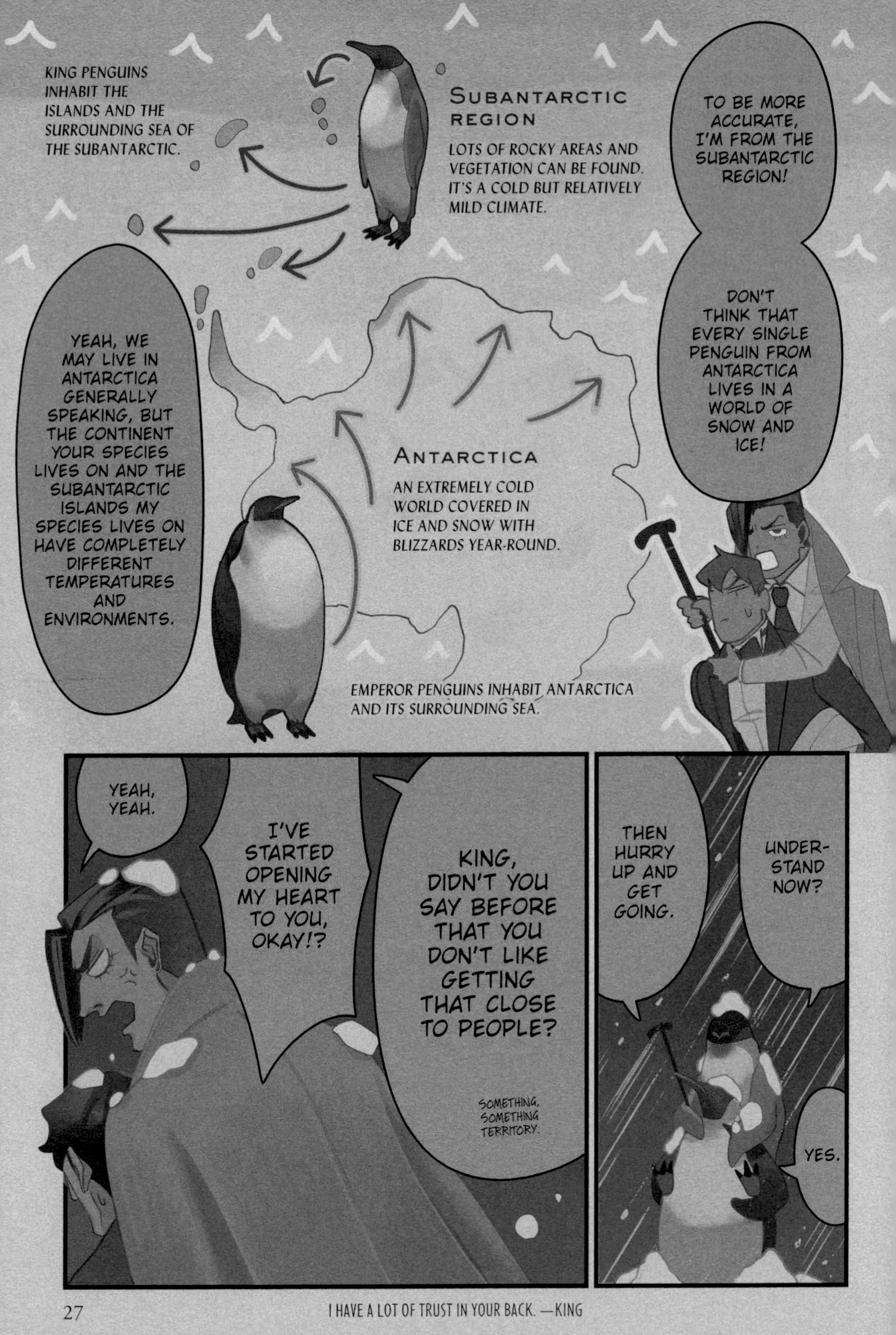
TO BE MORE ACCURATE, I'M FROM THE SUBANTARCTIC REGION!
DON'T THINK THAT EVERY SINGLE PENGUIN FROM ANTARCTICA LIVES IN A WORLD OF SNOW AND ICE!
SUBANTARCTIC REGION
LOTS OF ROCKY AREAS AND VEGETATION CAN BE FOUND. IT'S A COLD BUT RELATIVELY MILD CLIMATE.
KING PENGUINS INHABIT THE ISLANDS AND THE SURROUNDING SEA OF THE SUBANTARCTIC.
ANTARCTICA
AN EXTREMELY COLD WORLD COVERED IN ICE AND SNOW WITH BLIZZARDS YEAR-ROUND.
EMPEROR PENGUINS INHABIT ANTARCTICA AND ITS SURROUNDING SEA.
YEAH, WE MAY LIVE IN ANTARCTICA GENERALLY SPEAKING, BUT THE CONTINENT YOUR SPECIES LIVES ON AND THE SUBANTARCTIC ISLANDS MY SPECIES LIVES ON HAVE COMPLETELY DIFFERENT TEMPERATURES AND ENVIRONMENTS.
UNDER-STAND NOW?
THEN HURRY UP AND GET GOING.
YES.
KING, DIDN'T YOU SAY BEFORE THAT YOU DON'T LIKE GETTING THAT CLOSE TO PEOPLE?
SOMETHING, SOMETHING TERRITORY.
I'VE STARTED OPENING MY HEART TO YOU, OKAY!?
YEAH, YEAH.

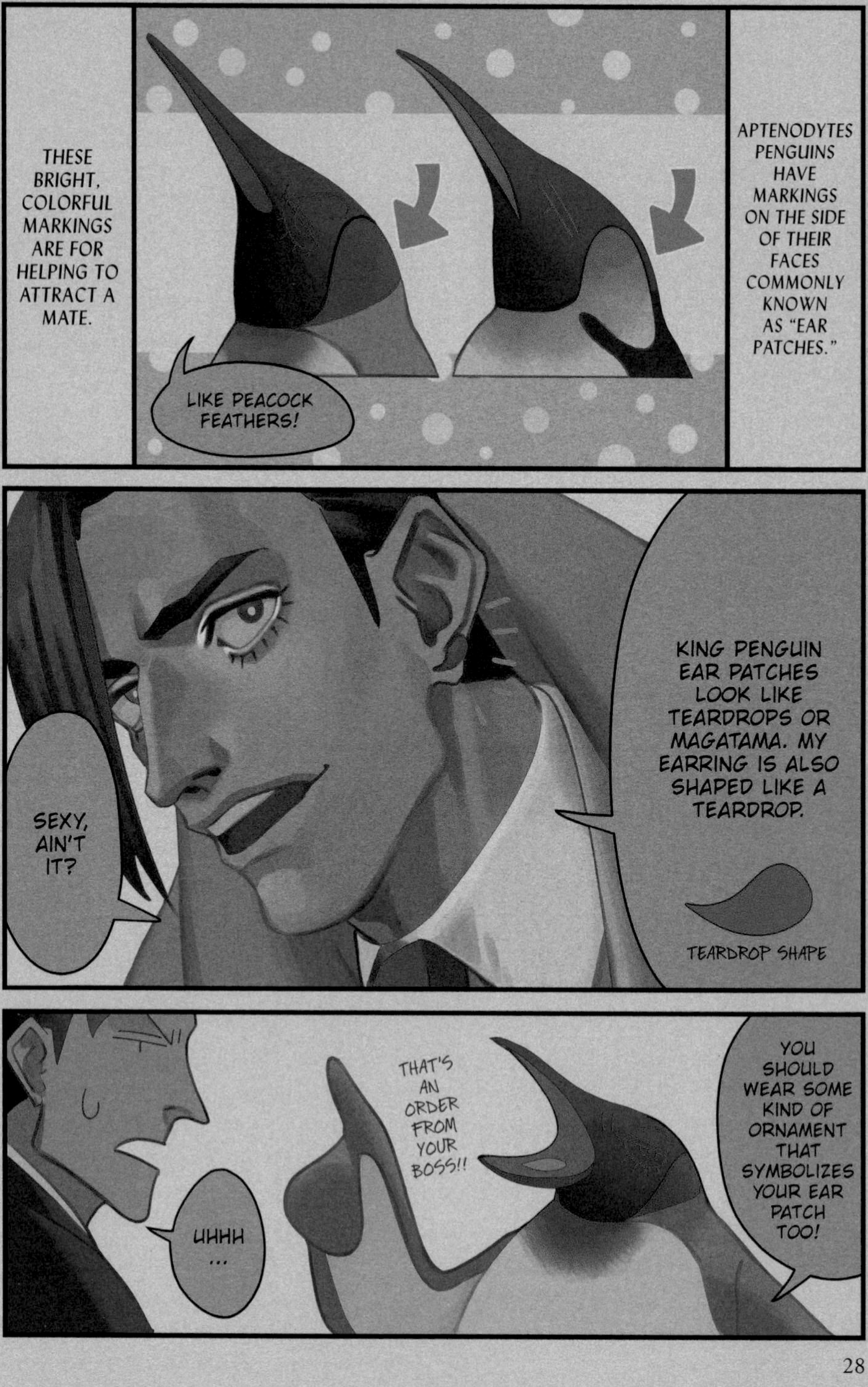
APTENODYTES PENGUINS HAVE MARKINGS ON THE SIDE OF THEIR FACES COMMONLY KNOWN AS "EAR PATCHES."
THESE BRIGHT, COLORFUL MARKINGS ARE FOR HELPING TO ATTRACT A MATE.
LIKE PEACOCK FEATHERS!
KING PENGUIN EAR PATCHES LOOK LIKE TEARDROPS OR MAGATAMA. MY EARRING IS ALSO SHAPED LIKE A TEARDROP.
TEARDROP SHAPE
SEXY, AIN'T IT?
YOU SHOULD WEAR SOME KIND OF ORNAMENT THAT SYMBOLIZES YOUR EAR PATCH TOO!
THAT'S AN ORDER FROM YOUR BOSS!!
UHHH...

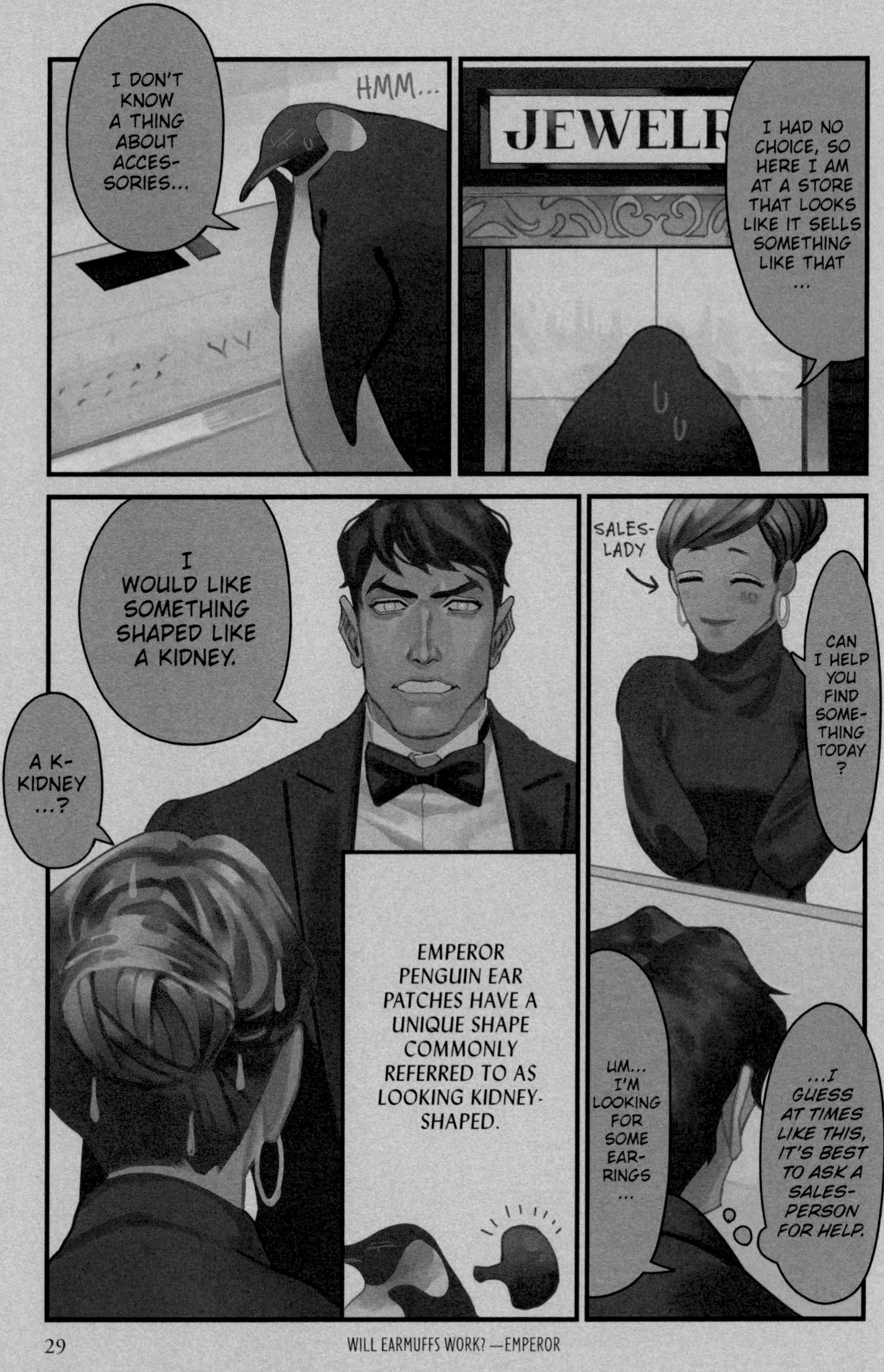
JEWELR
I HAD NO CHOICE, SO HERE I AM AT A STORE THAT LOOKS LIKE IT SELLS SOMETHING LIKE THAT...
HMM...
I DON'T KNOW A THING ABOUT ACCES-SORIES...
SALES-LADY
CAN I HELP YOU FIND SOME-THING TODAY?
...I GUESS AT TIMES LIKE THIS, IT'S BEST TO ASK A SALES-PERSON FOR HELP.
UM... I'M LOOKING FOR SOME EAR-RINGS...
I WOULD LIKE SOMETHING SHAPED LIKE A KIDNEY.
A K-KIDNEY...?
EMPEROR PENGUIN EAR PATCHES HAVE A UNIQUE SHAPE COMMONLY REFERRED TO AS LOOKING KIDNEY-SHAPED.

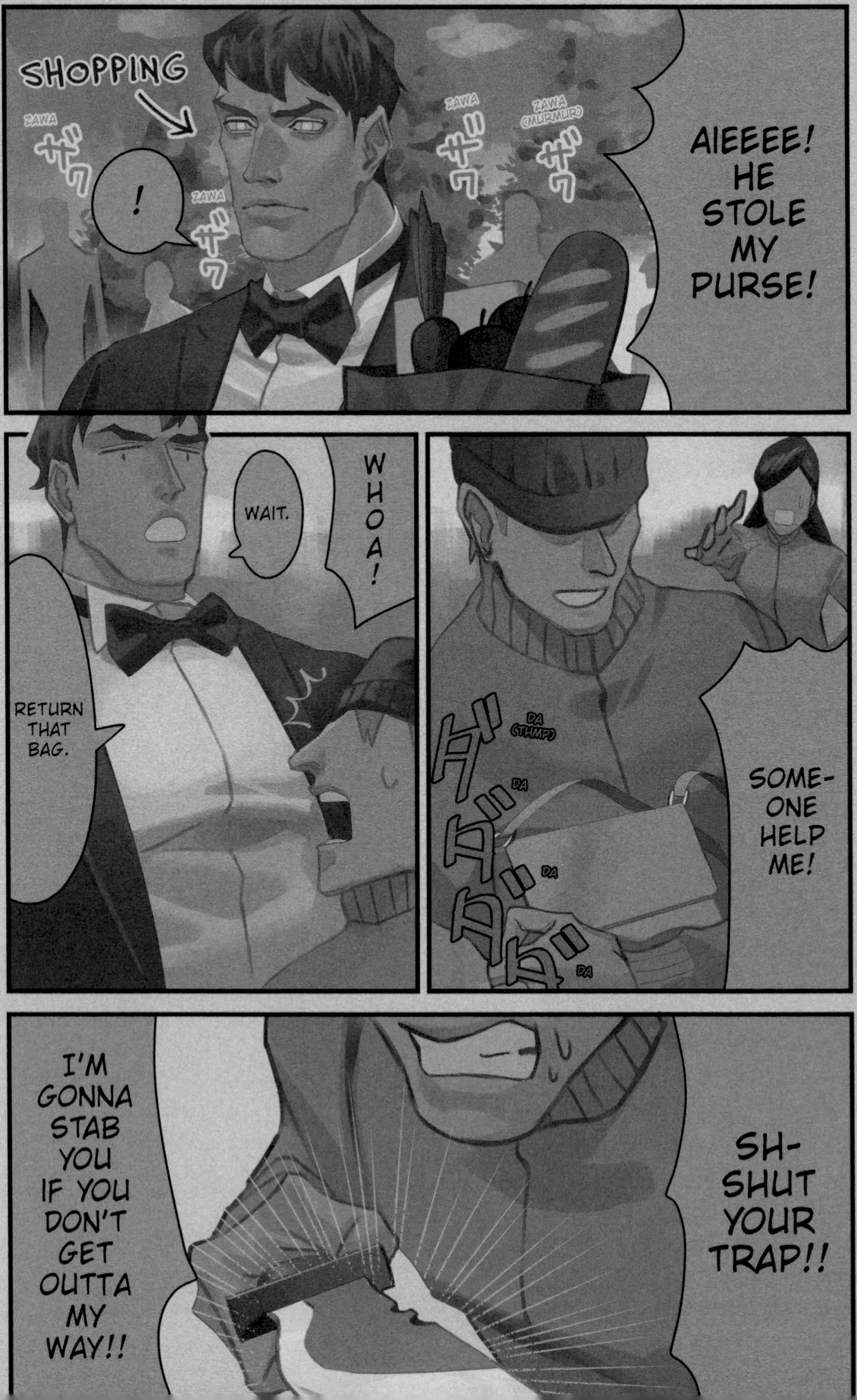
AIEEEE! HE STOLE MY PURSE!
ZAWA (MURMUR)
ZAWA
SHOPPING
ZAWA
!
ZAWA
SOME-ONE HELP ME!
DA (THMP)
DA
DA
DA
WHOA!
WAIT.
RETURN THAT BAG.
SH-SHUT YOUR TRAP!!
I'M GONNA STAB YOU IF YOU DON'T GET OUTTA MY WAY!!

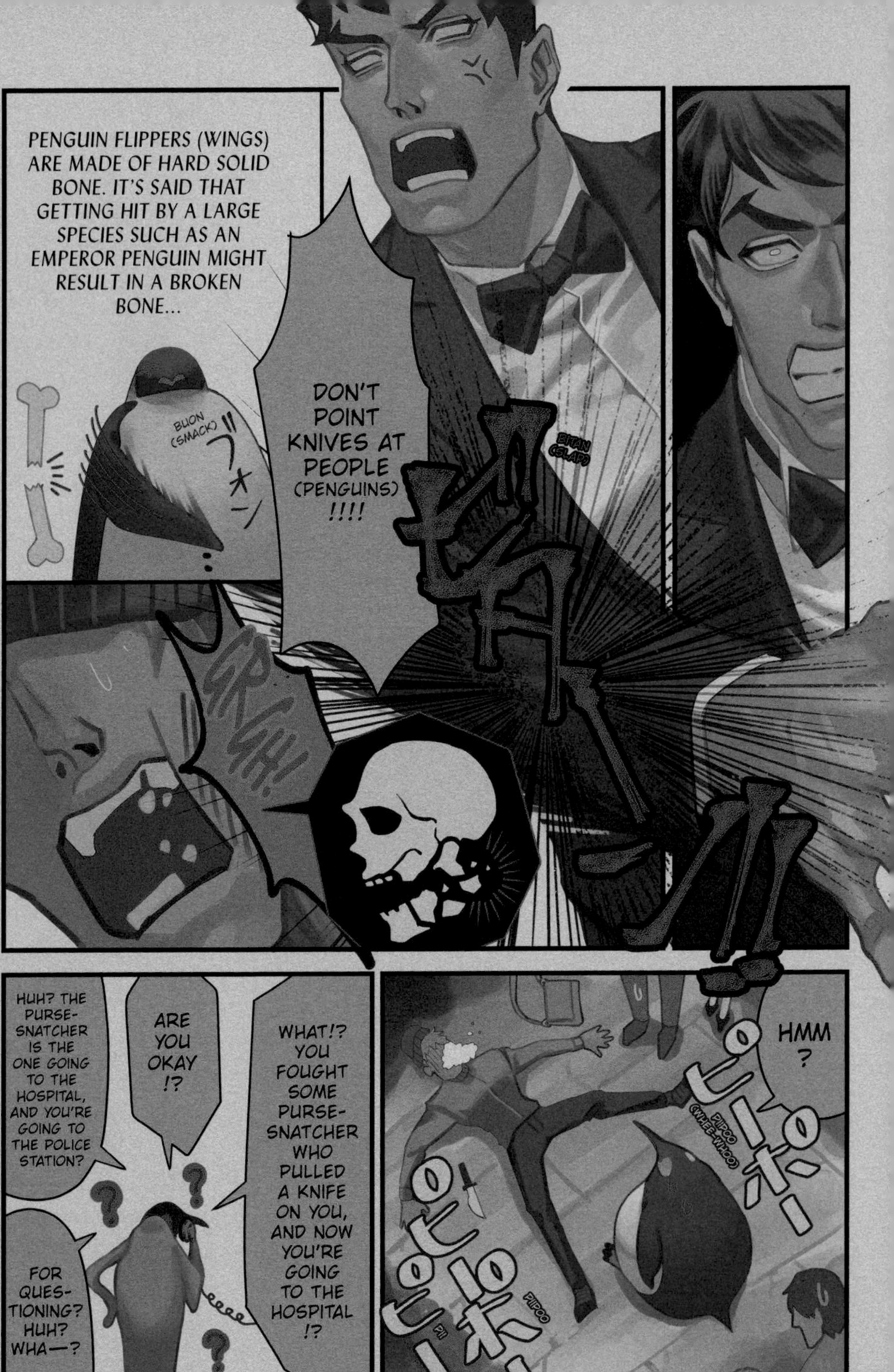
DON'T POINT KNIVES AT PEOPLE (PENGUINS) !!!!
PENGUIN FLIPPERS (WINGS) ARE MADE OF HARD SOLID BONE. IT'S SAID THAT GETTING HIT BY A LARGE SPECIES SUCH AS AN EMPEROR PENGUIN MIGHT RESULT IN A BROKEN BONE...
BUON (SMACK)
BITAN (SLAP)
GRGH!
HMM ?
PIPOO (WHEE-WHOO)
PIPOO
PI
WHAT!? YOU FOUGHT SOME PURSE-SNATCHER WHO PULLED A KNIFE ON YOU, AND NOW YOU'RE GOING TO THE HOSPITAL !?
ARE YOU OKAY !?
HUH? THE PURSE-SNATCHER IS THE ONE GOING TO THE HOSPITAL, AND YOU'RE GOING TO THE POLICE STATION?
FOR QUES-TIONING? HUH? WHA—?

EMPEROR PENGUIN SLAPS ARE TO BE FEARED. —KING

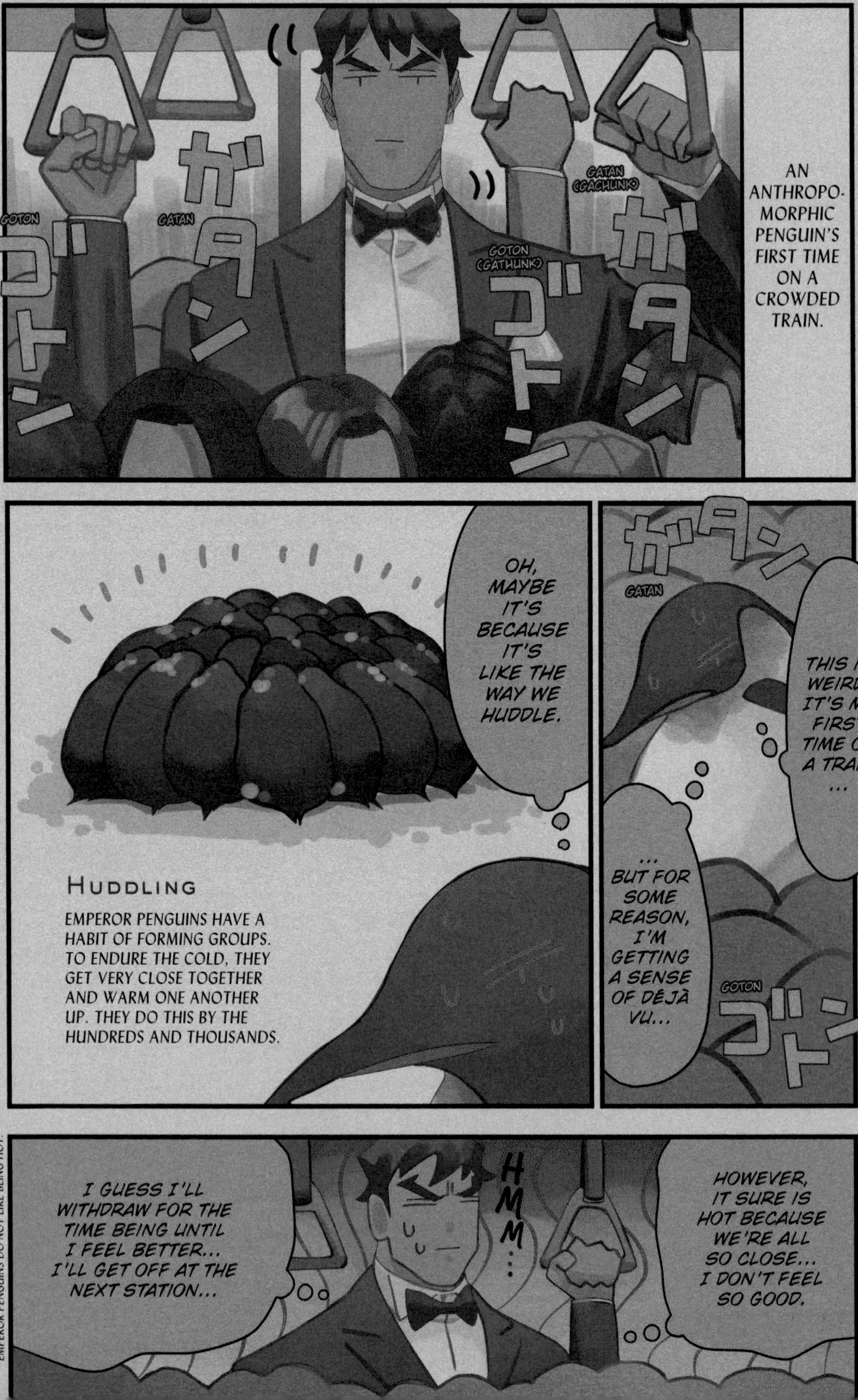
AN ANTHROPOMORPHIC PENGUIN'S FIRST TIME ON A CROWDED TRAIN.
GATAN (GACHUNK)
ガタン
GOTON (GATHUNK)
ゴトン
GATAN
ガタン
GOTON
ゴトン
GATAN
ガタン
THIS IS WEIRD. IT'S MY FIRST TIME ON A TRAIN ...
... BUT FOR SOME REASON, I'M GETTING A SENSE OF DÉJÀ VU...
GOTON
ゴトン
OH, MAYBE IT'S BECAUSE IT'S LIKE THE WAY WE HUDDLE.
HUDDLING
EMPEROR PENGUINS HAVE A HABIT OF FORMING GROUPS. TO ENDURE THE COLD, THEY GET VERY CLOSE TOGETHER AND WARM ONE ANOTHER UP. THEY DO THIS BY THE HUNDREDS AND THOUSANDS.
HOWEVER, IT SURE IS HOT BECAUSE WE'RE ALL SO CLOSE... I DON'T FEEL SO GOOD.
HMM...
I GUESS I'LL WITHDRAW FOR THE TIME BEING UNTIL I FEEL BETTER... I'LL GET OFF AT THE NEXT STATION...

*EMPEROR PENGUINS DO NOT LIKE BEING HOT.

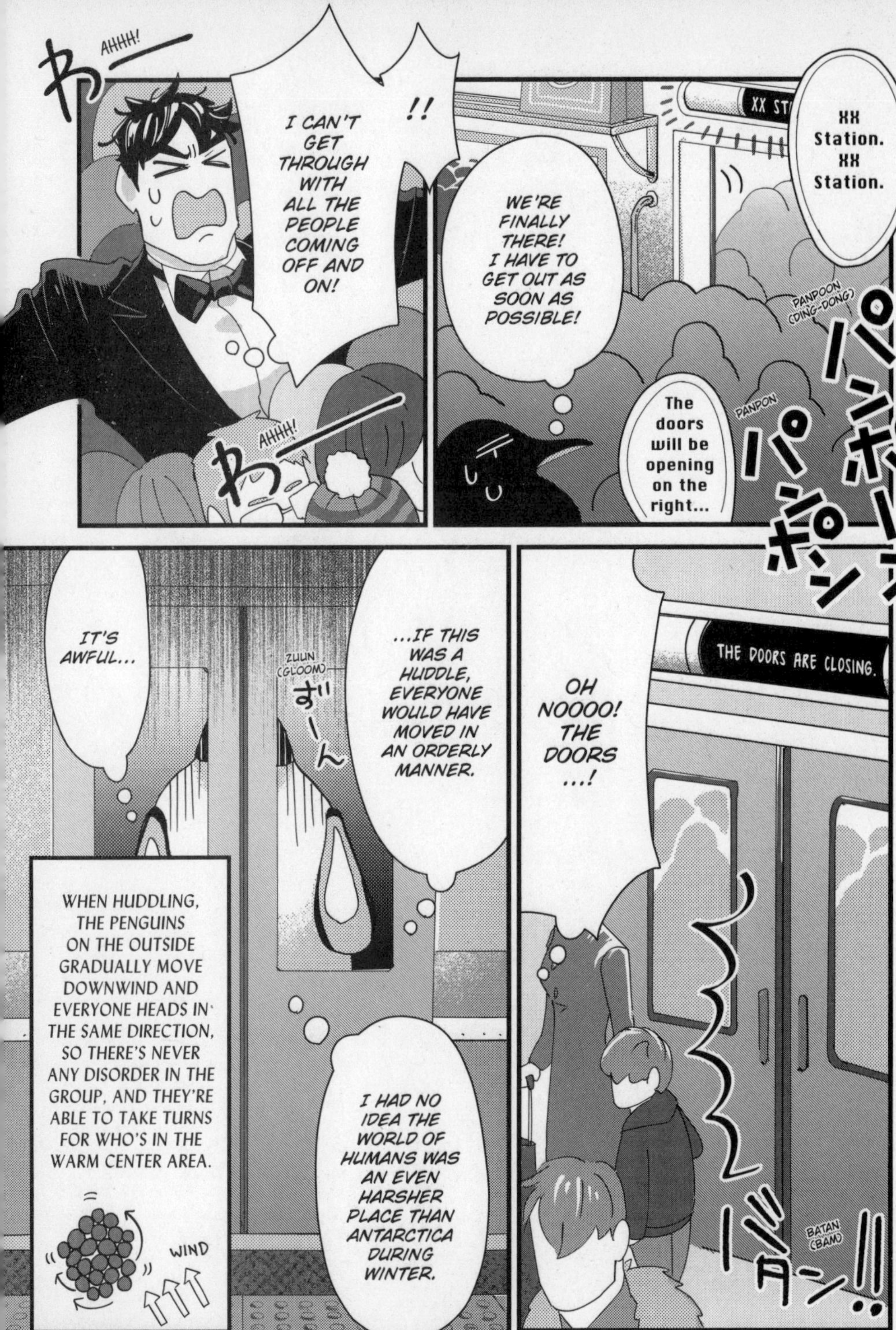
XX STATION
XX Station. XX Station.
WE'RE FINALLY THERE! I HAVE TO GET OUT AS SOON AS POSSIBLE!
パンポーン
PANPOON (DING-DONG)
パンポン
PANPON
The doors will be opening on the right...
わー
AHHH!
I CAN'T GET THROUGH WITH ALL THE PEOPLE COMING OFF AND ON!
!!
わー
AHHH!
THE DOORS ARE CLOSING.
OH NOOOO! THE DOORS ...!
バターン!!
BATAN (BAM)
IT'S AWFUL...
ずーん
ZUUN (GLOOM)
...IF THIS WAS A HUDDLE, EVERYONE WOULD HAVE MOVED IN AN ORDERLY MANNER.
I HAD NO IDEA THE WORLD OF HUMANS WAS AN EVEN HARSHER PLACE THAN ANTARCTICA DURING WINTER.
WHEN HUDDLING, THE PENGUINS ON THE OUTSIDE GRADUALLY MOVE DOWNWIND AND EVERYONE HEADS IN THE SAME DIRECTION, SO THERE'S NEVER ANY DISORDER IN THE GROUP, AND THEY'RE ABLE TO TAKE TURNS FOR WHO'S IN THE WARM CENTER AREA.
WIND

IF IT'S ABOUT 100 KM AWAY, I CAN JUST WALK.
—EMPEROR

Penguin Gentlemen

Chapter 2

We the Stylish

♦ *Do You Know the Pygoscelis Penguins?* ♦

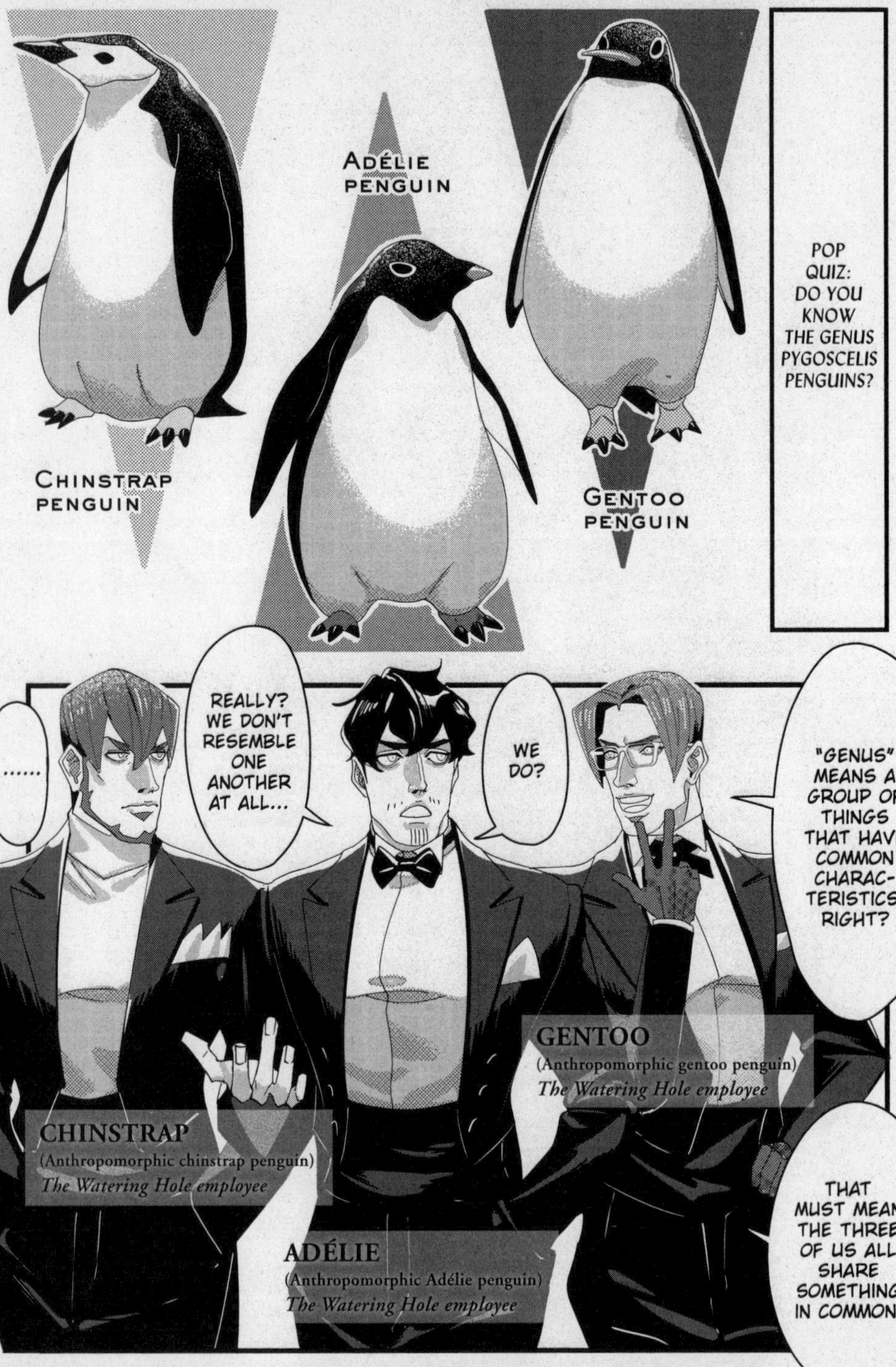
POP QUIZ: DO YOU KNOW THE GENUS PYGOSCELIS PENGUINS?
GENTOO PENGUIN
ADÉLIE PENGUIN
CHINSTRAP PENGUIN
"GENUS" MEANS A GROUP OF THINGS THAT HAVE COMMON CHARACTERISTICS, RIGHT?
THAT MUST MEAN THE THREE OF US ALL SHARE SOMETHING IN COMMON.
WE DO?
REALLY? WE DON'T RESEMBLE ONE ANOTHER AT ALL...
......
GENTOO (Anthropomorphic gentoo penguin) *The Watering Hole employee*
ADÉLIE (Anthropomorphic Adélie penguin) *The Watering Hole employee*
CHINSTRAP (Anthropomorphic chinstrap penguin) *The Watering Hole employee*

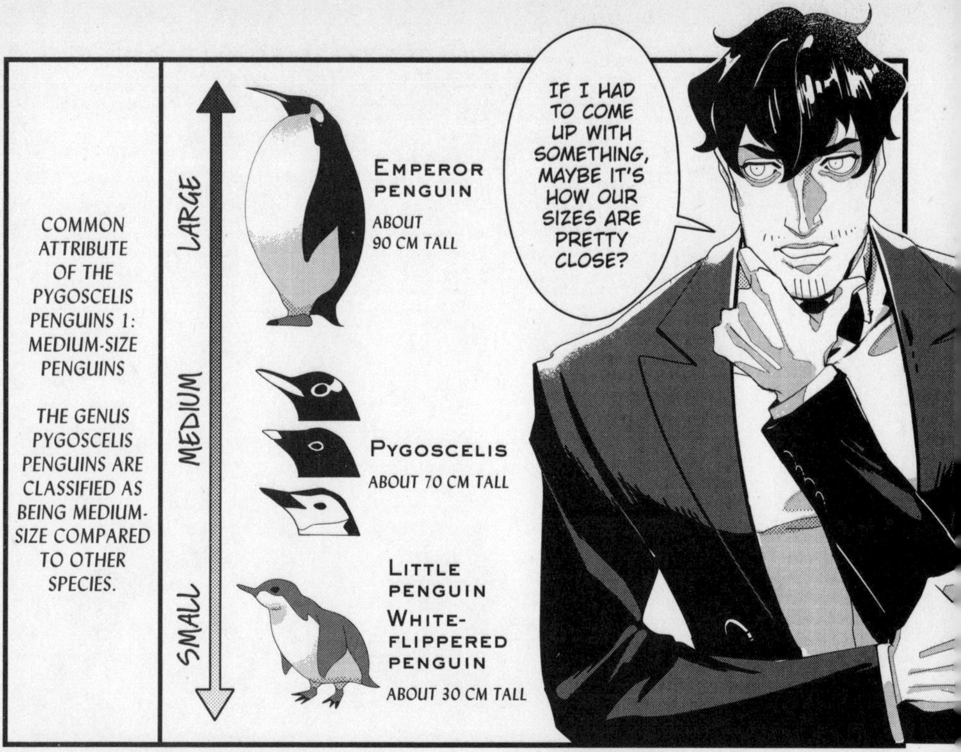
IF I HAD TO COME UP WITH SOMETHING, MAYBE IT'S HOW OUR SIZES ARE PRETTY CLOSE?
LARGE
Emperor penguin
ABOUT 90 CM TALL
MEDIUM
Pygoscelis
ABOUT 70 CM TALL
SMALL
Little penguin
White-flippered penguin
ABOUT 30 CM TALL
COMMON ATTRIBUTE OF THE PYGOSCELIS PENGUINS 1: MEDIUM-SIZE PENGUINS
THE GENUS PYGOSCELIS PENGUINS ARE CLASSIFIED AS BEING MEDIUM-SIZE COMPARED TO OTHER SPECIES.

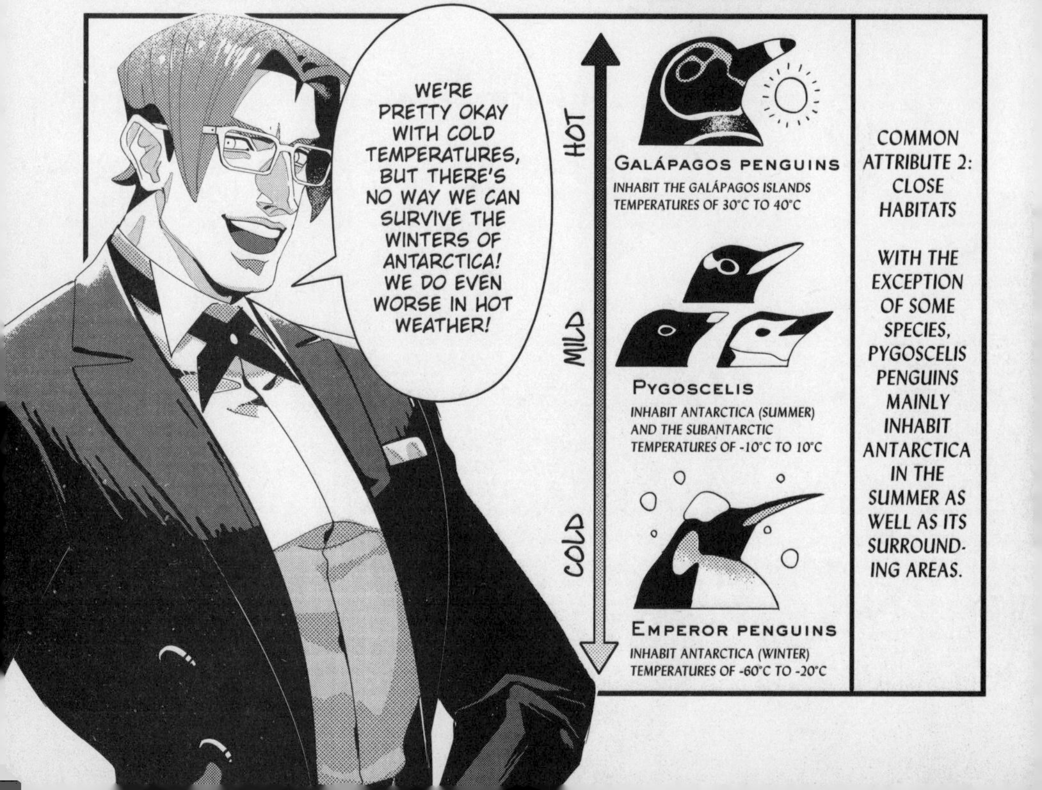
COMMON ATTRIBUTE 2: CLOSE HABITATS
WITH THE EXCEPTION OF SOME SPECIES, PYGOSCELIS PENGUINS MAINLY INHABIT ANTARCTICA IN THE SUMMER AS WELL AS ITS SURROUND-ING AREAS.
HOT
Galápagos penguins
INHABIT THE GALÁPAGOS ISLANDS
TEMPERATURES OF 30°C TO 40°C
MILD
Pygoscelis
INHABIT ANTARCTICA (SUMMER) AND THE SUBANTARCTIC
TEMPERATURES OF -10°C TO 10°C
COLD
Emperor penguins
INHABIT ANTARCTICA (WINTER)
TEMPERATURES OF -60°C TO -20°C
WE'RE PRETTY OKAY WITH COLD TEMPERATURES, BUT THERE'S NO WAY WE CAN SURVIVE THE WINTERS OF ANTARCTICA! WE DO EVEN WORSE IN HOT WEATHER!

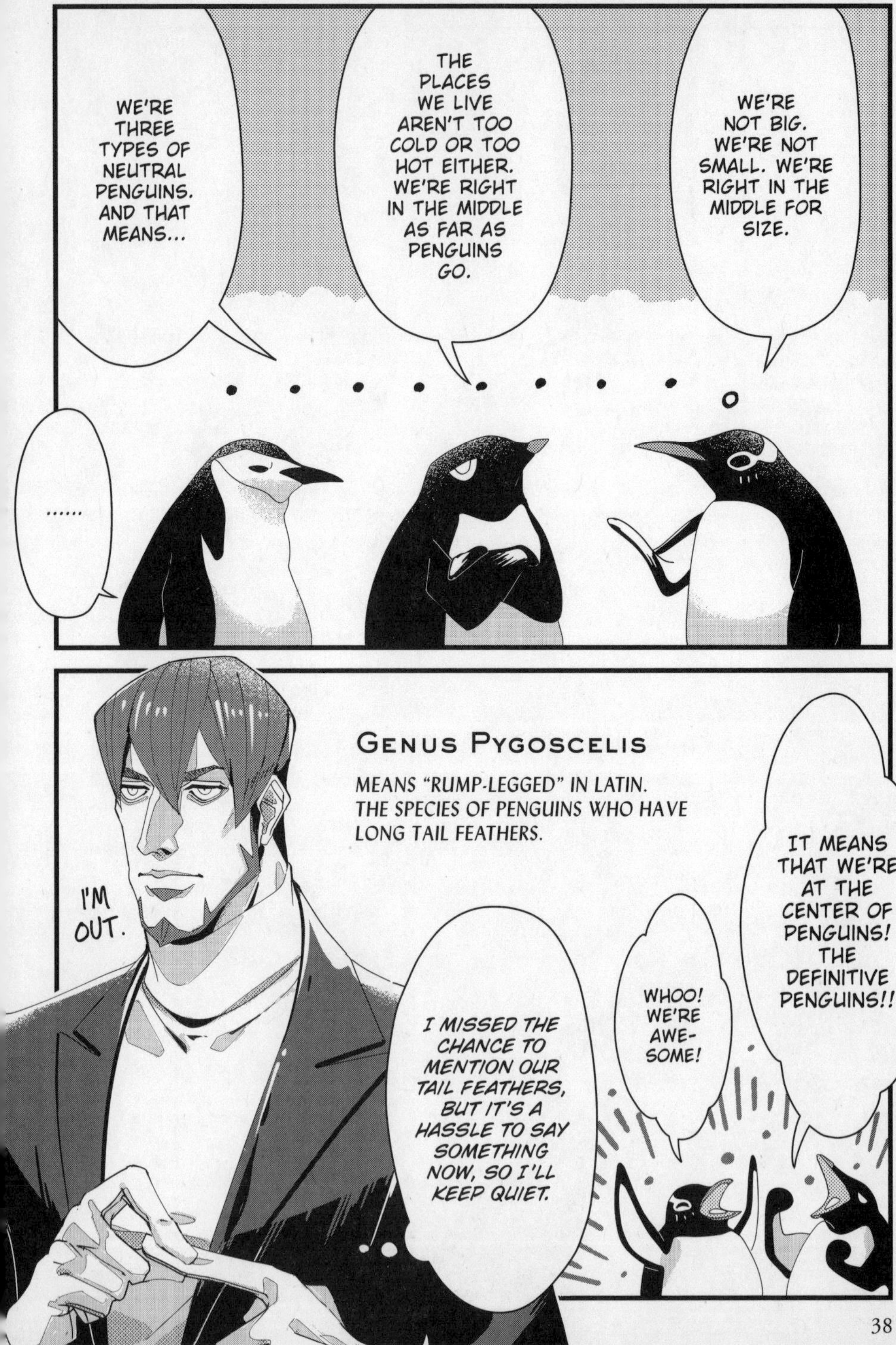

WE'RE NOT BIG. WE'RE NOT SMALL. WE'RE RIGHT IN THE MIDDLE FOR SIZE.
THE PLACES WE LIVE AREN'T TOO COLD OR TOO HOT EITHER. WE'RE RIGHT IN THE MIDDLE AS FAR AS PENGUINS GO.
WE'RE THREE TYPES OF NEUTRAL PENGUINS. AND THAT MEANS...
......
IT MEANS THAT WE'RE AT THE CENTER OF PENGUINS! THE DEFINITIVE PENGUINS!!
GENUS PYGOSCELIS
MEANS "RUMP-LEGGED" IN LATIN. THE SPECIES OF PENGUINS WHO HAVE LONG TAIL FEATHERS.
WHOO! WE'RE AWE-SOME!
I MISSED THE CHANCE TO MENTION OUR TAIL FEATHERS, BUT IT'S A HASSLE TO SAY SOMETHING NOW, SO I'LL KEEP QUIET.
I'M OUT.

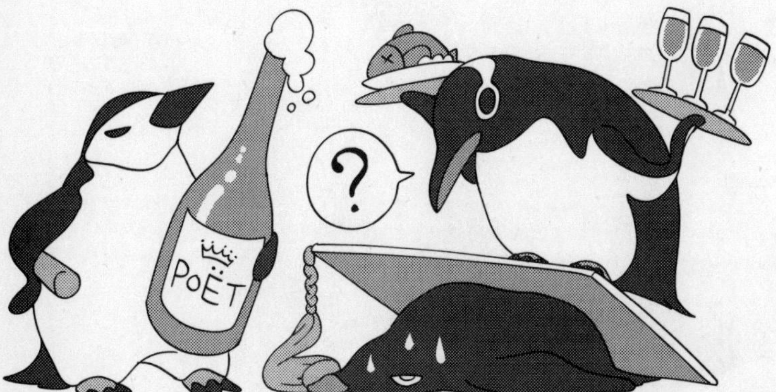
?
POËT

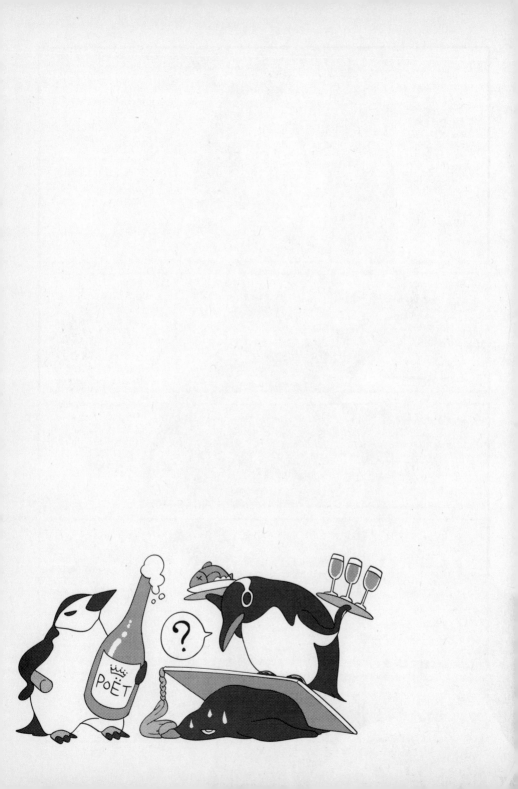

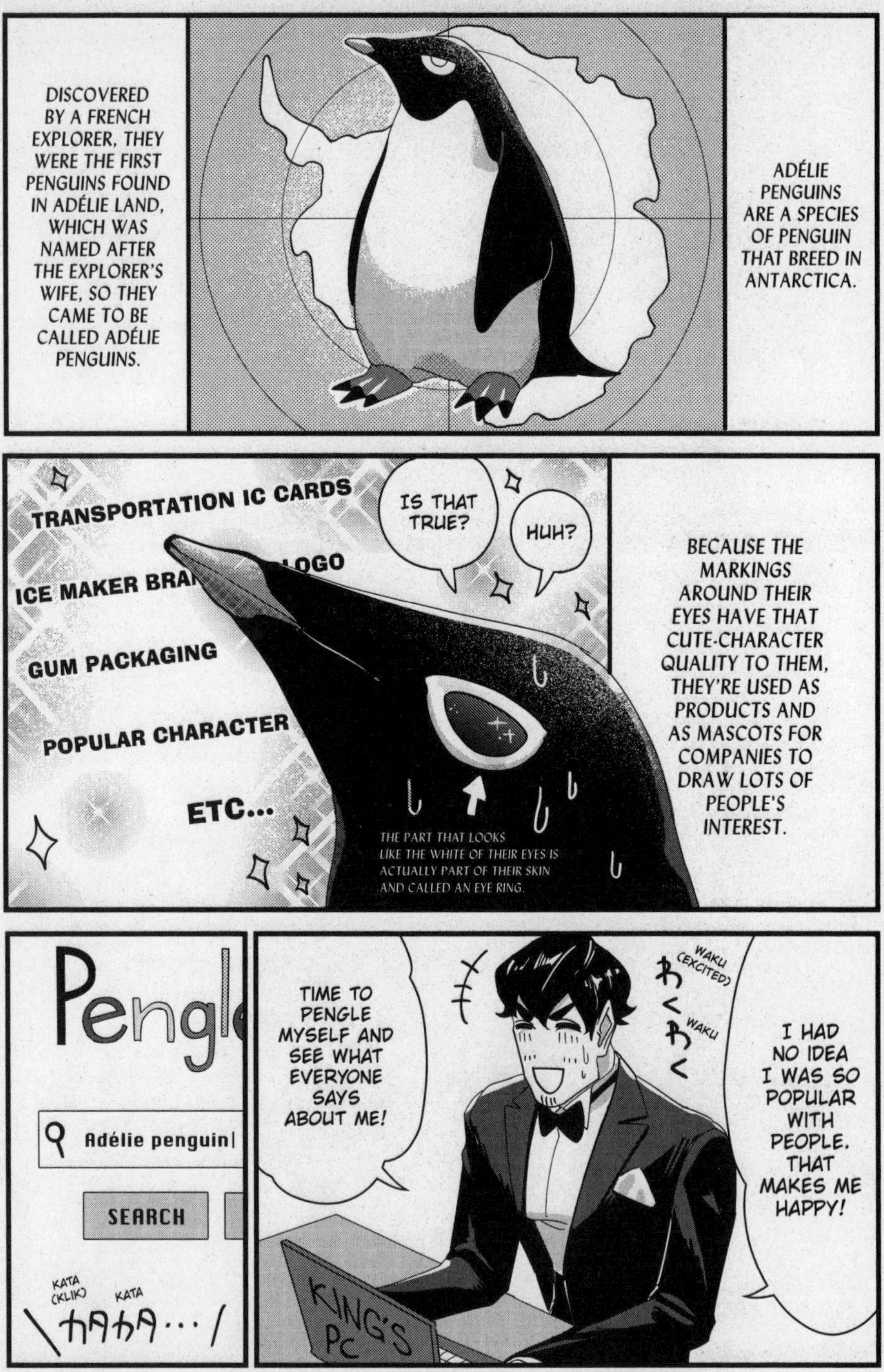
ADÉLIE PENGUINS ARE A SPECIES OF PENGUIN THAT BREED IN ANTARCTICA.
DISCOVERED BY A FRENCH EXPLORER, THEY WERE THE FIRST PENGUINS FOUND IN ADÉLIE LAND, WHICH WAS NAMED AFTER THE EXPLORER'S WIFE, SO THEY CAME TO BE CALLED ADÉLIE PENGUINS.
BECAUSE THE MARKINGS AROUND THEIR EYES HAVE THAT CUTE-CHARACTER QUALITY TO THEM, THEY'RE USED AS PRODUCTS AND AS MASCOTS FOR COMPANIES TO DRAW LOTS OF PEOPLE'S INTEREST.
HUH?
IS THAT TRUE?
TRANSPORTATION IC CARDS
ICE MAKER BRA
LOGO
GUM PACKAGING
POPULAR CHARACTER
ETC...
THE PART THAT LOOKS LIKE THE WHITE OF THEIR EYES IS ACTUALLY PART OF THEIR SKIN AND CALLED AN EYE RING.
I HAD NO IDEA I WAS SO POPULAR WITH PEOPLE. THAT MAKES ME HAPPY!
WAKU (EXCITED) WAKU
TIME TO PENGLE MYSELF AND SEE WHAT EVERYONE SAYS ABOUT ME!
KING'S PC
Pengle
Adélie penguin|
SEARCH
KATA (KLIK) KATA
カタカタ…

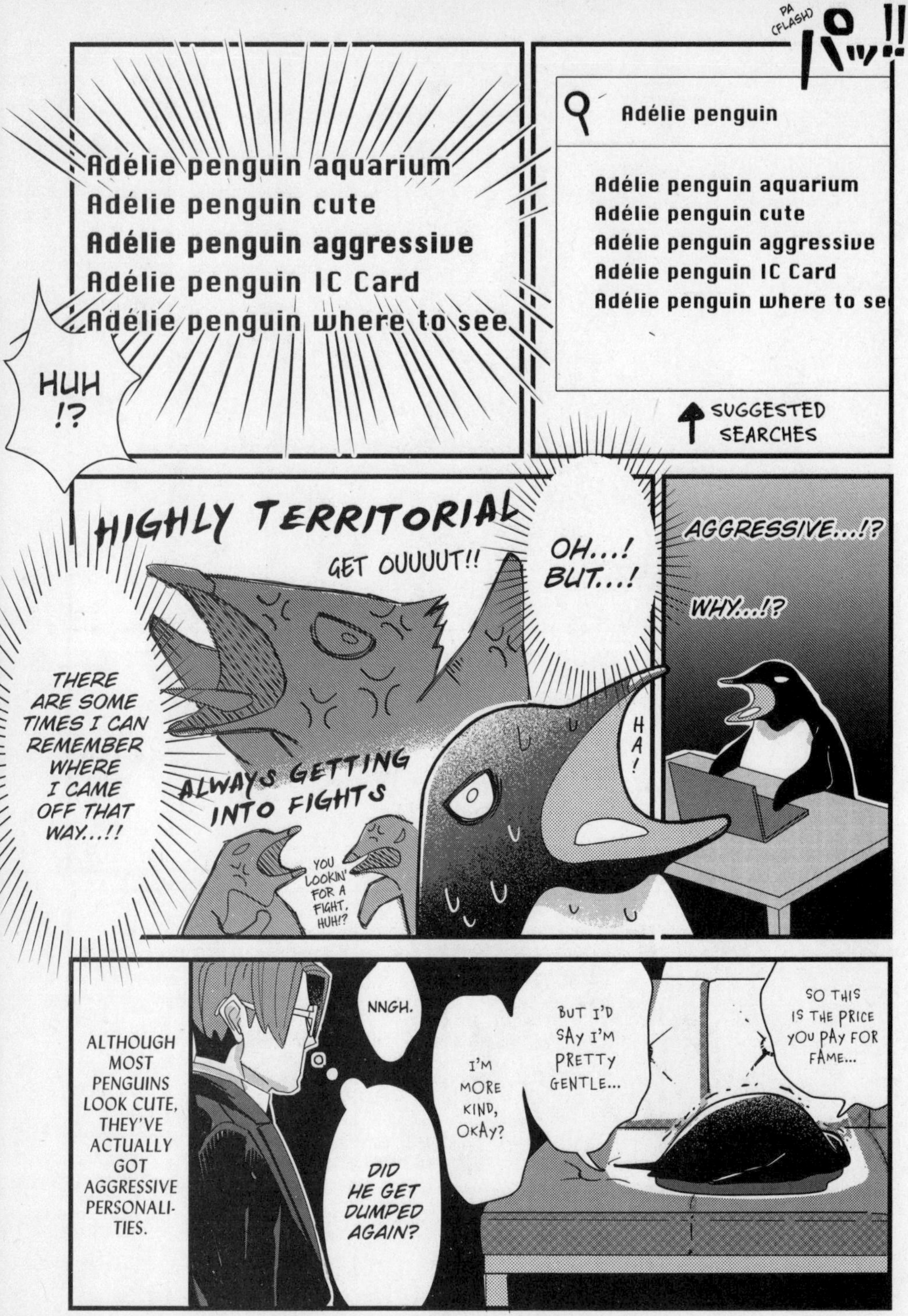
PA (FLASH)
パッ!!
Adélie penguin
Adélie penguin aquarium
Adélie penguin cute
Adélie penguin aggressive
Adélie penguin IC Card
Adélie penguin where to se
SUGGESTED SEARCHES
Adélie penguin aquarium
Adélie penguin cute
Adélie penguin aggressive
Adélie penguin IC Card
Adélie penguin where to see
HUH!?
AGGRESSIVE...!?
WHY...!?
OH...! BUT...!
HA!
HIGHLY TERRITORIAL
GET OUUUUT!!
ALWAYS GETTING INTO FIGHTS
YOU LOOKIN' FOR A FIGHT, HUH!?
THERE ARE SOME TIMES I CAN REMEMBER WHERE I CAME OFF THAT WAY...!!
SO THIS IS THE PRICE YOU PAY FOR FAME...
BUT I'D SAY I'M PRETTY GENTLE...
I'M MORE KIND, OKAY?
NNGH.
DID HE GET DUMPED AGAIN?
ALTHOUGH MOST PENGUINS LOOK CUTE, THEY'VE ACTUALLY GOT AGGRESSIVE PERSONALITIES.

IT'S NOT LIKE I CAN HELP BEING TERRITORIAL... —ADÉLIE

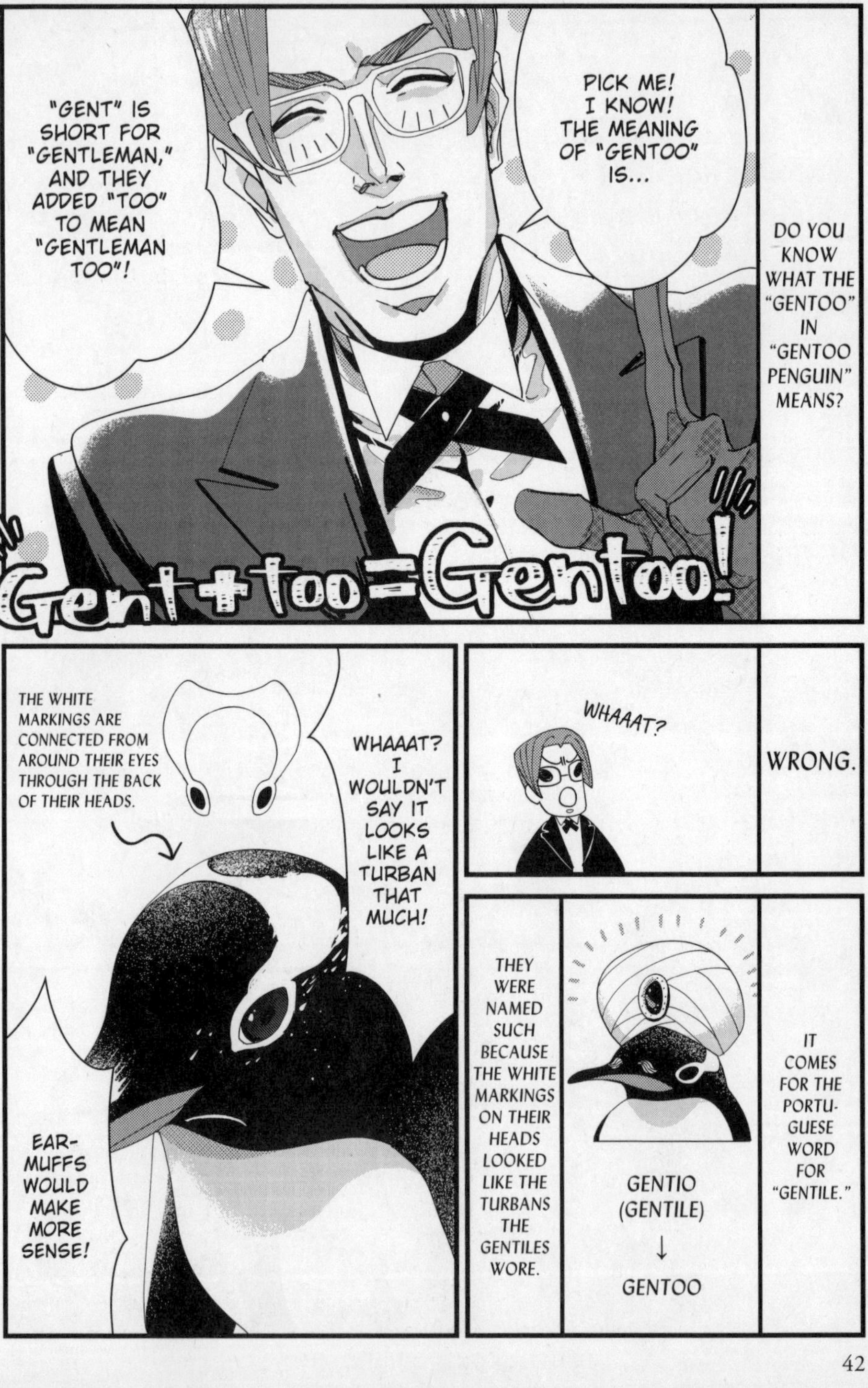
DO YOU KNOW WHAT THE "GENTOO" IN "GENTOO PENGUIN" MEANS?
PICK ME! I KNOW! THE MEANING OF "GENTOO" IS...
"GENT" IS SHORT FOR "GENTLEMAN," AND THEY ADDED "TOO" TO MEAN "GENTLEMAN TOO"!
Gent+too=Gentoo!
WRONG.
WHAAAT?
IT COMES FOR THE PORTU-GUESE WORD FOR "GENTILE."
GENTIO (GENTILE)
↓
GENTOO
THEY WERE NAMED SUCH BECAUSE THE WHITE MARKINGS ON THEIR HEADS LOOKED LIKE THE TURBANS THE GENTILES WORE.
WHAAAT? I WOULDN'T SAY IT LOOKS LIKE A TURBAN THAT MUCH!
THE WHITE MARKINGS ARE CONNECTED FROM AROUND THEIR EYES THROUGH THE BACK OF THEIR HEADS.
EAR-MUFFS WOULD MAKE MORE SENSE!

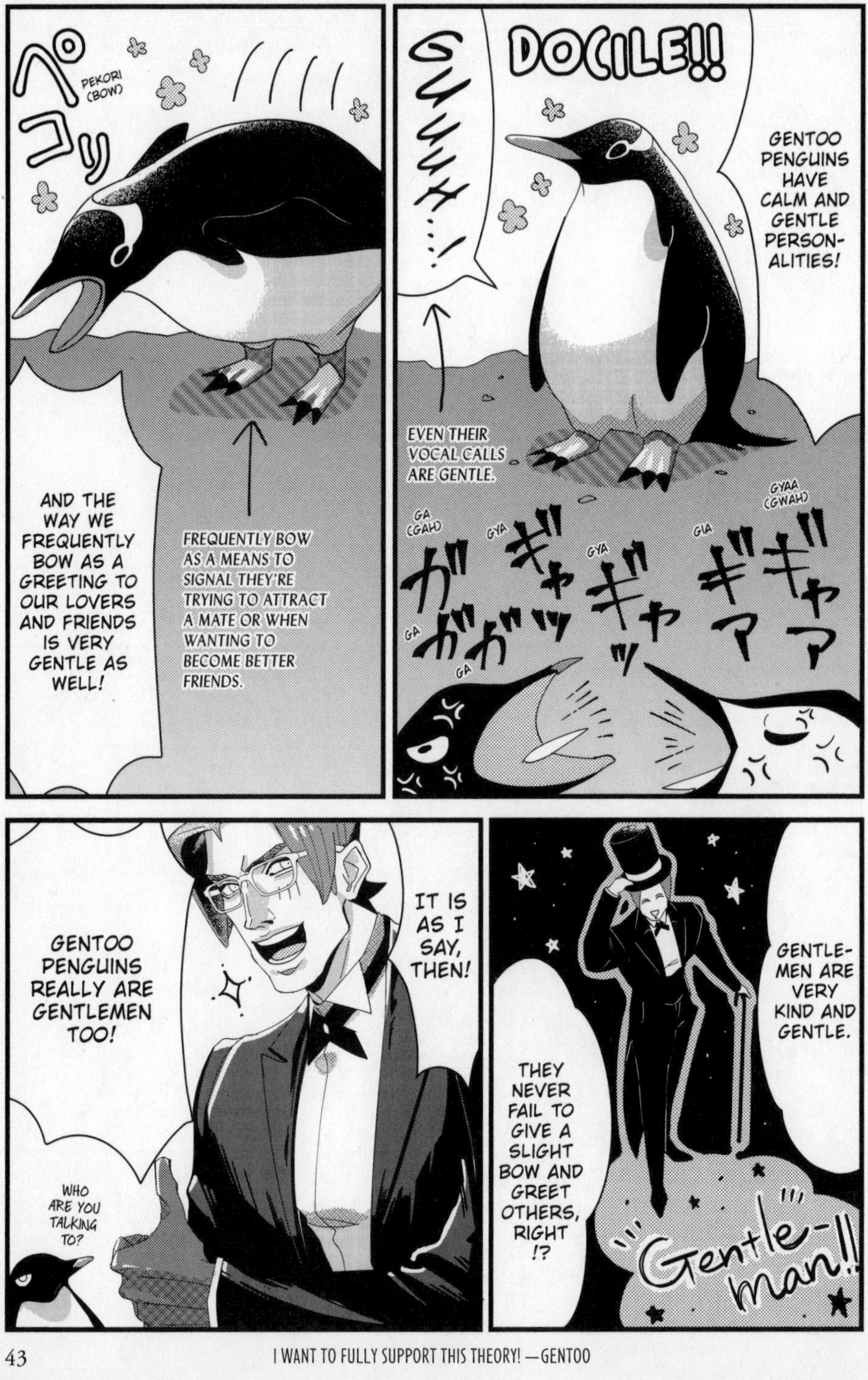
DOCILE!!
GENTOO PENGUINS HAVE CALM AND GENTLE PERSONALITIES!
GUUUUH...!
EVEN THEIR VOCAL CALLS ARE GENTLE.
GYAA (GWAH)
GIA
GYA
GYA
GA (GAH)
GA
GA
ペコリ
PEKORI (BOW)
FREQUENTLY BOW AS A MEANS TO SIGNAL THEY'RE TRYING TO ATTRACT A MATE OR WHEN WANTING TO BECOME BETTER FRIENDS.
AND THE WAY WE FREQUENTLY BOW AS A GREETING TO OUR LOVERS AND FRIENDS IS VERY GENTLE AS WELL!
GENTLE-MEN ARE VERY KIND AND GENTLE.
THEY NEVER FAIL TO GIVE A SLIGHT BOW AND GREET OTHERS, RIGHT!?
Gentle-man!!
IT IS AS I SAY, THEN!
GENTOO PENGUINS REALLY ARE GENTLEMEN TOO!
WHO ARE YOU TALKING TO?

◆ About Chinstraps ◆

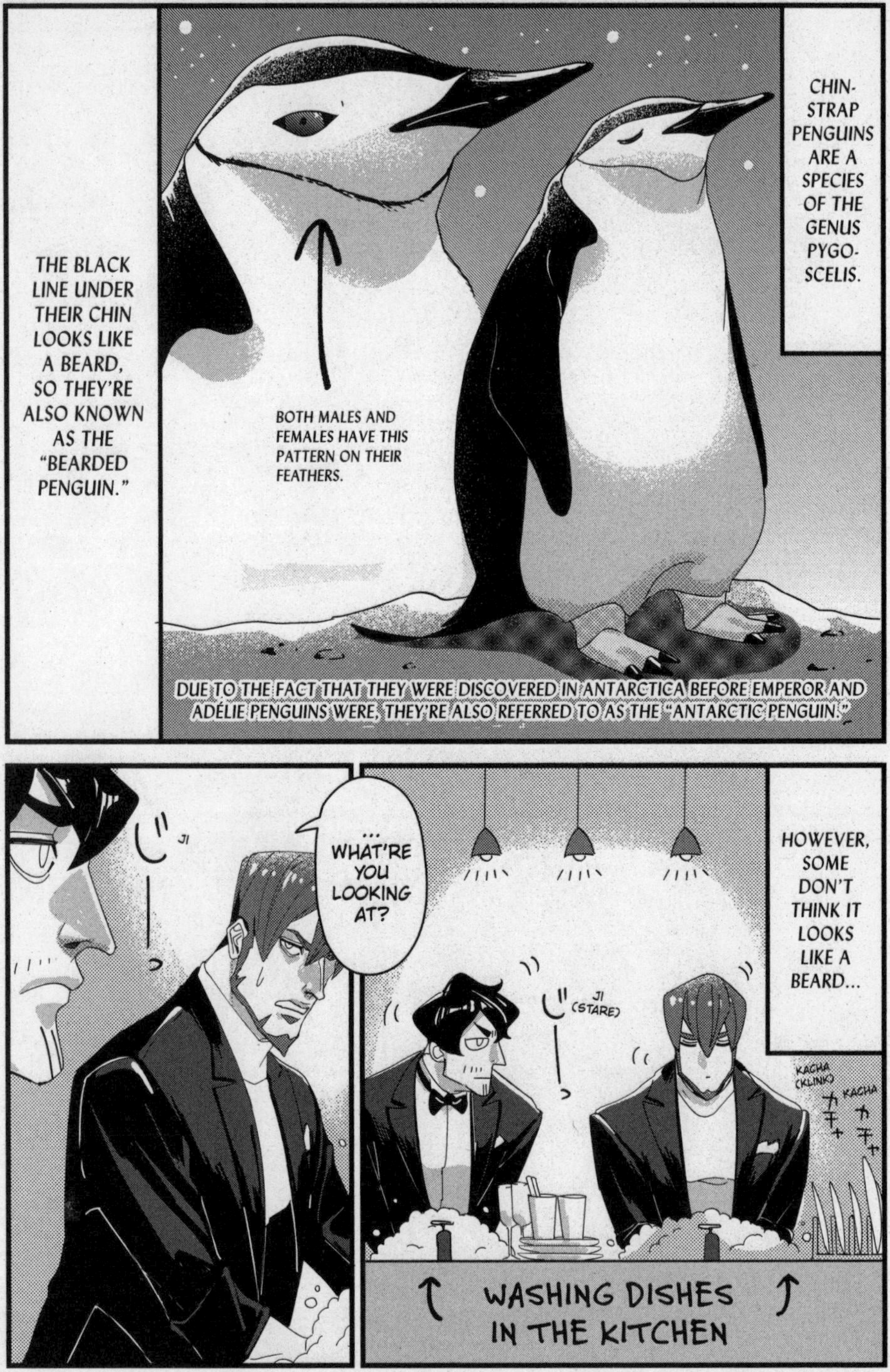
CHIN-STRAP PENGUINS ARE A SPECIES OF THE GENUS PYGO-SCELIS.
THE BLACK LINE UNDER THEIR CHIN LOOKS LIKE A BEARD, SO THEY'RE ALSO KNOWN AS THE "BEARDED PENGUIN."
BOTH MALES AND FEMALES HAVE THIS PATTERN ON THEIR FEATHERS.
DUE TO THE FACT THAT THEY WERE DISCOVERED IN ANTARCTICA BEFORE EMPEROR AND ADÉLIE PENGUINS WERE, THEY'RE ALSO REFERRED TO AS THE "ANTARCTIC PENGUIN."
HOWEVER, SOME DON'T THINK IT LOOKS LIKE A BEARD...
JI (STARE)
KACHA (KLINK)
KACHA
WASHING DISHES IN THE KITCHEN
JI
... WHAT'RE YOU LOOKING AT?

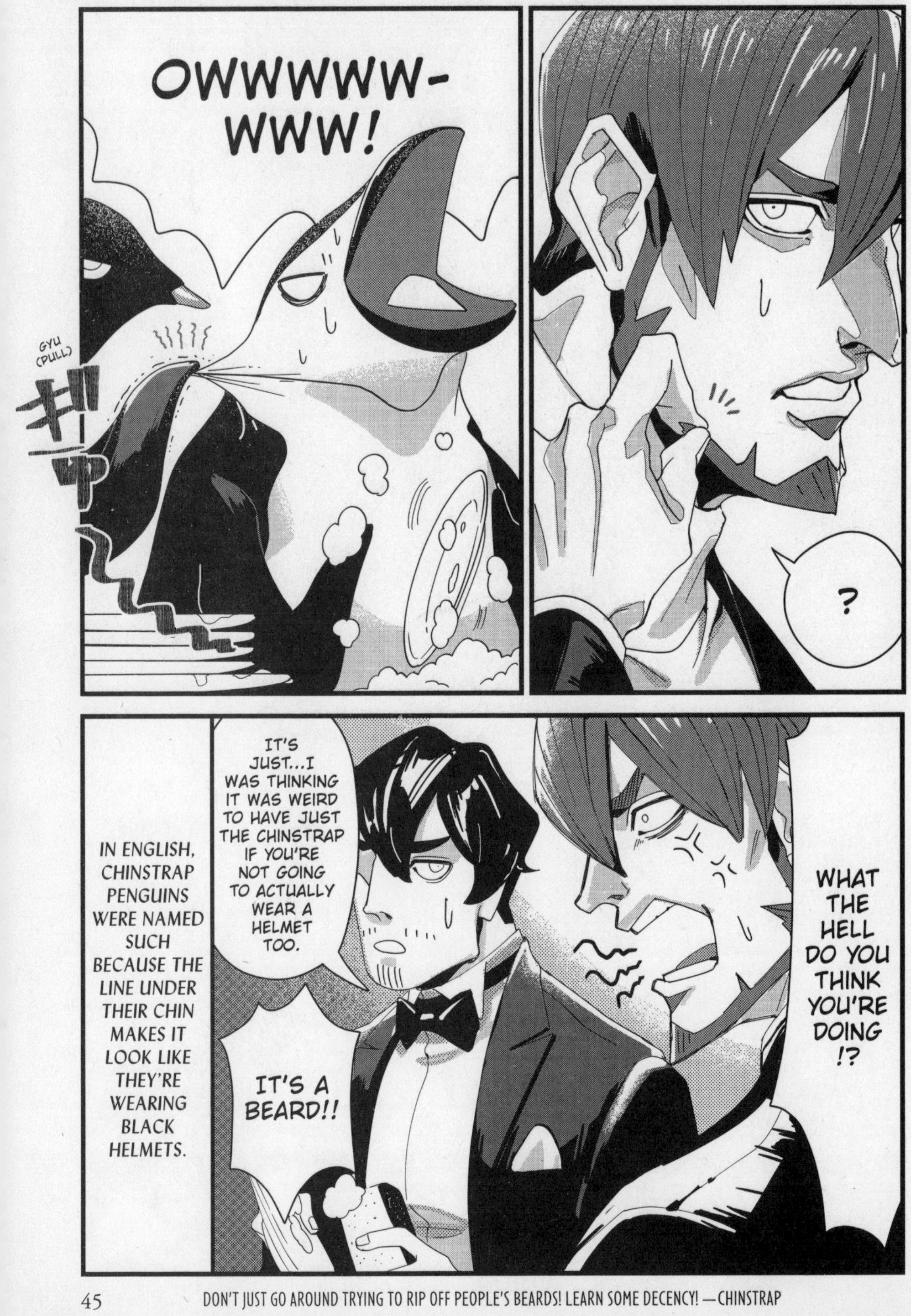
?
OWWWWW-WWW!
GYU (PULL)
WHAT THE HELL DO YOU THINK YOU'RE DOING!?
IT'S JUST...I WAS THINKING IT WAS WEIRD TO HAVE JUST THE CHINSTRAP IF YOU'RE NOT GOING TO ACTUALLY WEAR A HELMET TOO.
IT'S A BEARD!!
IN ENGLISH, CHINSTRAP PENGUINS WERE NAMED SUCH BECAUSE THE LINE UNDER THEIR CHIN MAKES IT LOOK LIKE THEY'RE WEARING BLACK HELMETS.

DON'T JUST GO AROUND TRYING TO RIP OFF PEOPLE'S BEARDS! LEARN SOME DECENCY! —CHINSTRAP

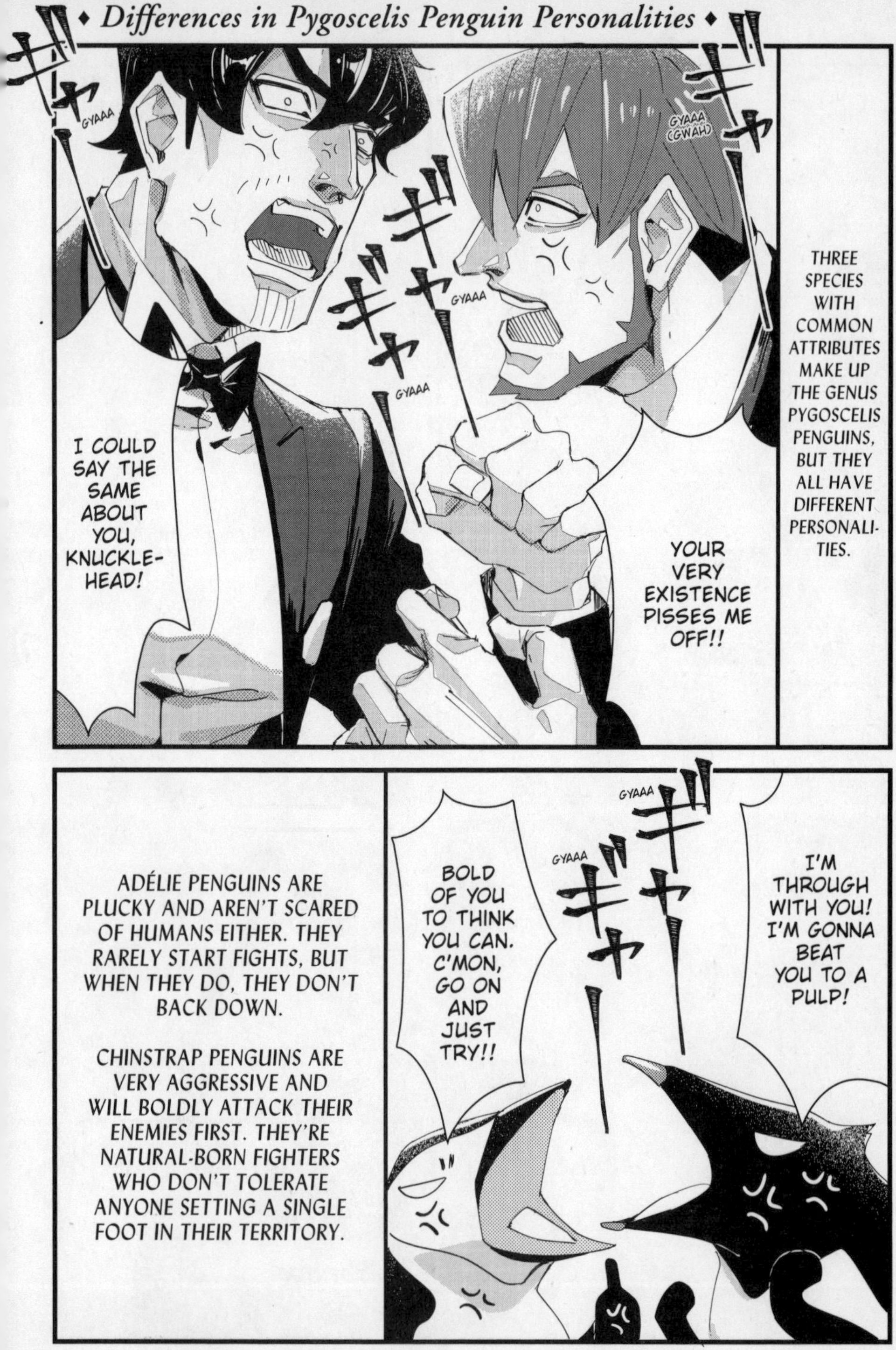
THREE SPECIES WITH COMMON ATTRIBUTES MAKE UP THE GENUS PYGOSCELIS PENGUINS, BUT THEY ALL HAVE DIFFERENT PERSONALITIES.
GYAAA (GWAH)
YOUR VERY EXISTENCE PISSES ME OFF!!
GYAAA
GYAAA
GYAAA
I COULD SAY THE SAME ABOUT YOU, KNUCKLEHEAD!
I'M THROUGH WITH YOU! I'M GONNA BEAT YOU TO A PULP!
GYAAA
GYAAA
BOLD OF YOU TO THINK YOU CAN. C'MON, GO ON AND JUST TRY!!
ADÉLIE PENGUINS ARE PLUCKY AND AREN'T SCARED OF HUMANS EITHER. THEY RARELY START FIGHTS, BUT WHEN THEY DO, THEY DON'T BACK DOWN.
CHINSTRAP PENGUINS ARE VERY AGGRESSIVE AND WILL BOLDLY ATTACK THEIR ENEMIES FIRST. THEY'RE NATURAL-BORN FIGHTERS WHO DON'T TOLERATE ANYONE SETTING A SINGLE FOOT IN THEIR TERRITORY.

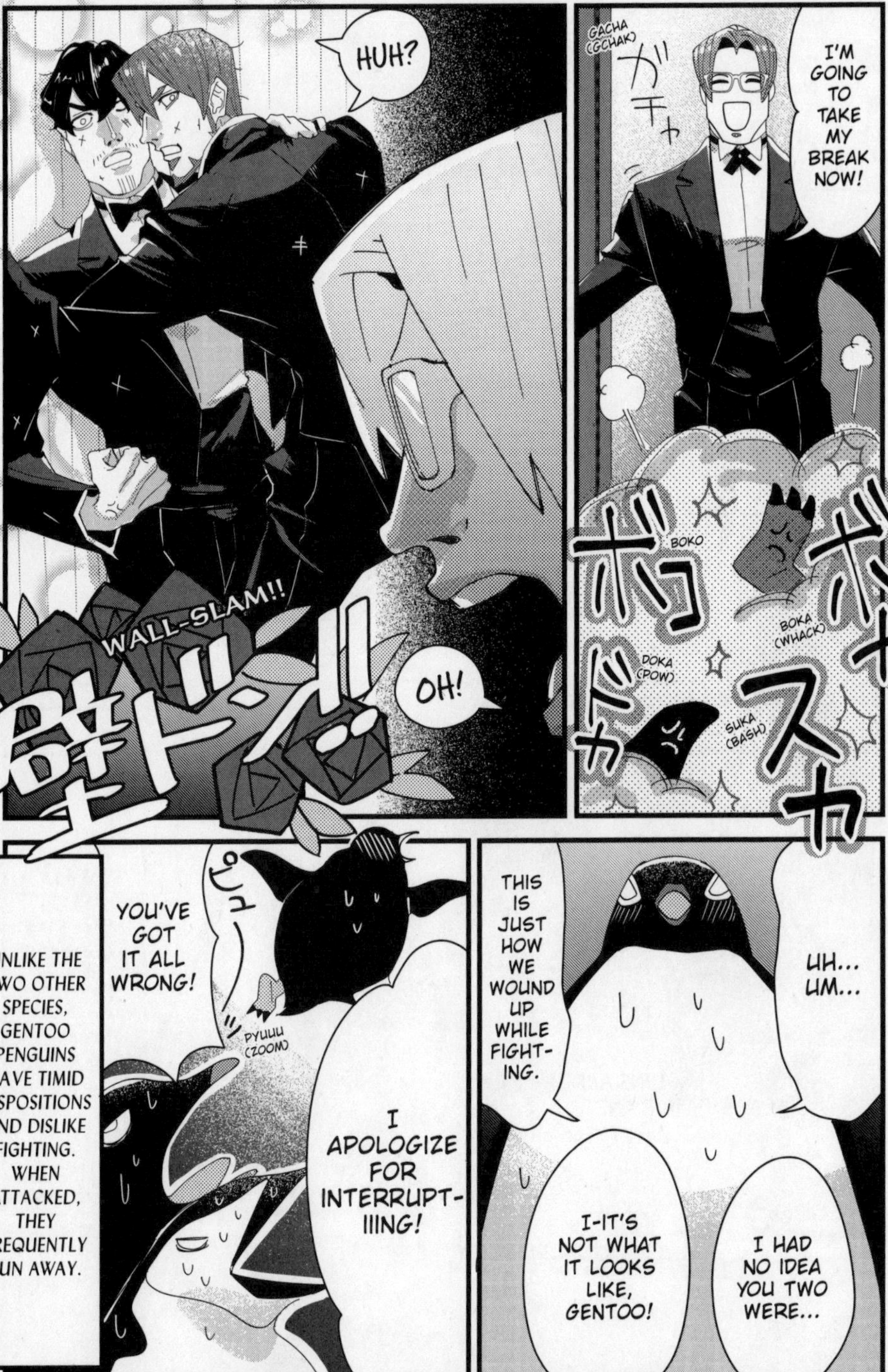
GACHA (GCHAK)
I'M GOING TO TAKE MY BREAK NOW!
BOKO
BOKA (WHACK)
DOKA (POW)
SUKA (BASH)
HUH?
WALL-SLAM!!
OH!
UH... UM...
THIS IS JUST HOW WE WOUND UP WHILE FIGHT-ING.
I HAD NO IDEA YOU TWO WERE...
I-IT'S NOT WHAT IT LOOKS LIKE, GENTOO!
YOU'VE GOT IT ALL WRONG!
PYUUU (ZOOM)
I APOLOGIZE FOR INTERRUPT-IIING!
UNLIKE THE TWO OTHER SPECIES, GENTOO PENGUINS HAVE TIMID DISPOSITIONS AND DISLIKE FIGHTING. WHEN ATTACKED, THEY FREQUENTLY RUN AWAY.

THE FACT THAT THEY FIGHT SO MUCH JUST MEANS THEY'RE CLOSE FRIENDS. —GENTOO

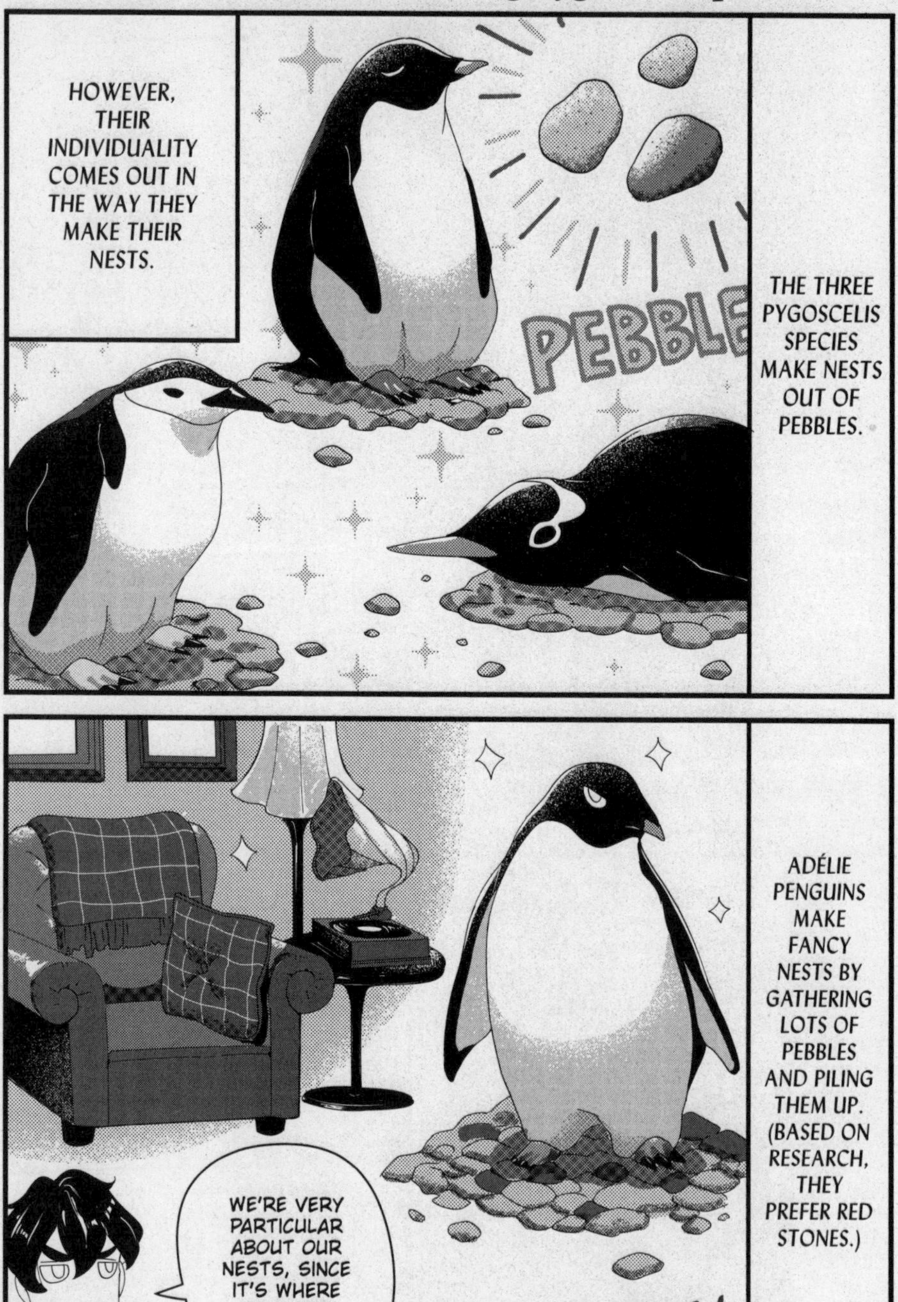
THE THREE PYGOSCELIS SPECIES MAKE NESTS OUT OF PEBBLES.
HOWEVER, THEIR INDIVIDUALITY COMES OUT IN THE WAY THEY MAKE THEIR NESTS.
PEBBLE
ADÉLIE PENGUINS MAKE FANCY NESTS BY GATHERING LOTS OF PEBBLES AND PILING THEM UP. (BASED ON RESEARCH, THEY PREFER RED STONES.)
WE'RE VERY PARTICULAR ABOUT OUR NESTS, SINCE IT'S WHERE WE INVITE THE LADIES.
TRADITIONAL NESTS!!

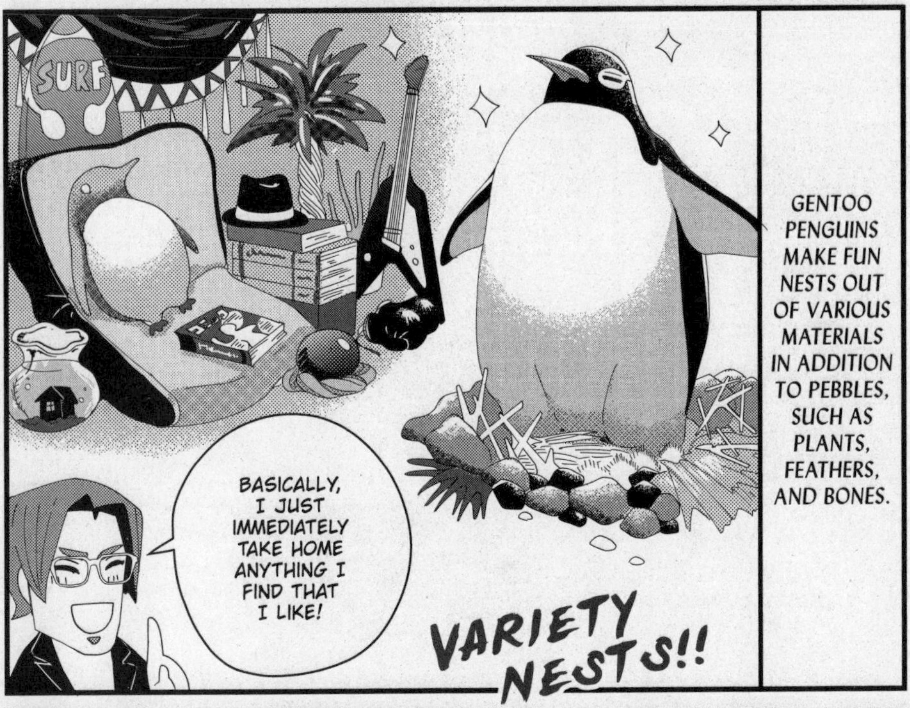
GENTOO PENGUINS MAKE FUN NESTS OUT OF VARIOUS MATERIALS IN ADDITION TO PEBBLES, SUCH AS PLANTS, FEATHERS, AND BONES.
VARIETY NESTS!!
SURF
BASICALLY, I JUST IMMEDIATELY TAKE HOME ANYTHING I FIND THAT I LIKE!

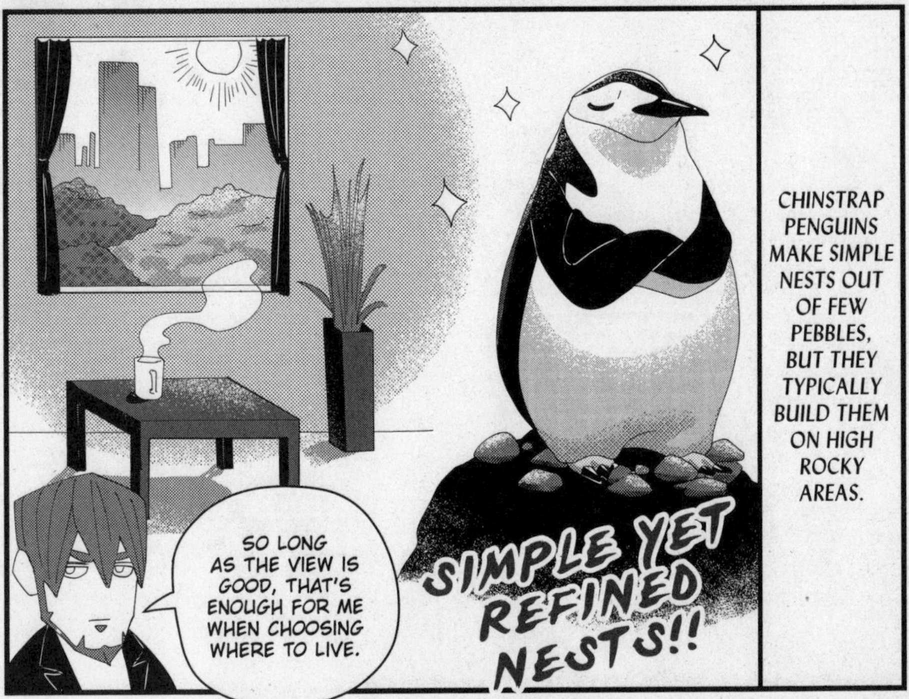
CHINSTRAP PENGUINS MAKE SIMPLE NESTS OUT OF FEW PEBBLES, BUT THEY TYPICALLY BUILD THEM ON HIGH ROCKY AREAS.
SIMPLE YET REFINED NESTS!!
SO LONG AS THE VIEW IS GOOD, THAT'S ENOUGH FOR ME WHEN CHOOSING WHERE TO LIVE.

THERE'S A LOT OF INDIVIDUALITY IN REGARDS TO WHERE PENGUINS LIVE TOO! —GENTOO

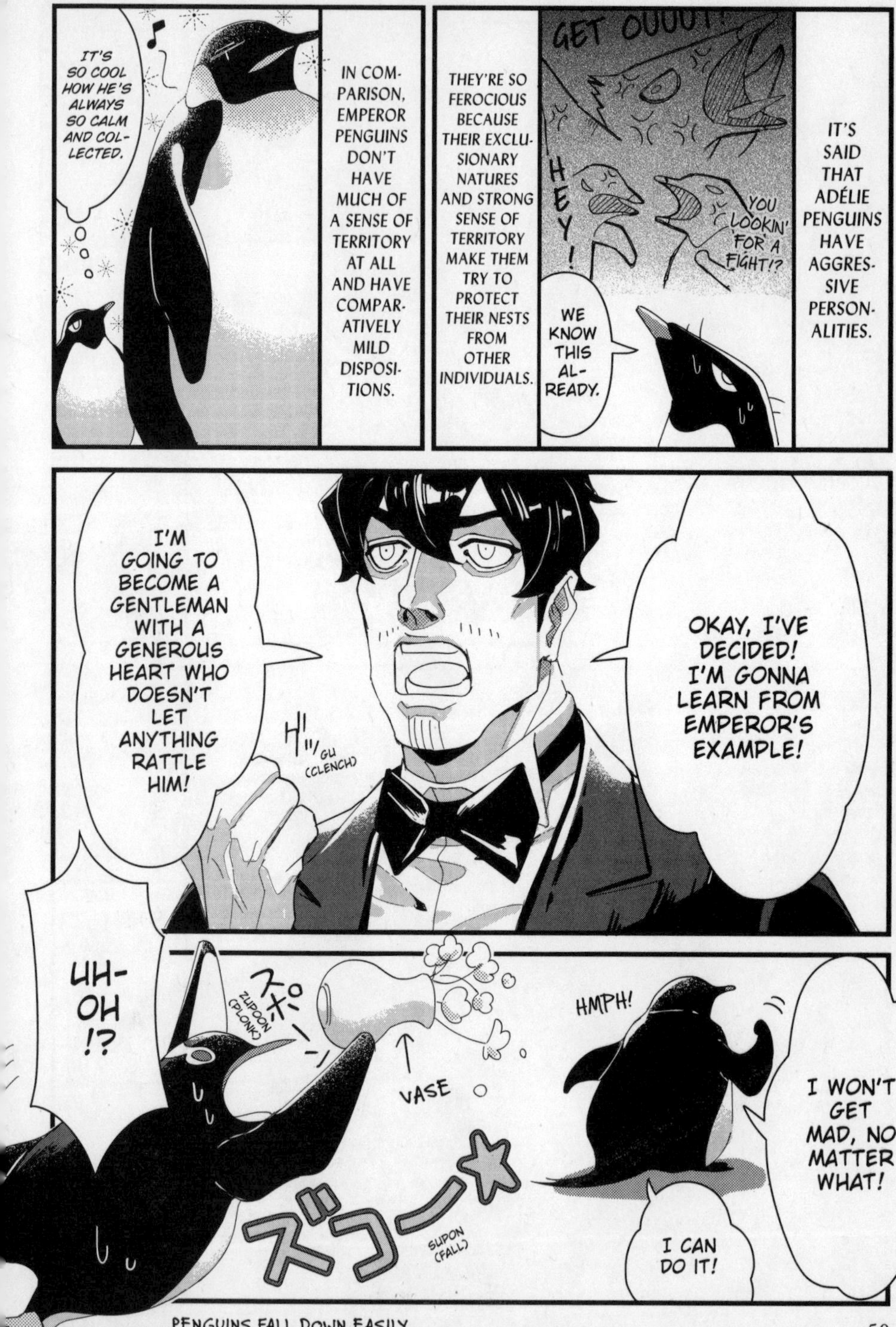
IT'S SAID THAT ADÉLIE PENGUINS HAVE AGGRESSIVE PERSONALITIES.
GET OUUUT!
HEY!
YOU LOOKIN' FOR A FIGHT!?
WE KNOW THIS ALREADY.
THEY'RE SO FEROCIOUS BECAUSE THEIR EXCLUSIONARY NATURES AND STRONG SENSE OF TERRITORY MAKE THEM TRY TO PROTECT THEIR NESTS FROM OTHER INDIVIDUALS.
IN COMPARISON, EMPEROR PENGUINS DON'T HAVE MUCH OF A SENSE OF TERRITORY AT ALL AND HAVE COMPARATIVELY MILD DISPOSITIONS.
IT'S SO COOL HOW HE'S ALWAYS SO CALM AND COLLECTED.
OKAY, I'VE DECIDED! I'M GONNA LEARN FROM EMPEROR'S EXAMPLE!
I'M GOING TO BECOME A GENTLEMAN WITH A GENEROUS HEART WHO DOESN'T LET ANYTHING RATTLE HIM!
GU (CLENCH)
I WON'T GET MAD, NO MATTER WHAT!
I CAN DO IT!
HMPH!
VASE
ZUPOON (PLONK)
SUPON (FALL)
UH-OH!?

PENGUINS FALL DOWN EASILY.

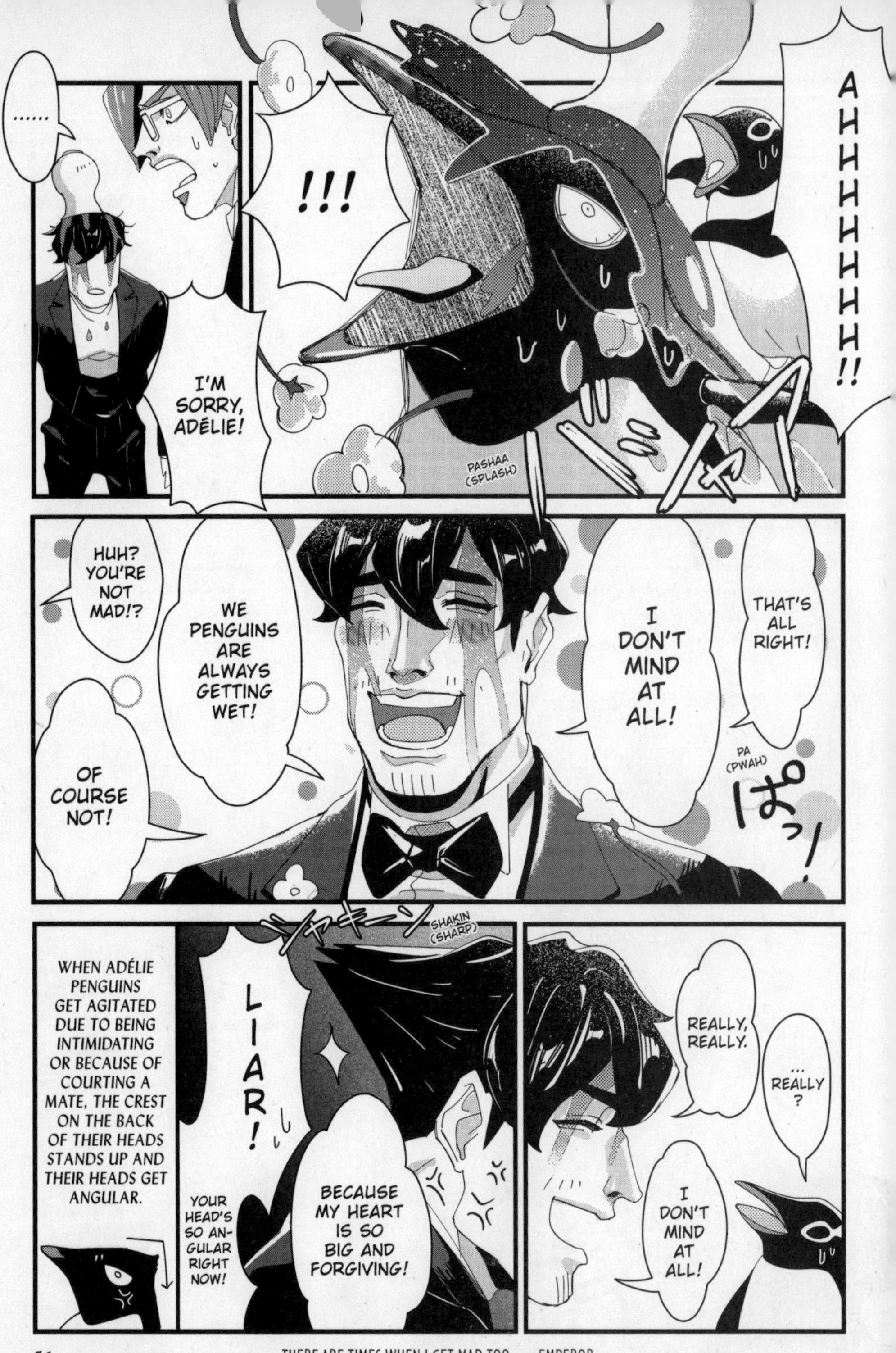

AHHHHHHHHH!!
!!!
PASHAA (SPLASH)
......
I'M SORRY, ADÉLIE!
THAT'S ALL RIGHT!
I DON'T MIND AT ALL!
PA (PWAH)
ぱっ!
WE PENGUINS ARE ALWAYS GETTING WET!
HUH? YOU'RE NOT MAD!?
OF COURSE NOT!
... REALLY?
REALLY, REALLY.
I DON'T MIND AT ALL!
SHAKIN (SHARP)
LIAR!
BECAUSE MY HEART IS SO BIG AND FORGIVING!
YOUR HEAD'S SO AN-GULAR RIGHT NOW!
WHEN ADÉLIE PENGUINS GET AGITATED DUE TO BEING INTIMIDATING OR BECAUSE OF COURTING A MATE, THE CREST ON THE BACK OF THEIR HEADS STANDS UP AND THEIR HEADS GET ANGULAR.

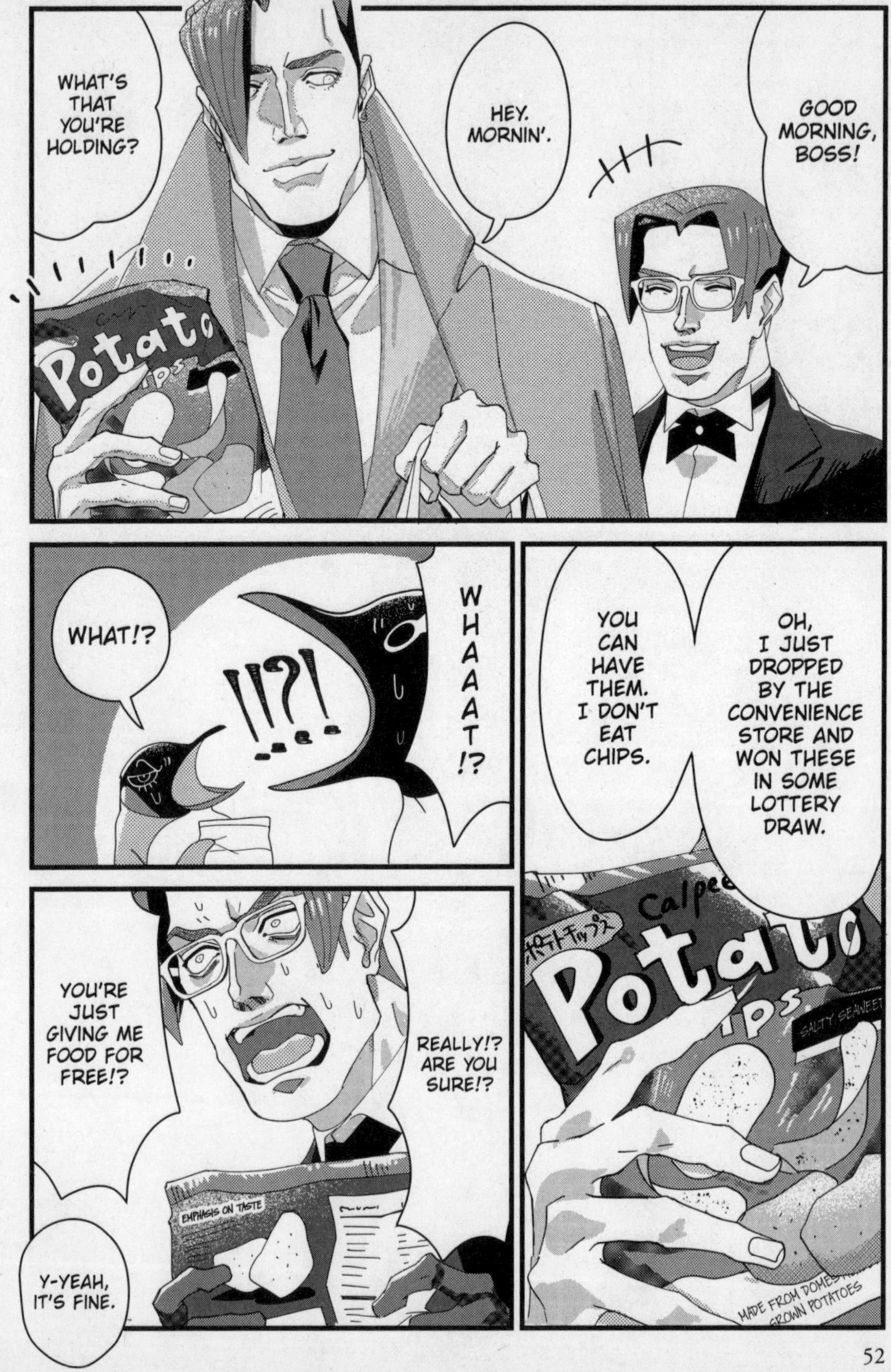
GOOD MORNING, BOSS!
HEY. MORNIN'.
WHAT'S THAT YOU'RE HOLDING?
Potato
OH, I JUST DROPPED BY THE CONVENIENCE STORE AND WON THESE IN SOME LOTTERY DRAW.
YOU CAN HAVE THEM. I DON'T EAT CHIPS.
Calpee
Potato
SALTY SEAWEED
WHAAAAT!?
!!?!
WHAT!?
REALLY!? ARE YOU SURE!?
YOU'RE JUST GIVING ME FOOD FOR FREE!?
EMPHASIS ON TASTE
Y-YEAH, IT'S FINE.

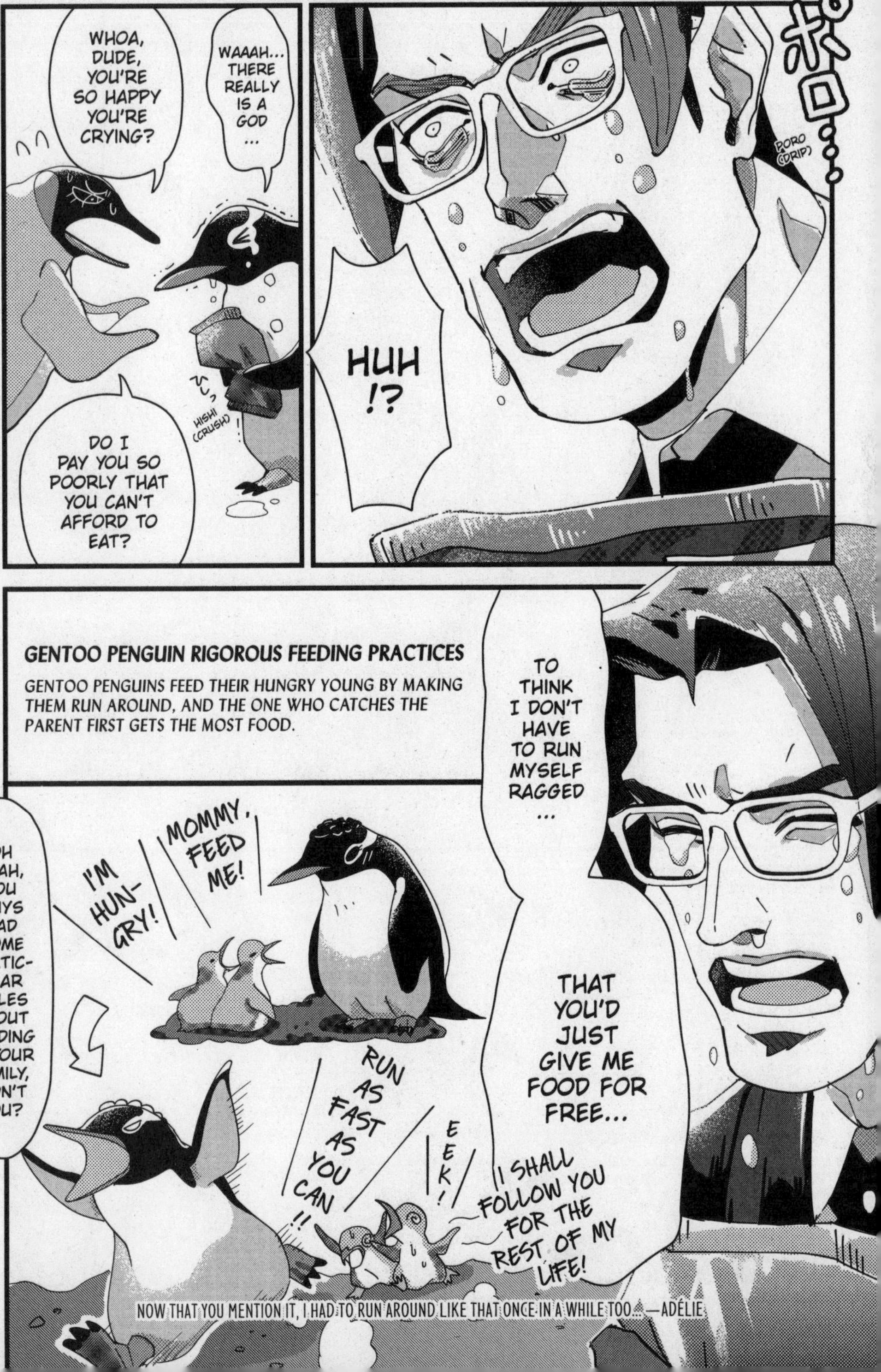
ポロ…
PORO (DRIP)
HUH !?
WAAAH... THERE REALLY IS A GOD...
WHOA, DUDE, YOU'RE SO HAPPY YOU'RE CRYING?
HISHI (CRUSH)
DO I PAY YOU SO POORLY THAT YOU CAN'T AFFORD TO EAT?
TO THINK I DON'T HAVE TO RUN MYSELF RAGGED...
THAT YOU'D JUST GIVE ME FOOD FOR FREE...
GENTOO PENGUIN RIGOROUS FEEDING PRACTICES
GENTOO PENGUINS FEED THEIR HUNGRY YOUNG BY MAKING THEM RUN AROUND, AND THE ONE WHO CATCHES THE PARENT FIRST GETS THE MOST FOOD.
MOMMY, FEED ME!
I'M HUNGRY!
OH YEAH, YOU GUYS HAD SOME PARTICULAR RULES ABOUT FEEDING IN YOUR FAMILY, DIDN'T YOU?
RUN AS FAST AS YOU CAN!!
EEK!
I SHALL FOLLOW YOU FOR THE REST OF MY LIFE!
NOW THAT YOU MENTION IT, I HAD TO RUN AROUND LIKE THAT ONCE IN A WHILE TOO... —ADÉLIE

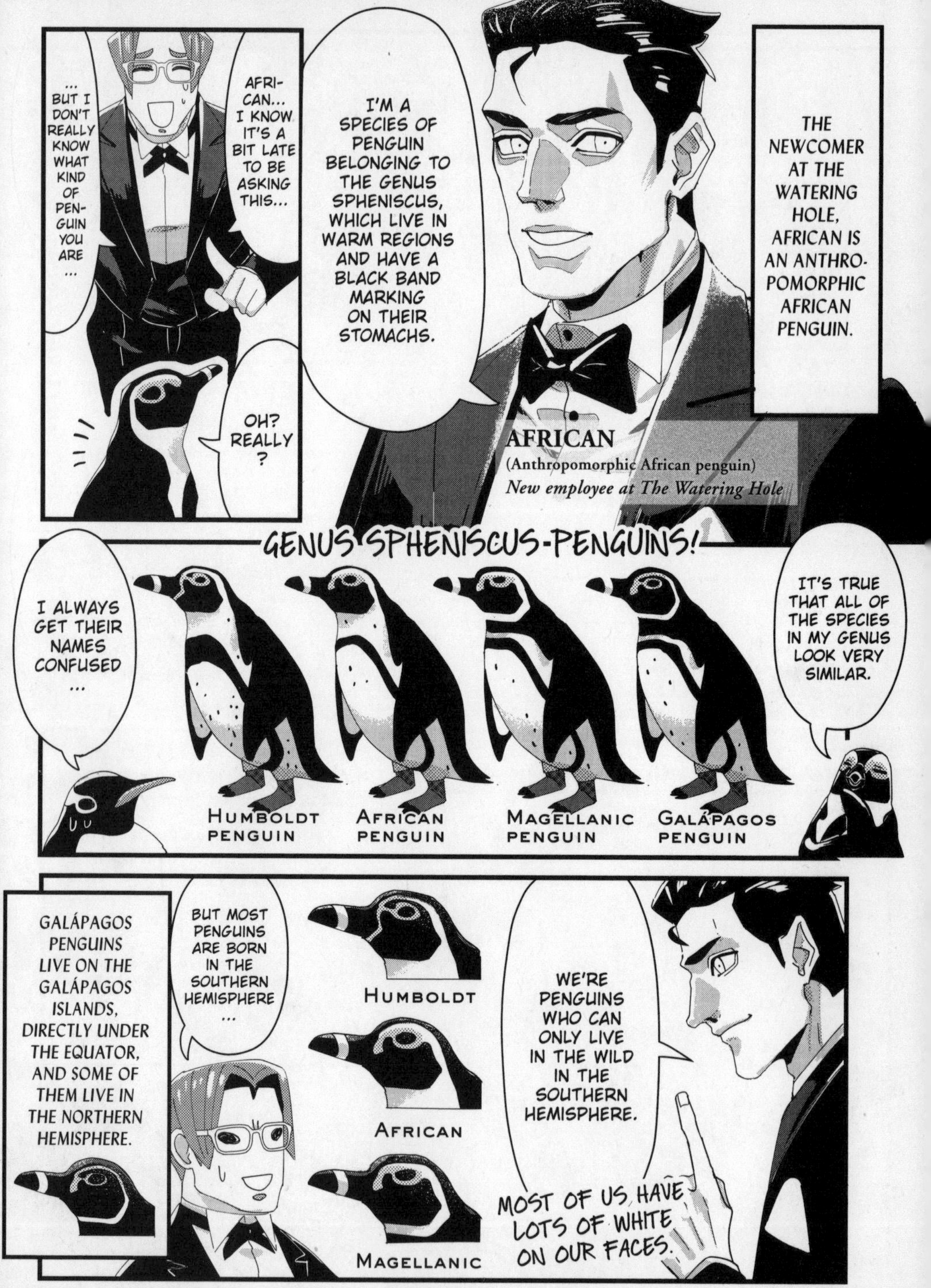
THE NEWCOMER AT THE WATERING HOLE, AFRICAN IS AN ANTHRO-POMORPHIC AFRICAN PENGUIN.
I'M A SPECIES OF PENGUIN BELONGING TO THE GENUS SPHENISCUS, WHICH LIVE IN WARM REGIONS AND HAVE A BLACK BAND MARKING ON THEIR STOMACHS.
AFRICAN
(Anthropomorphic African penguin)
New employee at The Watering Hole
AFRI-CAN... I KNOW IT'S A BIT LATE TO BE ASKING THIS...
...BUT I DON'T REALLY KNOW WHAT KIND OF PEN-GUIN YOU ARE...
OH? REALLY?
GENUS SPHENISCUS-PENGUINS!
IT'S TRUE THAT ALL OF THE SPECIES IN MY GENUS LOOK VERY SIMILAR.
HUMBOLDT PENGUIN
AFRICAN PENGUIN
MAGELLANIC PENGUIN
GALÁPAGOS PENGUIN
I ALWAYS GET THEIR NAMES CONFUSED...
WE'RE PENGUINS WHO CAN ONLY LIVE IN THE WILD IN THE SOUTHERN HEMISPHERE.
MOST OF US HAVE LOTS OF WHITE ON OUR FACES.
HUMBOLDT
AFRICAN
MAGELLANIC
BUT MOST PENGUINS ARE BORN IN THE SOUTHERN HEMISPHERE...
GALÁPAGOS PENGUINS LIVE ON THE GALÁPAGOS ISLANDS, DIRECTLY UNDER THE EQUATOR, AND SOME OF THEM LIVE IN THE NORTHERN HEMISPHERE.

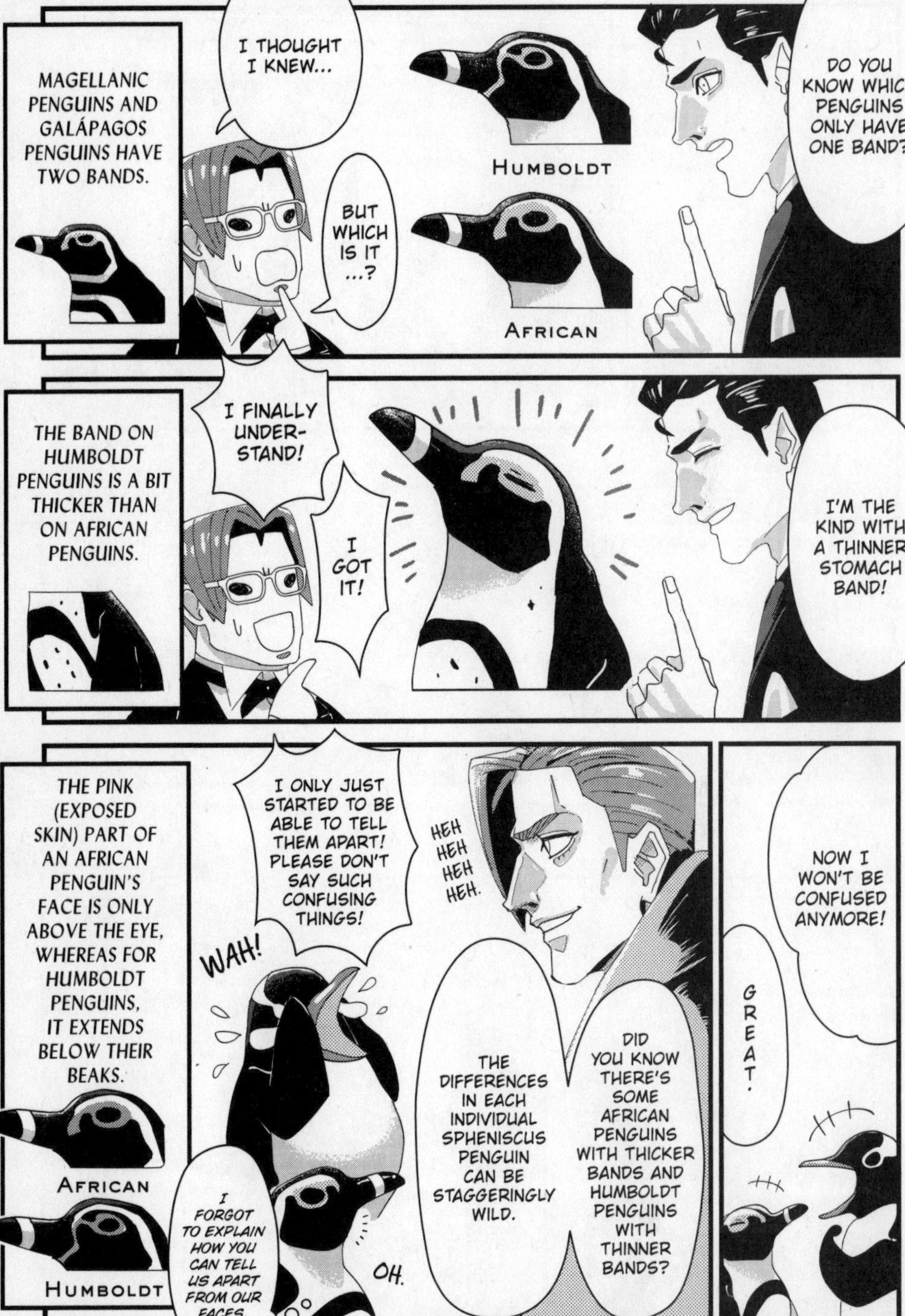
DO YOU KNOW WHICH PENGUINS ONLY HAVE ONE BAND?
HUMBOLDT
I THOUGHT I KNEW...
AFRICAN
BUT WHICH IS IT ...?
MAGELLANIC PENGUINS AND GALÁPAGOS PENGUINS HAVE TWO BANDS.
I'M THE KIND WITH A THINNER STOMACH BAND!
I FINALLY UNDER-STAND!
I GOT IT!
THE BAND ON HUMBOLDT PENGUINS IS A BIT THICKER THAN ON AFRICAN PENGUINS.
NOW I WON'T BE CONFUSED ANYMORE!
GREAT.
DID YOU KNOW THERE'S SOME AFRICAN PENGUINS WITH THICKER BANDS AND HUMBOLDT PENGUINS WITH THINNER BANDS?
THE DIFFERENCES IN EACH INDIVIDUAL SPHENISCUS PENGUIN CAN BE STAGGERINGLY WILD.
HEH HEH HEH HEH.
I ONLY JUST STARTED TO BE ABLE TO TELL THEM APART! PLEASE DON'T SAY SUCH CONFUSING THINGS!
WAH!
OH.
I FORGOT TO EXPLAIN HOW YOU CAN TELL US APART FROM OUR FACES.
THE PINK (EXPOSED SKIN) PART OF AN AFRICAN PENGUIN'S FACE IS ONLY ABOVE THE EYE, WHEREAS FOR HUMBOLDT PENGUINS, IT EXTENDS BELOW THEIR BEAKS.
AFRICAN
HUMBOLDT

THE SPOTS ON OUR STOMACHS ARE IN COMPLETELY DIFFERENT PLACES FOR ALL OF US. —AFRICAN

♦ African's Name ♦

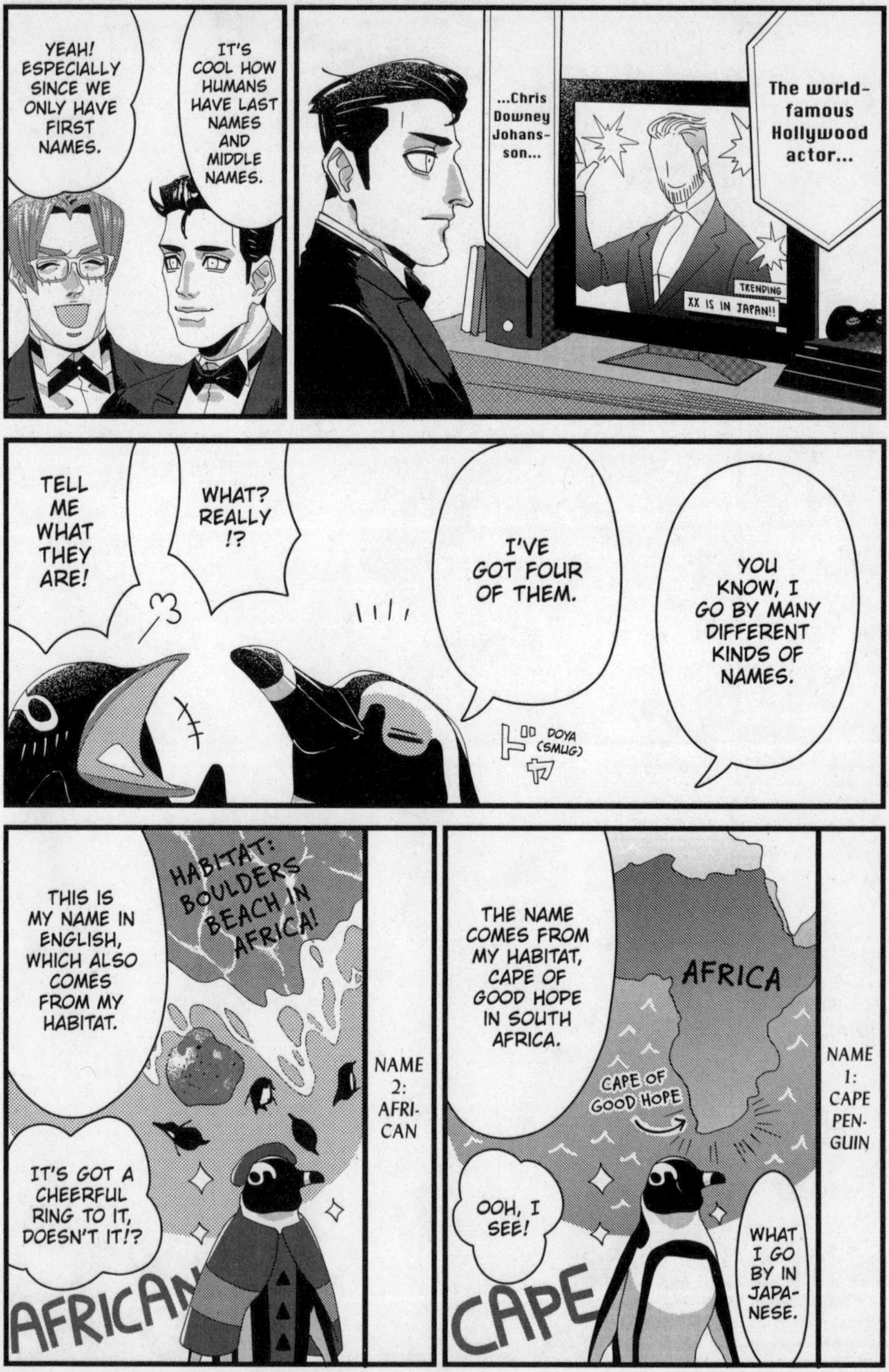
The world-famous Hollywood actor...
...Chris Downey Johansson...
TRENDING
XX IS IN JAPAN!!
IT'S COOL HOW HUMANS HAVE LAST NAMES AND MIDDLE NAMES.
YEAH! ESPECIALLY SINCE WE ONLY HAVE FIRST NAMES.
YOU KNOW, I GO BY MANY DIFFERENT KINDS OF NAMES.
I'VE GOT FOUR OF THEM.
DOYA (SMUG)
WHAT? REALLY!?
TELL ME WHAT THEY ARE!
NAME 1: CAPE PENGUIN
THE NAME COMES FROM MY HABITAT, CAPE OF GOOD HOPE IN SOUTH AFRICA.
AFRICA
CAPE OF GOOD HOPE
WHAT I GO BY IN JAPANESE.
OOH, I SEE!
CAPE
NAME 2: AFRICAN
HABITAT: BOULDERS BEACH IN AFRICA!
THIS IS MY NAME IN ENGLISH, WHICH ALSO COMES FROM MY HABITAT.
IT'S GOT A CHEERFUL RING TO IT, DOESN'T IT!?
AFRICAN

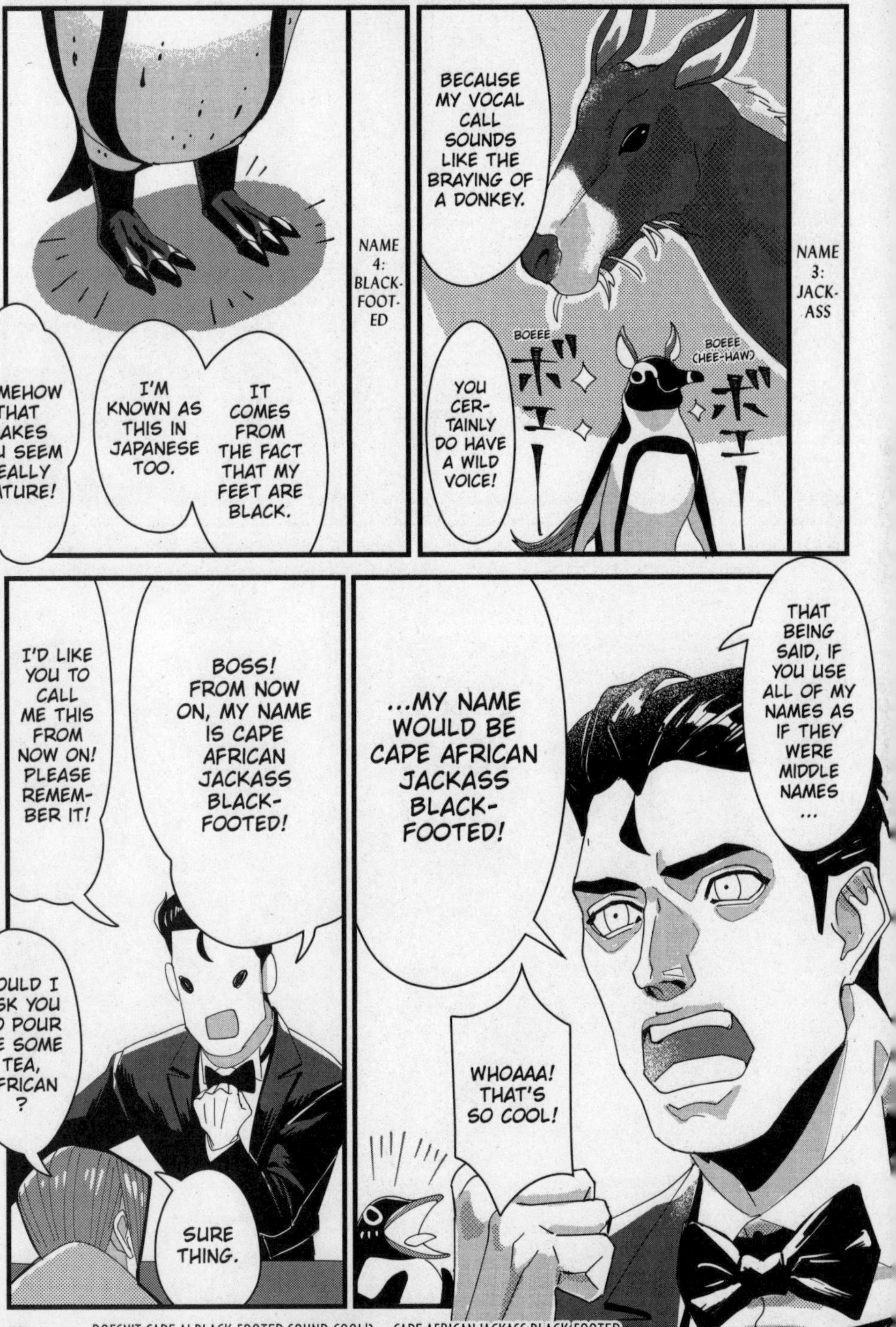
NAME 3: JACKASS
BECAUSE MY VOCAL CALL SOUNDS LIKE THE BRAYING OF A DONKEY.
BOEEE (CHEE-HAW)
BOEEE
YOU CERTAINLY DO HAVE A WILD VOICE!
NAME 4: BLACK-FOOTED
IT COMES FROM THE FACT THAT MY FEET ARE BLACK.
I'M KNOWN AS THIS IN JAPANESE TOO.
SOMEHOW THAT MAKES YOU SEEM REALLY MATURE!
THAT BEING SAID, IF YOU USE ALL OF MY NAMES AS IF THEY WERE MIDDLE NAMES...
...MY NAME WOULD BE CAPE AFRICAN JACKASS BLACK-FOOTED!
WHOAAA! THAT'S SO COOL!
BOSS! FROM NOW ON, MY NAME IS CAPE AFRICAN JACKASS BLACK-FOOTED!
I'D LIKE YOU TO CALL ME THIS FROM NOW ON! PLEASE REMEMBER IT!
COULD I ASK YOU TO POUR ME SOME TEA, AFRICAN?
SURE THING.

DOESN'T CAPE AJ BLACK-FOOTED SOUND COOL!? —CAPE AFRICAN JACKASS BLACK-FOOTED

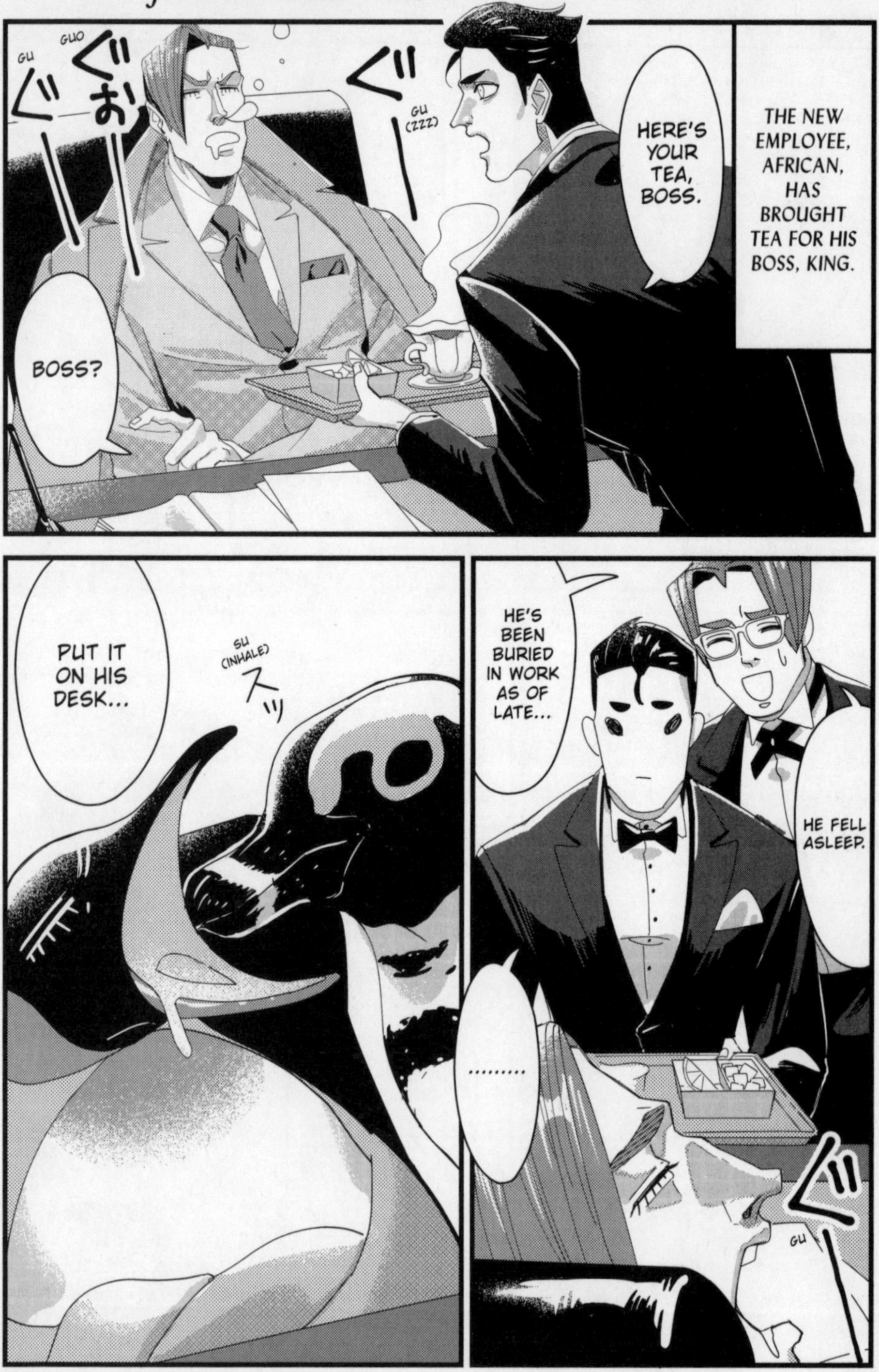
THE NEW EMPLOYEE, AFRICAN, HAS BROUGHT TEA FOR HIS BOSS, KING.
HERE'S YOUR TEA, BOSS.
GU (ZZZ)
GUO
GU
BOSS?
HE'S BEEN BURIED IN WORK AS OF LATE...
HE FELL ASLEEP.
....
GU
SU (INHALE)
PUT IT ON HIS DESK...

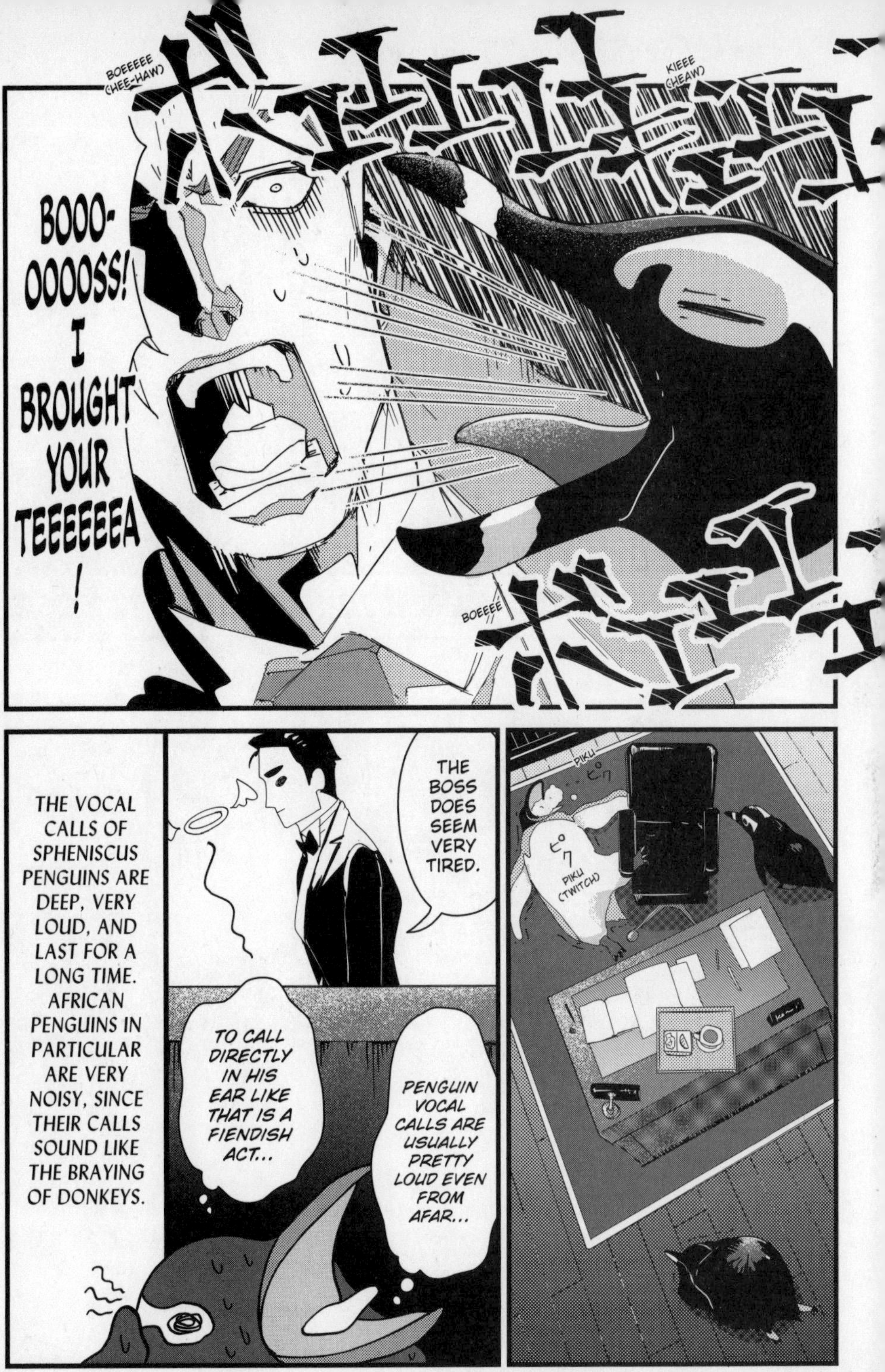
KIEEE (HEAW)
BOEEEEE (HEE-HAW)
BOOO-OOOOSS! I BROUGHT YOUR TEEEEEEA!
BOEEEE
PIKU
PIKU (TWITCH)
THE BOSS DOES SEEM VERY TIRED.
PENGUIN VOCAL CALLS ARE USUALLY PRETTY LOUD EVEN FROM AFAR...
TO CALL DIRECTLY IN HIS EAR LIKE THAT IS A FIENDISH ACT...
THE VOCAL CALLS OF SPHENISCUS PENGUINS ARE DEEP, VERY LOUD, AND LAST FOR A LONG TIME. AFRICAN PENGUINS IN PARTICULAR ARE VERY NOISY, SINCE THEIR CALLS SOUND LIKE THE BRAYING OF DONKEYS.

MY VOICE IS REALLY COOL, NO? I'M VERY CONFIDENT IN IT! —AFRICAN

♦ The Faces of Temperate Zone Penguins ♦

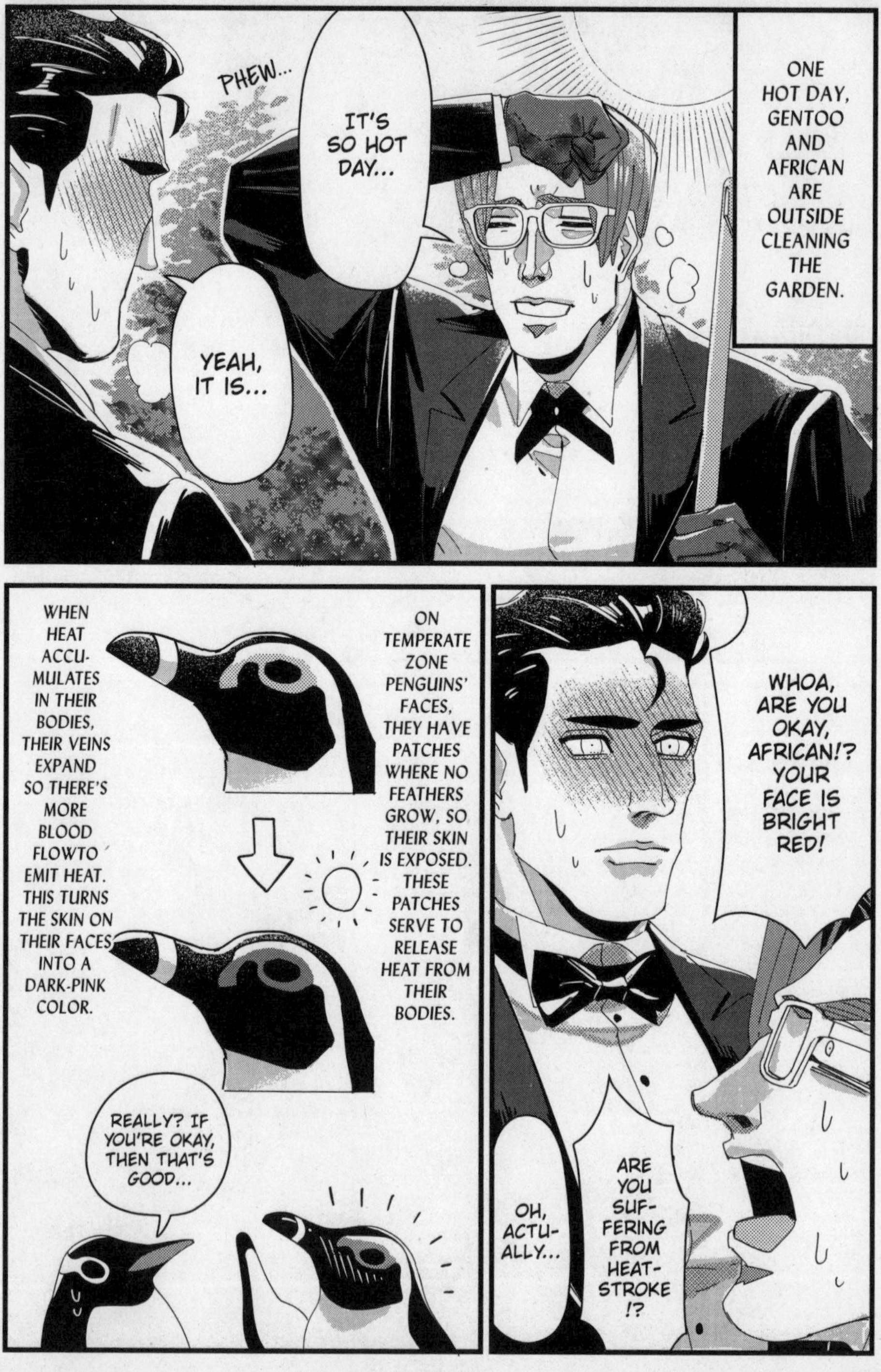
ONE HOT DAY, GENTOO AND AFRICAN ARE OUTSIDE CLEANING THE GARDEN.
PHEW...
IT'S SO HOT DAY...
YEAH, IT IS...
WHOA, ARE YOU OKAY, AFRICAN!? YOUR FACE IS BRIGHT RED!
ARE YOU SUFFERING FROM HEATSTROKE!?
OH, ACTUALLY...
ON TEMPERATE ZONE PENGUINS' FACES, THEY HAVE PATCHES WHERE NO FEATHERS GROW, SO THEIR SKIN IS EXPOSED. THESE PATCHES SERVE TO RELEASE HEAT FROM THEIR BODIES.
WHEN HEAT ACCUMULATES IN THEIR BODIES, THEIR VEINS EXPAND SO THERE'S MORE BLOOD FLOWTO EMIT HEAT. THIS TURNS THE SKIN ON THEIR FACES INTO A DARK-PINK COLOR.
REALLY? IF YOU'RE OKAY, THEN THAT'S GOOD...

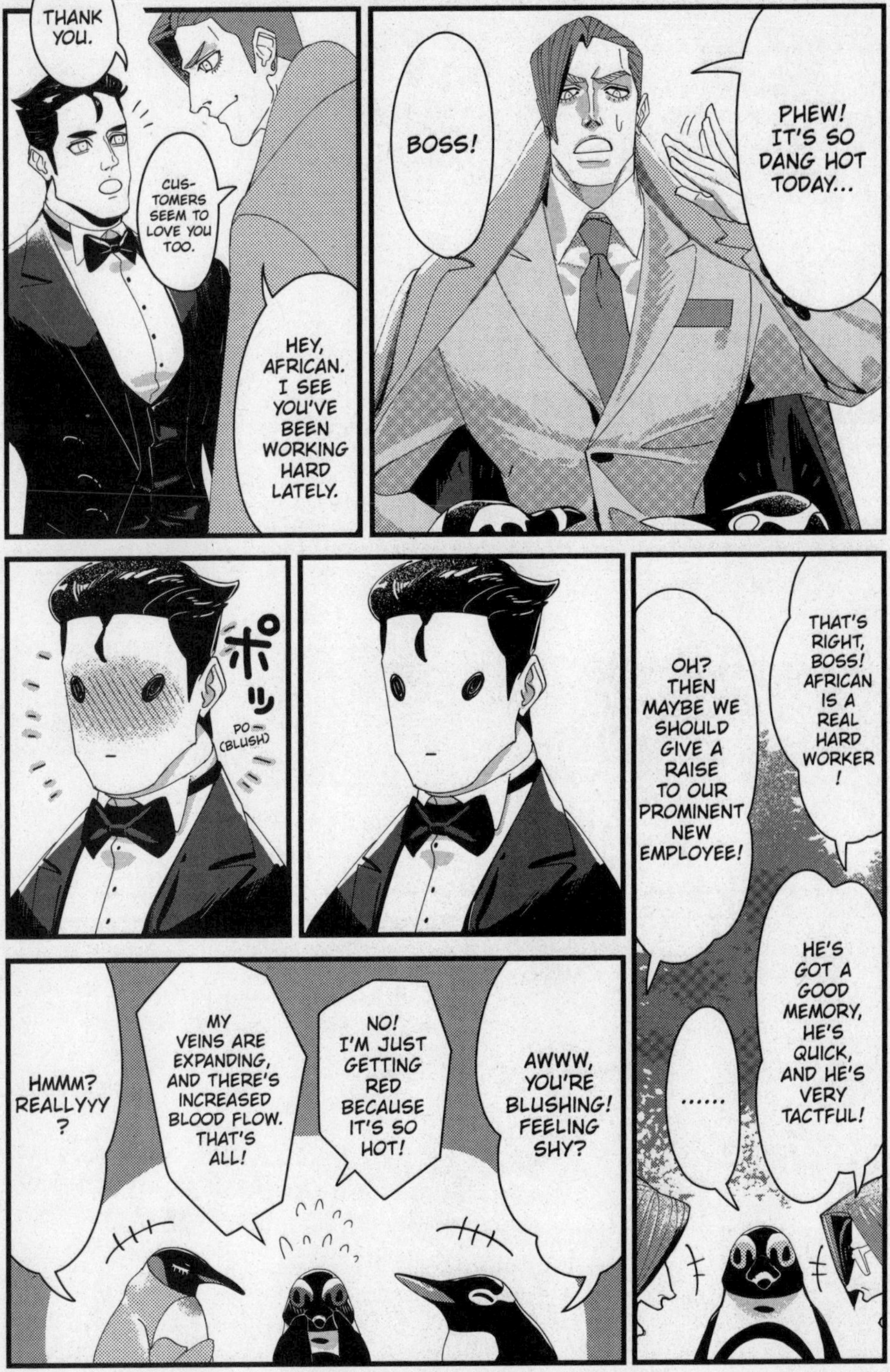
PHEW! IT'S SO DANG HOT TODAY...
BOSS!
HEY, AFRICAN. I SEE YOU'VE BEEN WORKING HARD LATELY.
CUS-TOMERS SEEM TO LOVE YOU TOO.
THANK YOU.
THAT'S RIGHT, BOSS! AFRICAN IS A REAL HARD WORKER!
OH? THEN MAYBE WE SHOULD GIVE A RAISE TO OUR PROMINENT NEW EMPLOYEE!
HE'S GOT A GOOD MEMORY, HE'S QUICK, AND HE'S VERY TACTFUL!
......
ポッ
PO— (BLUSH)
AWWW, YOU'RE BLUSHING! FEELING SHY?
NO! I'M JUST GETTING RED BECAUSE IT'S SO HOT!
MY VEINS ARE EXPANDING, AND THERE'S INCREASED BLOOD FLOW. THAT'S ALL!
HMMM? REALLYYY?

♦ How Many Species Are There in All? ♦

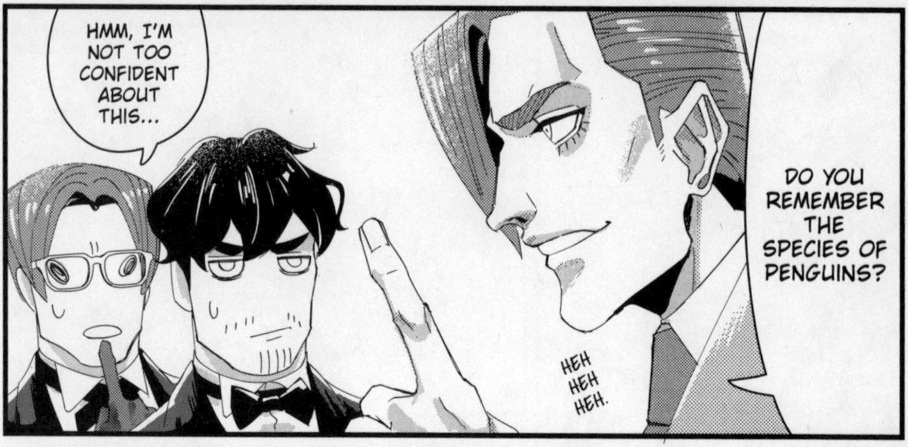
DO YOU REMEMBER THE SPECIES OF PENGUINS?
HEH HEH HEH.
HMM, I'M NOT TOO CONFIDENT ABOUT THIS...

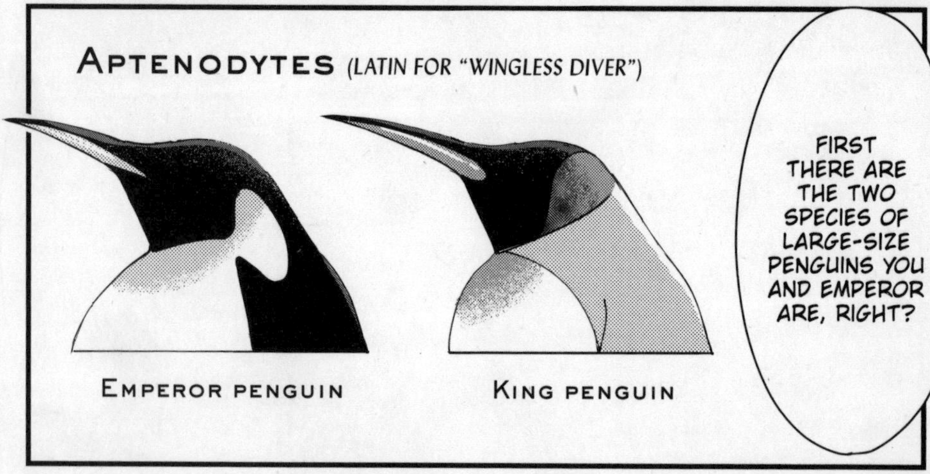
FIRST THERE ARE THE TWO SPECIES OF LARGE-SIZE PENGUINS YOU AND EMPEROR ARE, RIGHT?
APTENODYTES (LATIN FOR "WINGLESS DIVER")
KING PENGUIN
EMPEROR PENGUIN

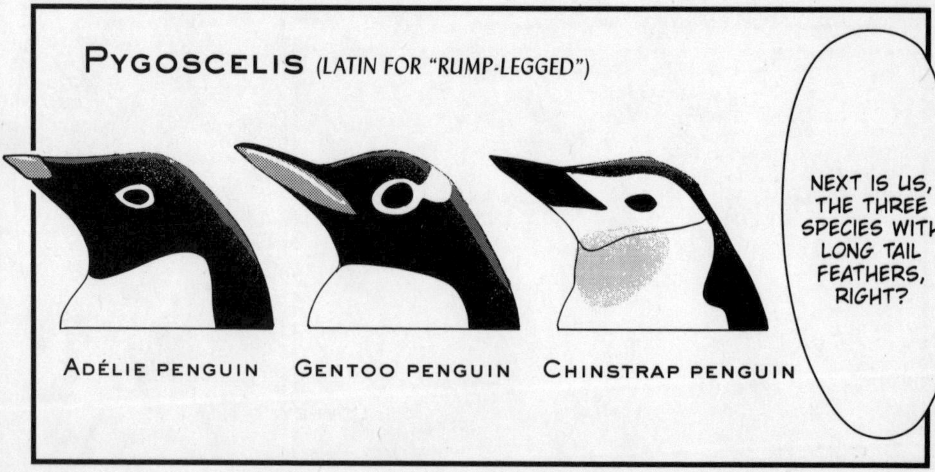
NEXT IS US, THE THREE SPECIES WITH LONG TAIL FEATHERS, RIGHT?
PYGOSCELIS (LATIN FOR "RUMP-LEGGED")
CHINSTRAP PENGUIN
GENTOO PENGUIN
ADÉLIE PENGUIN

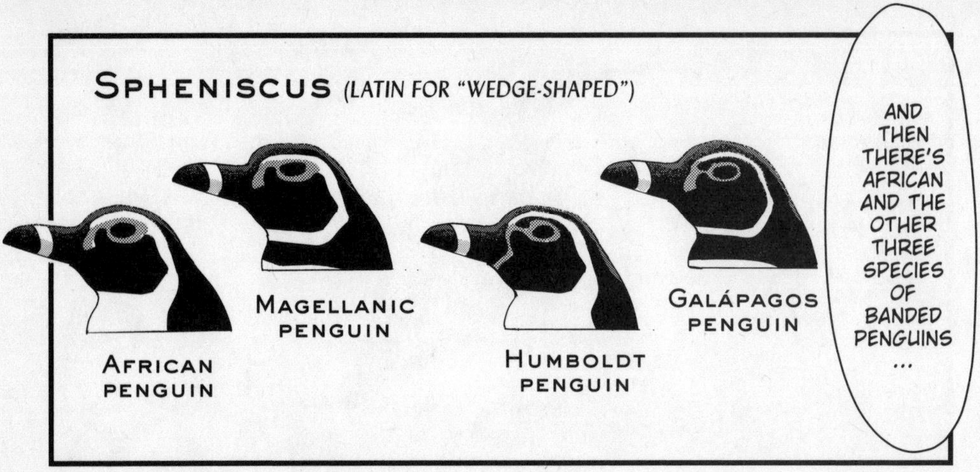
AND THEN THERE'S AFRICAN AND THE OTHER THREE SPECIES OF BANDED PENGUINS ...
SPHENISCUS (LATIN FOR "WEDGE-SHAPED")
GALÁPAGOS PENGUIN
HUMBOLDT PENGUIN
MAGELLANIC PENGUIN
AFRICAN PENGUIN

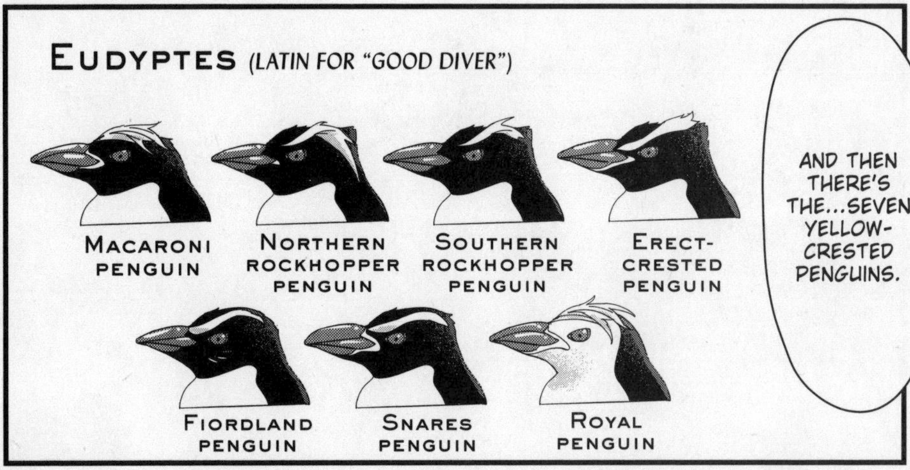
AND THEN THERE'S THE...SEVEN YELLOW-CRESTED PENGUINS.
EUDYPTES (LATIN FOR "GOOD DIVER")
MACARONI PENGUIN
NORTHERN ROCKHOPPER PENGUIN
SOUTHERN ROCKHOPPER PENGUIN
ERECT-CRESTED PENGUIN
FIORDLAND PENGUIN
SNARES PENGUIN
ROYAL PENGUIN

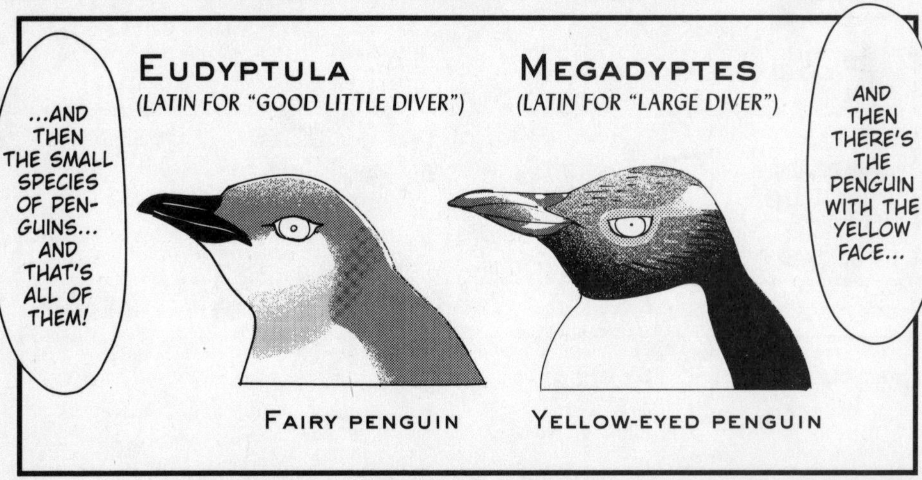
AND THEN THERE'S THE PENGUIN WITH THE YELLOW FACE...
...AND THEN THE SMALL SPECIES OF PEN-GUINS... AND THAT'S ALL OF THEM!
EUDYPTULA
(LATIN FOR "GOOD LITTLE DIVER")
MEGADYPTES
(LATIN FOR "LARGE DIVER")
FAIRY PENGUIN
YELLOW-EYED PENGUIN

*THE NORTHERN AND SOUTHERN ROCKHOPPER PENGUINS USED TO BE CATEGORIZED AS A SINGLE SPECIES. THE GENUS EUDYPTULA INCLUDES ANOTHER SPECIES CALLED THE WHITE-FLIPPERED PENGUIN.

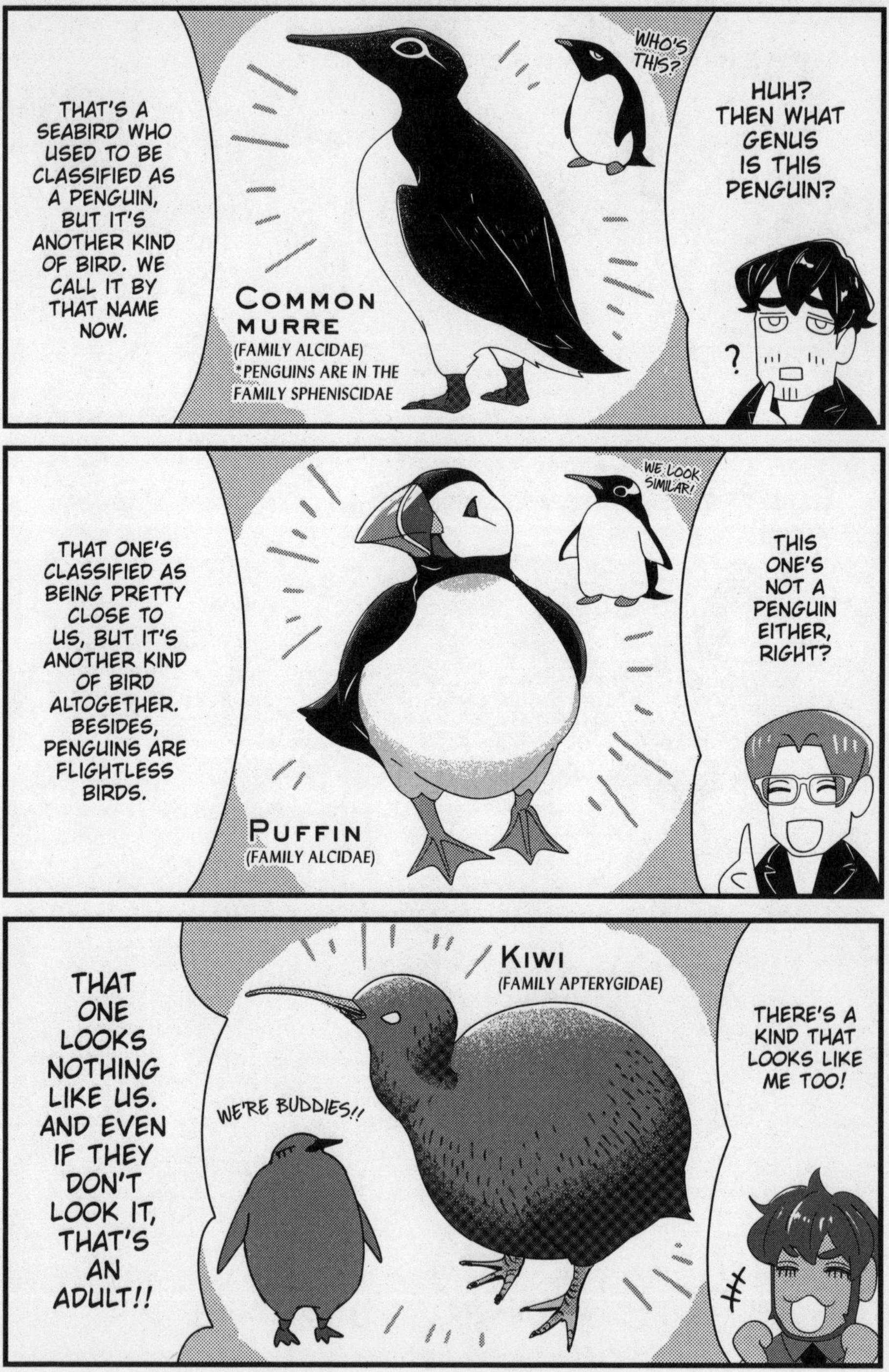
HUH? THEN WHAT GENUS IS THIS PENGUIN?
WHO'S THIS?
COMMON MURRE
(FAMILY ALCIDAE)
*PENGUINS ARE IN THE FAMILY SPHENISCIDAE
?
THAT'S A SEABIRD WHO USED TO BE CLASSIFIED AS A PENGUIN, BUT IT'S ANOTHER KIND OF BIRD. WE CALL IT BY THAT NAME NOW.
THIS ONE'S NOT A PENGUIN EITHER, RIGHT?
WE LOOK SIMILAR!
PUFFIN
(FAMILY ALCIDAE)
THAT ONE'S CLASSIFIED AS BEING PRETTY CLOSE TO US, BUT IT'S ANOTHER KIND OF BIRD ALTOGETHER. BESIDES, PENGUINS ARE FLIGHTLESS BIRDS.
THERE'S A KIND THAT LOOKS LIKE ME TOO!
KIWI
(FAMILY APTERYGIDAE)
WE'RE BUDDIES!!
THAT ONE LOOKS NOTHING LIKE US. AND EVEN IF THEY DON'T LOOK IT, THAT'S AN ADULT!!

THERE'S EIGHTEEN SPECIES OF PENGUINS IN TOTAL! YOU BETTER REMEMBER THEM ALL! —KING

Penguin Gentlemen

Chapter 3

Magnificent Daily Life

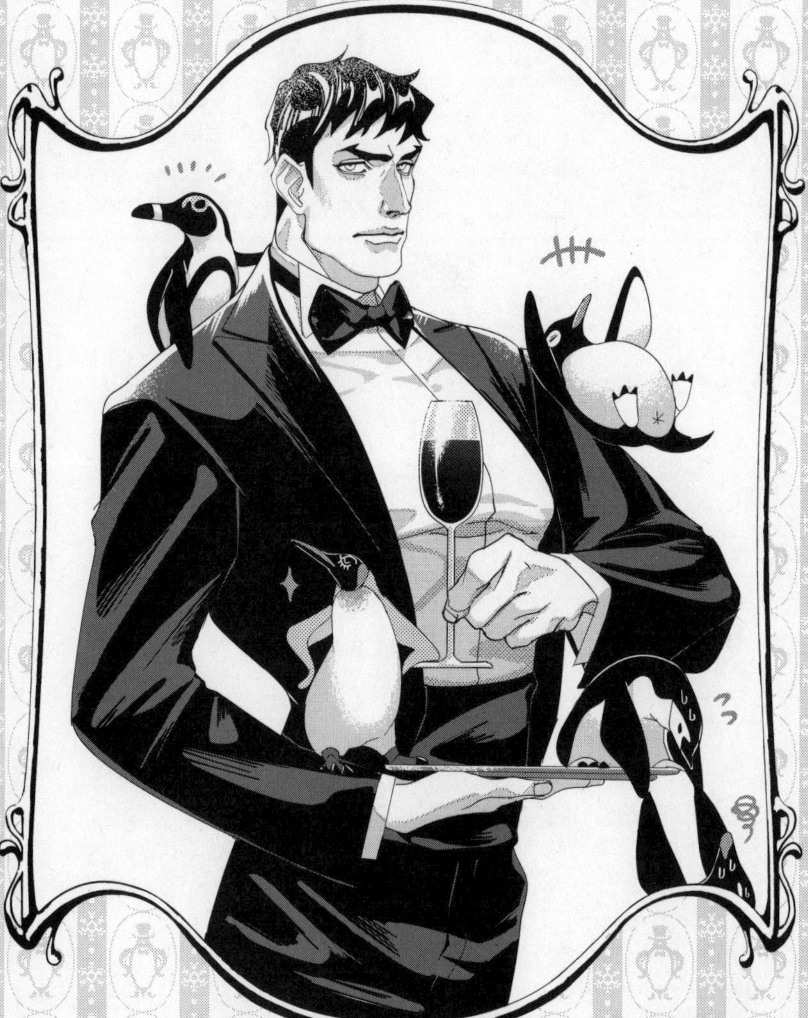

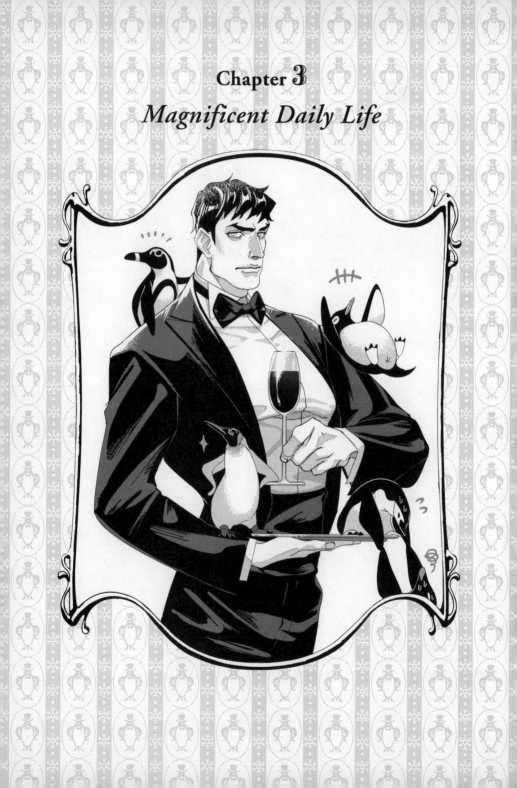

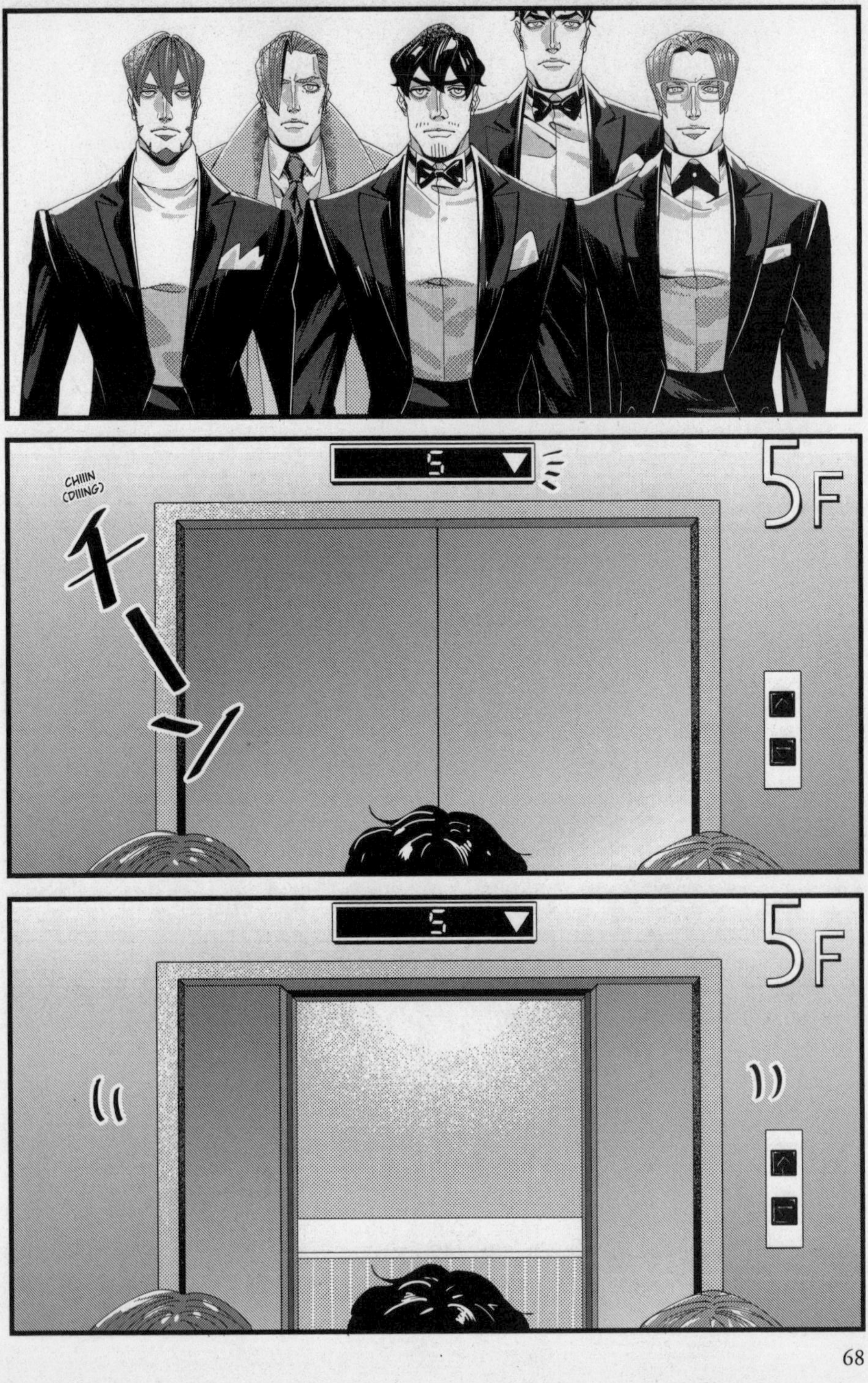
5F
CHIIIN (DIIING)
5F

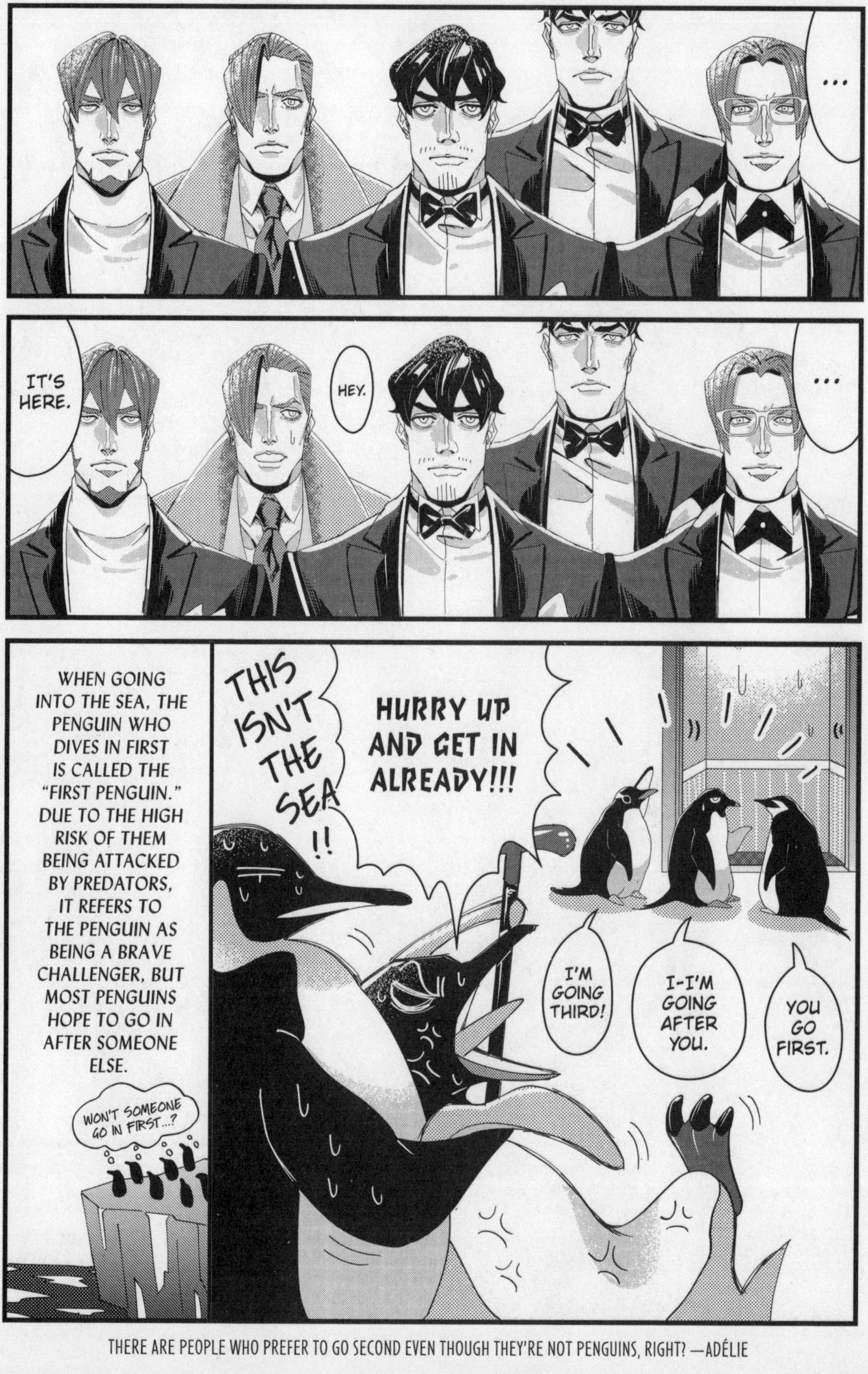
...
...
HEY.
IT'S HERE.
HURRY UP AND GET IN ALREADY!!!
THIS ISN'T THE SEA!!
YOU GO FIRST.
I-I'M GOING AFTER YOU.
I'M GOING THIRD!
WHEN GOING INTO THE SEA, THE PENGUIN WHO DIVES IN FIRST IS CALLED THE "FIRST PENGUIN." DUE TO THE HIGH RISK OF THEM BEING ATTACKED BY PREDATORS, IT REFERS TO THE PENGUIN AS BEING A BRAVE CHALLENGER, BUT MOST PENGUINS HOPE TO GO IN AFTER SOMEONE ELSE.
WON'T SOMEONE GO IN FIRST...?

THERE ARE PEOPLE WHO PREFER TO GO SECOND EVEN THOUGH THEY'RE NOT PENGUINS, RIGHT? —ADÉLIE

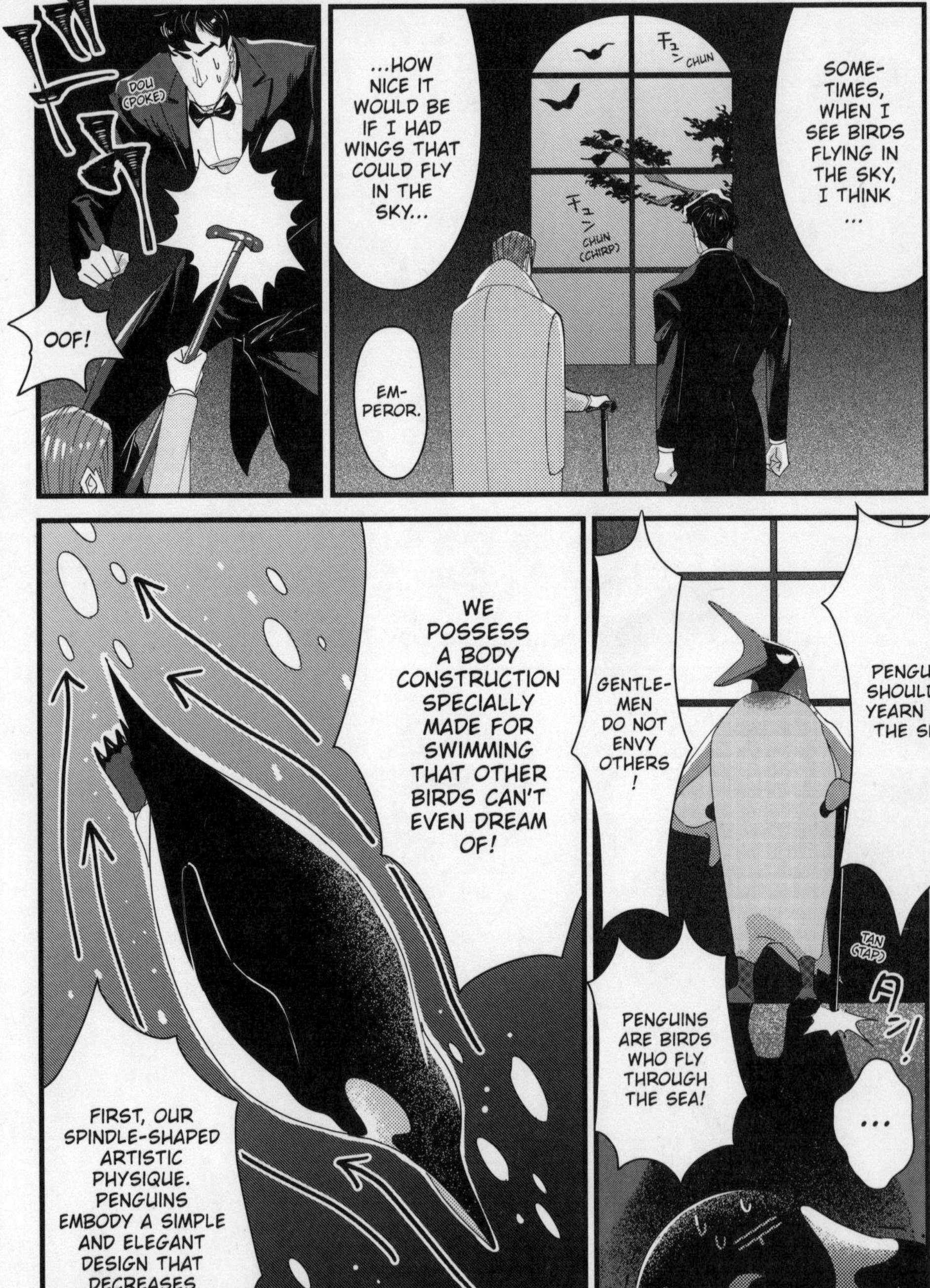
SOMETIMES, WHEN I SEE BIRDS FLYING IN THE SKY, I THINK ...
チュン CHUN
...HOW NICE IT WOULD BE IF I HAD WINGS THAT COULD FLY IN THE SKY...
チュン CHUN (CHIRP)
EMPEROR.
DOU (POKE)
OOF!
PENGUINS SHOULDN'T YEARN FOR THE SKY!
GENTLEMEN DO NOT ENVY OTHERS!
TAN (TAP)
PENGUINS ARE BIRDS WHO FLY THROUGH THE SEA!
...
WE POSSESS A BODY CONSTRUCTION SPECIALLY MADE FOR SWIMMING THAT OTHER BIRDS CAN'T EVEN DREAM OF!
FIRST, OUR SPINDLE-SHAPED ARTISTIC PHYSIQUE. PENGUINS EMBODY A SIMPLE AND ELEGANT DESIGN THAT DECREASES RESISTANCE IN THE WATER TO THE MAX!

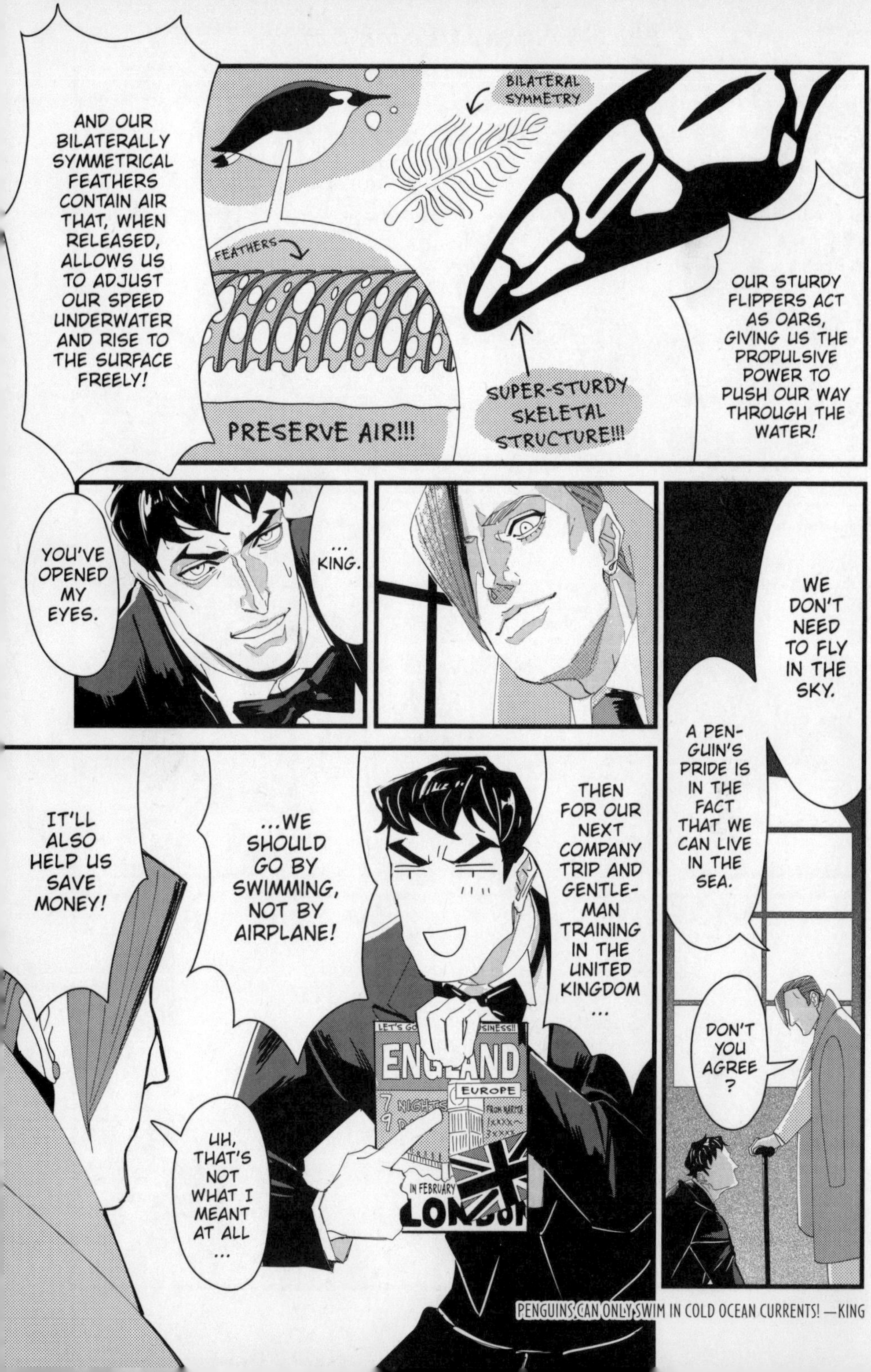
OUR STURDY FLIPPERS ACT AS OARS, GIVING US THE PROPULSIVE POWER TO PUSH OUR WAY THROUGH THE WATER!
SUPER-STURDY SKELETAL STRUCTURE!!!
BILATERAL SYMMETRY
FEATHERS
PRESERVE AIR!!!
AND OUR BILATERALLY SYMMETRICAL FEATHERS CONTAIN AIR THAT, WHEN RELEASED, ALLOWS US TO ADJUST OUR SPEED UNDERWATER AND RISE TO THE SURFACE FREELY!
WE DON'T NEED TO FLY IN THE SKY.
A PENGUIN'S PRIDE IS IN THE FACT THAT WE CAN LIVE IN THE SEA.
DON'T YOU AGREE?
...KING.
YOU'VE OPENED MY EYES.
THEN FOR OUR NEXT COMPANY TRIP AND GENTLEMAN TRAINING IN THE UNITED KINGDOM...
...WE SHOULD GO BY SWIMMING, NOT BY AIRPLANE!
IT'LL ALSO HELP US SAVE MONEY!
ENGLAND
EUROPE
IN FEBRUARY
UH, THAT'S NOT WHAT I MEANT AT ALL...

PENGUINS CAN ONLY SWIM IN COLD OCEAN CURRENTS! —KING

◆ *Stumpy Legs* ◆

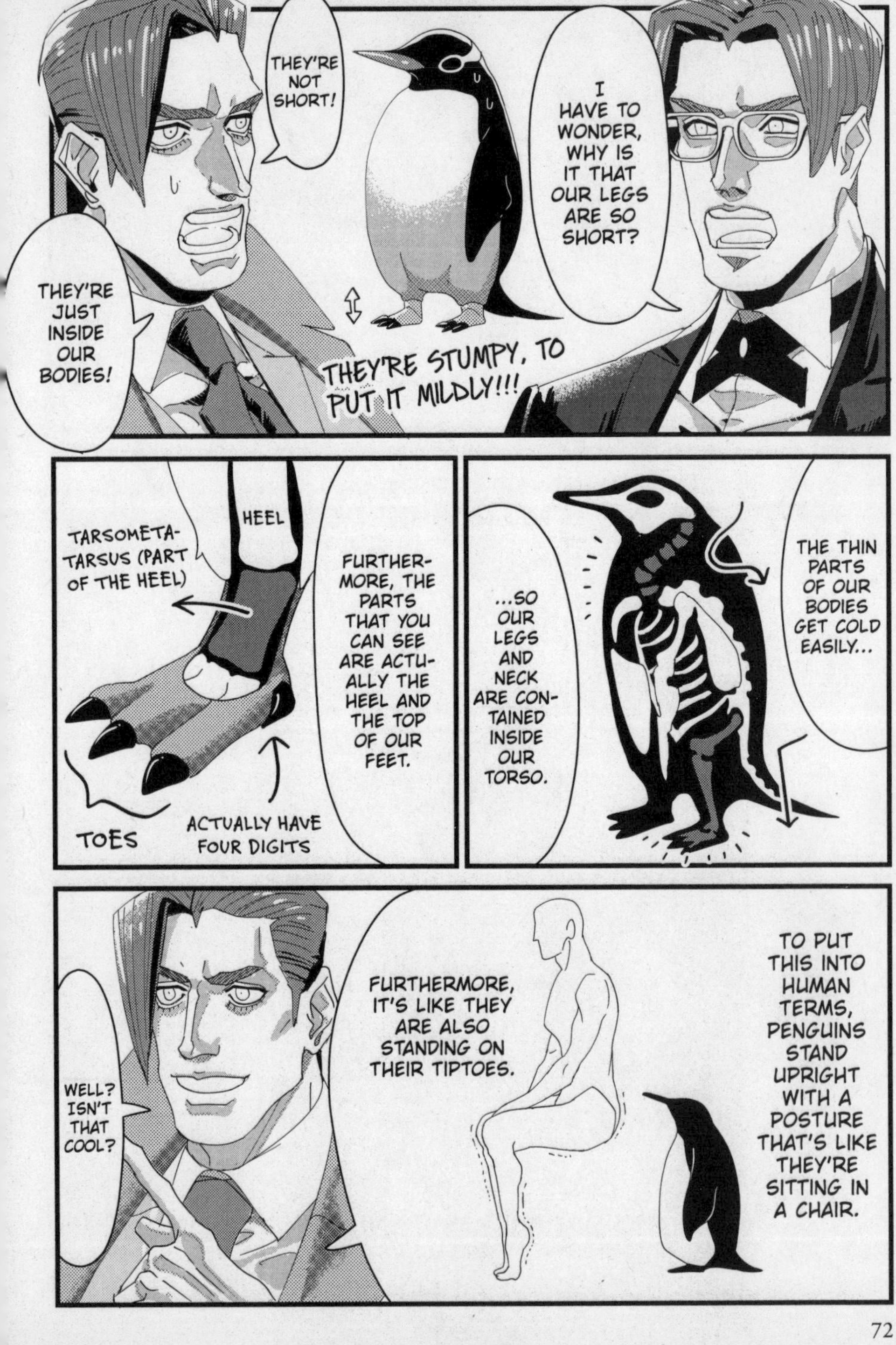
I HAVE TO WONDER, WHY IS IT THAT OUR LEGS ARE SO SHORT?
THEY'RE STUMPY, TO PUT IT MILDLY!!!
THEY'RE NOT SHORT!
THEY'RE JUST INSIDE OUR BODIES!
THE THIN PARTS OF OUR BODIES GET COLD EASILY...
...SO OUR LEGS AND NECK ARE CONTAINED INSIDE OUR TORSO.
FURTHERMORE, THE PARTS THAT YOU CAN SEE ARE ACTUALLY THE HEEL AND THE TOP OF OUR FEET.
HEEL
TARSOMETATARSUS (PART OF THE HEEL)
ACTUALLY HAVE FOUR DIGITS
TOES
TO PUT THIS INTO HUMAN TERMS, PENGUINS STAND UPRIGHT WITH A POSTURE THAT'S LIKE THEY'RE SITTING IN A CHAIR.
FURTHERMORE, IT'S LIKE THEY ARE ALSO STANDING ON THEIR TIPTOES.
WELL? ISN'T THAT COOL?

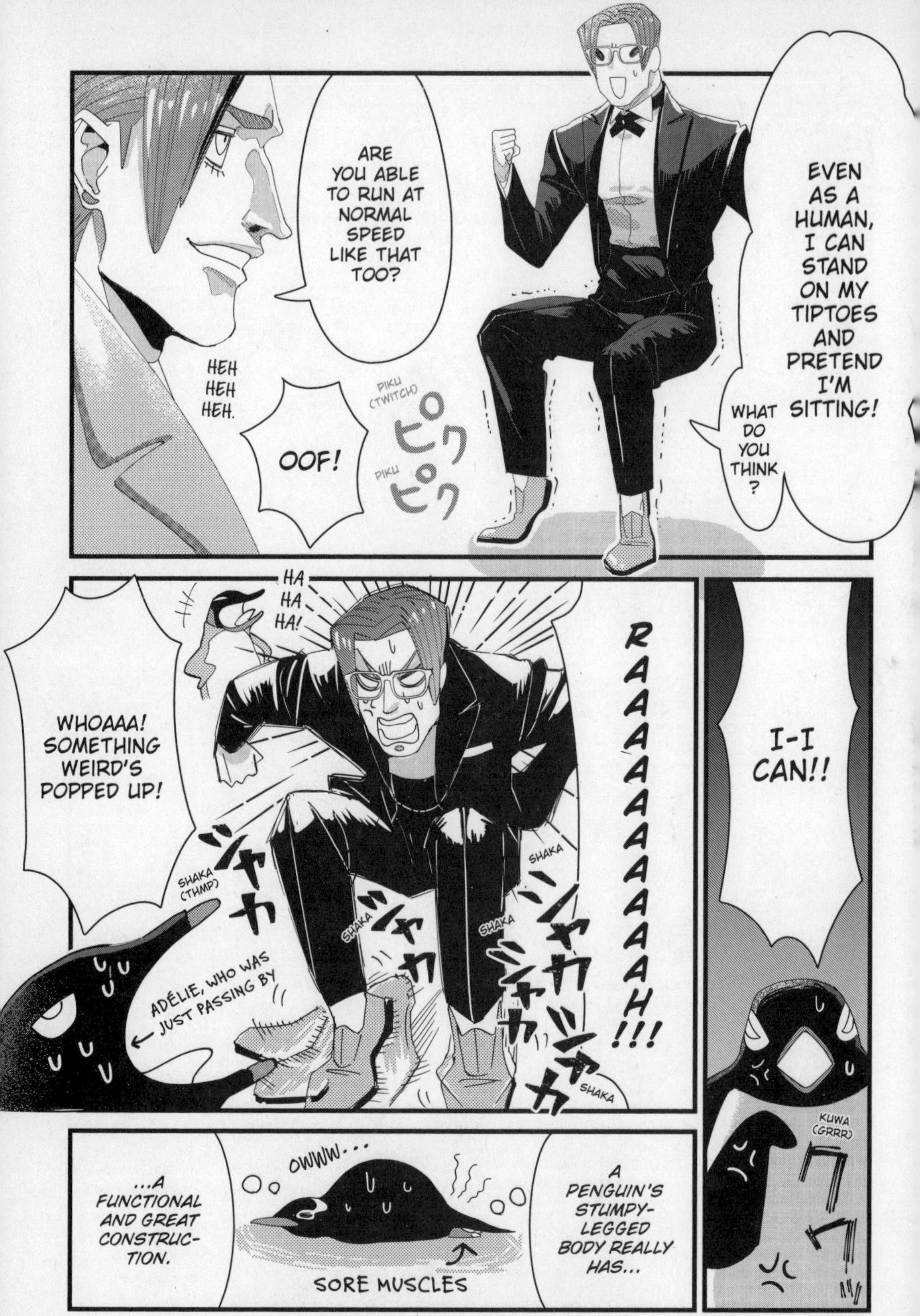
EVEN AS A HUMAN, I CAN STAND ON MY TIPTOES AND PRETEND I'M SITTING!
WHAT DO YOU THINK?
ARE YOU ABLE TO RUN AT NORMAL SPEED LIKE THAT TOO?
PIKU (TWITCH)
ピクピク
PIKU
OOF!
HEH HEH HEH.
I-I CAN!!
KUWA (GRRR)
RAAAAAAAAAAAAAH!!!
HA HA HA!
SHAKA
SHAKA
SHAKA
SHAKA (THMP)
SHAKA
WHOAAA! SOMETHING WEIRD'S POPPED UP!
ADÉLIE, WHO WAS JUST PASSING BY
A PENGUIN'S STUMPY-LEGGED BODY REALLY HAS...
OWWW...
SORE MUSCLES
...A FUNCTIONAL AND GREAT CONSTRUCTION.

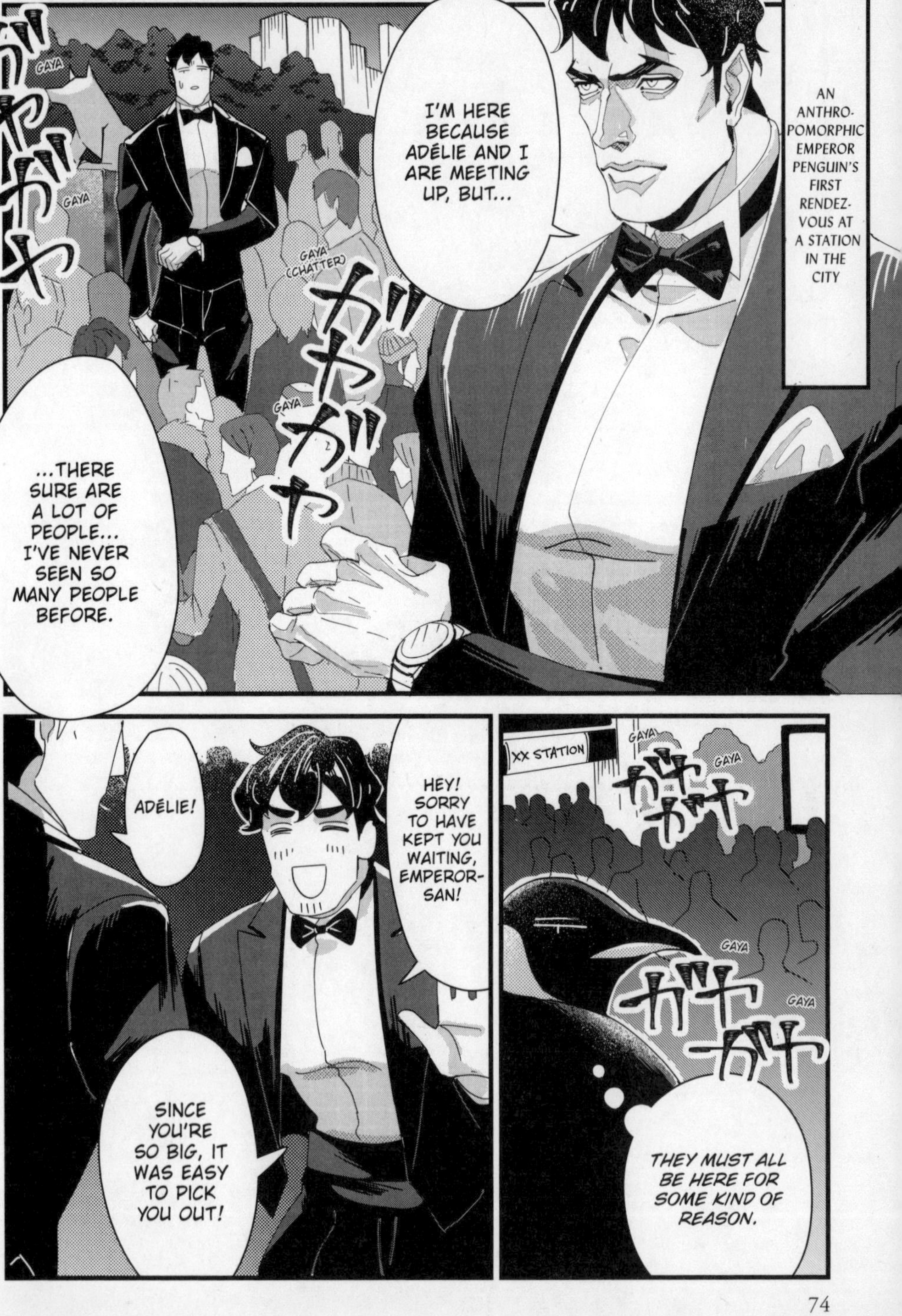
AN ANTHRO-POMORPHIC EMPEROR PENGUIN'S FIRST RENDEZ-VOUS AT A STATION IN THE CITY
I'M HERE BECAUSE ADÉLIE AND I ARE MEETING UP, BUT...
GAYA (CHATTER)
...THERE SURE ARE A LOT OF PEOPLE... I'VE NEVER SEEN SO MANY PEOPLE BEFORE.
XX STATION
GAYA
THEY MUST ALL BE HERE FOR SOME KIND OF REASON.
HEY! SORRY TO HAVE KEPT YOU WAITING, EMPEROR-SAN!
ADÉLIE!
SINCE YOU'RE SO BIG, IT WAS EASY TO PICK YOU OUT!

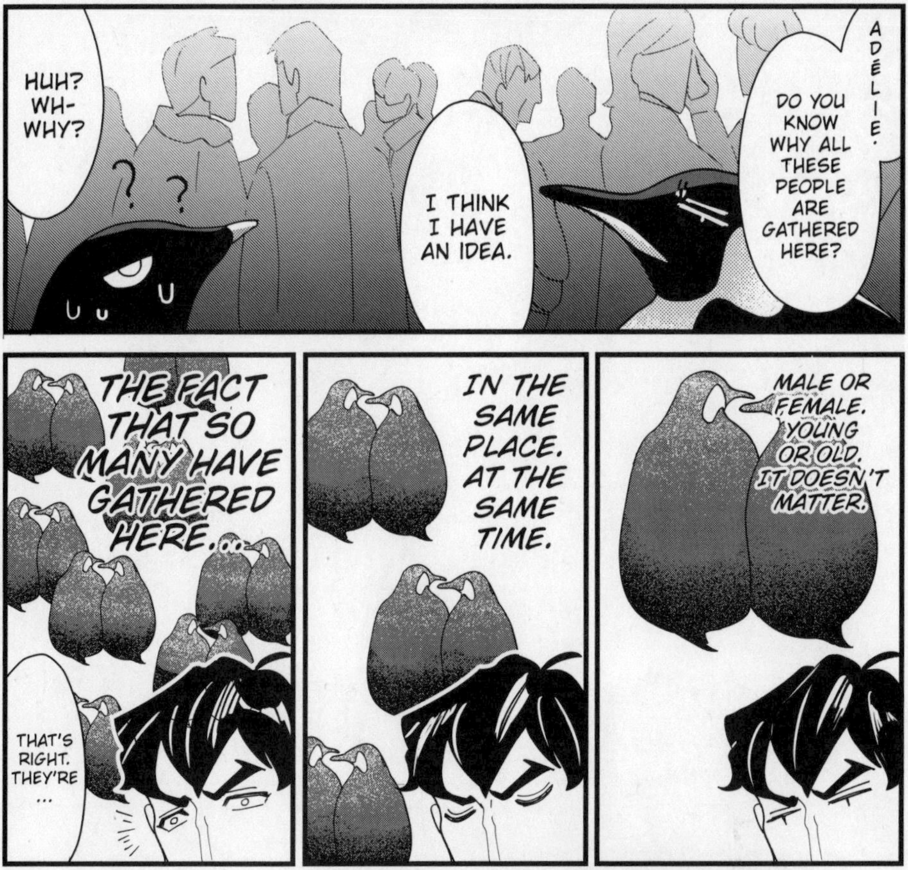
ADÉLIE.
DO YOU KNOW WHY ALL THESE PEOPLE ARE GATHERED HERE?
I THINK I HAVE AN IDEA.
HUH? WH-WHY?
MALE OR FEMALE. YOUNG OR OLD. IT DOESN'T MATTER.
IN THE SAME PLACE. AT THE SAME TIME.
THE FACT THAT SO MANY HAVE GATHERED HERE...
THAT'S RIGHT. THEY'RE ...

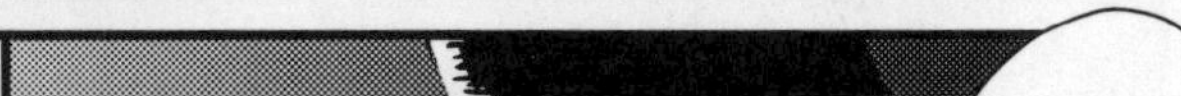
... MATING, NO DOUBT!
THESE HUMANS ARE LOOK-ING FOR SOMEONE TO COP-ULATE WITH.
THE BOSS AND THE OTHERS ARE WAITING FOR US. LET'S GO!

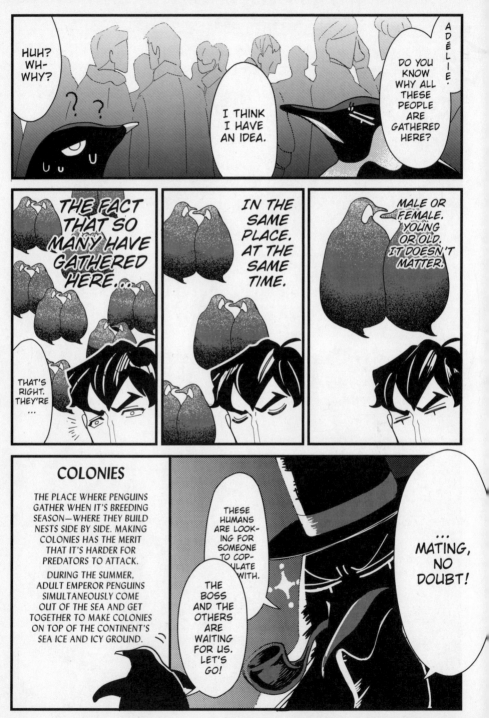

COLONIES

THE PLACE WHERE PENGUINS GATHER WHEN IT'S BREEDING SEASON—WHERE THEY BUILD NESTS SIDE BY SIDE. MAKING COLONIES HAS THE MERIT THAT IT'S HARDER FOR PREDATORS TO ATTACK.

DURING THE SUMMER, ADULT EMPEROR PENGUINS SIMULTANEOUSLY COME OUT OF THE SEA AND GET TOGETHER TO MAKE COLONIES ON TOP OF THE CONTINENT'S SEA ICE AND ICY GROUND.

THEY CALL A BIG COLONY MADE UP OF SEVERAL COLONIES A "ROOKERY." —KING

♦ *Walking in a Line* ♦

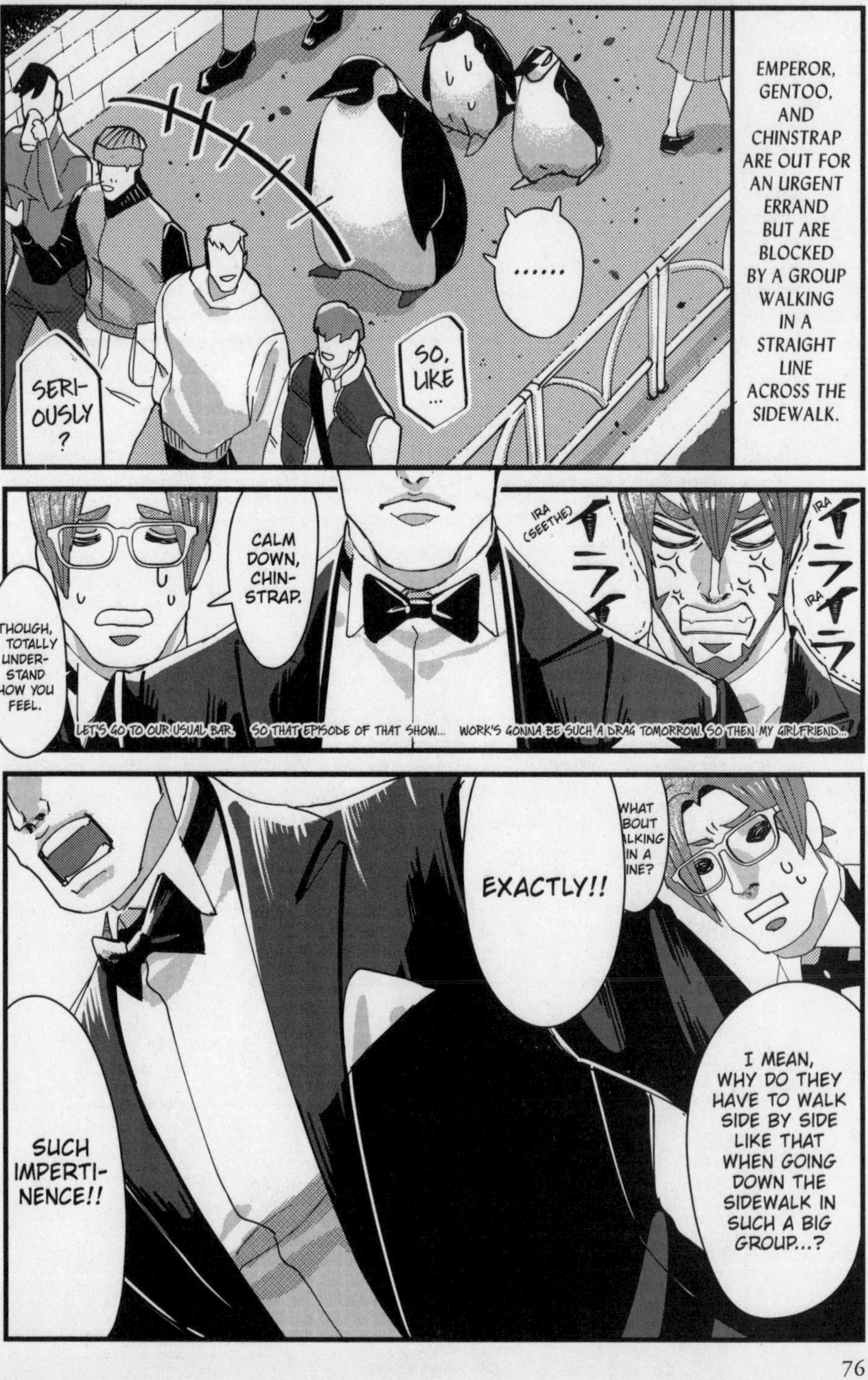

EMPEROR, GENTOO, AND CHINSTRAP ARE OUT FOR AN URGENT ERRAND BUT ARE BLOCKED BY A GROUP WALKING IN A STRAIGHT LINE ACROSS THE SIDEWALK.
......
SO, LIKE...
SERI-OUSLY?
IRA
IRA
IRA (SEETHE)
CALM DOWN, CHIN-STRAP.
THOUGH, I TOTALLY UNDER-STAND HOW YOU FEEL.
LET'S GO TO OUR USUAL BAR.
SO THAT EPISODE OF THAT SHOW...
WORK'S GONNA BE SUCH A DRAG TOMORROW.
SO THEN MY GIRLFRIEND...
WHAT BOUT ALKING IN A INE?
I MEAN, WHY DO THEY HAVE TO WALK SIDE BY SIDE LIKE THAT WHEN GOING DOWN THE SIDEWALK IN SUCH A BIG GROUP...?
EXACTLY!!
SUCH IMPERTI-NENCE!!

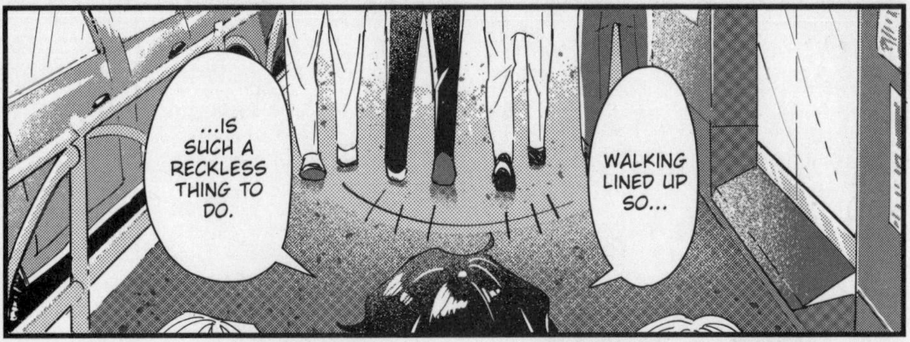
WALKING LINED UP SO...
...IS SUCH A RECKLESS THING TO DO.

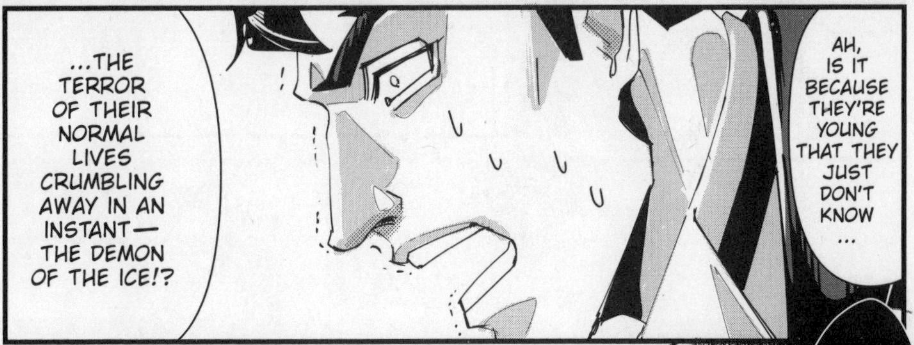
AH, IS IT BECAUSE THEY'RE YOUNG THAT THEY JUST DON'T KNOW...
...THE TERROR OF THEIR NORMAL LIVES CRUMBLING AWAY IN AN INSTANT— THE DEMON OF THE ICE!?

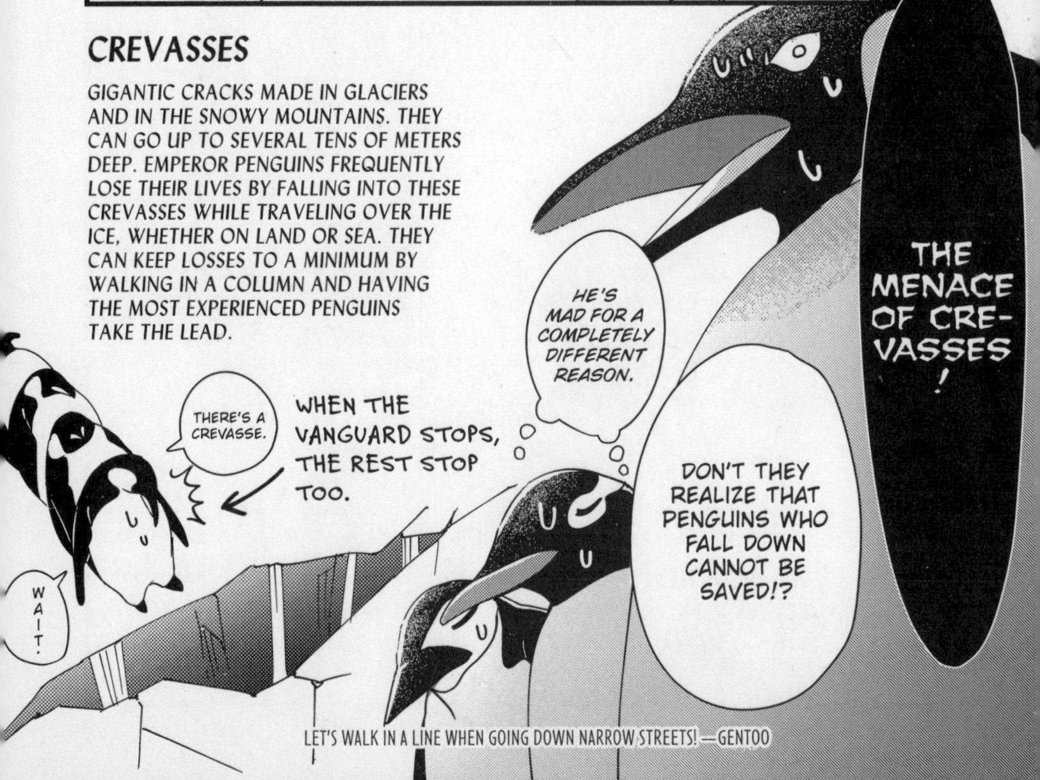
THE MENACE OF CRE-VASSES!
DON'T THEY REALIZE THAT PENGUINS WHO FALL DOWN CANNOT BE SAVED!?
HE'S MAD FOR A COMPLETELY DIFFERENT REASON.
WHEN THE VANGUARD STOPS, THE REST STOP TOO.
THERE'S A CREVASSE.
WAIT.

CREVASSES

GIGANTIC CRACKS MADE IN GLACIERS AND IN THE SNOWY MOUNTAINS. THEY CAN GO UP TO SEVERAL TENS OF METERS DEEP. EMPEROR PENGUINS FREQUENTLY LOSE THEIR LIVES BY FALLING INTO THESE CREVASSES WHILE TRAVELING OVER THE ICE, WHETHER ON LAND OR SEA. THEY CAN KEEP LOSSES TO A MINIMUM BY WALKING IN A COLUMN AND HAVING THE MOST EXPERIENCED PENGUINS TAKE THE LEAD.

LET'S WALK IN A LINE WHEN GOING DOWN NARROW STREETS! —GENTOO

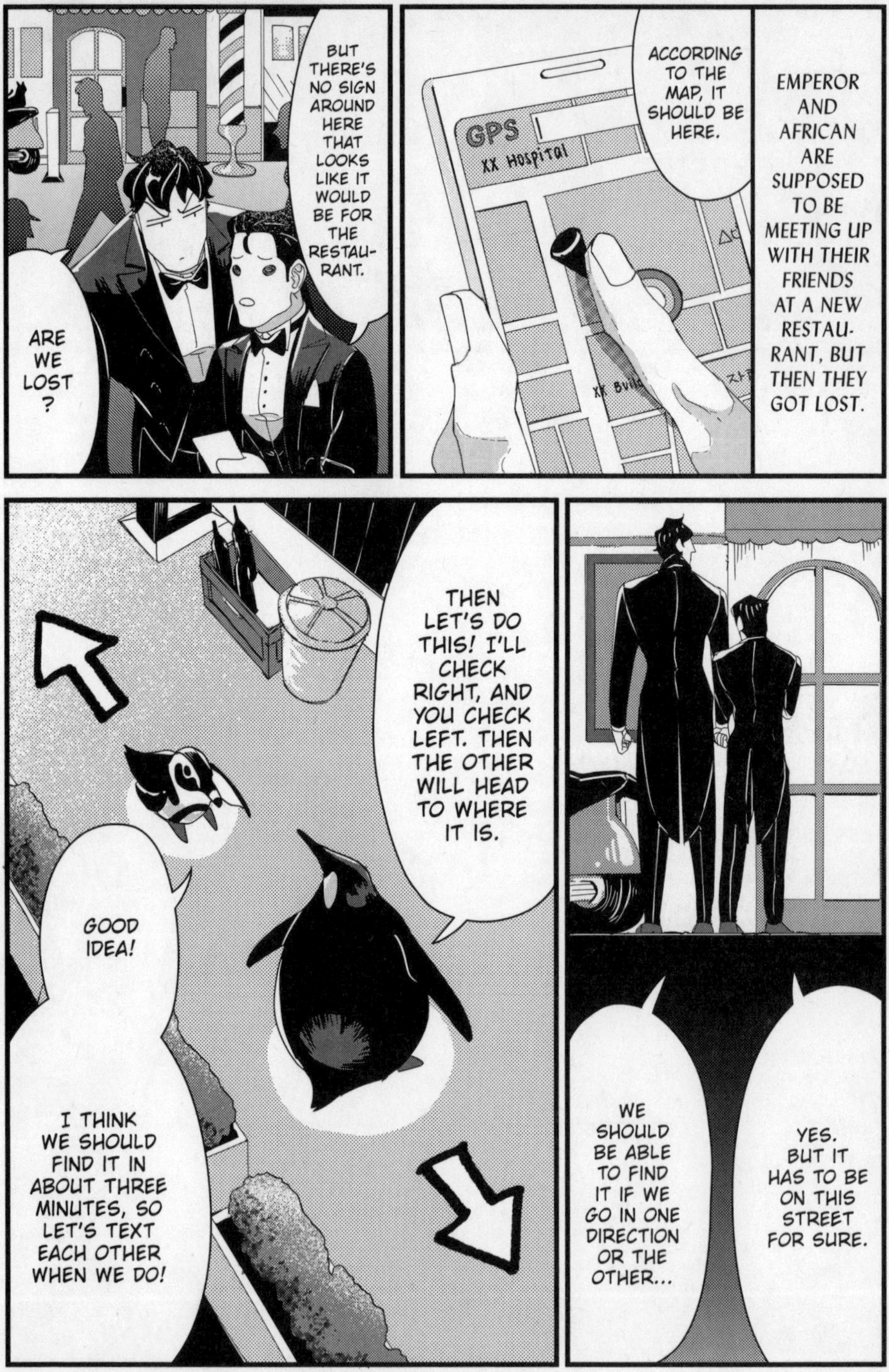
EMPEROR AND AFRICAN ARE SUPPOSED TO BE MEETING UP WITH THEIR FRIENDS AT A NEW RESTAU-RANT, BUT THEN THEY GOT LOST.
ACCORDING TO THE MAP, IT SHOULD BE HERE.
GPS
XX Hospital
XX Build
BUT THERE'S NO SIGN AROUND HERE THAT LOOKS LIKE IT WOULD BE FOR THE RESTAU-RANT.
ARE WE LOST?
YES. BUT IT HAS TO BE ON THIS STREET FOR SURE.
WE SHOULD BE ABLE TO FIND IT IF WE GO IN ONE DIRECTION OR THE OTHER...
THEN LET'S DO THIS! I'LL CHECK RIGHT, AND YOU CHECK LEFT. THEN THE OTHER WILL HEAD TO WHERE IT IS.
GOOD IDEA!
I THINK WE SHOULD FIND IT IN ABOUT THREE MINUTES, SO LET'S TEXT EACH OTHER WHEN WE DO!

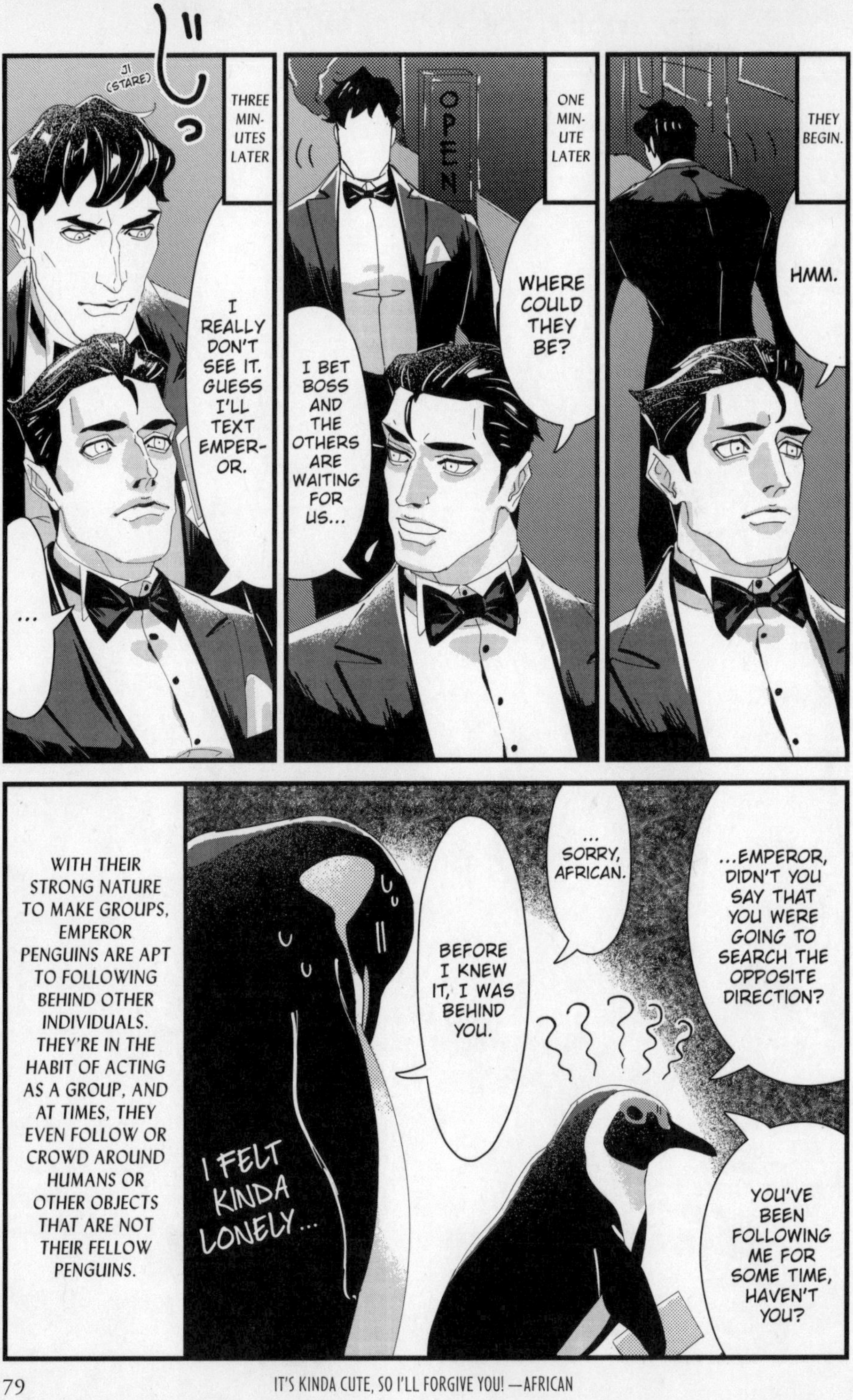
THEY BEGIN.
HMM.
ONE MIN-UTE LATER
WHERE COULD THEY BE?
I BET BOSS AND THE OTHERS ARE WAITING FOR US...
THREE MIN-UTES LATER
JI (STARE)
I REALLY DON'T SEE IT. GUESS I'LL TEXT EMPER-OR.
...
...EMPEROR, DIDN'T YOU SAY THAT YOU WERE GOING TO SEARCH THE OPPOSITE DIRECTION?
... SORRY, AFRICAN.
BEFORE I KNEW IT, I WAS BEHIND YOU.
YOU'VE BEEN FOLLOWING ME FOR SOME TIME, HAVEN'T YOU?
I FELT KINDA LONELY...
WITH THEIR STRONG NATURE TO MAKE GROUPS, EMPEROR PENGUINS ARE APT TO FOLLOWING BEHIND OTHER INDIVIDUALS. THEY'RE IN THE HABIT OF ACTING AS A GROUP, AND AT TIMES, THEY EVEN FOLLOW OR CROWD AROUND HUMANS OR OTHER OBJECTS THAT ARE NOT THEIR FELLOW PENGUINS.

IT'S KINDA CUTE, SO I'LL FORGIVE YOU! —AFRICAN

♦ Sleeping While Standing ♦

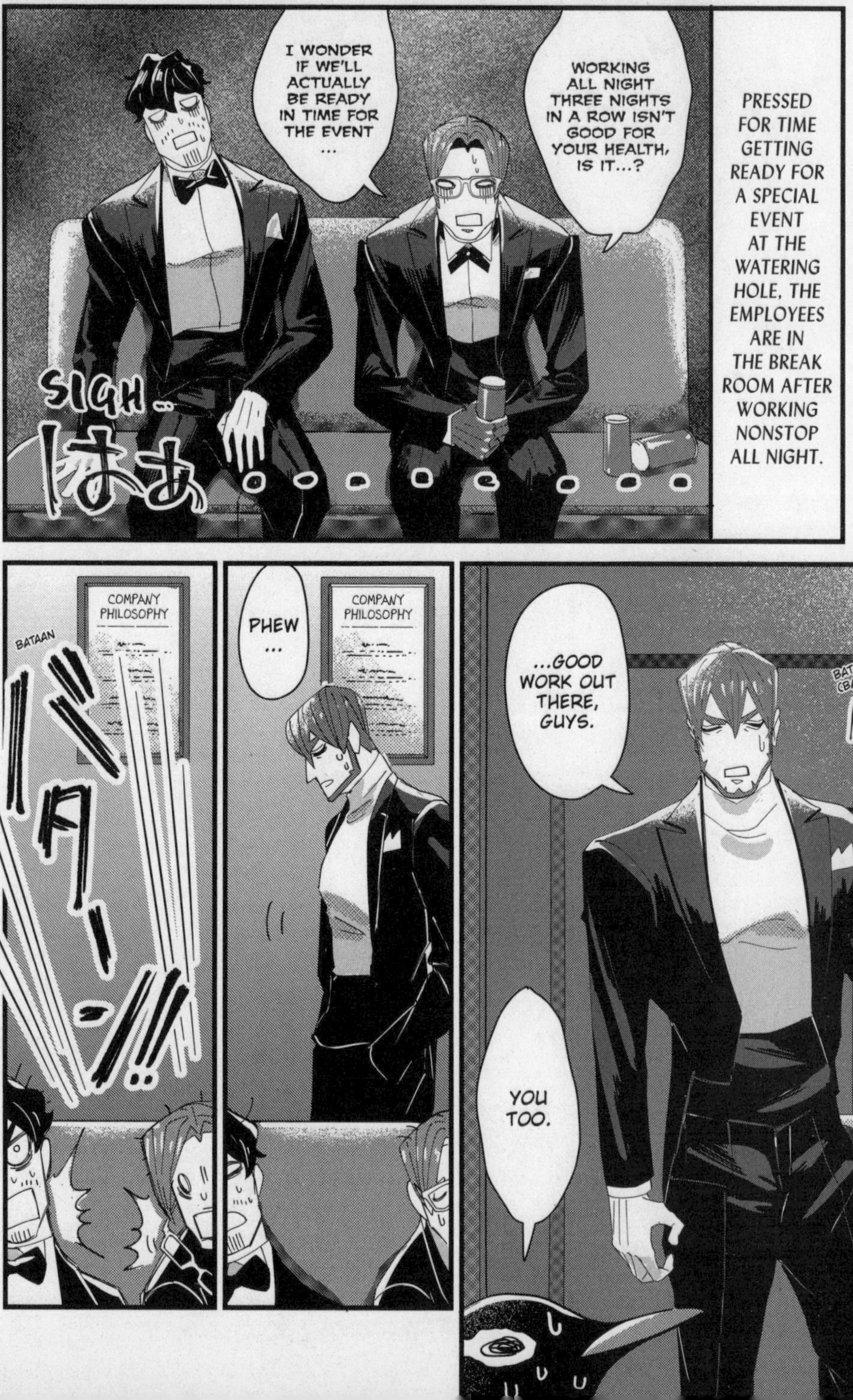
PRESSED FOR TIME GETTING READY FOR A SPECIAL EVENT AT THE WATERING HOLE, THE EMPLOYEES ARE IN THE BREAK ROOM AFTER WORKING NONSTOP ALL NIGHT.
WORKING ALL NIGHT THREE NIGHTS IN A ROW ISN'T GOOD FOR YOUR HEALTH, IS IT...?
I WONDER IF WE'LL ACTUALLY BE READY IN TIME FOR THE EVENT ...
SIGH...
はあ
BATAN (BAM)
...GOOD WORK OUT THERE, GUYS.
YOU TOO.
COMPANY PHILOSOPHY
PHEW ...
COMPANY PHILOSOPHY
BATAAN

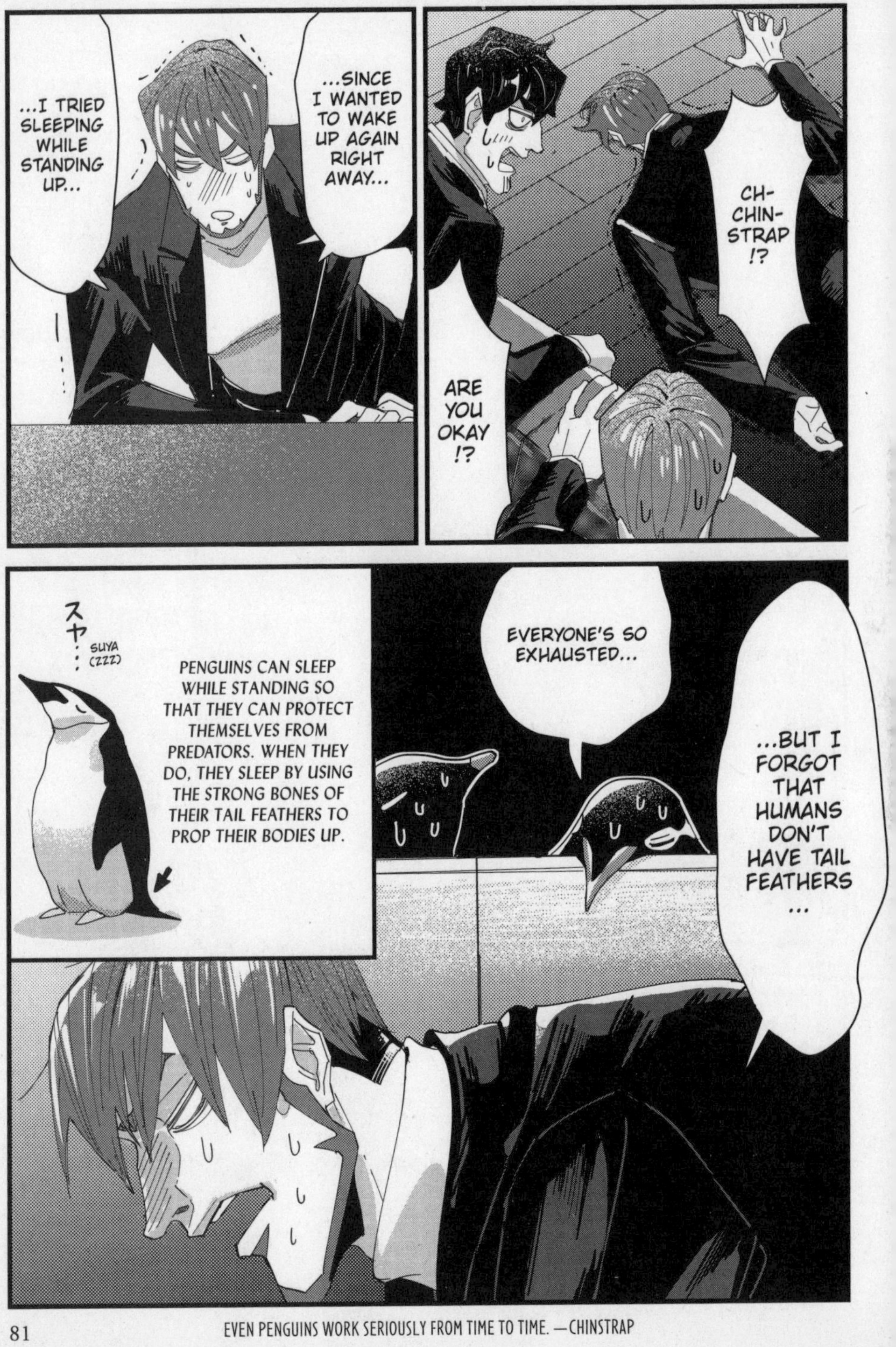
CH-CHIN-STRAP!?
ARE YOU OKAY!?
...SINCE I WANTED TO WAKE UP AGAIN RIGHT AWAY...
...I TRIED SLEEPING WHILE STANDING UP...
...BUT I FORGOT THAT HUMANS DON'T HAVE TAIL FEATHERS...
EVERYONE'S SO EXHAUSTED...
スヤ・・
SUYA (ZZZ)
PENGUINS CAN SLEEP WHILE STANDING SO THAT THEY CAN PROTECT THEMSELVES FROM PREDATORS. WHEN THEY DO, THEY SLEEP BY USING THE STRONG BONES OF THEIR TAIL FEATHERS TO PROP THEIR BODIES UP.

♦ Skating? ♦

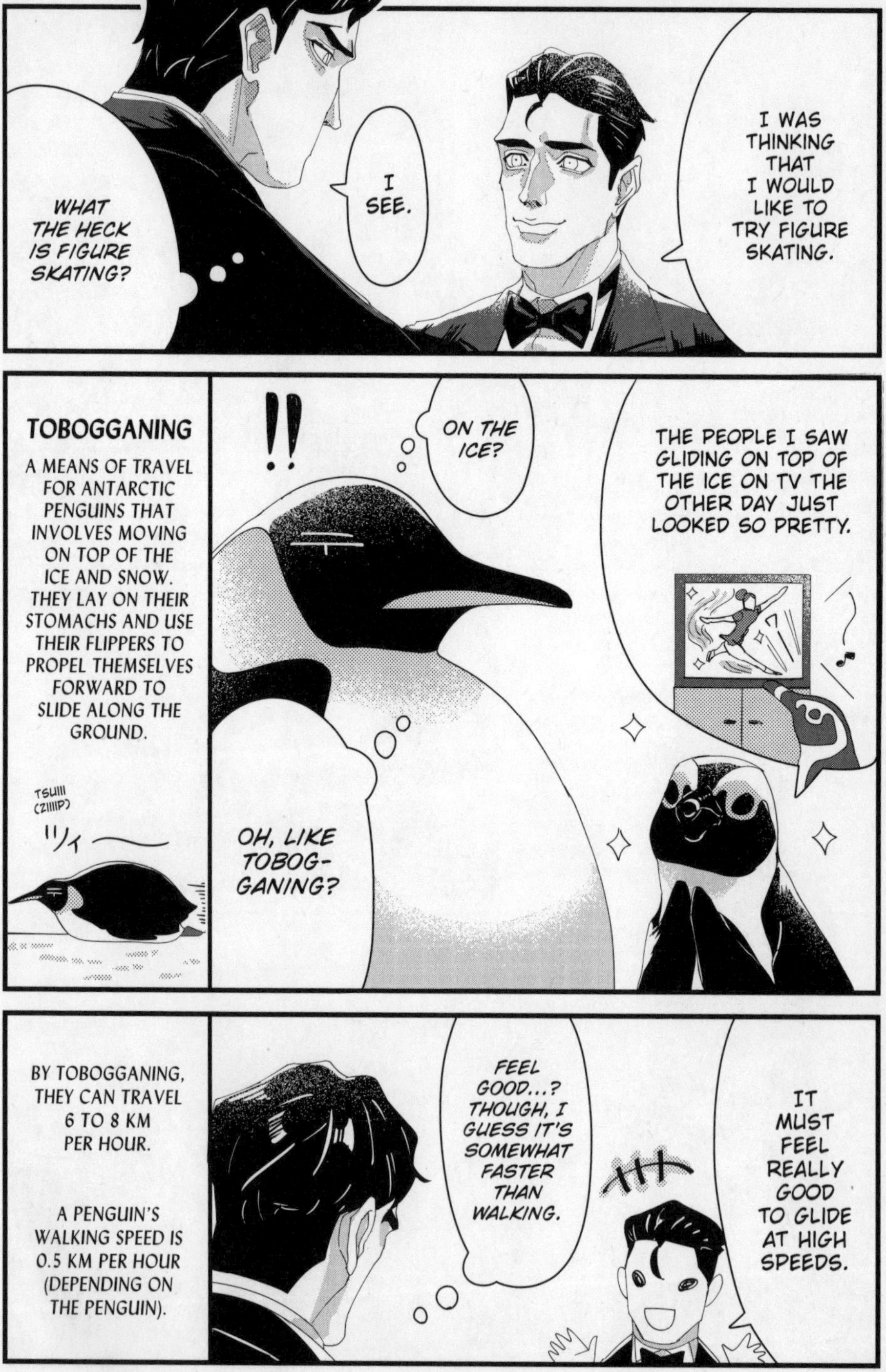

I WAS THINKING THAT I WOULD LIKE TO TRY FIGURE SKATING.
I SEE.
WHAT THE HECK IS FIGURE SKATING?
THE PEOPLE I SAW GLIDING ON TOP OF THE ICE ON TV THE OTHER DAY JUST LOOKED SO PRETTY.
ON THE ICE?
!!
OH, LIKE TOBOG-GANING?
TOBOGGANING
A MEANS OF TRAVEL FOR ANTARCTIC PENGUINS THAT INVOLVES MOVING ON TOP OF THE ICE AND SNOW. THEY LAY ON THEIR STOMACHS AND USE THEIR FLIPPERS TO PROPEL THEMSELVES FORWARD TO SLIDE ALONG THE GROUND.
TSUIII (ZIIIP)
IT MUST FEEL REALLY GOOD TO GLIDE AT HIGH SPEEDS.
FEEL GOOD...? THOUGH, I GUESS IT'S SOMEWHAT FASTER THAN WALKING.
BY TOBOGGANING, THEY CAN TRAVEL 6 TO 8 KM PER HOUR.
A PENGUIN'S WALKING SPEED IS 0.5 KM PER HOUR (DEPENDING ON THE PENGUIN).

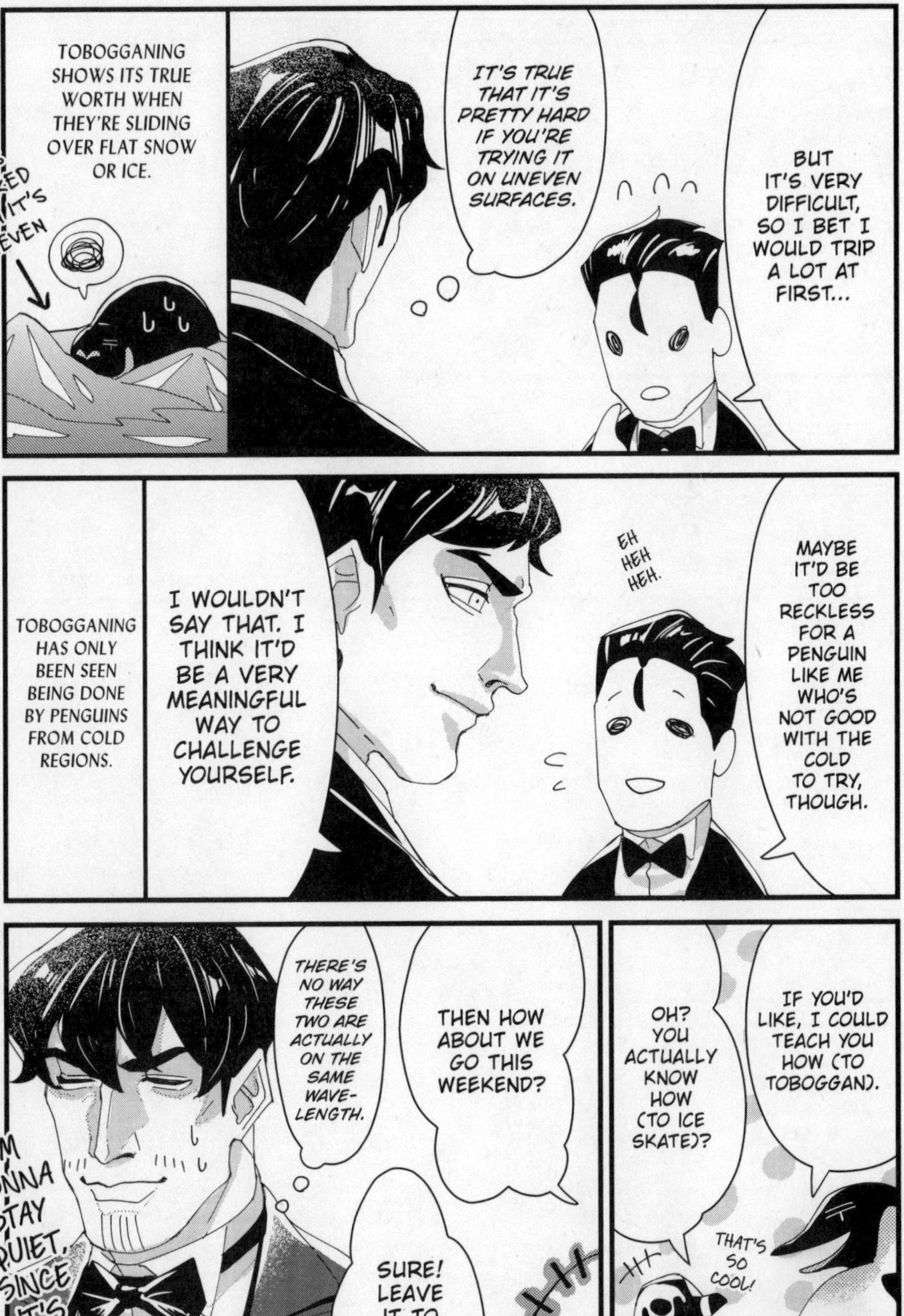
BUT IT'S VERY DIFFICULT, SO I BET I WOULD TRIP A LOT AT FIRST...
IT'S TRUE THAT IT'S PRETTY HARD IF YOU'RE TRYING IT ON UNEVEN SURFACES.
TOBOGGANING SHOWS ITS TRUE WORTH WHEN THEY'RE SLIDING OVER FLAT SNOW OR ICE.
GETS BLOCKED WHEN IT'S UNEVEN
MAYBE IT'D BE TOO RECKLESS FOR A PENGUIN LIKE ME WHO'S NOT GOOD WITH THE COLD TO TRY, THOUGH.
EH HEH HEH.
I WOULDN'T SAY THAT. I THINK IT'D BE A VERY MEANINGFUL WAY TO CHALLENGE YOURSELF.
TOBOGGANING HAS ONLY BEEN SEEN BEING DONE BY PENGUINS FROM COLD REGIONS.
IF YOU'D LIKE, I COULD TEACH YOU HOW (TO TOBOGGAN).
OH? YOU ACTUALLY KNOW HOW (TO ICE SKATE)?
THAT'S SO COOL!
THEN HOW ABOUT WE GO THIS WEEKEND?
THERE'S NO WAY THESE TWO ARE ACTUALLY ON THE SAME WAVE-LENGTH.
SURE! LEAVE IT TO ME!
I'M GONNA STAY QUIET, SINCE IT'S FUNNY.

I TREMBLED WITH FEAR WHEN HE SUDDENLY GOT ON HIS STOMACH ON THE SKATING RINK. —AFRICAN

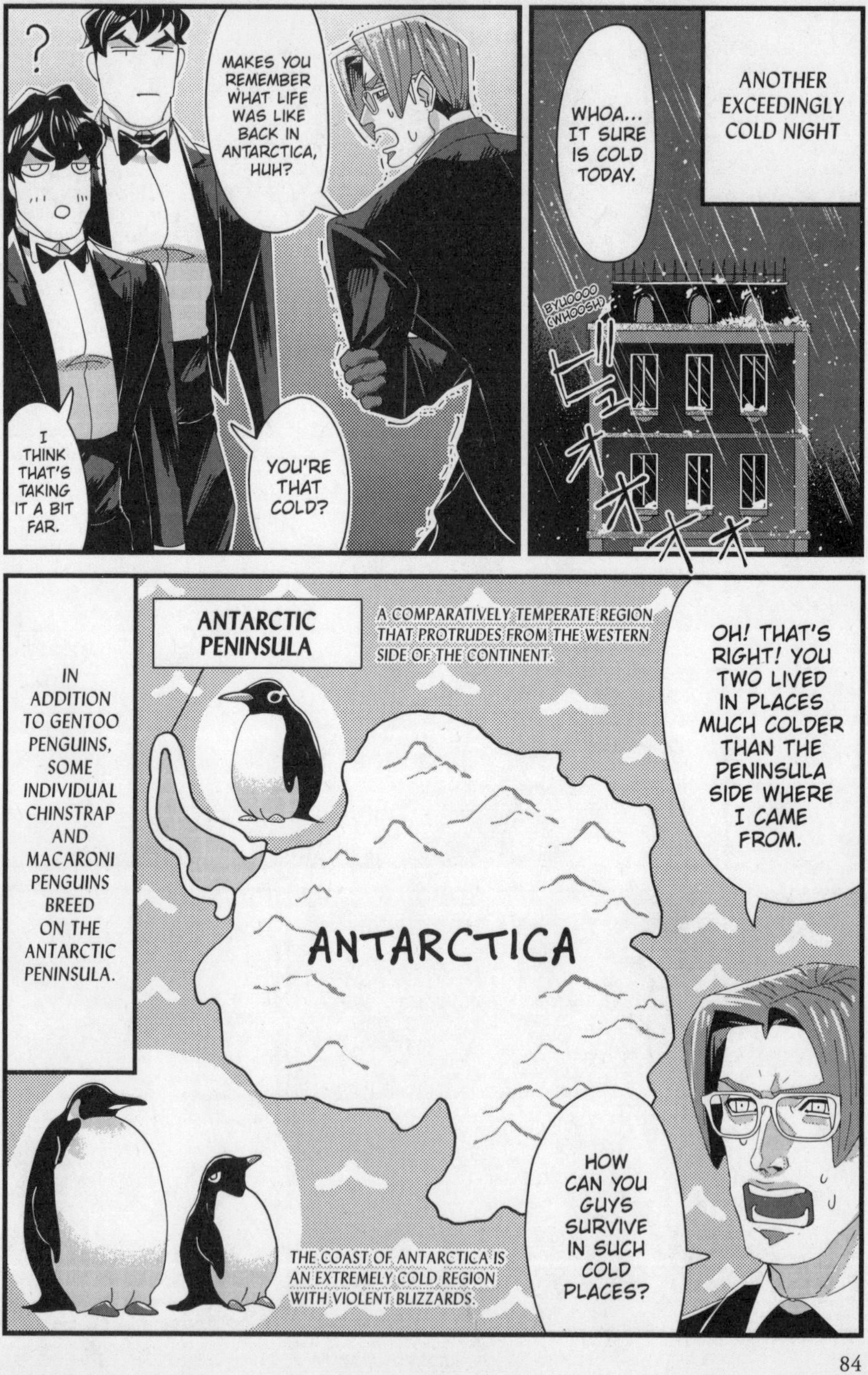
ANOTHER EXCEEDINGLY COLD NIGHT
WHOA... IT SURE IS COLD TODAY.
BYUOOOO (WHOOSH)
MAKES YOU REMEMBER WHAT LIFE WAS LIKE BACK IN ANTARCTICA, HUH?
YOU'RE THAT COLD?
I THINK THAT'S TAKING IT A BIT FAR.
OH! THAT'S RIGHT! YOU TWO LIVED IN PLACES MUCH COLDER THAN THE PENINSULA SIDE WHERE I CAME FROM.
A COMPARATIVELY TEMPERATE REGION THAT PROTRUDES FROM THE WESTERN SIDE OF THE CONTINENT.
ANTARCTIC PENINSULA
IN ADDITION TO GENTOO PENGUINS, SOME INDIVIDUAL CHINSTRAP AND MACARONI PENGUINS BREED ON THE ANTARCTIC PENINSULA.
ANTARCTICA
HOW CAN YOU GUYS SURVIVE IN SUCH COLD PLACES?
THE COAST OF ANTARCTICA IS AN EXTREMELY COLD REGION WITH VIOLENT BLIZZARDS.

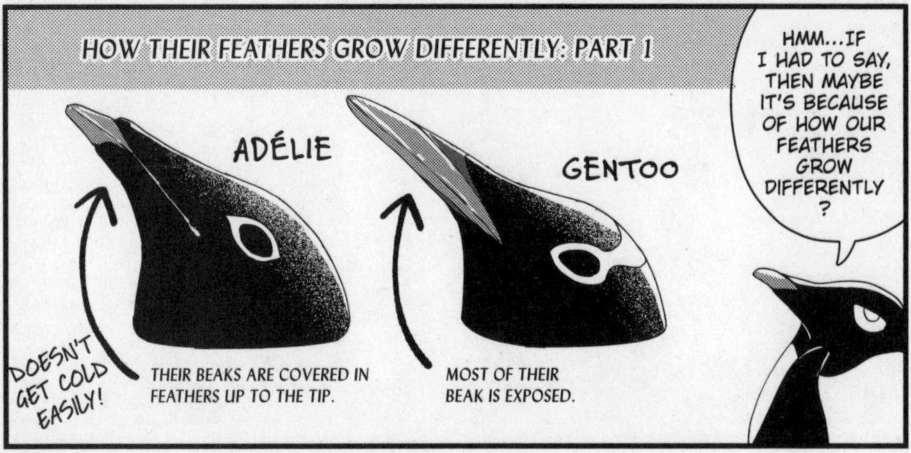
HMM...IF I HAD TO SAY, THEN MAYBE IT'S BECAUSE OF HOW OUR FEATHERS GROW DIFFERENTLY?
HOW THEIR FEATHERS GROW DIFFERENTLY: PART 1
GENTOO
MOST OF THEIR BEAK IS EXPOSED.
ADÉLIE
THEIR BEAKS ARE COVERED IN FEATHERS UP TO THE TIP.
DOESN'T GET COLD EASILY!

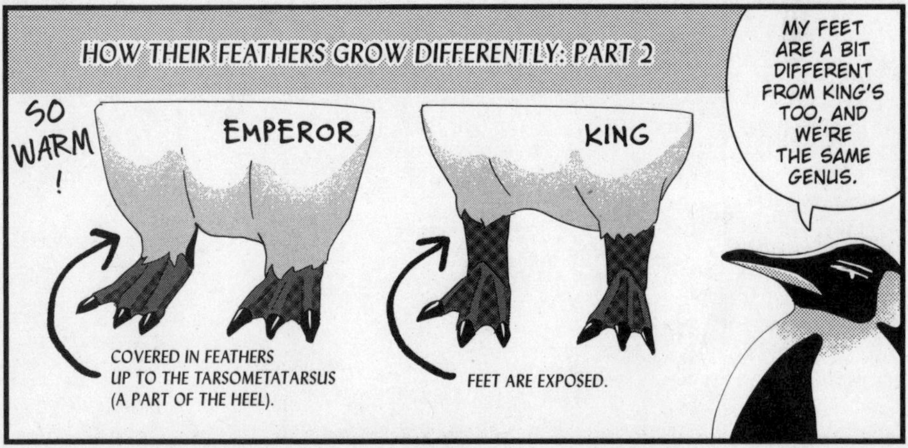
MY FEET ARE A BIT DIFFERENT FROM KING'S TOO, AND WE'RE THE SAME GENUS.
HOW THEIR FEATHERS GROW DIFFERENTLY: PART 2
KING
FEET ARE EXPOSED.
EMPEROR
COVERED IN FEATHERS UP TO THE TARSOMETATARSUS (A PART OF THE HEEL).
SO WARM!

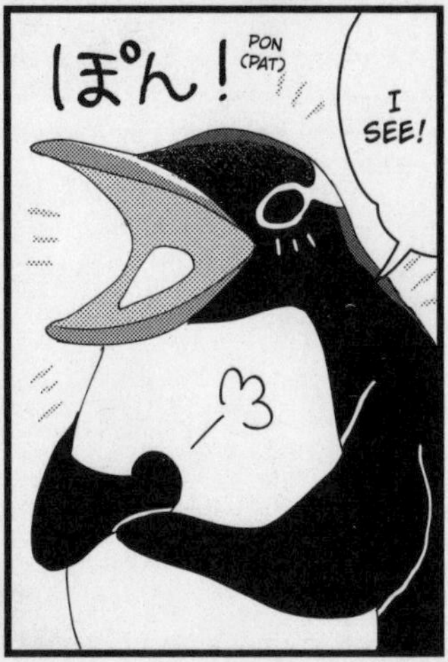
I SEE!
PON (PAT)
ぽん!

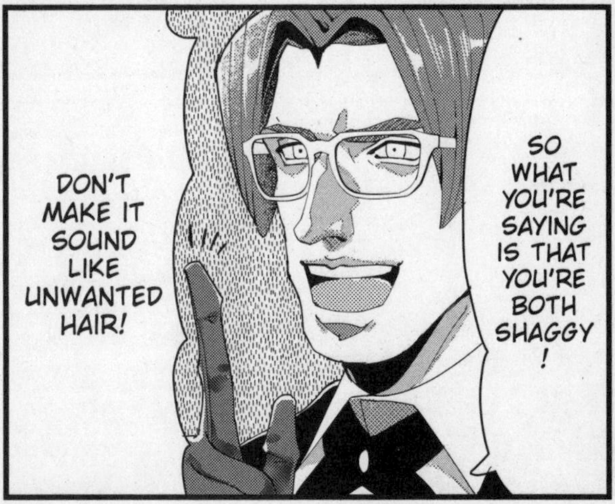
SO WHAT YOU'RE SAYING IS THAT YOU'RE BOTH SHAGGY!
DON'T MAKE IT SOUND LIKE UNWANTED HAIR!

♦ They Don't Like the Heat, Since They're from Antarctica ♦

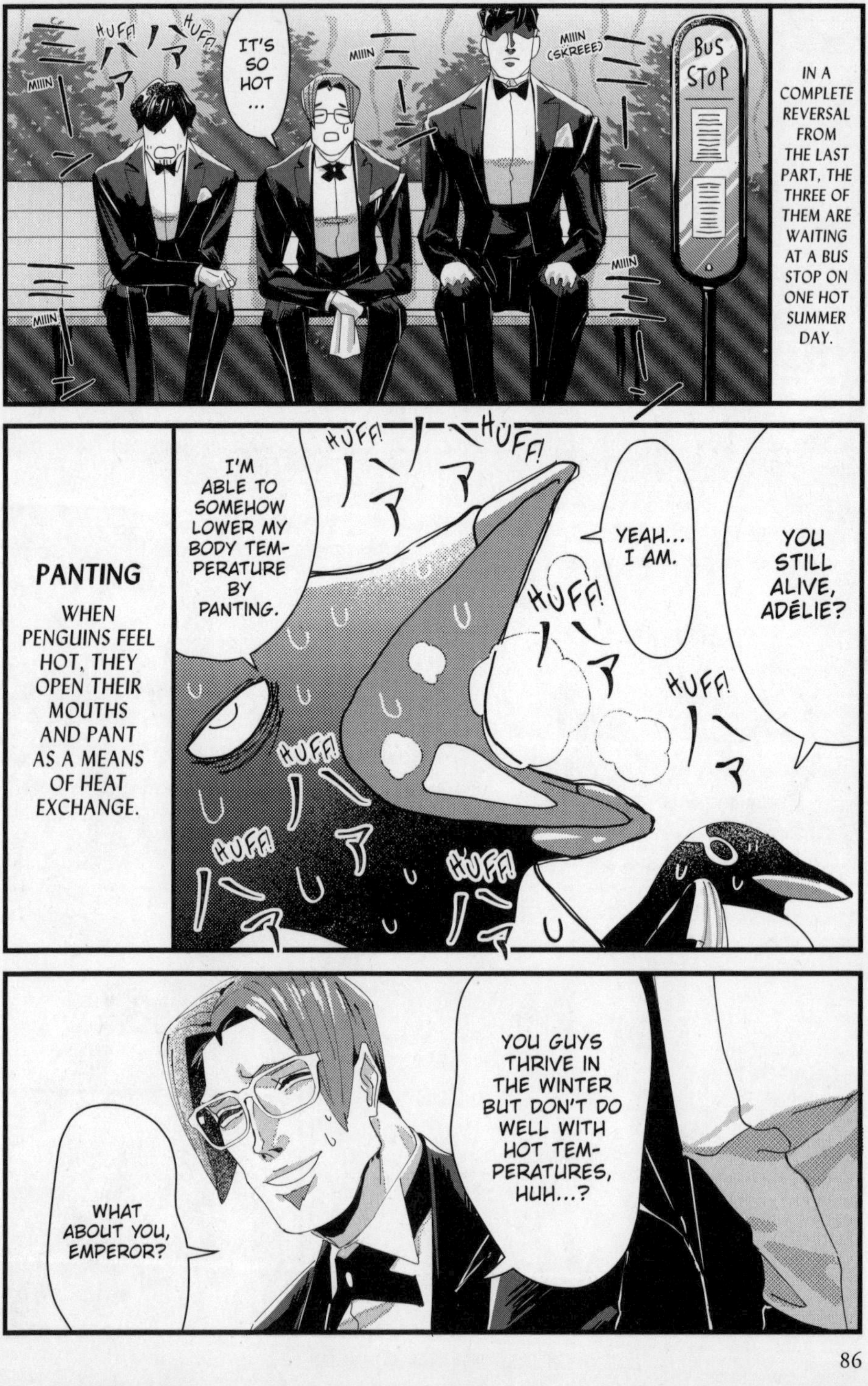
IN A COMPLETE REVERSAL FROM THE LAST PART, THE THREE OF THEM ARE WAITING AT A BUS STOP ON ONE HOT SUMMER DAY.
BUS STOP
MIIN (SKREEE)
MIIN
IT'S SO HOT...
HUFF! HUFF!
MIIN
MIIN
MIIN
MIIN
YOU STILL ALIVE, ADÉLIE?
YEAH... I AM.
HUFF!
HUFF!
HUFF! HUFF!
I'M ABLE TO SOMEHOW LOWER MY BODY TEMPERATURE BY PANTING.
HUFF!
HUFF!
HUFF!
PANTING
WHEN PENGUINS FEEL HOT, THEY OPEN THEIR MOUTHS AND PANT AS A MEANS OF HEAT EXCHANGE.
YOU GUYS THRIVE IN THE WINTER BUT DON'T DO WELL WITH HOT TEMPERATURES, HUH...?
WHAT ABOUT YOU, EMPEROR?

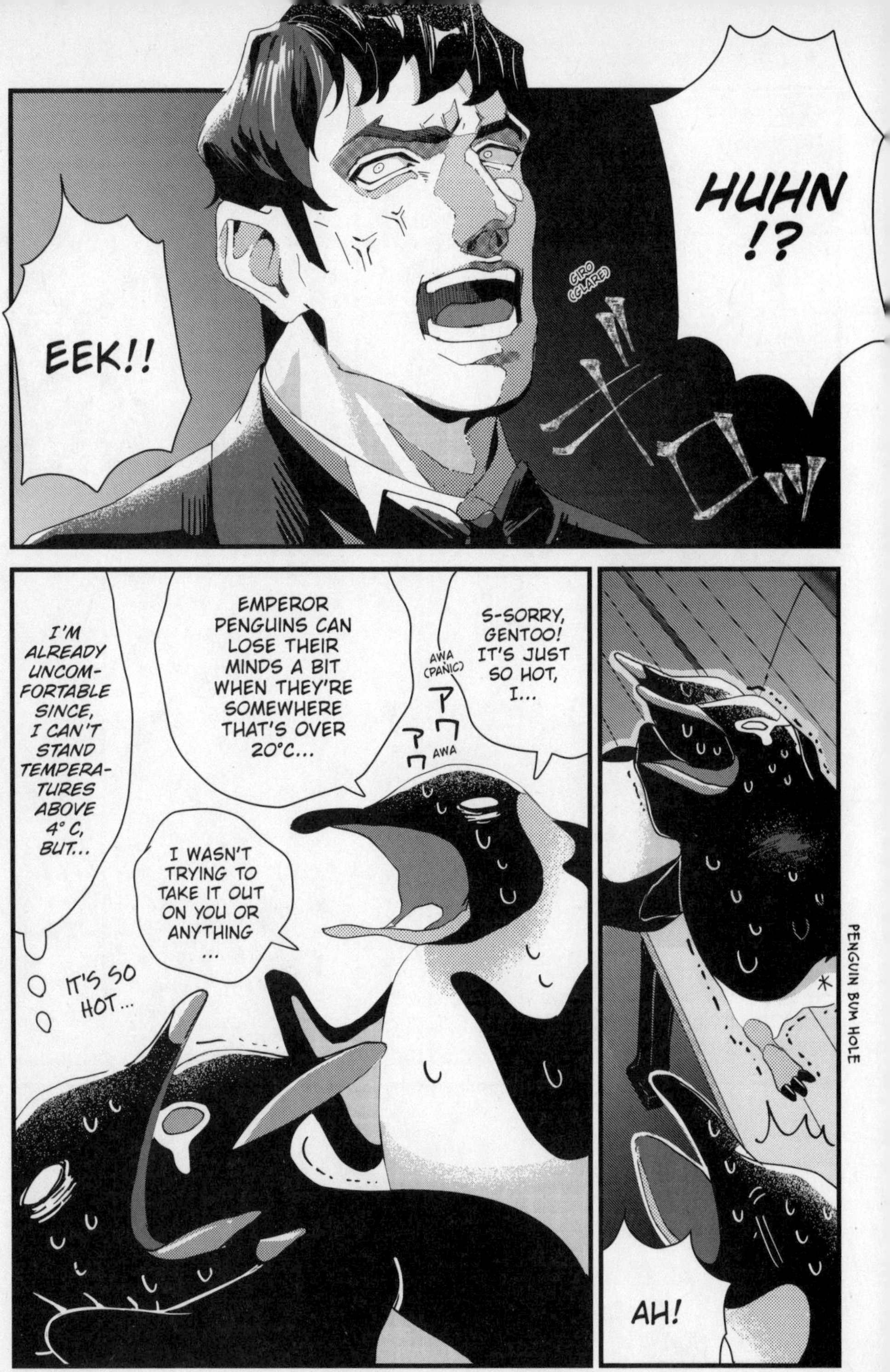
HUHN!?
GIRO (GLARE)
EEK!!
PENGUIN BUM HOLE
AH!
S-SORRY, GENTOO! IT'S JUST SO HOT, I...
AWA (PANIC)
AWA
EMPEROR PENGUINS CAN LOSE THEIR MINDS A BIT WHEN THEY'RE SOMEWHERE THAT'S OVER 20°C...
I'M ALREADY UNCOMFORTABLE SINCE, I CAN'T STAND TEMPERATURES ABOVE 4° C, BUT...
I WASN'T TRYING TO TAKE IT OUT ON YOU OR ANYTHING...
IT'S SO HOT...

◆ *Preening* ◆

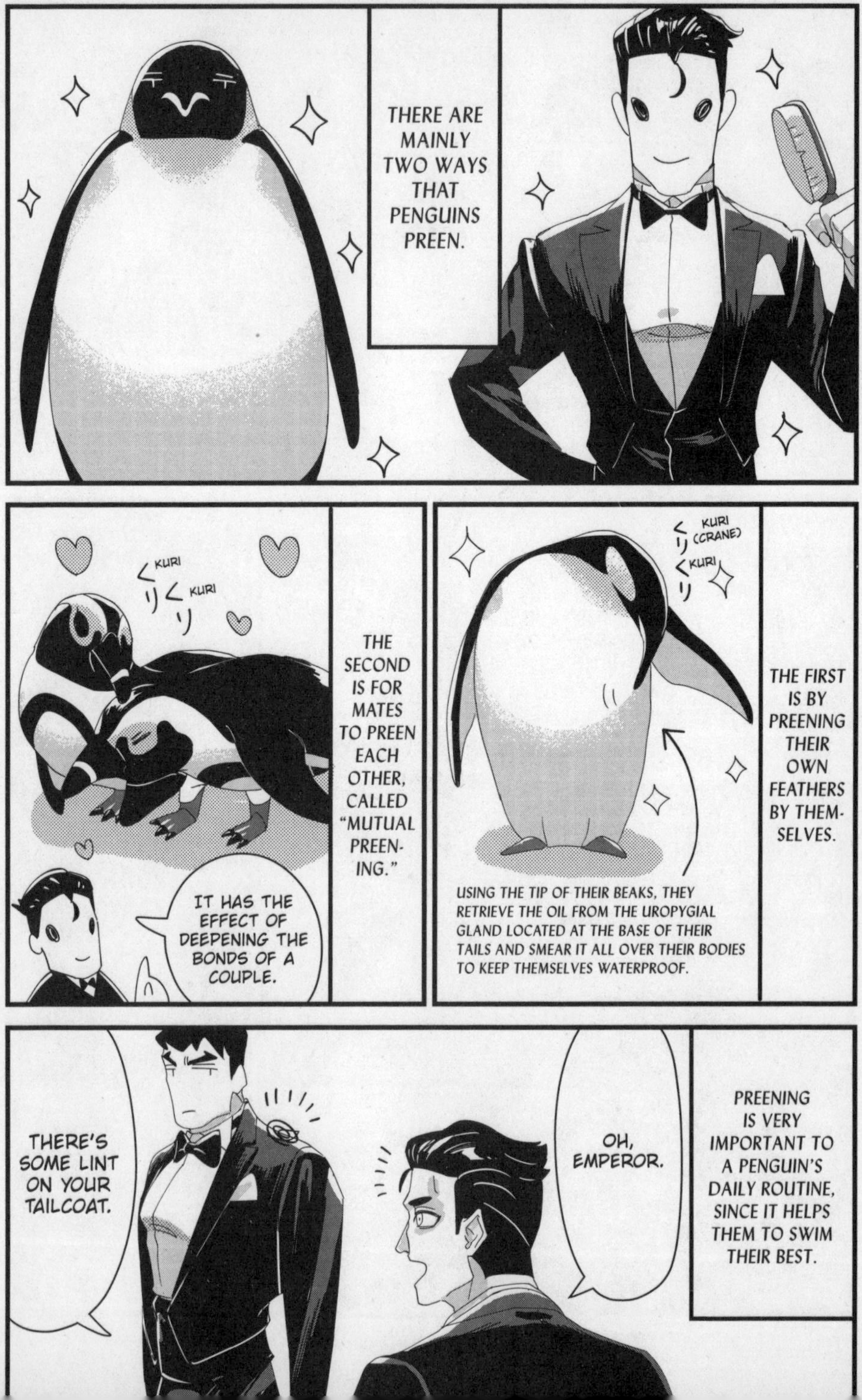
THERE ARE MAINLY TWO WAYS THAT PENGUINS PREEN.
THE FIRST IS BY PREENING THEIR OWN FEATHERS BY THEMSELVES.
くりくり KURI (CRANE) KURI
USING THE TIP OF THEIR BEAKS, THEY RETRIEVE THE OIL FROM THE UROPYGIAL GLAND LOCATED AT THE BASE OF THEIR TAILS AND SMEAR IT ALL OVER THEIR BODIES TO KEEP THEMSELVES WATERPROOF.
THE SECOND IS FOR MATES TO PREEN EACH OTHER, CALLED "MUTUAL PREENING."
くりくり KURI KURI
IT HAS THE EFFECT OF DEEPENING THE BONDS OF A COUPLE.
PREENING IS VERY IMPORTANT TO A PENGUIN'S DAILY ROUTINE, SINCE IT HELPS THEM TO SWIM THEIR BEST.
OH, EMPEROR.
THERE'S SOME LINT ON YOUR TAILCOAT.

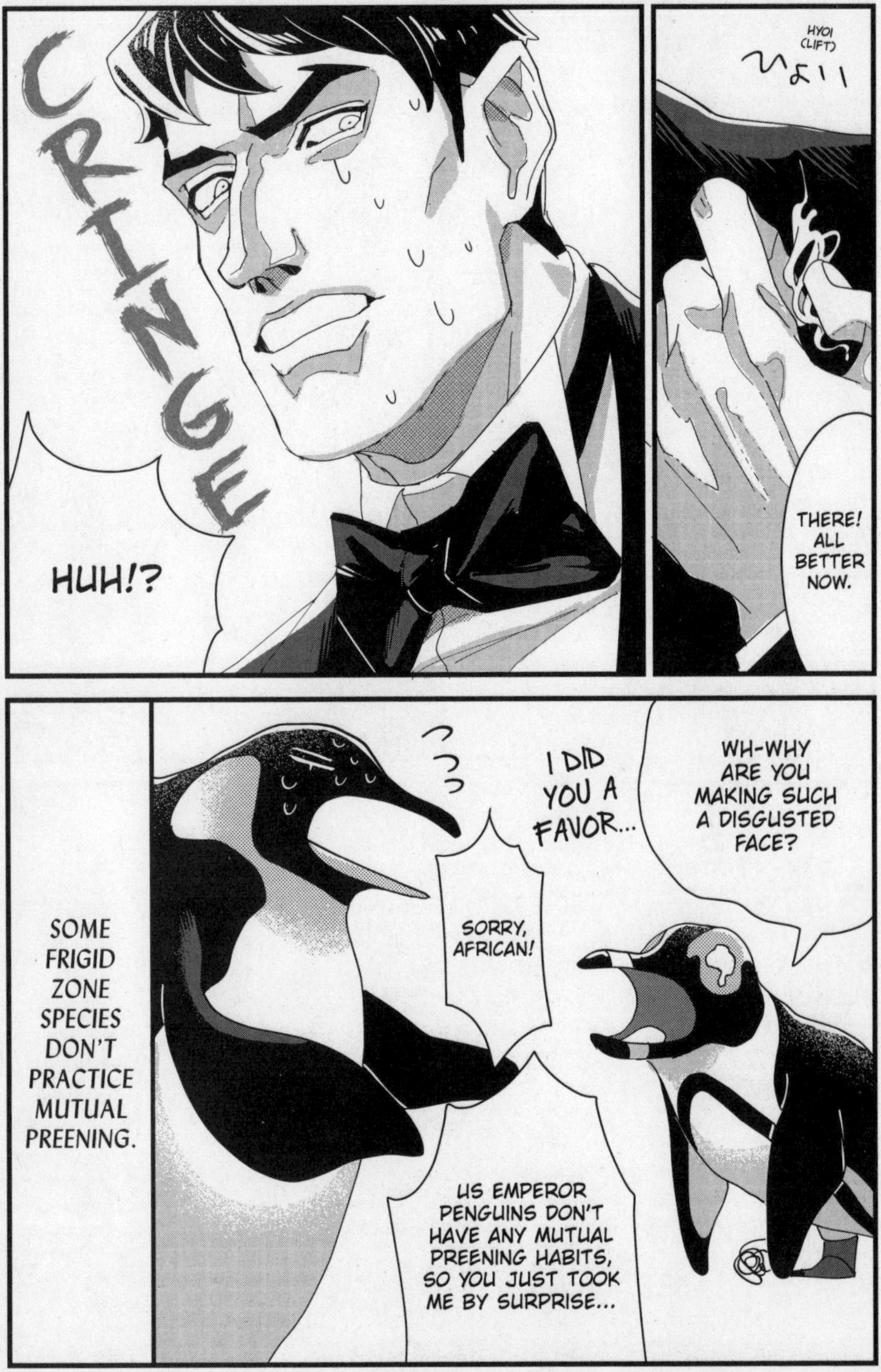
HYOI (LIFT)
ひょい
THERE! ALL BETTER NOW.
CRINGE
HUH!?
WH-WHY ARE YOU MAKING SUCH A DISGUSTED FACE?
I DID YOU A FAVOR...
SORRY, AFRICAN!
US EMPEROR PENGUINS DON'T HAVE ANY MUTUAL PREENING HABITS, SO YOU JUST TOOK ME BY SURPRISE...
SOME FRIGID ZONE SPECIES DON'T PRACTICE MUTUAL PREENING.

PENGUINS ARE GENTLEMEN, SO WE MUSTN'T FAIL TO TAKE CARE OF OUR ONLY GOOD SUIT. —KING

◆ Molting ◆

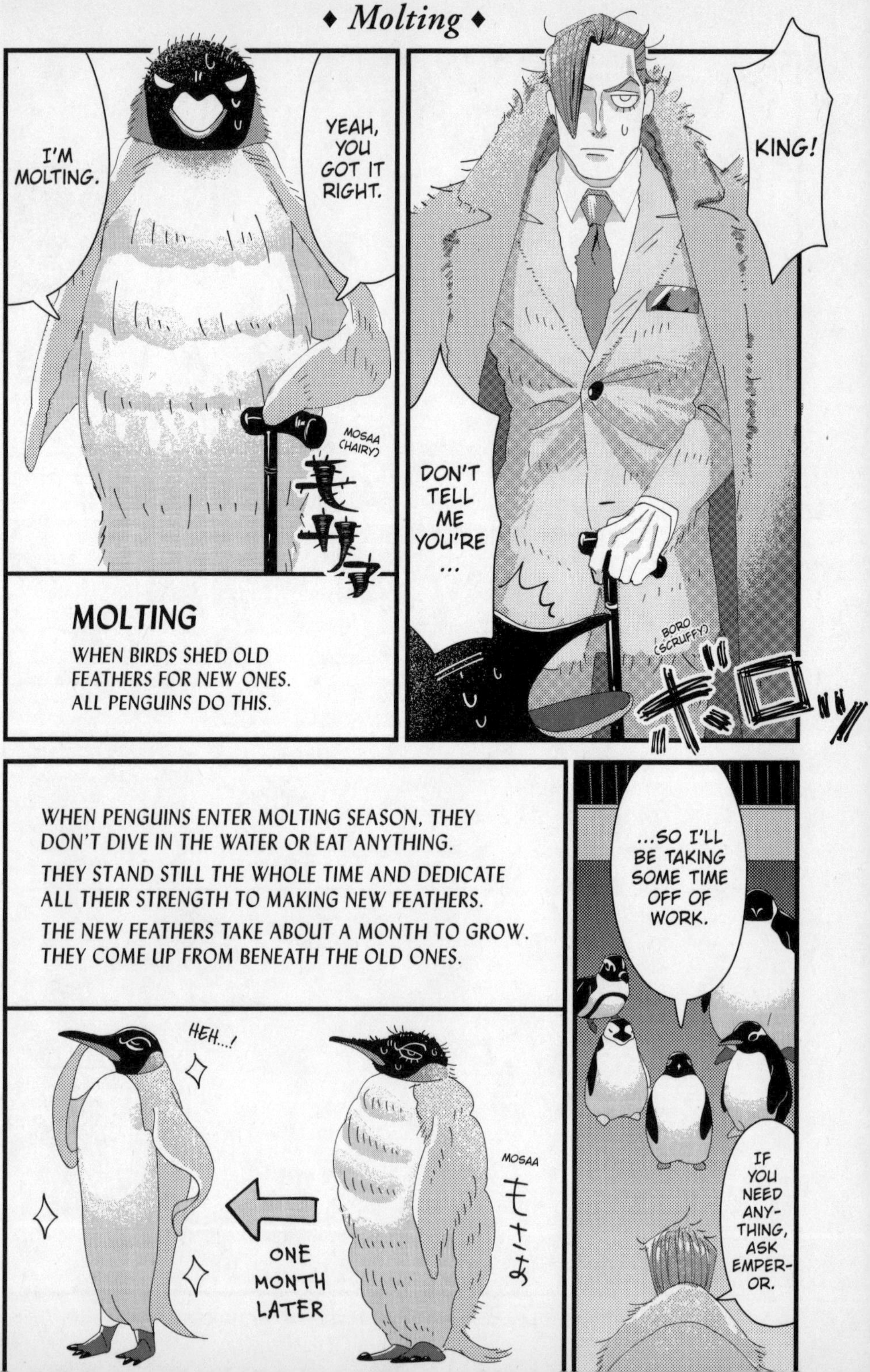
KING!
DON'T TELL ME YOU'RE ...
BORO (SCRUFFY)
YEAH, YOU GOT IT RIGHT.
I'M MOLTING.
MOSAA (HAIRY)
MOLTING
WHEN BIRDS SHED OLD FEATHERS FOR NEW ONES. ALL PENGUINS DO THIS.
...SO I'LL BE TAKING SOME TIME OFF OF WORK.
IF YOU NEED ANY-THING, ASK EMPER-OR.
WHEN PENGUINS ENTER MOLTING SEASON, THEY DON'T DIVE IN THE WATER OR EAT ANYTHING.
THEY STAND STILL THE WHOLE TIME AND DEDICATE ALL THEIR STRENGTH TO MAKING NEW FEATHERS.
THE NEW FEATHERS TAKE ABOUT A MONTH TO GROW. THEY COME UP FROM BENEATH THE OLD ONES.
MOSAA
HEH...!
ONE MONTH LATER

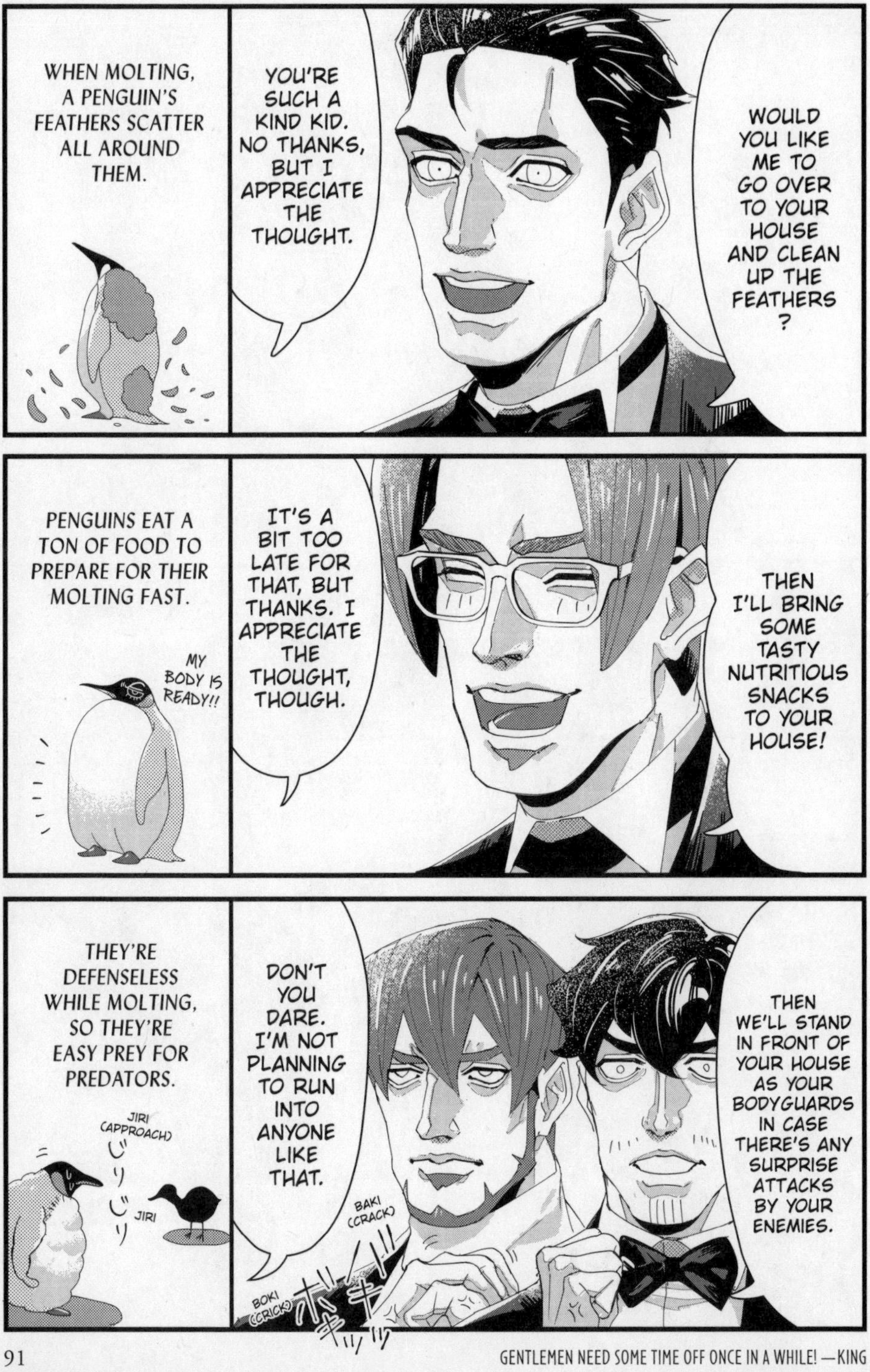
WOULD YOU LIKE ME TO GO OVER TO YOUR HOUSE AND CLEAN UP THE FEATHERS ?
YOU'RE SUCH A KIND KID. NO THANKS, BUT I APPRECIATE THE THOUGHT.
WHEN MOLTING, A PENGUIN'S FEATHERS SCATTER ALL AROUND THEM.
THEN I'LL BRING SOME TASTY NUTRITIOUS SNACKS TO YOUR HOUSE!
IT'S A BIT TOO LATE FOR THAT, BUT THANKS. I APPRECIATE THE THOUGHT, THOUGH.
PENGUINS EAT A TON OF FOOD TO PREPARE FOR THEIR MOLTING FAST.
MY BODY IS READY!!
THEN WE'LL STAND IN FRONT OF YOUR HOUSE AS YOUR BODYGUARDS IN CASE THERE'S ANY SURPRISE ATTACKS BY YOUR ENEMIES.
DON'T YOU DARE. I'M NOT PLANNING TO RUN INTO ANYONE LIKE THAT.
BAKI (CRACK)
BOKI (CRICK)
THEY'RE DEFENSELESS WHILE MOLTING, SO THEY'RE EASY PREY FOR PREDATORS.
JIRI (APPROACH)
JIRI

GENTLEMEN NEED SOME TIME OFF ONCE IN A WHILE! —KING

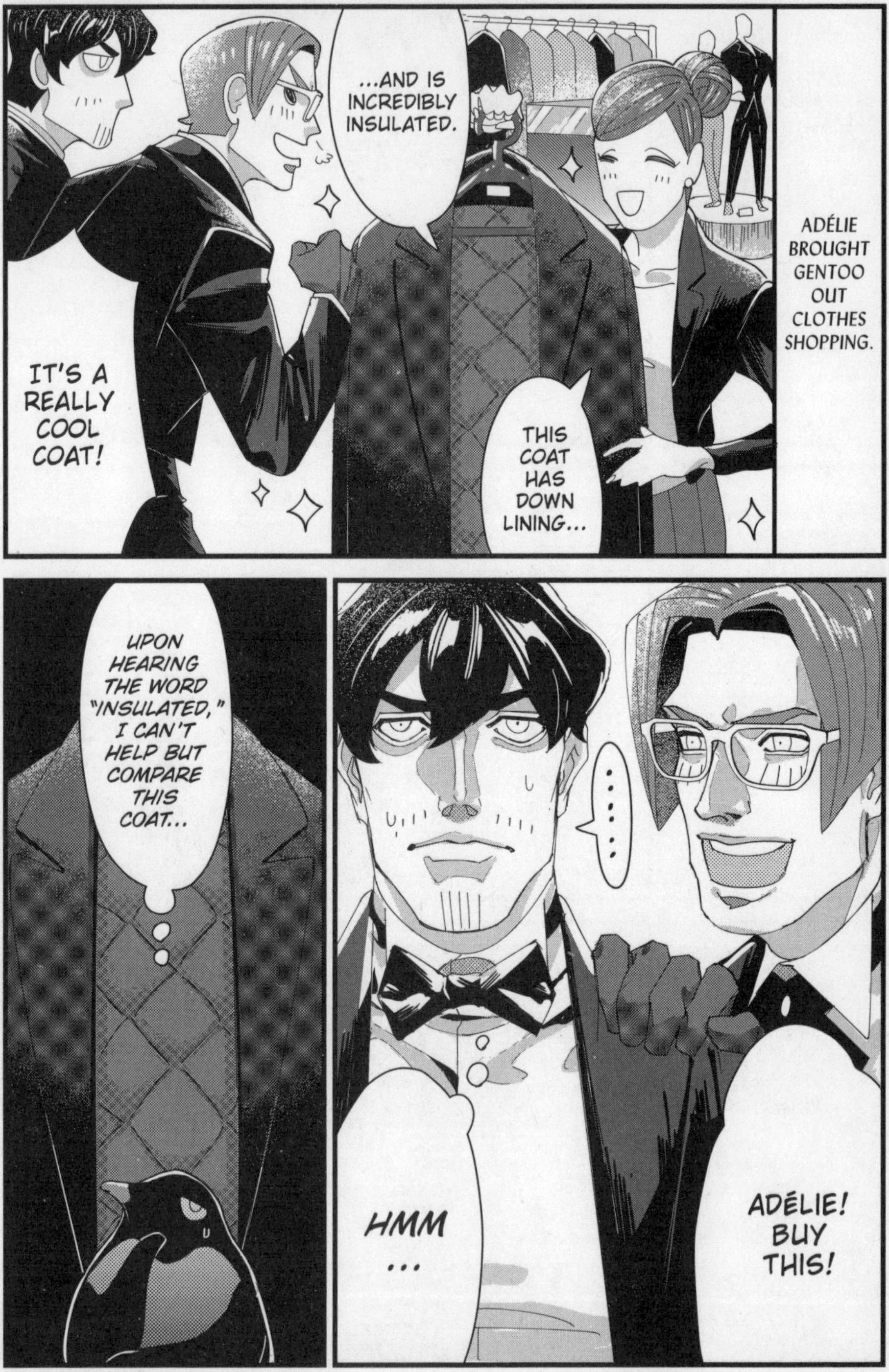
ADÉLIE BROUGHT GENTOO OUT CLOTHES SHOPPING.
THIS COAT HAS DOWN LINING...
...AND IS INCREDIBLY INSULATED.
IT'S A REALLY COOL COAT!
ADÉLIE! BUY THIS!
......
HMM ...
UPON HEARING THE WORD "INSULATED," I CAN'T HELP BUT COMPARE THIS COAT...

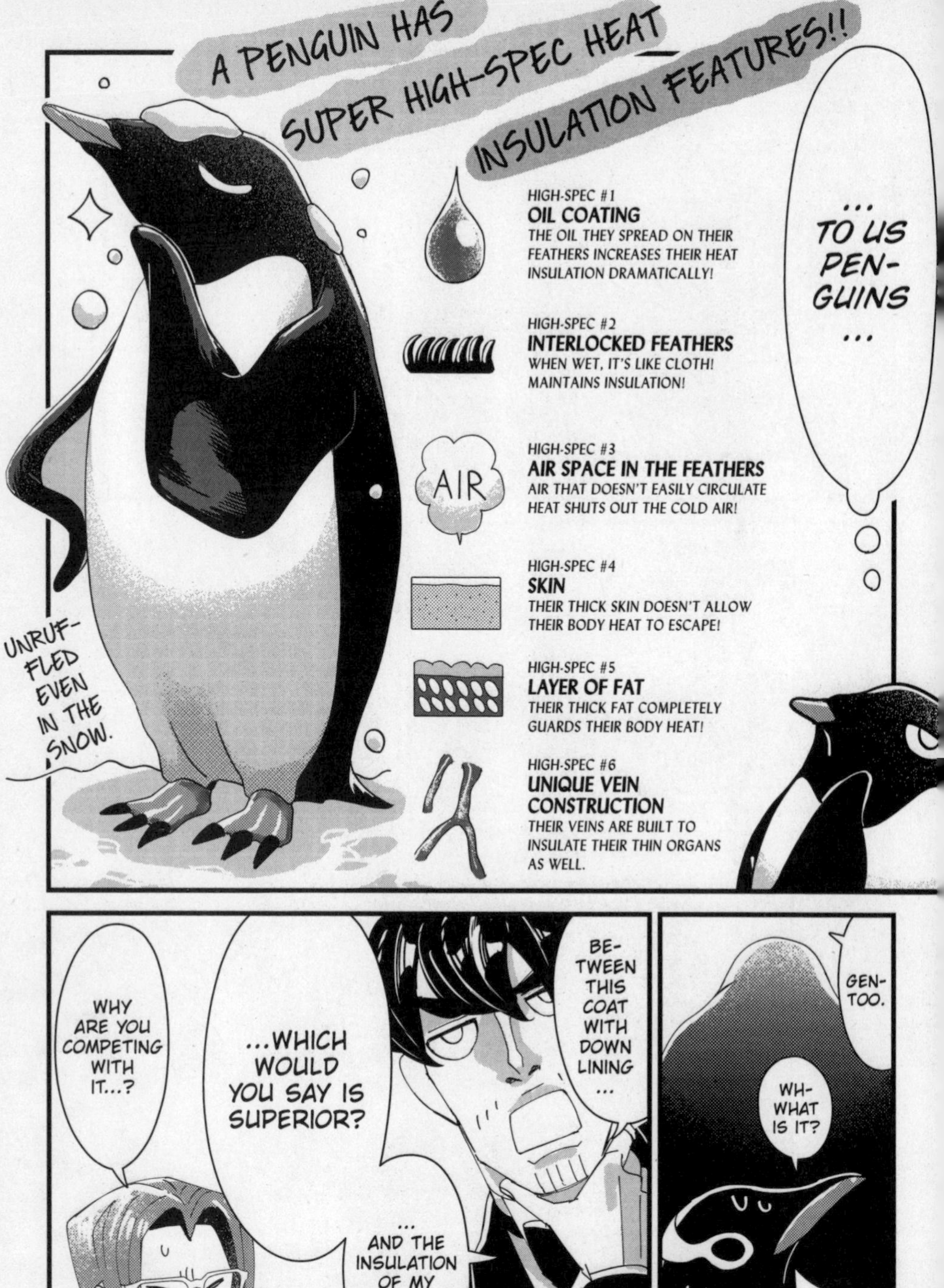

... TO US PEN-GUINS ...
A PENGUIN HAS SUPER HIGH-SPEC HEAT INSULATION FEATURES!!
HIGH-SPEC #1
OIL COATING
THE OIL THEY SPREAD ON THEIR FEATHERS INCREASES THEIR HEAT INSULATION DRAMATICALLY!
HIGH-SPEC #2
INTERLOCKED FEATHERS
WHEN WET, IT'S LIKE CLOTH! MAINTAINS INSULATION!
AIR
HIGH-SPEC #3
AIR SPACE IN THE FEATHERS
AIR THAT DOESN'T EASILY CIRCULATE HEAT SHUTS OUT THE COLD AIR!
HIGH-SPEC #4
SKIN
THEIR THICK SKIN DOESN'T ALLOW THEIR BODY HEAT TO ESCAPE!
HIGH-SPEC #5
LAYER OF FAT
THEIR THICK FAT COMPLETELY GUARDS THEIR BODY HEAT!
HIGH-SPEC #6
UNIQUE VEIN CONSTRUCTION
THEIR VEINS ARE BUILT TO INSULATE THEIR THIN ORGANS AS WELL.
UNRUF-FLED EVEN IN THE SNOW.
GEN-TOO.
WH-WHAT IS IT?
BE-TWEEN THIS COAT WITH DOWN LINING ...
... AND THE INSULATION OF MY BODY...
...WHICH WOULD YOU SAY IS SUPERIOR?
WHY ARE YOU COMPETING WITH IT...?

AFTER MULLING IT OVER FOR TWO HOURS, HE DECIDED TO GO WITH SOMETHING ELSE... —GENTOO

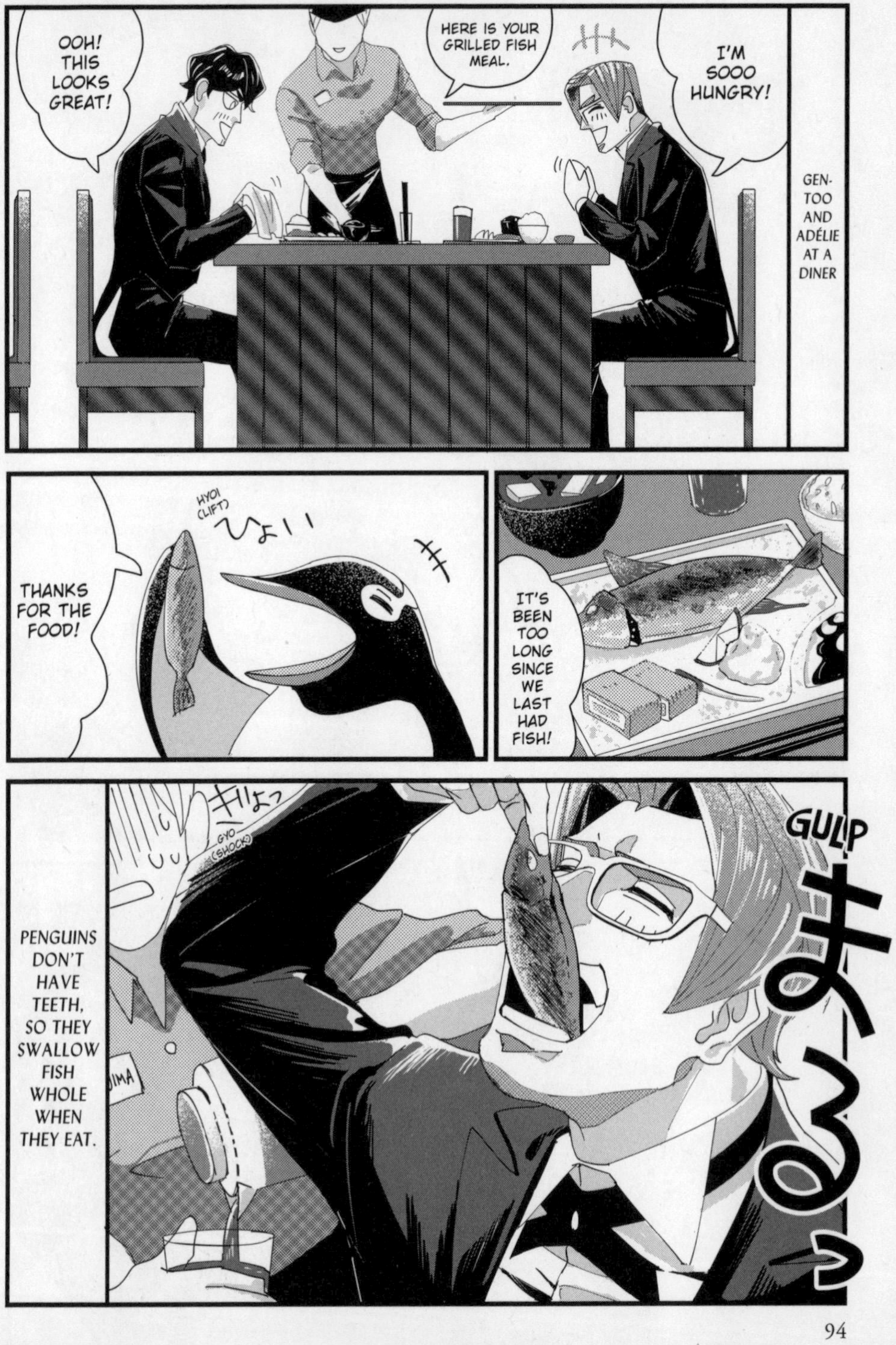
GEN-TOO AND ADÉLIE AT A DINER
I'M SOOO HUNGRY!
HERE IS YOUR GRILLED FISH MEAL.
OOH! THIS LOOKS GREAT!
IT'S BEEN TOO LONG SINCE WE LAST HAD FISH!
HYOI (LIFT)
THANKS FOR THE FOOD!
GULP
GYO (SHOCK)
PENGUINS DON'T HAVE TEETH, SO THEY SWALLOW FISH WHOLE WHEN THEY EAT.

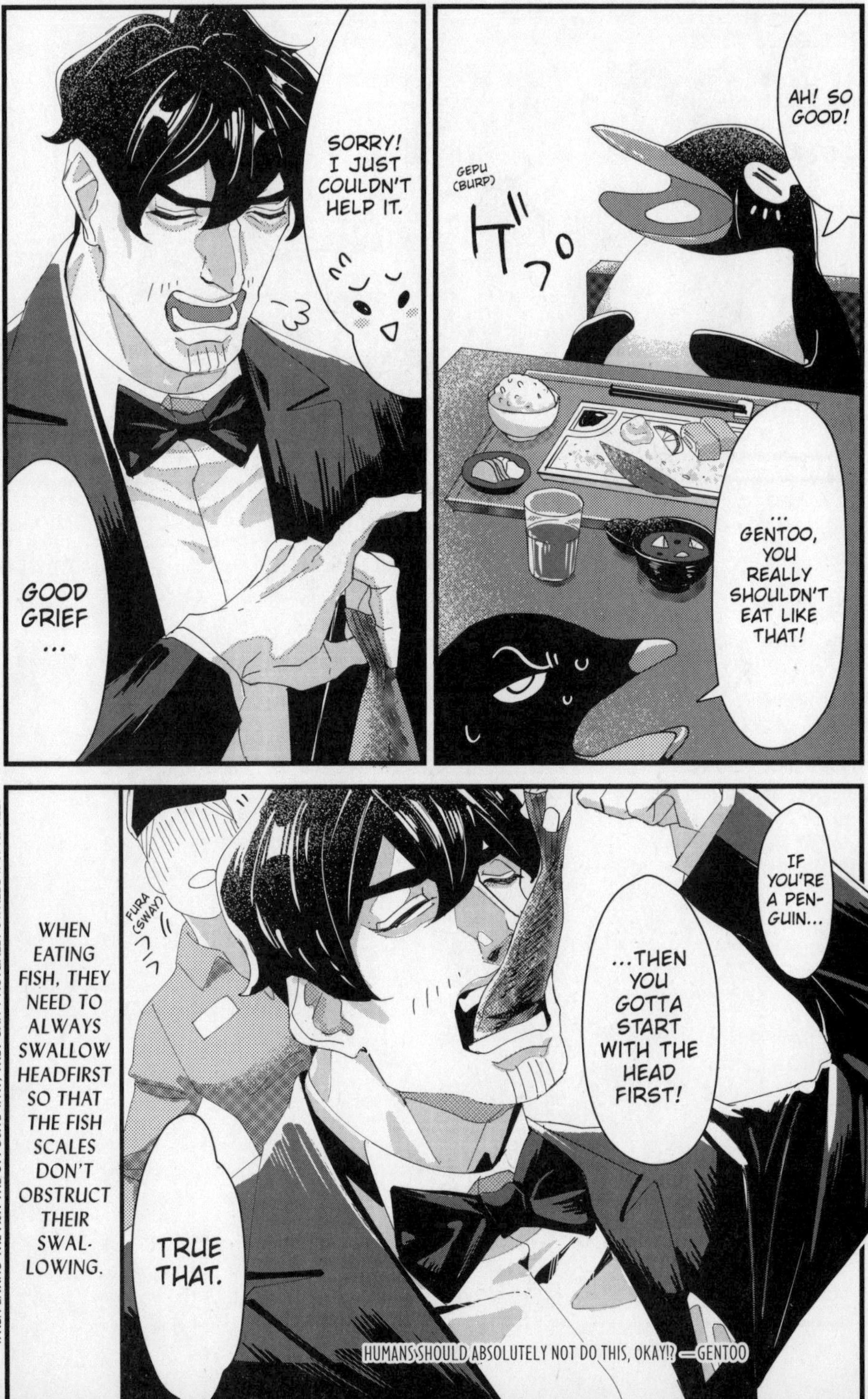

AH! SO GOOD!
GEPU (BURP)
...GENTOO, YOU REALLY SHOULDN'T EAT LIKE THAT!
SORRY! I JUST COULDN'T HELP IT.
GOOD GRIEF...
IF YOU'RE A PENGUIN...
...THEN YOU GOTTA START WITH THE HEAD FIRST!
FURA (SWAY)
WHEN EATING FISH, THEY NEED TO ALWAYS SWALLOW HEADFIRST SO THAT THE FISH SCALES DON'T OBSTRUCT THEIR SWALLOWING.
TRUE THAT.
HUMANS SHOULD ABSOLUTELY NOT DO THIS, OKAY!? —GENTOO

*WHEN EATING THE FISH THE OPPOSITE WAY, THEY CAN'T ACTUALLY SWALLOW IT AT ALL.

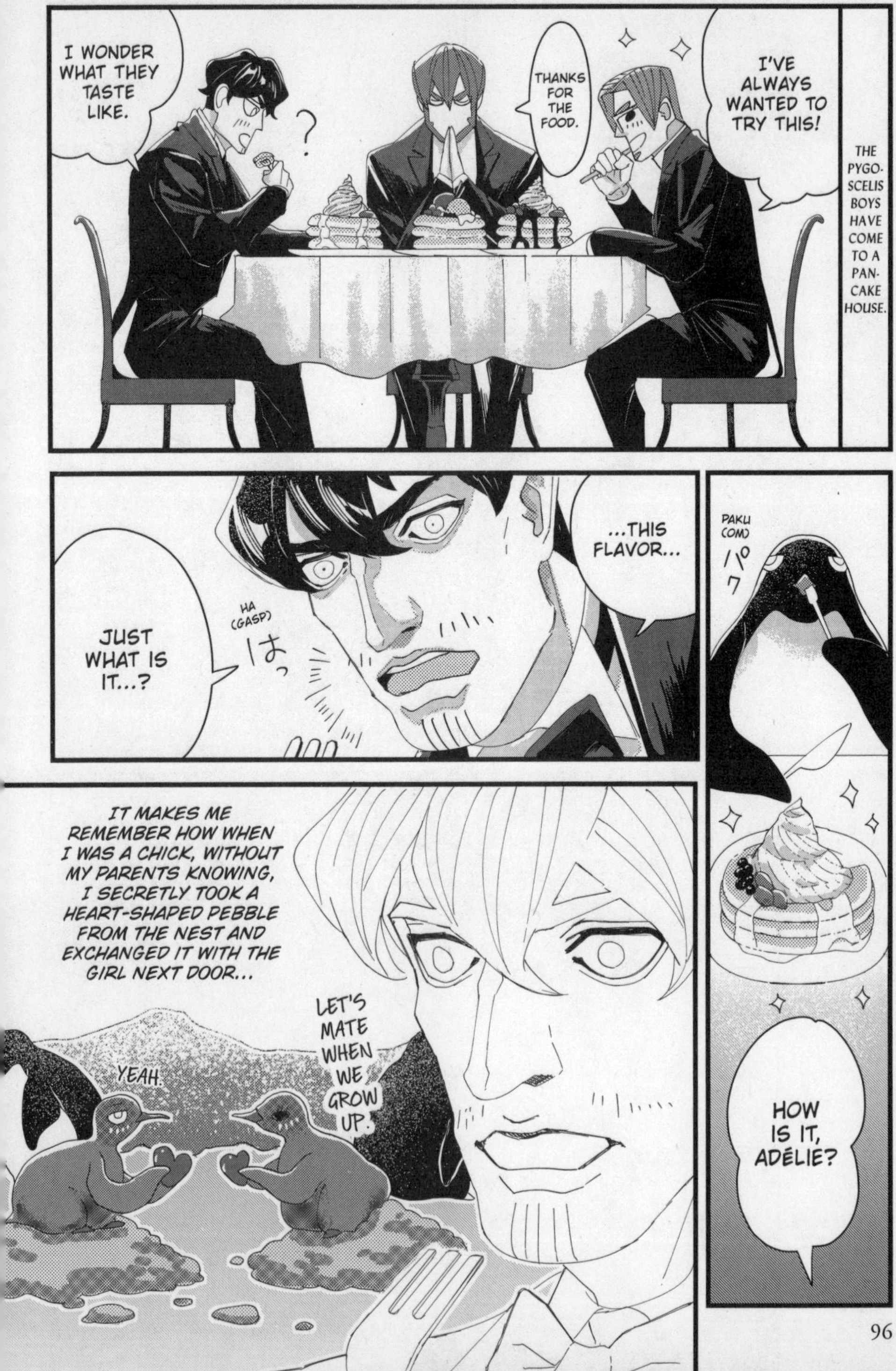
THE PYGOSCELIS BOYS HAVE COME TO A PANCAKE HOUSE.
I'VE ALWAYS WANTED TO TRY THIS!
THANKS FOR THE FOOD.
I WONDER WHAT THEY TASTE LIKE.
?
PAKU (OM) パク
HOW IS IT, ADÉLIE?
...THIS FLAVOR...
HA (GASP) はっ
JUST WHAT IS IT...?
IT MAKES ME REMEMBER HOW WHEN I WAS A CHICK, WITHOUT MY PARENTS KNOWING, I SECRETLY TOOK A HEART-SHAPED PEBBLE FROM THE NEST AND EXCHANGED IT WITH THE GIRL NEXT DOOR...
LET'S MATE WHEN WE GROW UP.
YEAH.

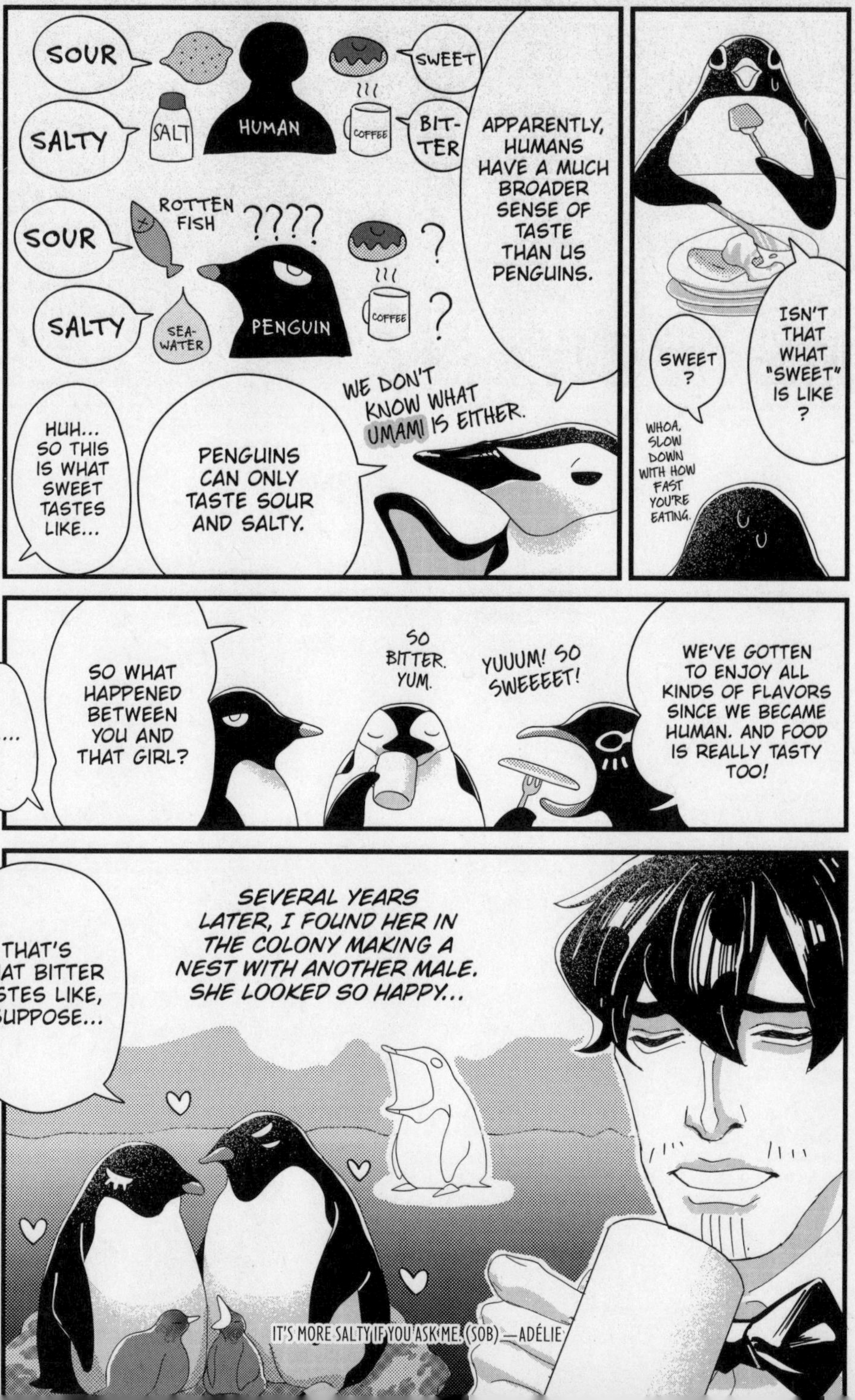
ISN'T THAT WHAT "SWEET" IS LIKE?
SWEET?
WHOA, SLOW DOWN WITH HOW FAST YOU'RE EATING.
APPARENTLY, HUMANS HAVE A MUCH BROADER SENSE OF TASTE THAN US PENGUINS.
SWEET
BIT-TER
COFFEE
HUMAN
SALT
SOUR
SALTY
?
?
????
COFFEE
PENGUIN
ROTTEN FISH
SEA-WATER
SOUR
SALTY
WE DON'T KNOW WHAT UMAMI IS EITHER.
PENGUINS CAN ONLY TASTE SOUR AND SALTY.
HUH... SO THIS IS WHAT SWEET TASTES LIKE...
WE'VE GOTTEN TO ENJOY ALL KINDS OF FLAVORS SINCE WE BECAME HUMAN. AND FOOD IS REALLY TASTY TOO!
YUUUM! SO SWEEEET!
SO BITTER. YUM.
SO WHAT HAPPENED BETWEEN YOU AND THAT GIRL?
......
SEVERAL YEARS LATER, I FOUND HER IN THE COLONY MAKING A NEST WITH ANOTHER MALE. SHE LOOKED SO HAPPY...
THAT'S WHAT BITTER TASTES LIKE, I SUPPOSE...
IT'S MORE SALTY IF YOU ASK ME. (SOB) —ADÉLIE

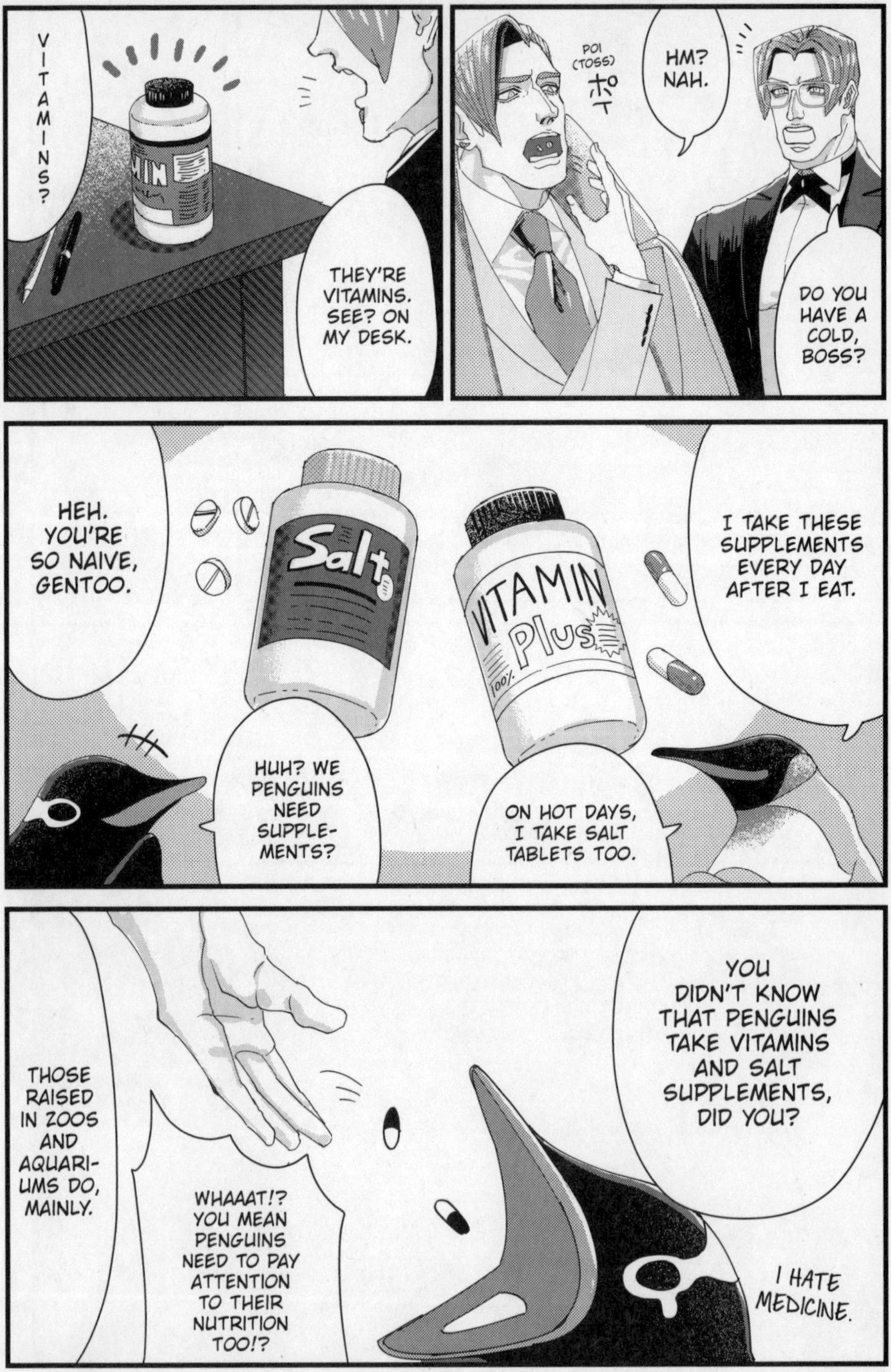
DO YOU HAVE A COLD, BOSS?
HM? NAH.
POI (TOSS)
ポイ
VITAMINS?
THEY'RE VITAMINS. SEE? ON MY DESK.
I TAKE THESE SUPPLEMENTS EVERY DAY AFTER I EAT.
VITAMIN Plus
100%
Salt
ON HOT DAYS, I TAKE SALT TABLETS TOO.
HUH? WE PENGUINS NEED SUPPLE-MENTS?
HEH. YOU'RE SO NAIVE, GENTOO.
YOU DIDN'T KNOW THAT PENGUINS TAKE VITAMINS AND SALT SUPPLEMENTS, DID YOU?
I HATE MEDICINE.
WHAAAT!? YOU MEAN PENGUINS NEED TO PAY ATTENTION TO THEIR NUTRITION TOO!?
THOSE RAISED IN ZOOS AND AQUARI-UMS DO, MAINLY.

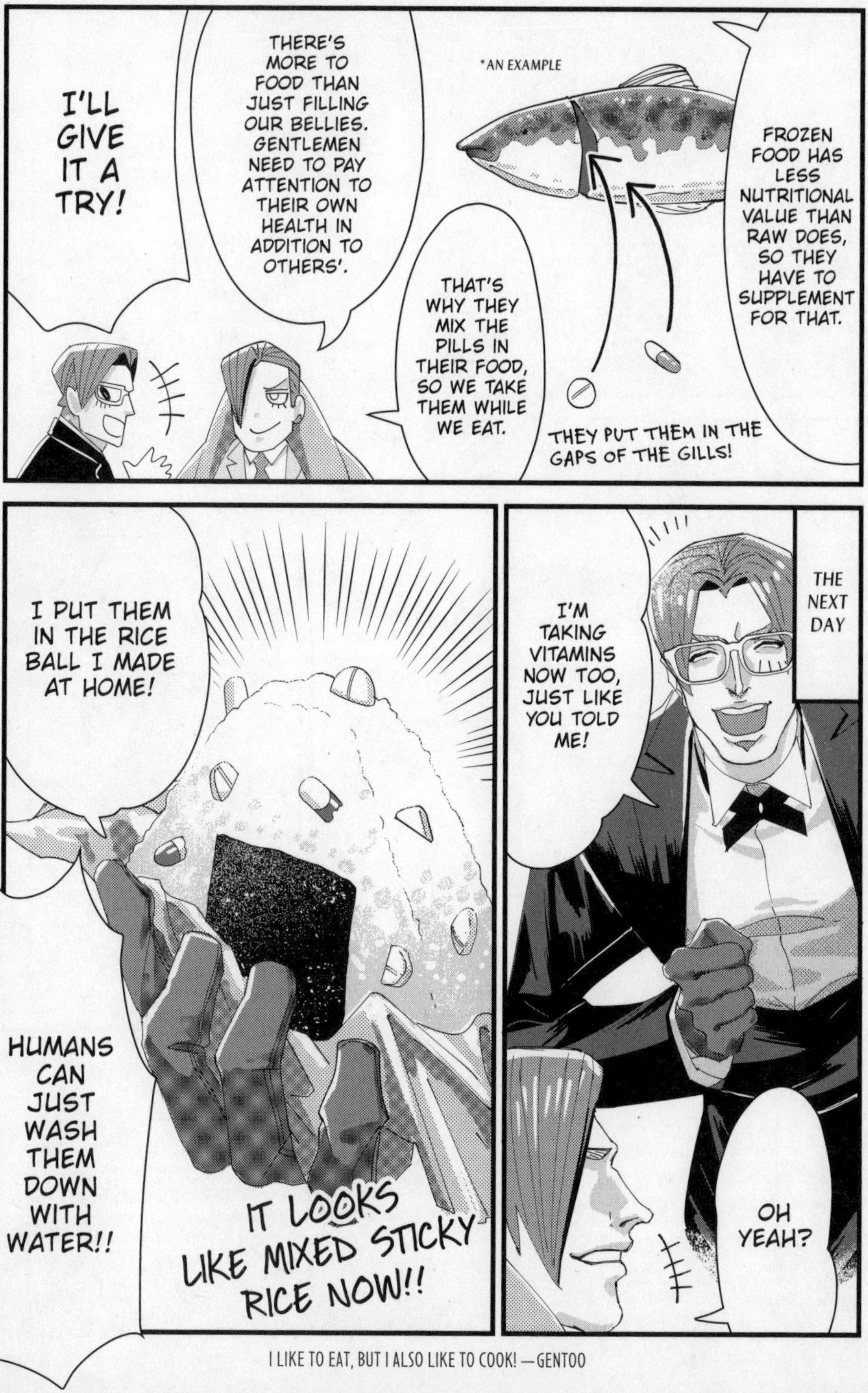
FROZEN FOOD HAS LESS NUTRITIONAL VALUE THAN RAW DOES, SO THEY HAVE TO SUPPLEMENT FOR THAT.
*AN EXAMPLE
THEY PUT THEM IN THE GAPS OF THE GILLS!
THAT'S WHY THEY MIX THE PILLS IN THEIR FOOD, SO WE TAKE THEM WHILE WE EAT.
THERE'S MORE TO FOOD THAN JUST FILLING OUR BELLIES. GENTLEMEN NEED TO PAY ATTENTION TO THEIR OWN HEALTH IN ADDITION TO OTHERS'.
I'LL GIVE IT A TRY!
THE NEXT DAY
I'M TAKING VITAMINS NOW TOO, JUST LIKE YOU TOLD ME!
OH YEAH?
I PUT THEM IN THE RICE BALL I MADE AT HOME!
IT LOOKS LIKE MIXED STICKY RICE NOW!!
HUMANS CAN JUST WASH THEM DOWN WITH WATER!!

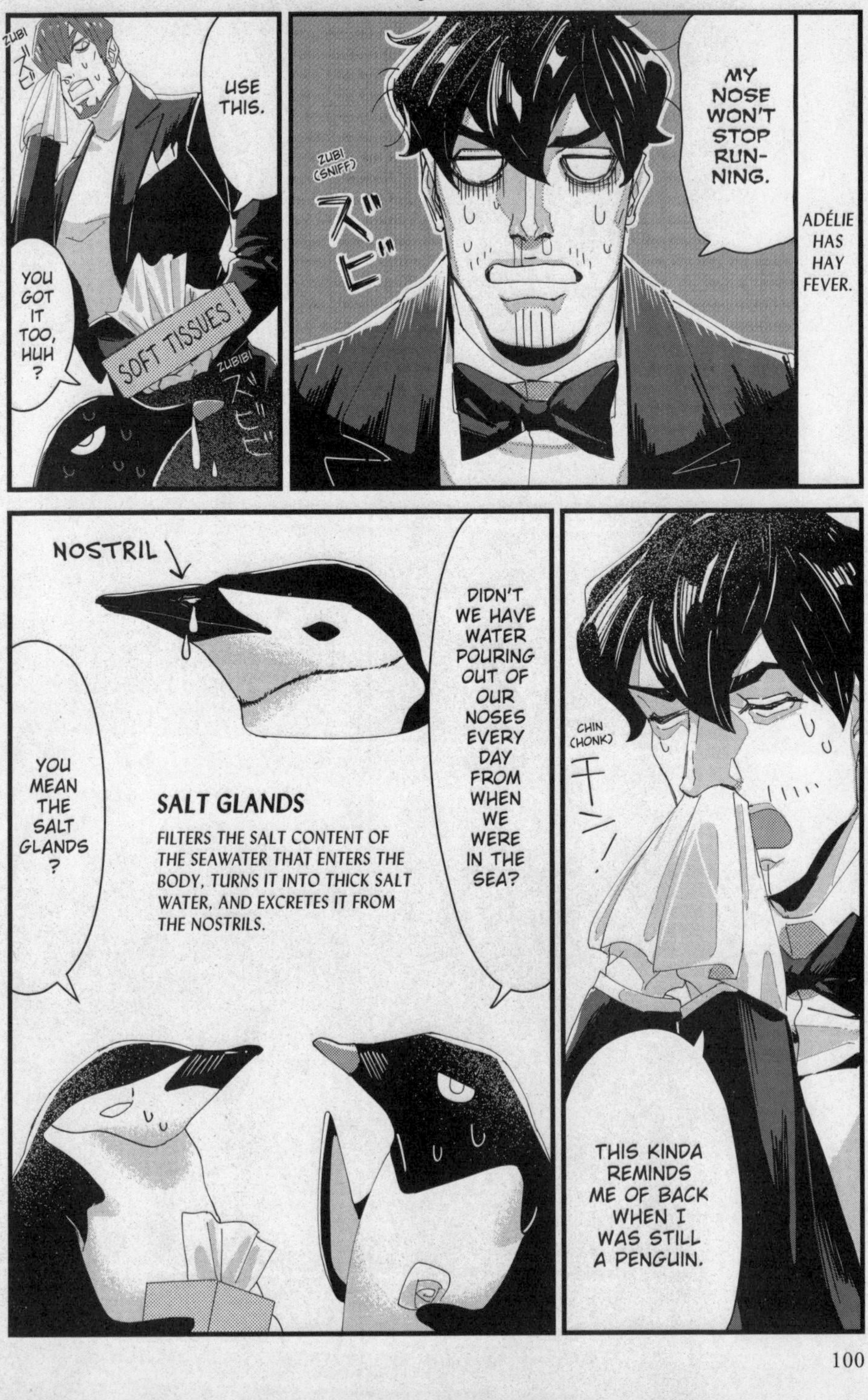
ADÉLIE HAS HAY FEVER.
MY NOSE WON'T STOP RUNNING.
ZUBI (SNIFF)
USE THIS.
ZUBI
YOU GOT IT TOO, HUH?
SOFT TISSUES!
ZUBIBI
CHIN (HONK)
THIS KINDA REMINDS ME OF BACK WHEN I WAS STILL A PENGUIN.
DIDN'T WE HAVE WATER POURING OUT OF OUR NOSES EVERY DAY FROM WHEN WE WERE IN THE SEA?
YOU MEAN THE SALT GLANDS?
NOSTRIL
SALT GLANDS
FILTERS THE SALT CONTENT OF THE SEAWATER THAT ENTERS THE BODY, TURNS IT INTO THICK SALT WATER, AND EXCRETES IT FROM THE NOSTRILS.

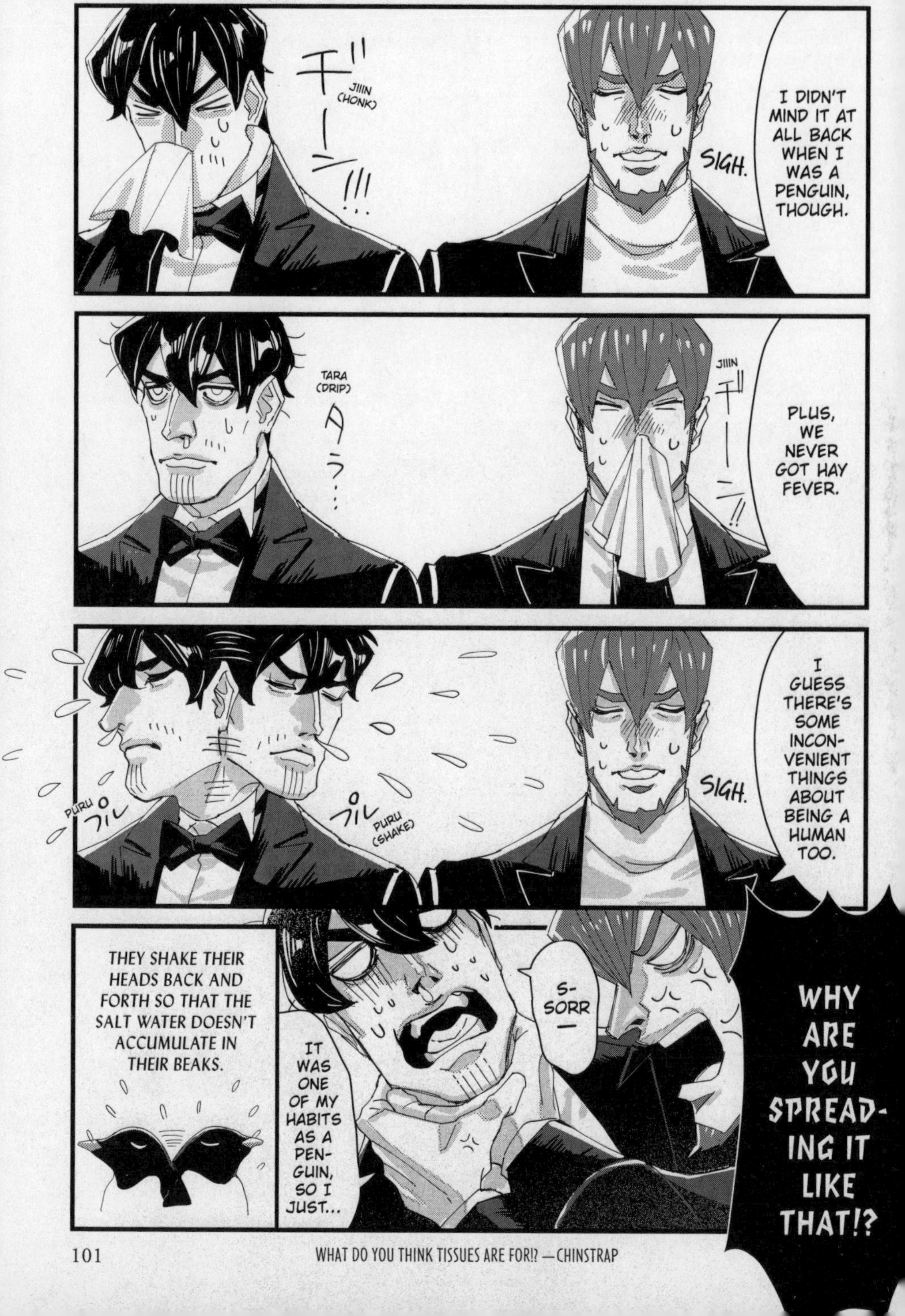

I DIDN'T MIND IT AT ALL BACK WHEN I WAS A PENGUIN, THOUGH.
SIGH.
JIIIN (HONK)
PLUS, WE NEVER GOT HAY FEVER.
JIIIN
TARA (DRIP)
I GUESS THERE'S SOME INCON-VENIENT THINGS ABOUT BEING A HUMAN TOO.
SIGH.
PURU (SHAKE)
PURU
WHY ARE YOU SPREAD-ING IT LIKE THAT!?
S-SORR—
IT WAS ONE OF MY HABITS AS A PEN-GUIN, SO I JUST...
THEY SHAKE THEIR HEADS BACK AND FORTH SO THAT THE SALT WATER DOESN'T ACCUMULATE IN THEIR BEAKS.

WHAT DO YOU THINK TISSUES ARE FOR!? —CHINSTRAP

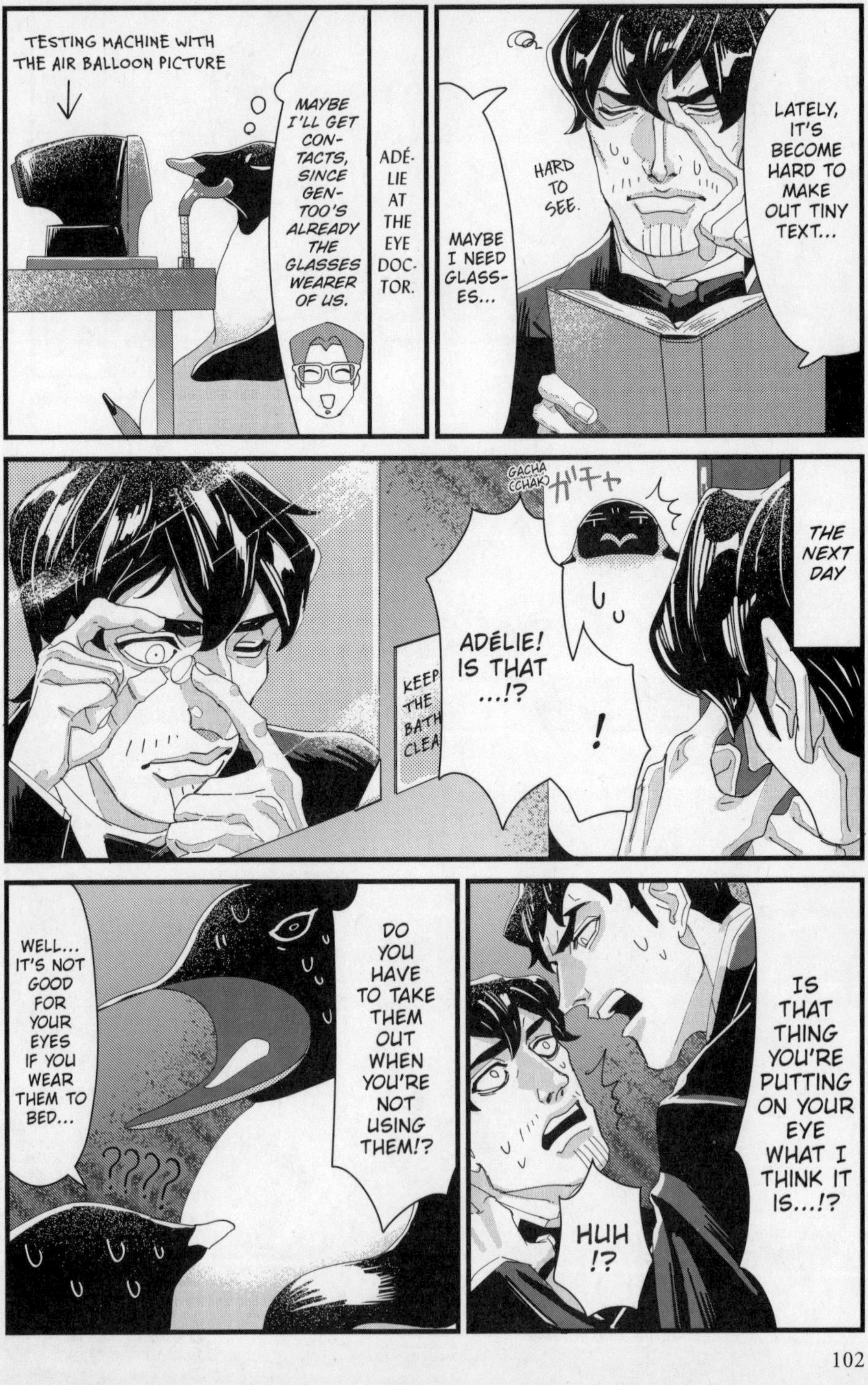
LATELY, IT'S BECOME HARD TO MAKE OUT TINY TEXT...
HARD TO SEE.
MAYBE I NEED GLASSES...
ADÉLIE AT THE EYE DOCTOR.
MAYBE I'LL GET CONTACTS, SINCE GENTOO'S ALREADY THE GLASSES WEARER OF US.
TESTING MACHINE WITH THE AIR BALLOON PICTURE
THE NEXT DAY
GACHA (CHAK)
ガチャ
ADÉLIE! IS THAT ...!?
!
KEEP THE BATH CLEA
IS THAT THING YOU'RE PUTTING ON YOUR EYE WHAT I THINK IT IS...!?
HUH !?
DO YOU HAVE TO TAKE THEM OUT WHEN YOU'RE NOT USING THEM!?
WELL... IT'S NOT GOOD FOR YOUR EYES IF YOU WEAR THEM TO BED...
????

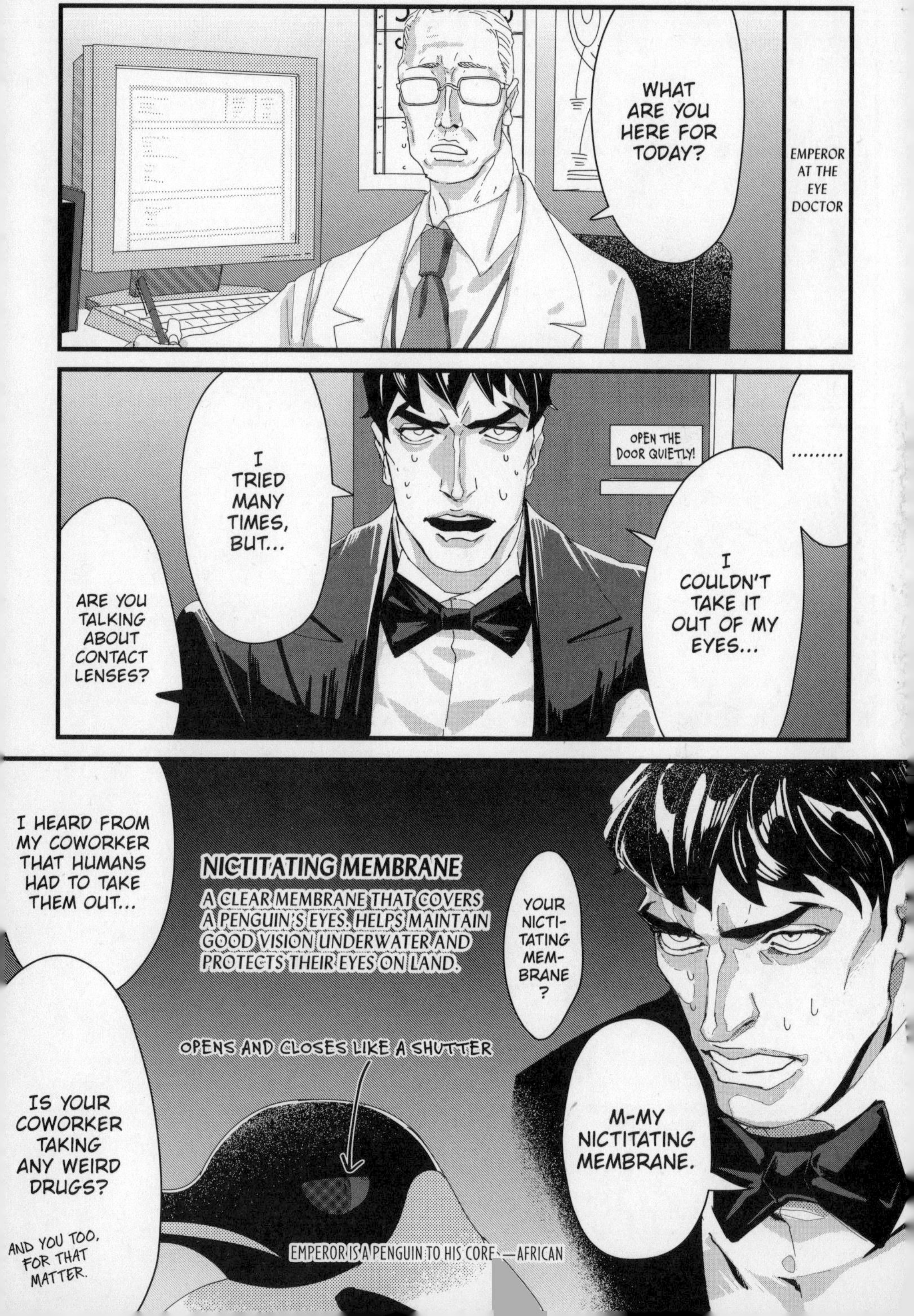
EMPEROR AT THE EYE DOCTOR
WHAT ARE YOU HERE FOR TODAY?
....
I COULDN'T TAKE IT OUT OF MY EYES...
OPEN THE DOOR QUIETLY!
I TRIED MANY TIMES, BUT...
ARE YOU TALKING ABOUT CONTACT LENSES?
M-MY NICTITATING MEMBRANE.
YOUR NICTI-TATING MEM-BRANE?
NICTITATING MEMBRANE
A CLEAR MEMBRANE THAT COVERS A PENGUIN'S EYES. HELPS MAINTAIN GOOD VISION UNDERWATER AND PROTECTS THEIR EYES ON LAND.
OPENS AND CLOSES LIKE A SHUTTER
I HEARD FROM MY COWORKER THAT HUMANS HAD TO TAKE THEM OUT...
IS YOUR COWORKER TAKING ANY WEIRD DRUGS?
AND YOU TOO, FOR THAT MATTER.
EMPEROR IS A PENGUIN TO HIS CORE.—AFRICAN

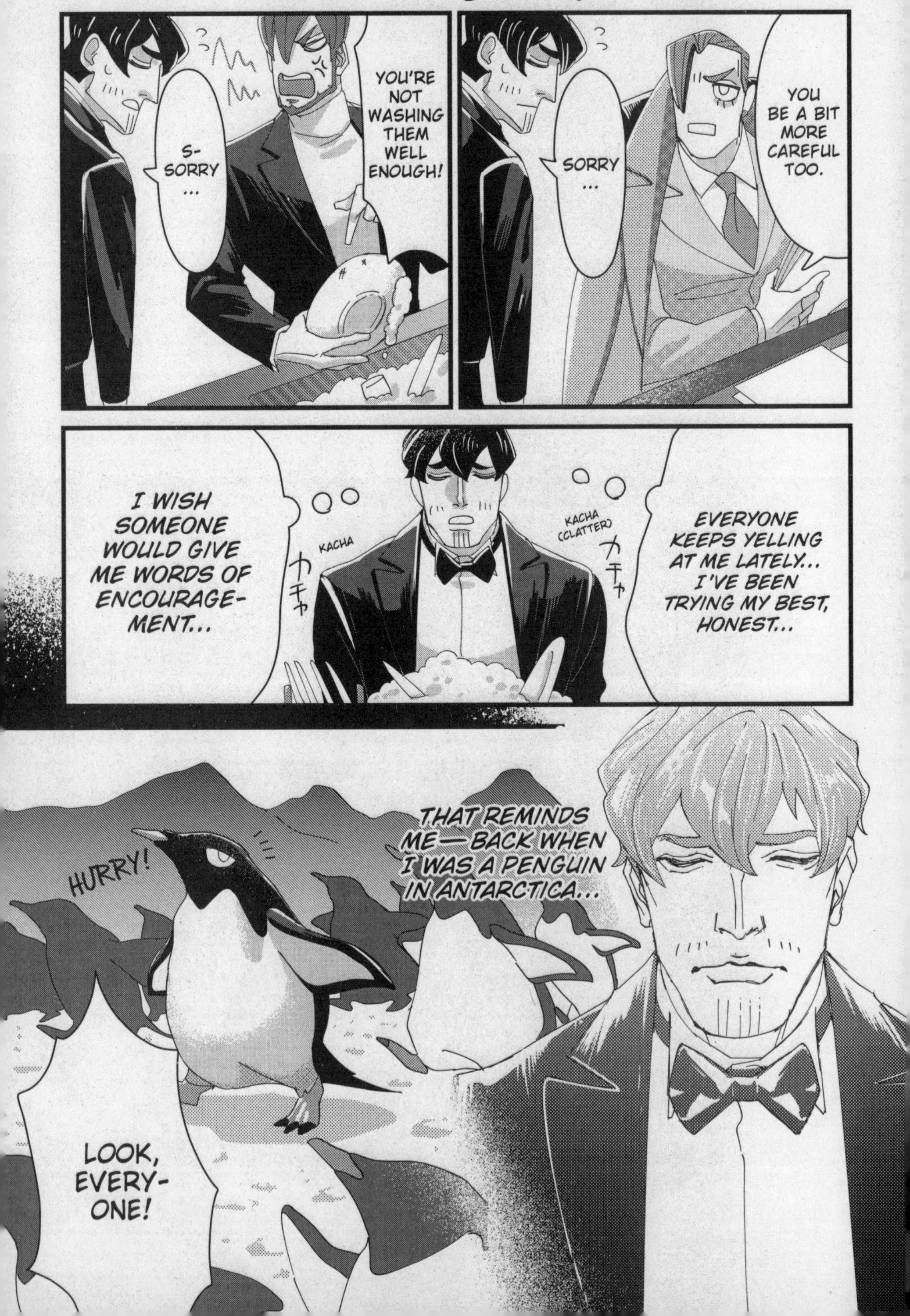
YOU BE A BIT MORE CAREFUL TOO.
SORRY ...
YOU'RE NOT WASHING THEM WELL ENOUGH!
S-SORRY ...
EVERYONE KEEPS YELLING AT ME LATELY... I'VE BEEN TRYING MY BEST, HONEST...
KACHA (CLATTER)
カチャ
KACHA
カチャ
I WISH SOMEONE WOULD GIVE ME WORDS OF ENCOURAGE-MENT...
THAT REMINDS ME—BACK WHEN I WAS A PENGUIN IN ANTARCTICA...
HURRY!
LOOK, EVERY-ONE!

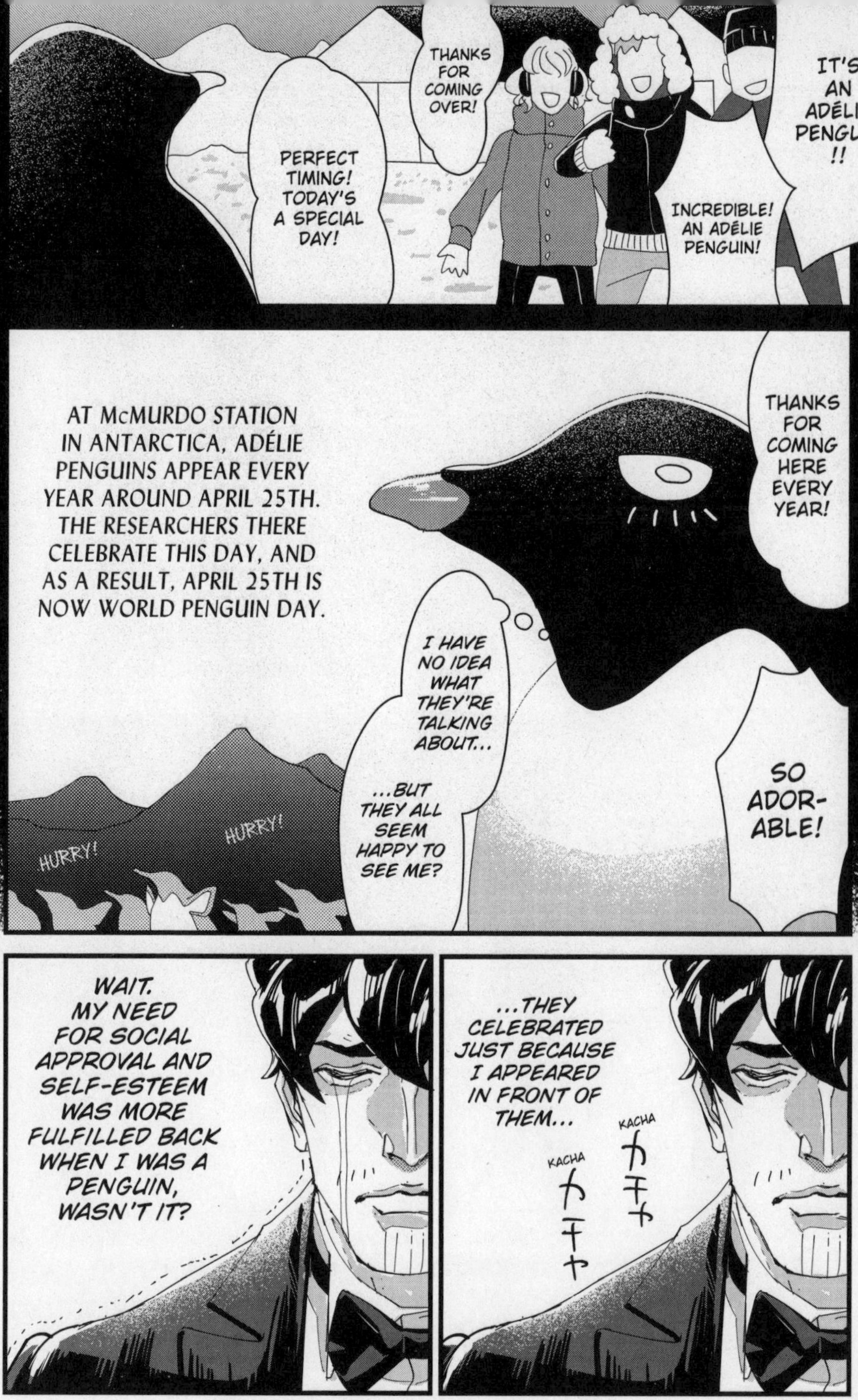
IT'S AN ADÉLIE PENGUIN!!
INCREDIBLE! AN ADÉLIE PENGUIN!
THANKS FOR COMING OVER!
PERFECT TIMING! TODAY'S A SPECIAL DAY!
THANKS FOR COMING HERE EVERY YEAR!
AT McMURDO STATION IN ANTARCTICA, ADÉLIE PENGUINS APPEAR EVERY YEAR AROUND APRIL 25TH. THE RESEARCHERS THERE CELEBRATE THIS DAY, AND AS A RESULT, APRIL 25TH IS NOW WORLD PENGUIN DAY.
I HAVE NO IDEA WHAT THEY'RE TALKING ABOUT...
SO ADORABLE!
...BUT THEY ALL SEEM HAPPY TO SEE ME?
HURRY!
HURRY!
...THEY CELEBRATED JUST BECAUSE I APPEARED IN FRONT OF THEM...
KACHA カチャ
KACHA カチャ
WAIT. MY NEED FOR SOCIAL APPROVAL AND SELF-ESTEEM WAS MORE FULFILLED BACK WHEN I WAS A PENGUIN, WASN'T IT?

♦ A Penguin's Anger: Emperor ♦

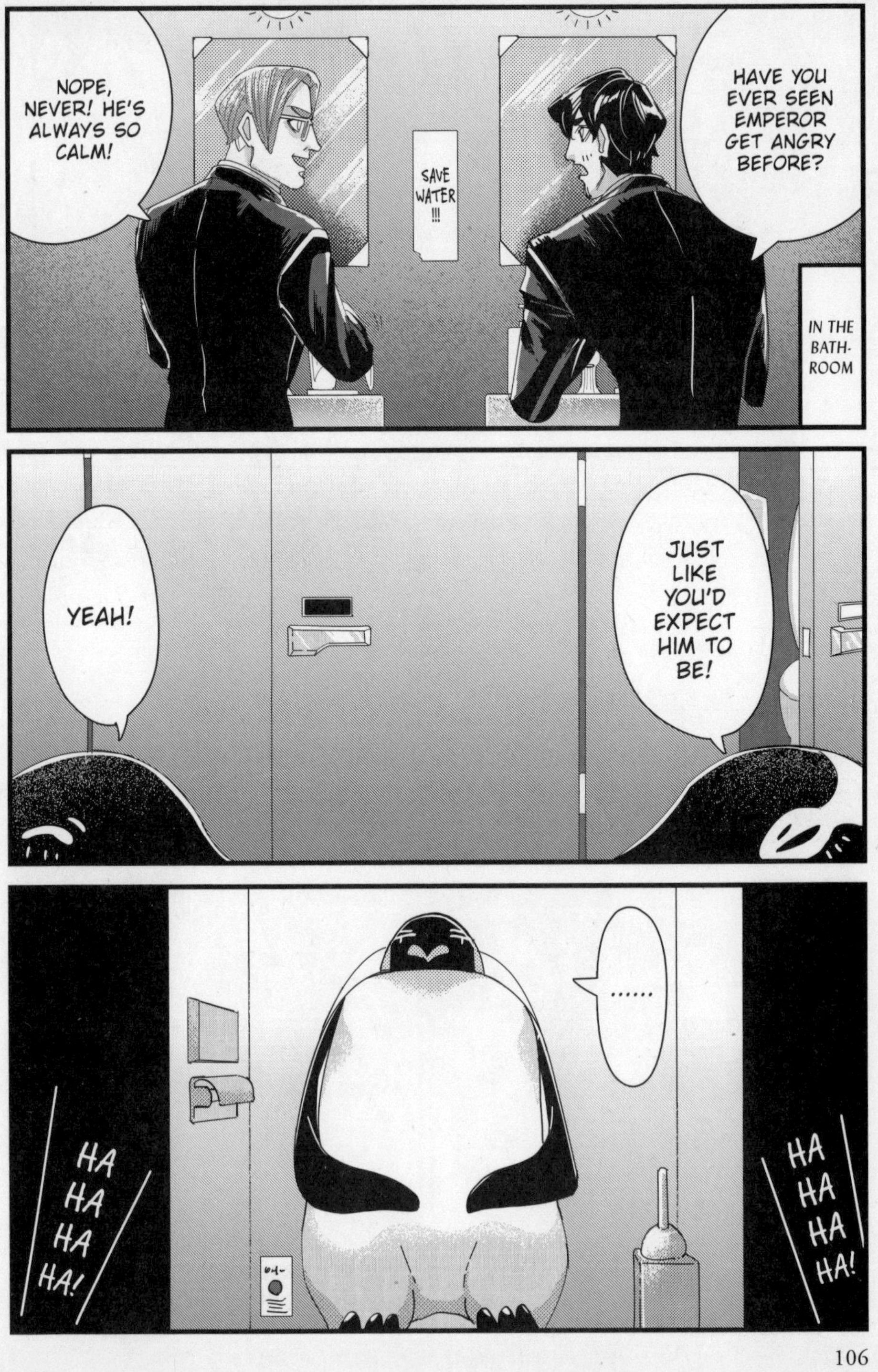
HAVE YOU EVER SEEN EMPEROR GET ANGRY BEFORE?
IN THE BATH-ROOM
SAVE WATER !!!
NOPE, NEVER! HE'S ALWAYS SO CALM!
JUST LIKE YOU'D EXPECT HIM TO BE!
YEAH!
......
HA HA HA HA!
HA HA HA HA!

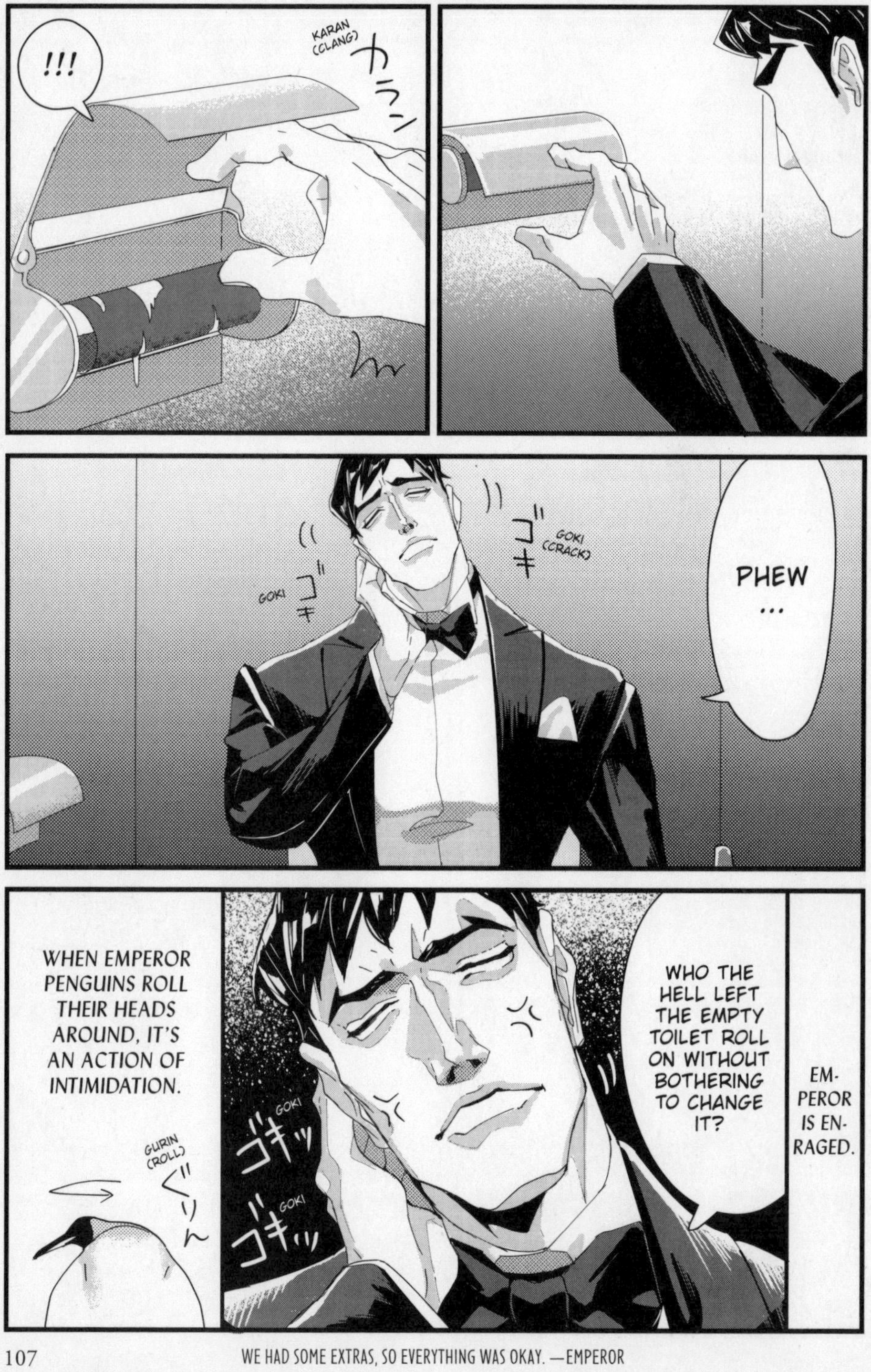
!!!
KARAN (CLANG)
カラン
PHEW…
GOKI (CRACK)
ゴキ
GOKI
ゴキ
EMPEROR IS ENRAGED.
WHO THE HELL LEFT THE EMPTY TOILET ROLL ON WITHOUT BOTHERING TO CHANGE IT?
GOKI
ゴキッ
GOKI
ゴキッ
WHEN EMPEROR PENGUINS ROLL THEIR HEADS AROUND, IT'S AN ACTION OF INTIMIDATION.
GURIN (ROLL)
ぐりん

WE HAD SOME EXTRAS, SO EVERYTHING WAS OKAY. —EMPEROR

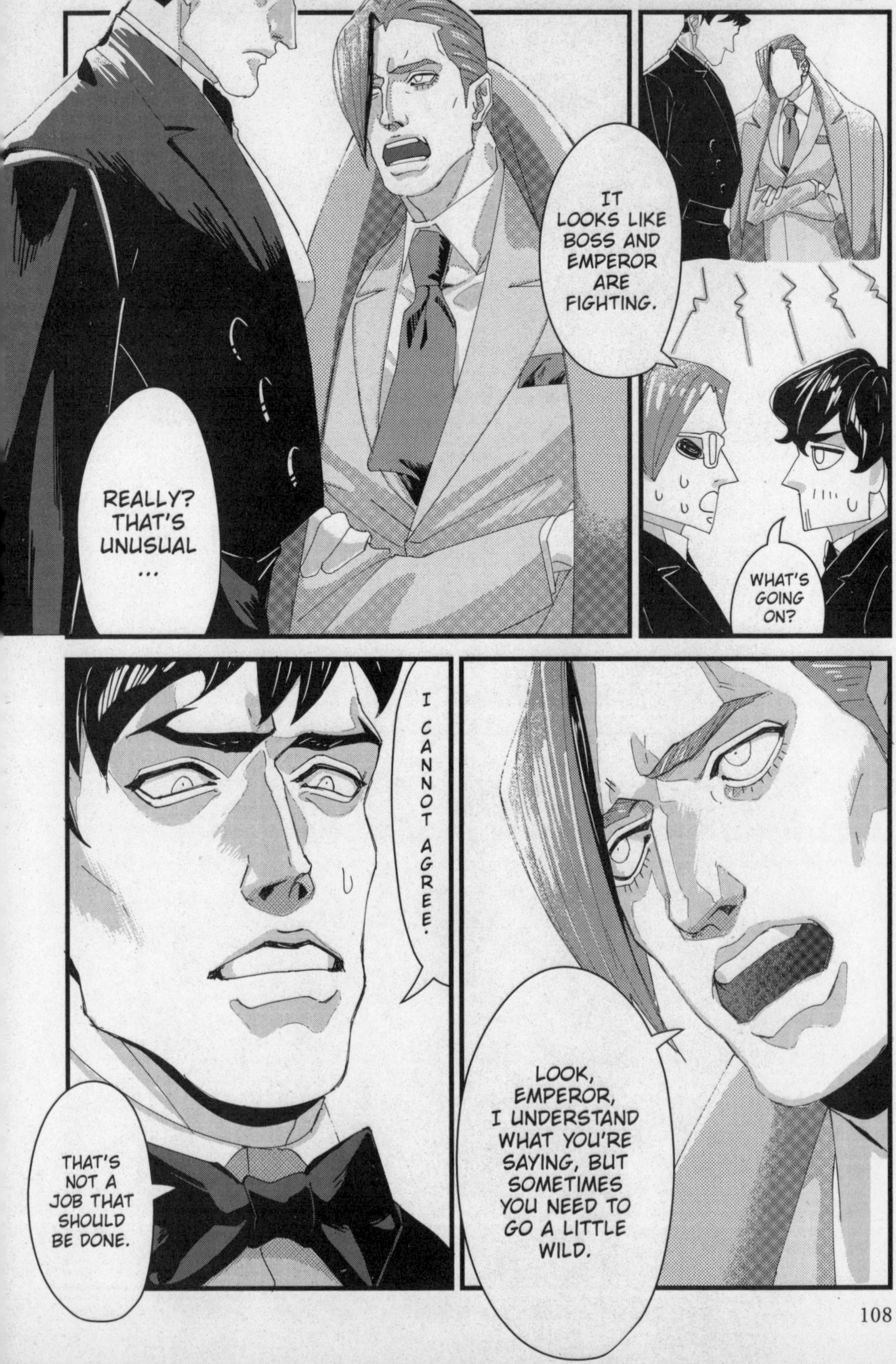
WHAT'S GOING ON?
IT LOOKS LIKE BOSS AND EMPEROR ARE FIGHTING.
REALLY? THAT'S UNUSUAL...
LOOK, EMPEROR, I UNDERSTAND WHAT YOU'RE SAYING, BUT SOMETIMES YOU NEED TO GO A LITTLE WILD.
I CANNOT AGREE.
THAT'S NOT A JOB THAT SHOULD BE DONE.

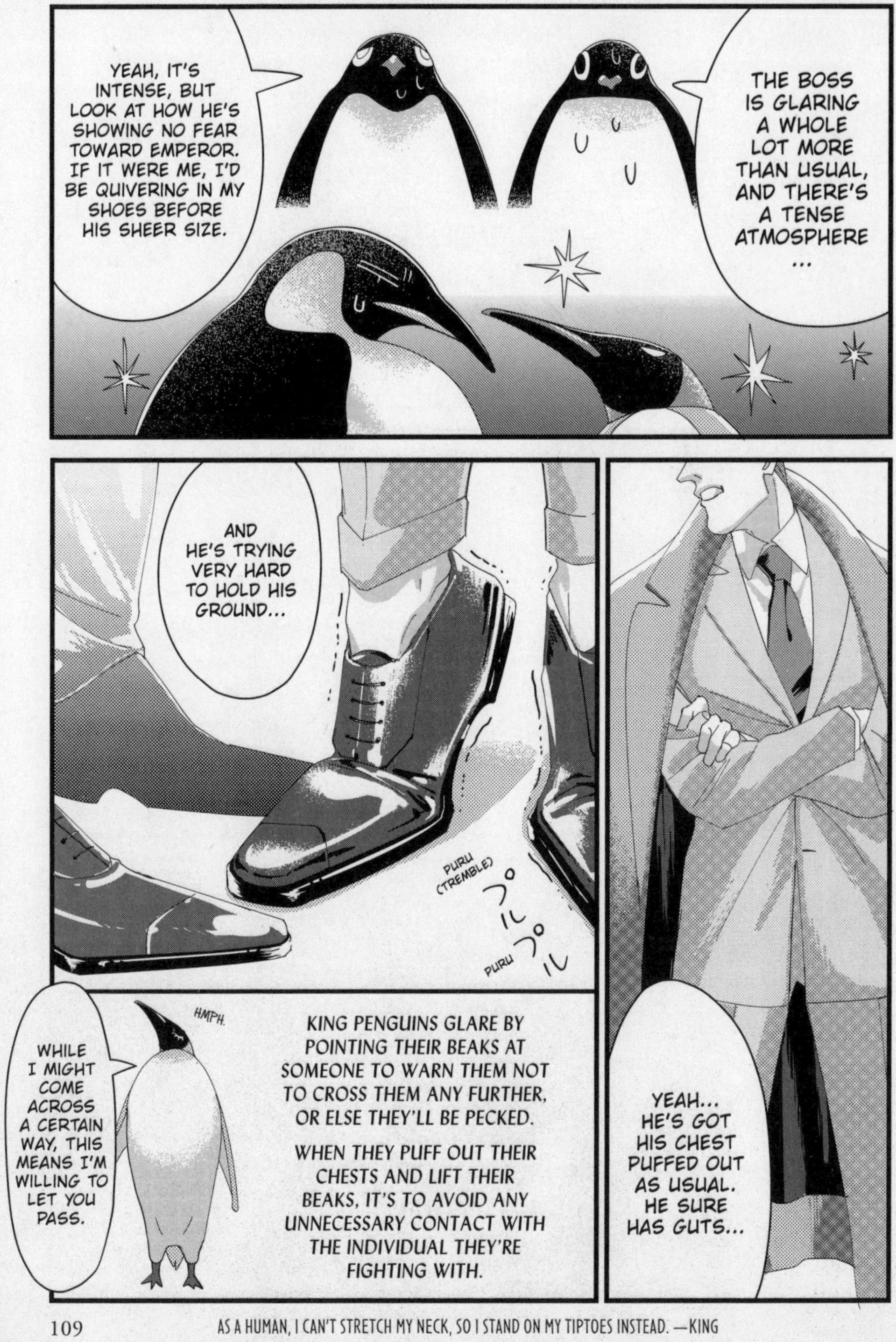
THE BOSS IS GLARING A WHOLE LOT MORE THAN USUAL, AND THERE'S A TENSE ATMOSPHERE ...
YEAH, IT'S INTENSE, BUT LOOK AT HOW HE'S SHOWING NO FEAR TOWARD EMPEROR. IF IT WERE ME, I'D BE QUIVERING IN MY SHOES BEFORE HIS SHEER SIZE.
YEAH... HE'S GOT HIS CHEST PUFFED OUT AS USUAL. HE SURE HAS GUTS...
AND HE'S TRYING VERY HARD TO HOLD HIS GROUND...
PURU (TREMBLE)
プルプル
PURU
KING PENGUINS GLARE BY POINTING THEIR BEAKS AT SOMEONE TO WARN THEM NOT TO CROSS THEM ANY FURTHER, OR ELSE THEY'LL BE PECKED.
WHEN THEY PUFF OUT THEIR CHESTS AND LIFT THEIR BEAKS, IT'S TO AVOID ANY UNNECESSARY CONTACT WITH THE INDIVIDUAL THEY'RE FIGHTING WITH.
HMPH.
WHILE I MIGHT COME ACROSS A CERTAIN WAY, THIS MEANS I'M WILLING TO LET YOU PASS.

AS A HUMAN, I CAN'T STRETCH MY NECK, SO I STAND ON MY TIPTOES INSTEAD. —KING

♦ A Penguin's Anger: African ♦

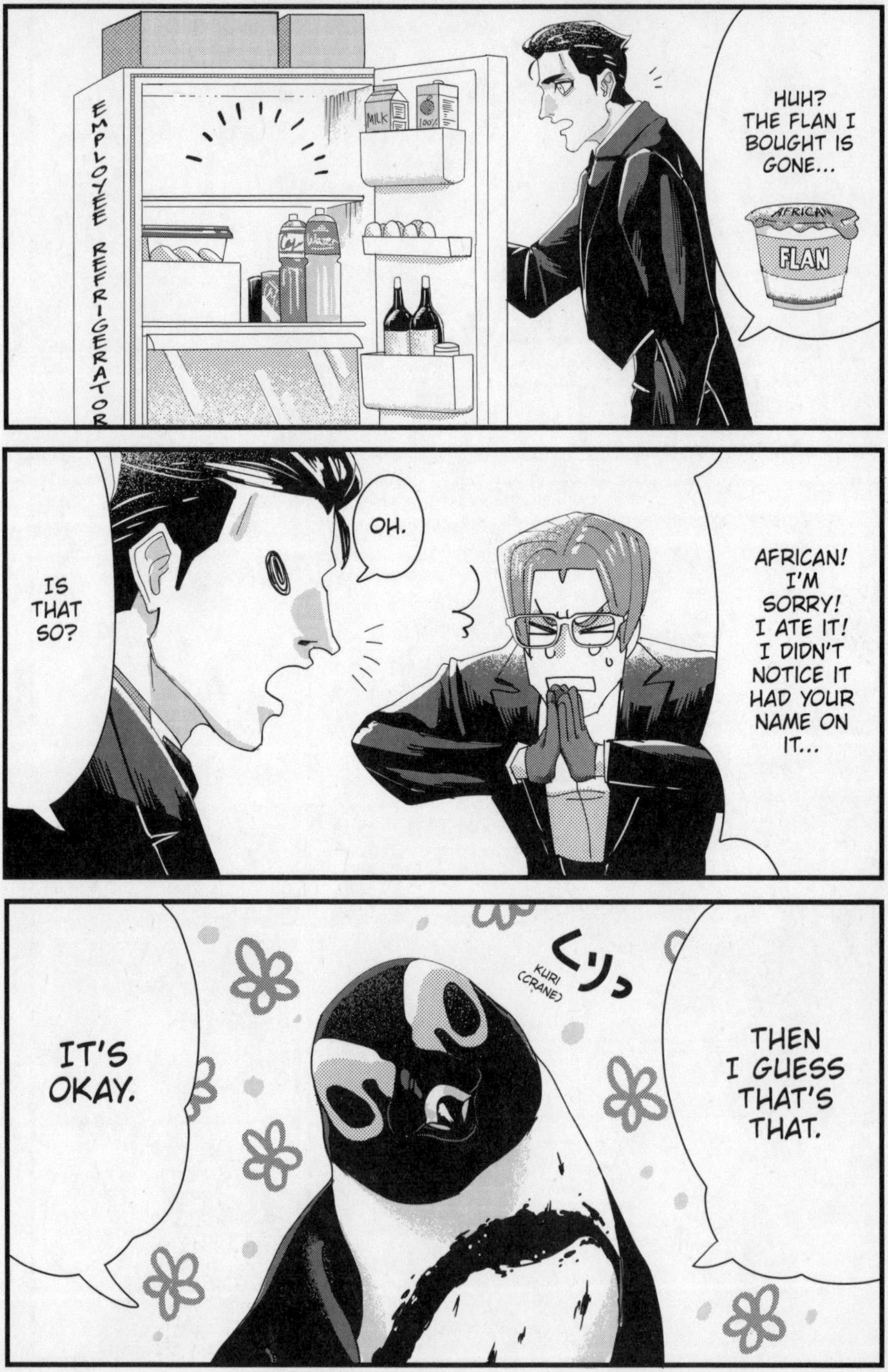
EMPLOYEE REFRIGERATOR
MILK
100%
HUH? THE FLAN I BOUGHT IS GONE...
AFRICAN
FLAN
AFRICAN! I'M SORRY! I ATE IT! I DIDN'T NOTICE IT HAD YOUR NAME ON IT...
OH.
IS THAT SO?
THEN I GUESS THAT'S THAT.
くりっ
KURI (CRANE)
IT'S OKAY.

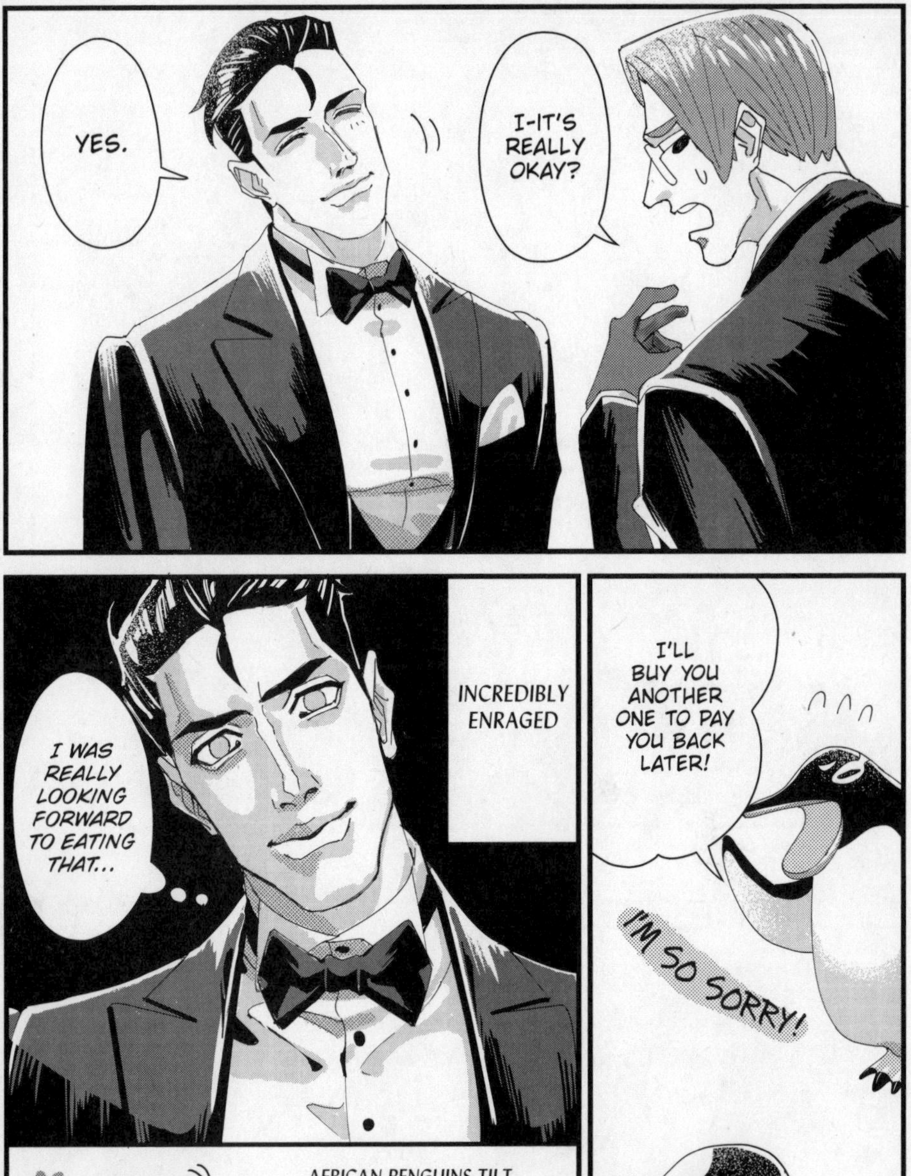
I-IT'S REALLY OKAY?
YES.
I'LL BUY YOU ANOTHER ONE TO PAY YOU BACK LATER!
I'M SO SORRY!
INCREDIBLY ENRAGED
I WAS REALLY LOOKING FORWARD TO EATING THAT...
...
AFRICAN PENGUINS TILT THEIR HEADS AND GLARE TO INTIMIDATE OTHERS.
FROM THE OUTSIDE, IT LOOKS CUTE—LIKE A PUPPY TILTING ITS HEAD—SO IT DOESN'T COME OFF AS AN ACTION INDICATING ANGER.
くりっ
KURI

KING TOLD ME THE TRUTH, SO I BOUGHT HIM ANOTHER ONE IMMEDIATELY... —GENTOO

◆ A Penguin's Anger: Pygoscelis Penguins ◆

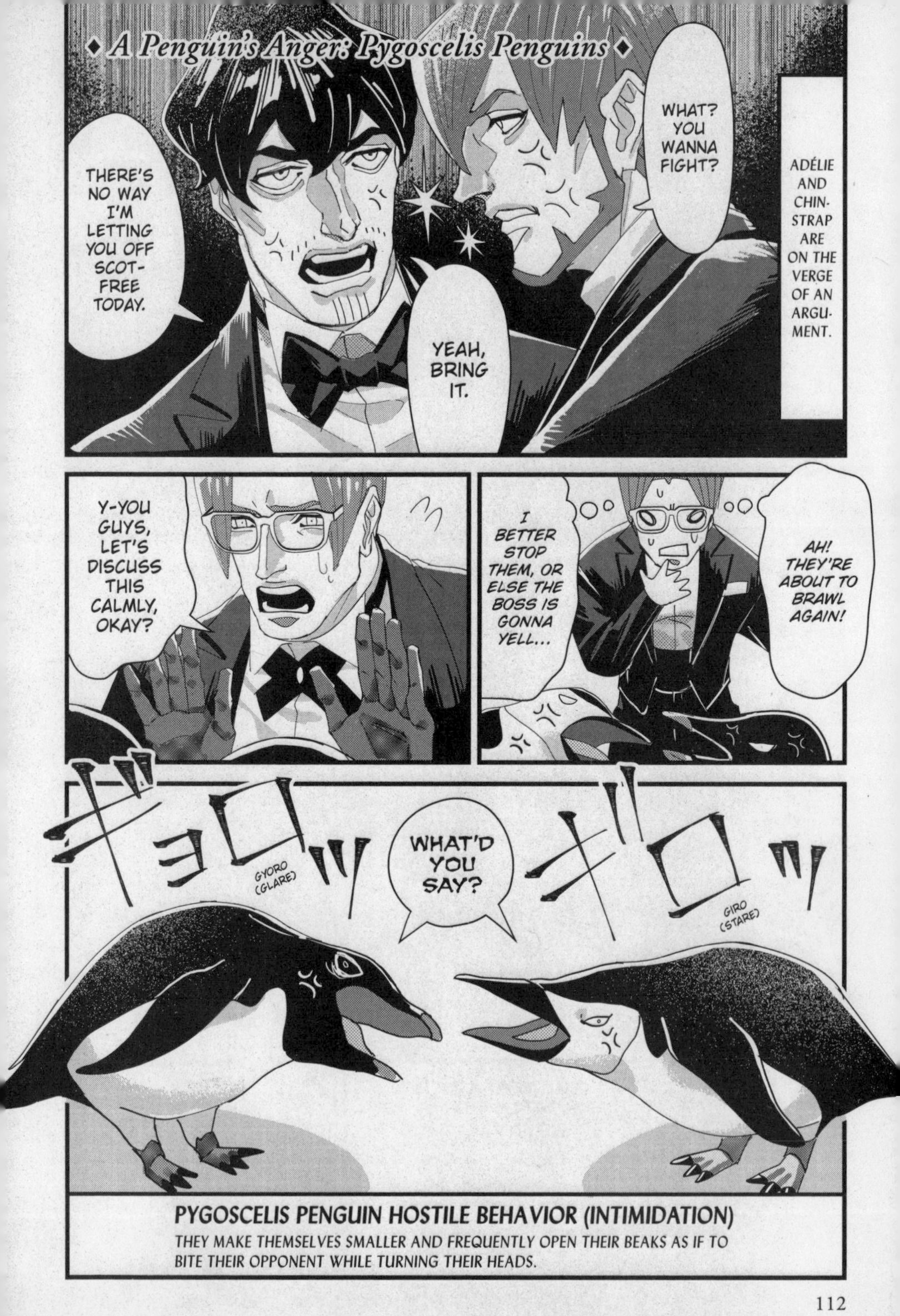
ADÉLIE AND CHINSTRAP ARE ON THE VERGE OF AN ARGUMENT.
WHAT? YOU WANNA FIGHT?
THERE'S NO WAY I'M LETTING YOU OFF SCOT-FREE TODAY.
YEAH, BRING IT.
AH! THEY'RE ABOUT TO BRAWL AGAIN!
I BETTER STOP THEM, OR ELSE THE BOSS IS GONNA YELL...
Y-YOU GUYS, LET'S DISCUSS THIS CALMLY, OKAY?
ギロッ
GIRO (STARE)
WHAT'D YOU SAY?
ギョロッ
GYORO (GLARE)

PYGOSCELIS PENGUIN HOSTILE BEHAVIOR (INTIMIDATION)

THEY MAKE THEMSELVES SMALLER AND FREQUENTLY OPEN THEIR BEAKS AS IF TO BITE THEIR OPPONENT WHILE TURNING THEIR HEADS.

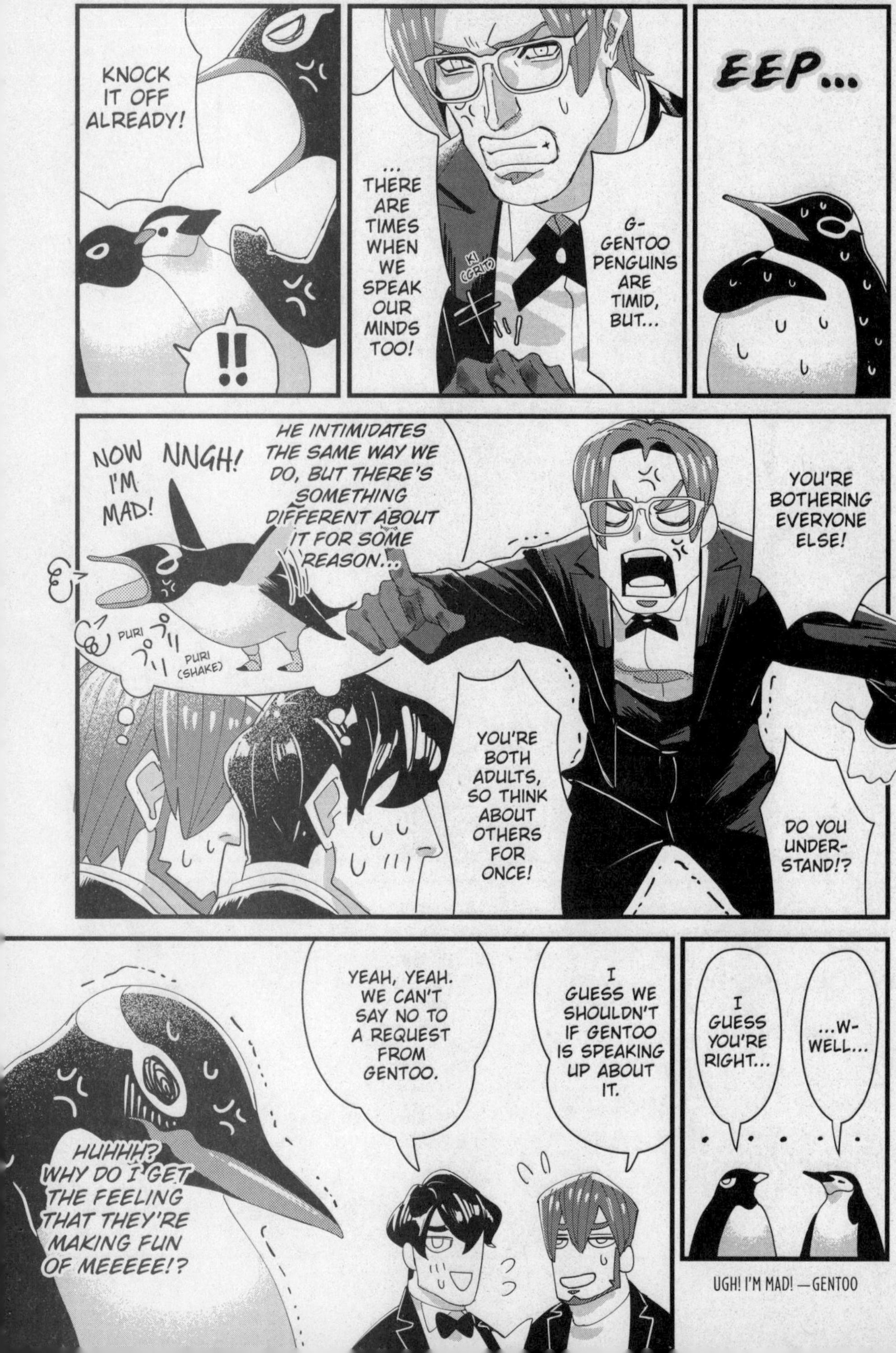
EEP...
G-GENTOO PENGUINS ARE TIMID, BUT...
KI (GRIT)
...THERE ARE TIMES WHEN WE SPEAK OUR MINDS TOO!
KNOCK IT OFF ALREADY!
!!
YOU'RE BOTHERING EVERYONE ELSE!
HE INTIMIDATES THE SAME WAY WE DO, BUT THERE'S SOMETHING DIFFERENT ABOUT IT FOR SOME REASON...
NNGH!
NOW I'M MAD!
PURI PURI (SHAKE)
DO YOU UNDERSTAND!?
YOU'RE BOTH ADULTS, SO THINK ABOUT OTHERS FOR ONCE!
...W-WELL...
I GUESS YOU'RE RIGHT...
I GUESS WE SHOULDN'T IF GENTOO IS SPEAKING UP ABOUT IT.
YEAH, YEAH. WE CAN'T SAY NO TO A REQUEST FROM GENTOO.
HUHHH? WHY DO I GET THE FEELING THAT THEY'RE MAKING FUN OF MEEEEE!?

UGH! I'M MAD! —GENTOO

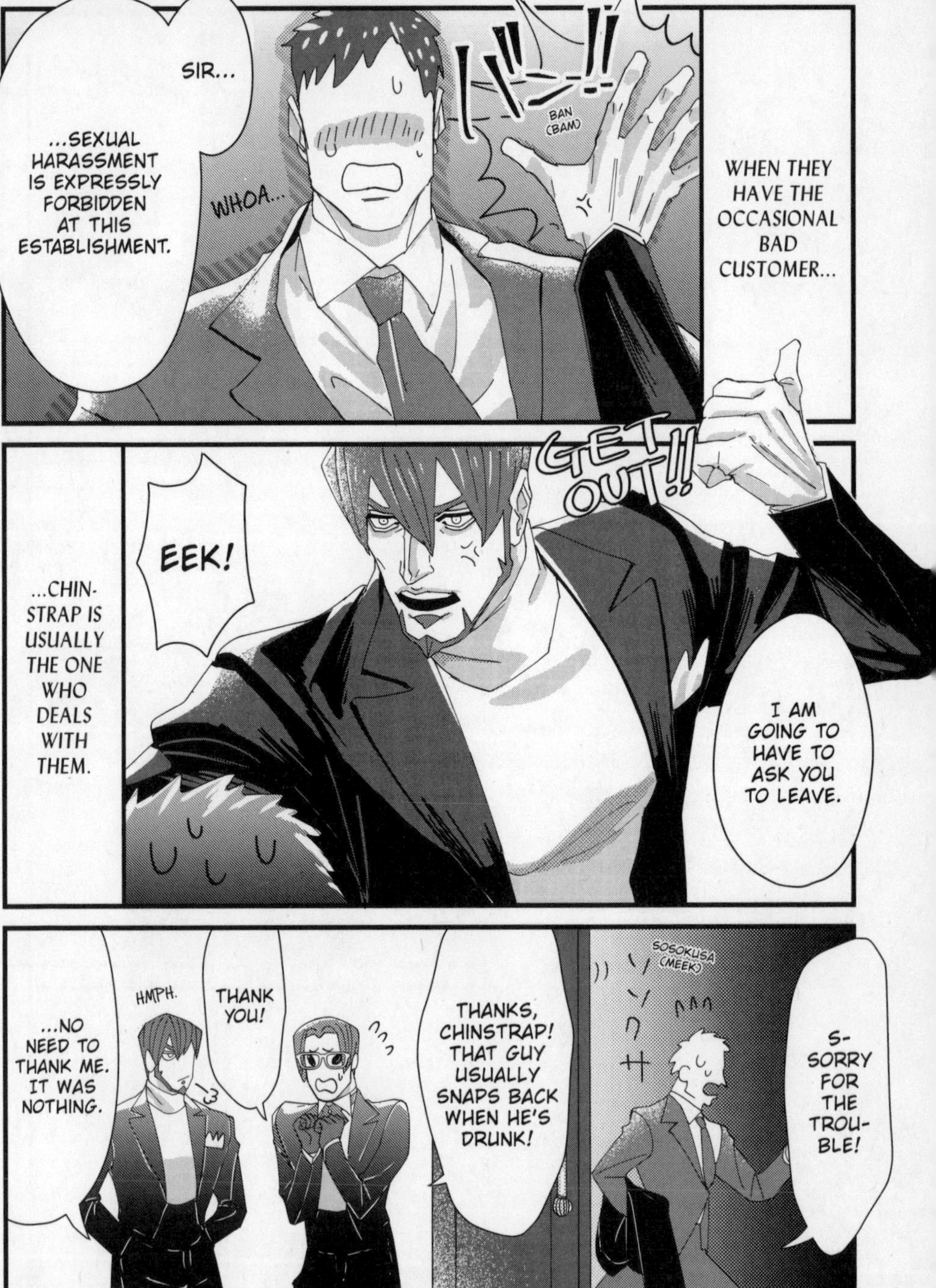
WHEN THEY HAVE THE OCCASIONAL BAD CUSTOMER...
BAN (BAM)
WHOA...
SIR...
...SEXUAL HARASSMENT IS EXPRESSLY FORBIDDEN AT THIS ESTABLISHMENT.
GET OUT!!
I AM GOING TO HAVE TO ASK YOU TO LEAVE.
EEK!
...CHIN-STRAP IS USUALLY THE ONE WHO DEALS WITH THEM.
S-SORRY FOR THE TROU-BLE!
SOSOKUSA (MEEK)
DOOR
THANKS, CHINSTRAP! THAT GUY USUALLY SNAPS BACK WHEN HE'S DRUNK!
THANK YOU!
HMPH.
...NO NEED TO THANK ME. IT WAS NOTHING.

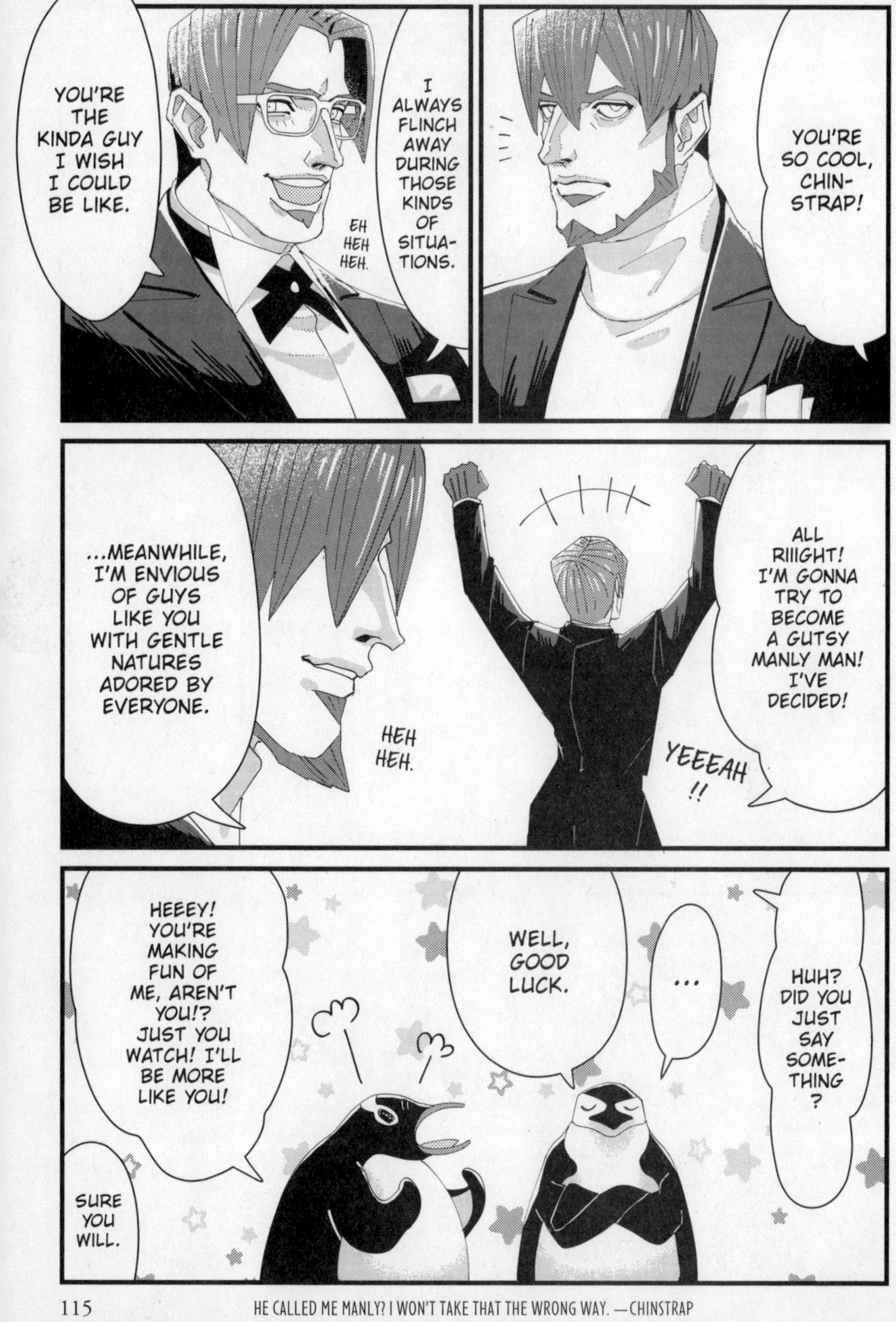
YOU'RE SO COOL, CHIN-STRAP!
I ALWAYS FLINCH AWAY DURING THOSE KINDS OF SITUA-TIONS.
EH HEH HEH.
YOU'RE THE KINDA GUY I WISH I COULD BE LIKE.
ALL RIIIGHT! I'M GONNA TRY TO BECOME A GUTSY MANLY MAN! I'VE DECIDED!
YEEEAH !!
HEH HEH.
...MEANWHILE, I'M ENVIOUS OF GUYS LIKE YOU WITH GENTLE NATURES ADORED BY EVERYONE.
HUH? DID YOU JUST SAY SOME-THING?
...
WELL, GOOD LUCK.
HEEEY! YOU'RE MAKING FUN OF ME, AREN'T YOU!? JUST YOU WATCH! I'LL BE MORE LIKE YOU!
SURE YOU WILL.

◆ *Friends Who Respect Each Other* ② ◆

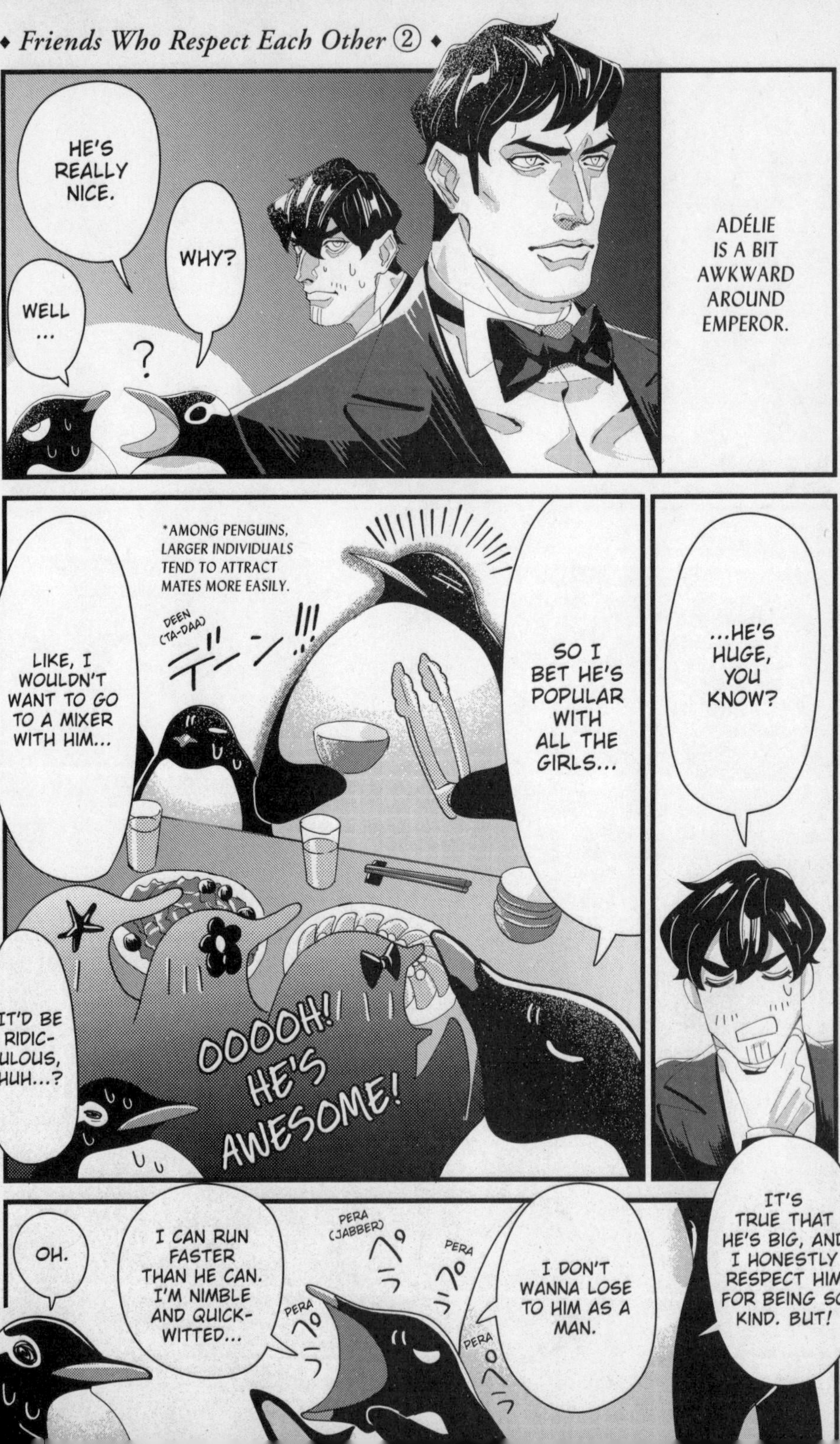
ADÉLIE IS A BIT AWKWARD AROUND EMPEROR.
HE'S REALLY NICE.
WHY?
WELL ...
?
...HE'S HUGE, YOU KNOW?
SO I BET HE'S POPULAR WITH ALL THE GIRLS...
*AMONG PENGUINS, LARGER INDIVIDUALS TEND TO ATTRACT MATES MORE EASILY.
DEEN (TA-DAA)
デーン!!!
OOOOH! HE'S AWESOME!
LIKE, I WOULDN'T WANT TO GO TO A MIXER WITH HIM...
IT'D BE RIDICULOUS, HUH...?
IT'S TRUE THAT HE'S BIG, AND I HONESTLY RESPECT HIM FOR BEING SO KIND. BUT!
I DON'T WANNA LOSE TO HIM AS A MAN.
PERA
PERA
PERA (JABBER)
PERA
I CAN RUN FASTER THAN HE CAN. I'M NIMBLE AND QUICK-WITTED...
OH.

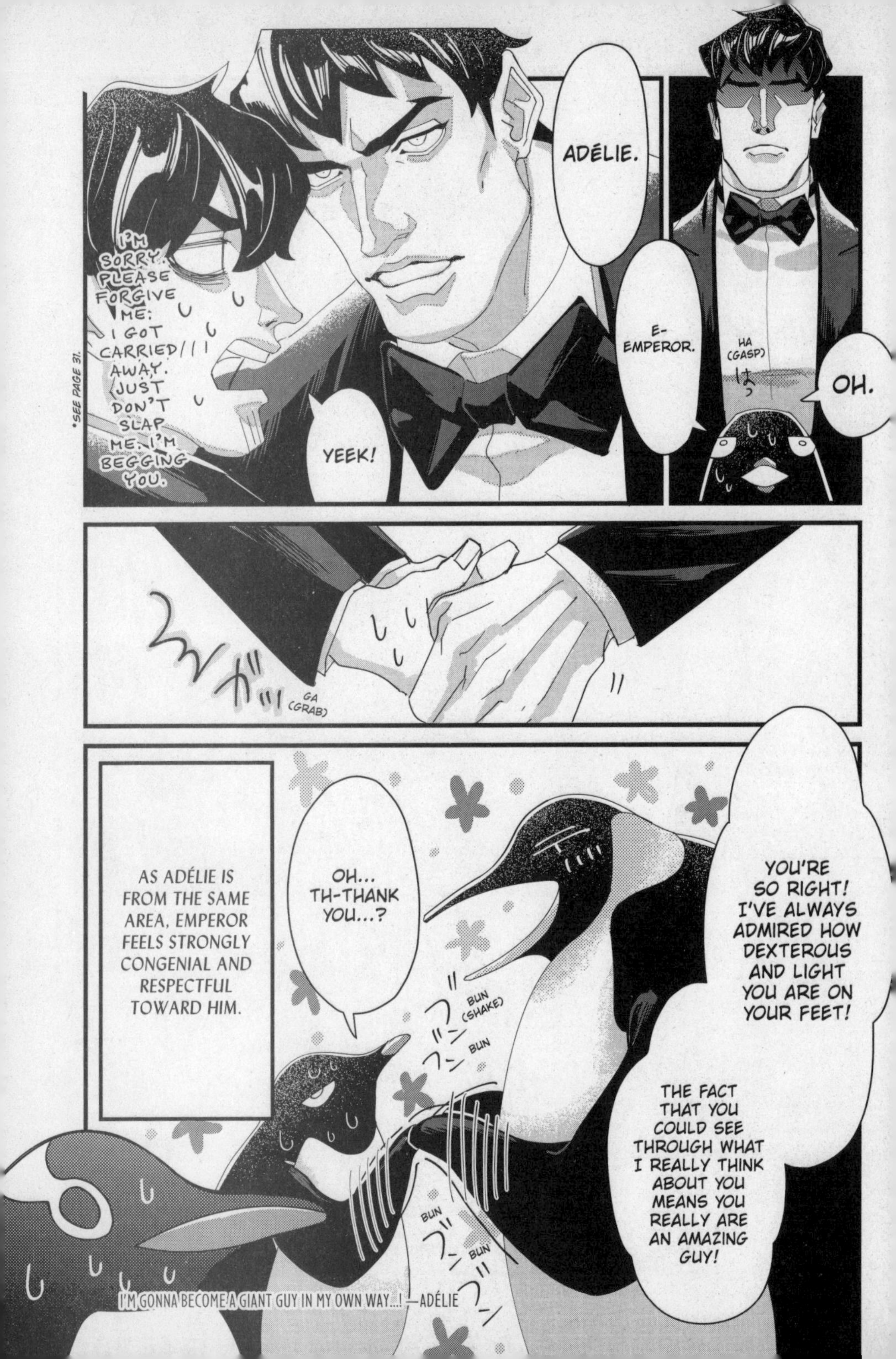

OH.
HA (GASP)
ADÉLIE.
E-EMPEROR.
YEEK!
I'M SORRY. PLEASE FORGIVE ME: I GOT CARRIED AWAY. JUST DON'T SLAP ME. I'M BEGGING YOU.
*SEE PAGE 31.
GA (GRAB)
YOU'RE SO RIGHT! I'VE ALWAYS ADMIRED HOW DEXTEROUS AND LIGHT YOU ARE ON YOUR FEET!
THE FACT THAT YOU COULD SEE THROUGH WHAT I REALLY THINK ABOUT YOU MEANS YOU REALLY ARE AN AMAZING GUY!
OH... TH-THANK YOU...?
BUN (SHAKE)
BUN
BUN
BUN
AS ADÉLIE IS FROM THE SAME AREA, EMPEROR FEELS STRONGLY CONGENIAL AND RESPECTFUL TOWARD HIM.
I'M GONNA BECOME A GIANT GUY IN MY OWN WAY...! —ADÉLIE

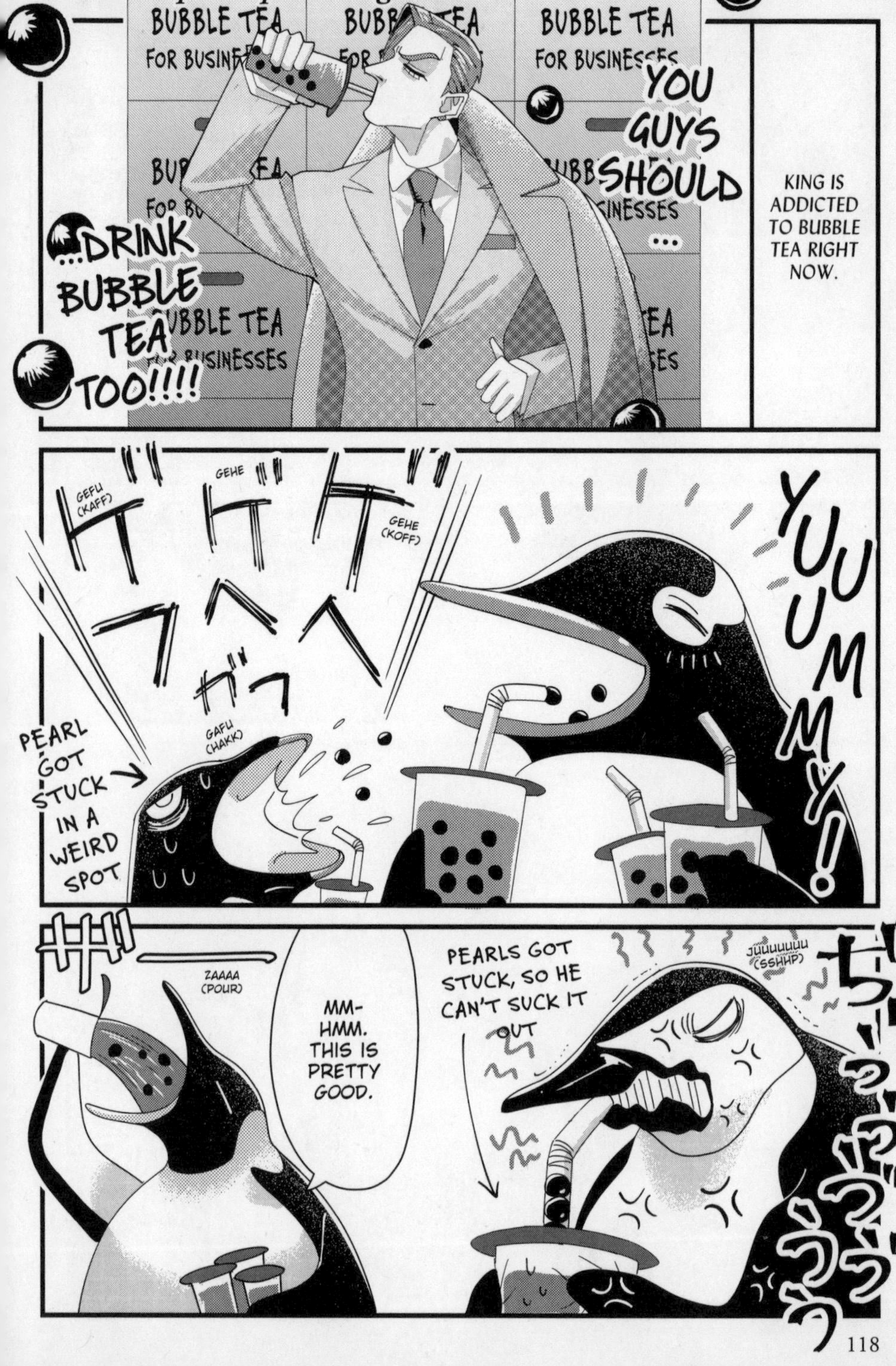
KING IS ADDICTED TO BUBBLE TEA RIGHT NOW.
BUBBLE TEA FOR BUSINESSES
YOU GUYS SHOULD...
...DRINK BUBBLE TEA TOO!!!!
YUUUMMY—!
GEHE (KOFF)
GEHE
GEFU (KAFF)
GAFU (HAKK)
PEARL GOT STUCK IN A WEIRD SPOT
JUUUUUUU (SSHHP)
PEARLS GOT STUCK, SO HE CAN'T SUCK IT OUT
MM-HMM. THIS IS PRETTY GOOD.
ZAAAA (POUR)

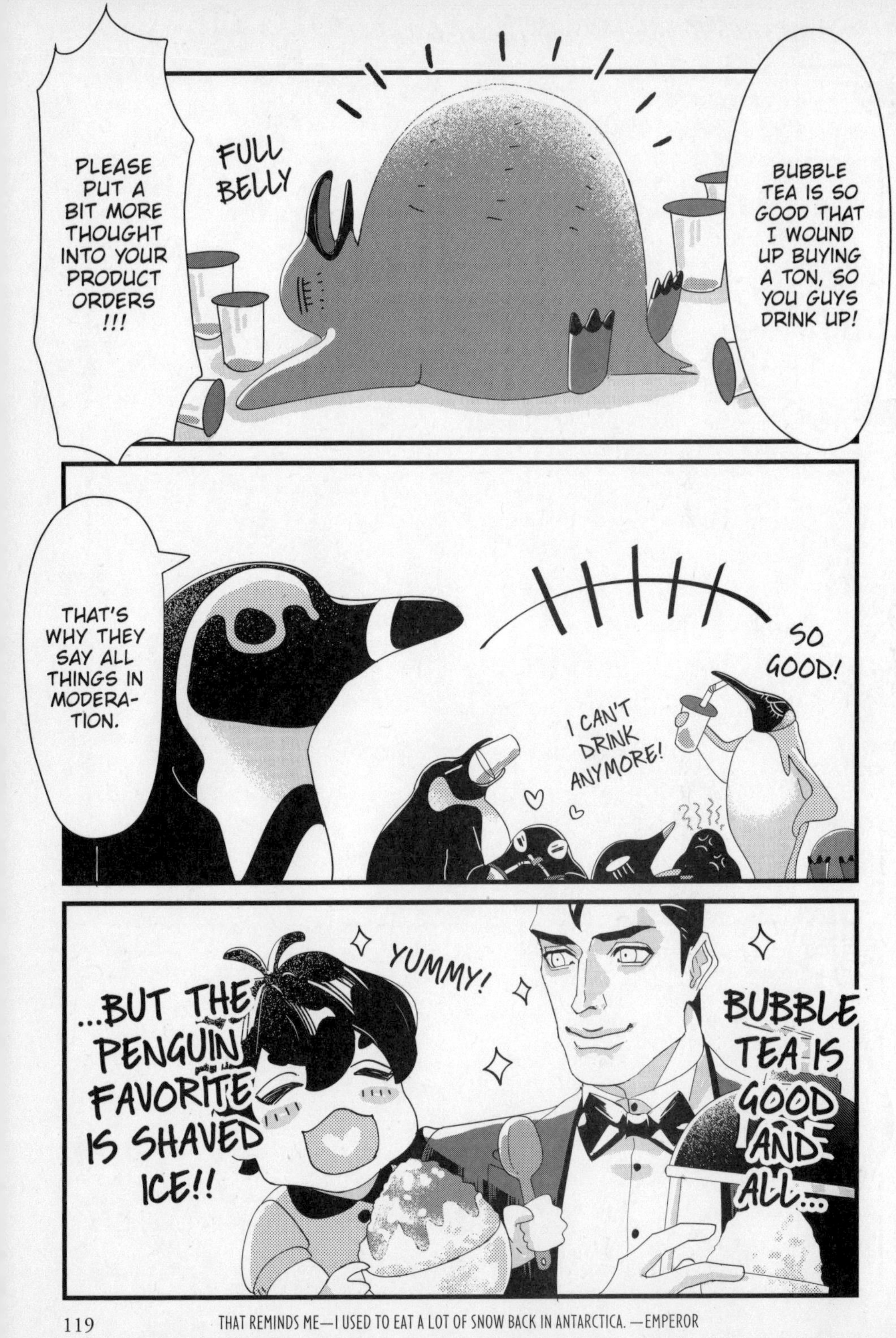
BUBBLE TEA IS SO GOOD THAT I WOUND UP BUYING A TON, SO YOU GUYS DRINK UP!
FULL BELLY
PLEASE PUT A BIT MORE THOUGHT INTO YOUR PRODUCT ORDERS!!!
SO GOOD!
I CAN'T DRINK ANYMORE!
THAT'S WHY THEY SAY ALL THINGS IN MODERATION.
BUBBLE TEA IS GOOD AND ALL...
YUMMY!
...BUT THE PENGUIN FAVORITE IS SHAVED ICE!!

THAT REMINDS ME—I USED TO EAT A LOT OF SNOW BACK IN ANTARCTICA. —EMPEROR

Penguin Gentlemen

Chapter 4
The Ways They Love

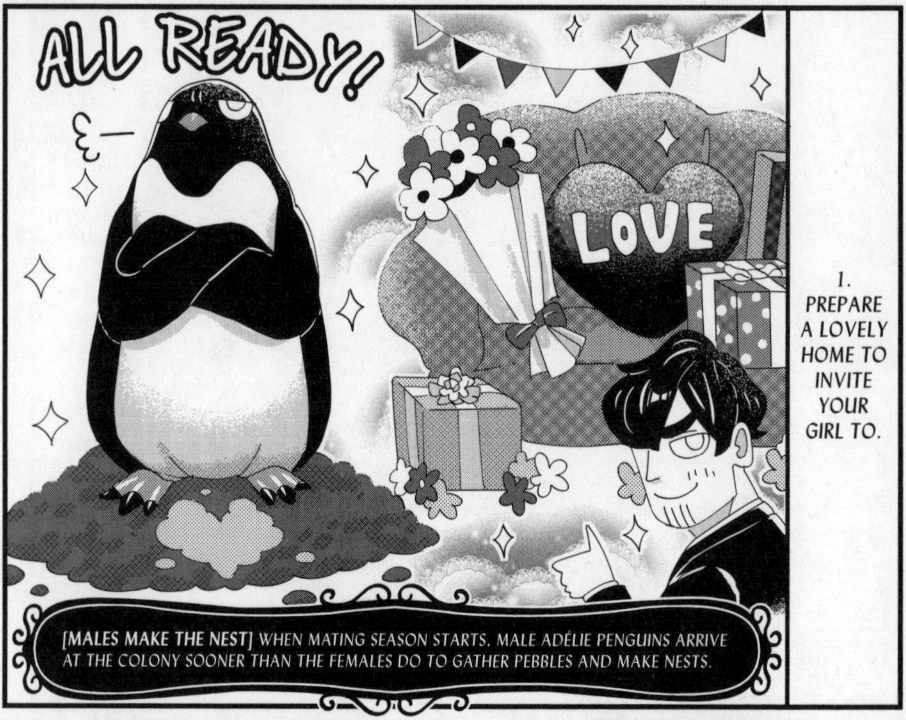
1. PREPARE A LOVELY HOME TO INVITE YOUR GIRL TO.
ALL READY!
LOVE
[MALES MAKE THE NEST] WHEN MATING SEASON STARTS, MALE ADÉLIE PENGUINS ARRIVE AT THE COLONY SOONER THAN THE FEMALES DO TO GATHER PEBBLES AND MAKE NESTS.

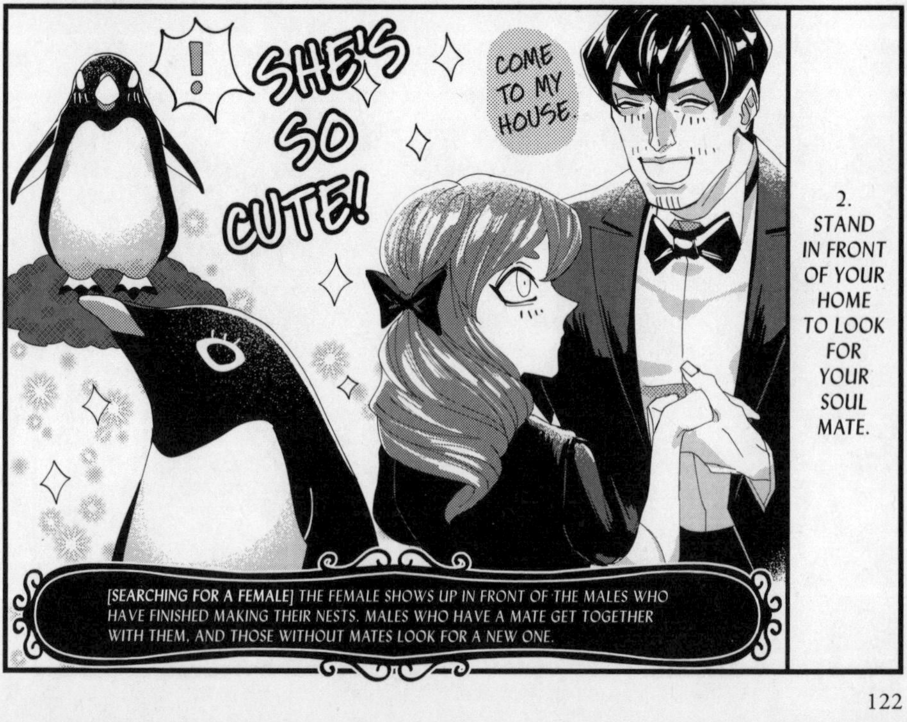
2. STAND IN FRONT OF YOUR HOME TO LOOK FOR YOUR SOUL MATE.
COME TO MY HOUSE.
SHE'S SO CUTE!
!
[SEARCHING FOR A FEMALE] THE FEMALE SHOWS UP IN FRONT OF THE MALES WHO HAVE FINISHED MAKING THEIR NESTS. MALES WHO HAVE A MATE GET TOGETHER WITH THEM, AND THOSE WITHOUT MATES LOOK FOR A NEW ONE.

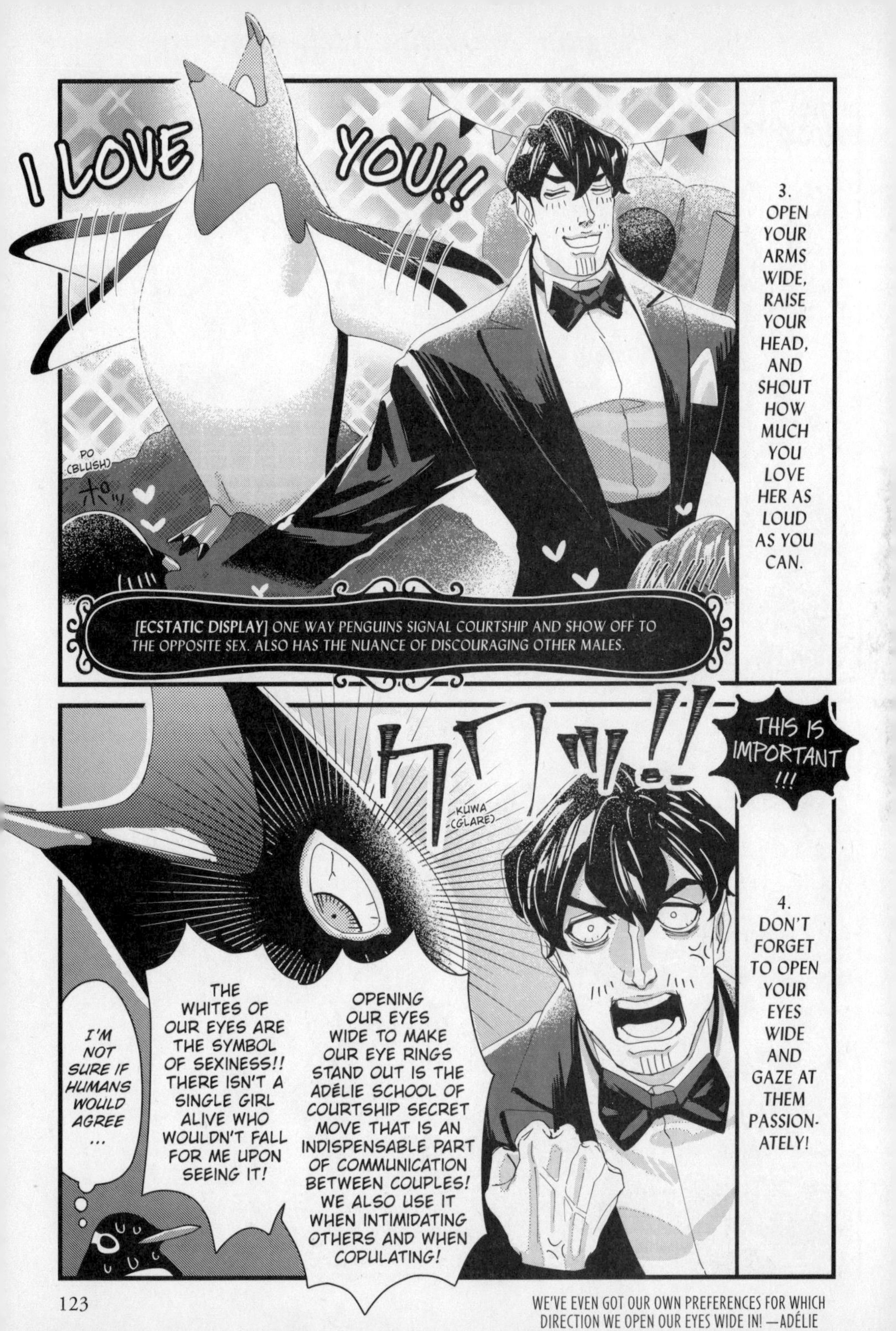
3. OPEN YOUR ARMS WIDE, RAISE YOUR HEAD, AND SHOUT HOW MUCH YOU LOVE HER AS LOUD AS YOU CAN.
I LOVE YOU!!
PO (BLUSH)
[ECSTATIC DISPLAY] ONE WAY PENGUINS SIGNAL COURTSHIP AND SHOW OFF TO THE OPPOSITE SEX. ALSO HAS THE NUANCE OF DISCOURAGING OTHER MALES.
THIS IS IMPORTANT!!!
KUWA (GLARE)
4. DON'T FORGET TO OPEN YOUR EYES WIDE AND GAZE AT THEM PASSION-ATELY!
OPENING OUR EYES WIDE TO MAKE OUR EYE RINGS STAND OUT IS THE ADÉLIE SCHOOL OF COURTSHIP SECRET MOVE THAT IS AN INDISPENSABLE PART OF COMMUNICATION BETWEEN COUPLES! WE ALSO USE IT WHEN INTIMIDATING OTHERS AND WHEN COPULATING!
THE WHITES OF OUR EYES ARE THE SYMBOL OF SEXINESS!! THERE ISN'T A SINGLE GIRL ALIVE WHO WOULDN'T FALL FOR ME UPON SEEING IT!
I'M NOT SURE IF HUMANS WOULD AGREE...

WE'VE EVEN GOT OUR OWN PREFERENCES FOR WHICH DIRECTION WE OPEN OUR EYES WIDE IN! —ADÉLIE

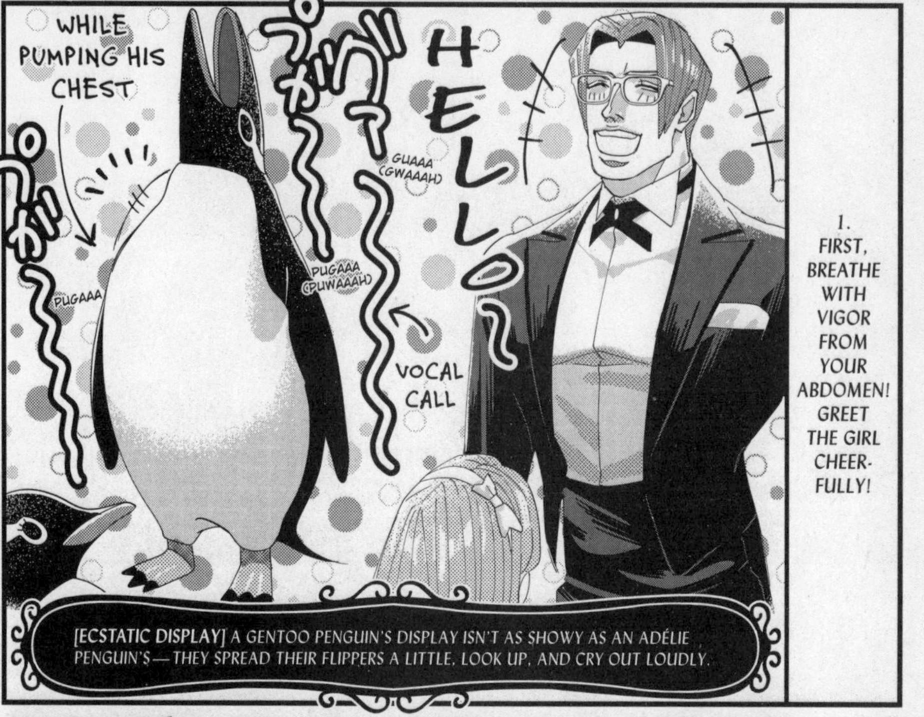
1. FIRST, BREATHE WITH VIGOR FROM YOUR ABDOMEN! GREET THE GIRL CHEERFULLY!
HELLO~
GUAAA (GWAAAH)
PUGAAA (PUWAAAH)
VOCAL CALL
WHILE PUMPING HIS CHEST
PUGAAA
[ECSTATIC DISPLAY] A GENTOO PENGUIN'S DISPLAY ISN'T AS SHOWY AS AN ADÉLIE PENGUIN'S—THEY SPREAD THEIR FLIPPERS A LITTLE, LOOK UP, AND CRY OUT LOUDLY.

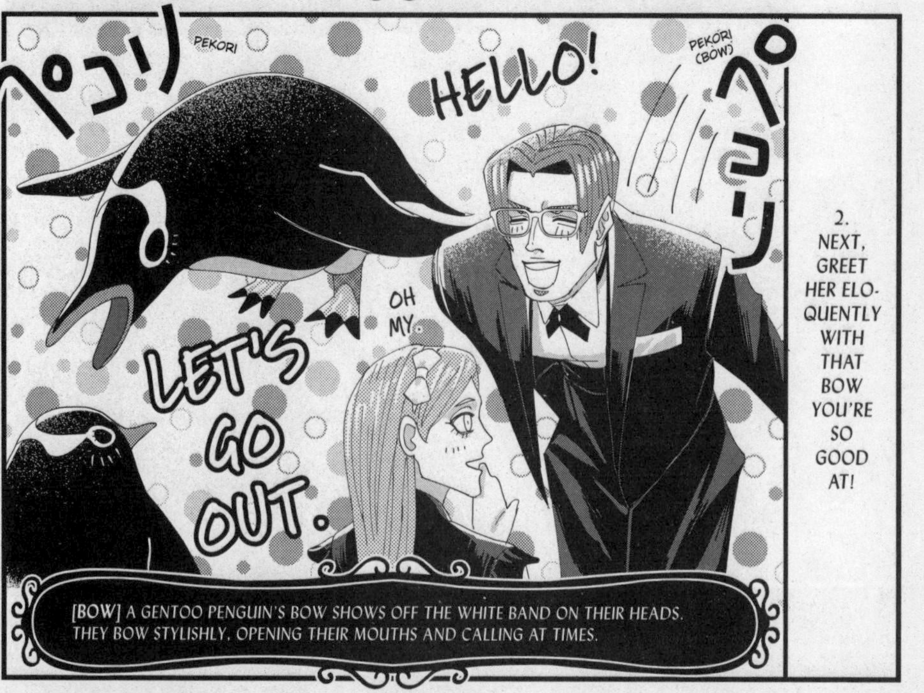
2. NEXT, GREET HER ELOQUENTLY WITH THAT BOW YOU'RE SO GOOD AT!
PEKORI (BOW)
HELLO!
OH MY
PEKORI
LET'S GO OUT.
[BOW] A GENTOO PENGUIN'S BOW SHOWS OFF THE WHITE BAND ON THEIR HEADS. THEY BOW STYLISHLY, OPENING THEIR MOUTHS AND CALLING AT TIMES.

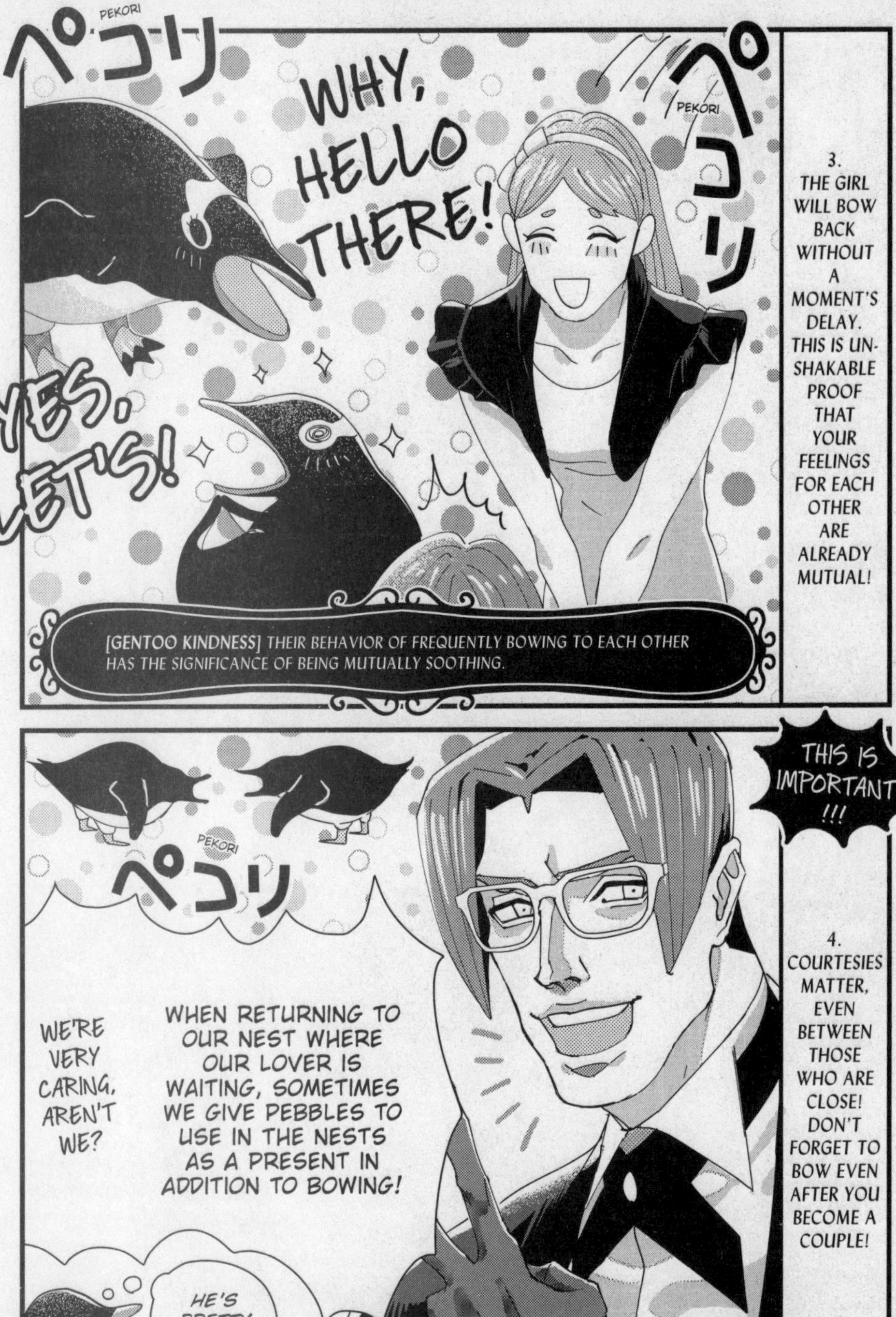
3.
THE GIRL WILL BOW BACK WITHOUT A MOMENT'S DELAY. THIS IS UNSHAKABLE PROOF THAT YOUR FEELINGS FOR EACH OTHER ARE ALREADY MUTUAL!
ペコリ PEKORI
WHY, HELLO THERE!
ペコリ PEKORI
YES, LET'S!
[GENTOO KINDNESS] THEIR BEHAVIOR OF FREQUENTLY BOWING TO EACH OTHER HAS THE SIGNIFICANCE OF BEING MUTUALLY SOOTHING.
THIS IS IMPORTANT!!!
4.
COURTESIES MATTER, EVEN BETWEEN THOSE WHO ARE CLOSE! DON'T FORGET TO BOW EVEN AFTER YOU BECOME A COUPLE!
ペコリ PEKORI
WHEN RETURNING TO OUR NEST WHERE OUR LOVER IS WAITING, SOMETIMES WE GIVE PEBBLES TO USE IN THE NESTS AS A PRESENT IN ADDITION TO BOWING!
WE'RE VERY CARING, AREN'T WE?
HE'S PRETTY SUAVE.

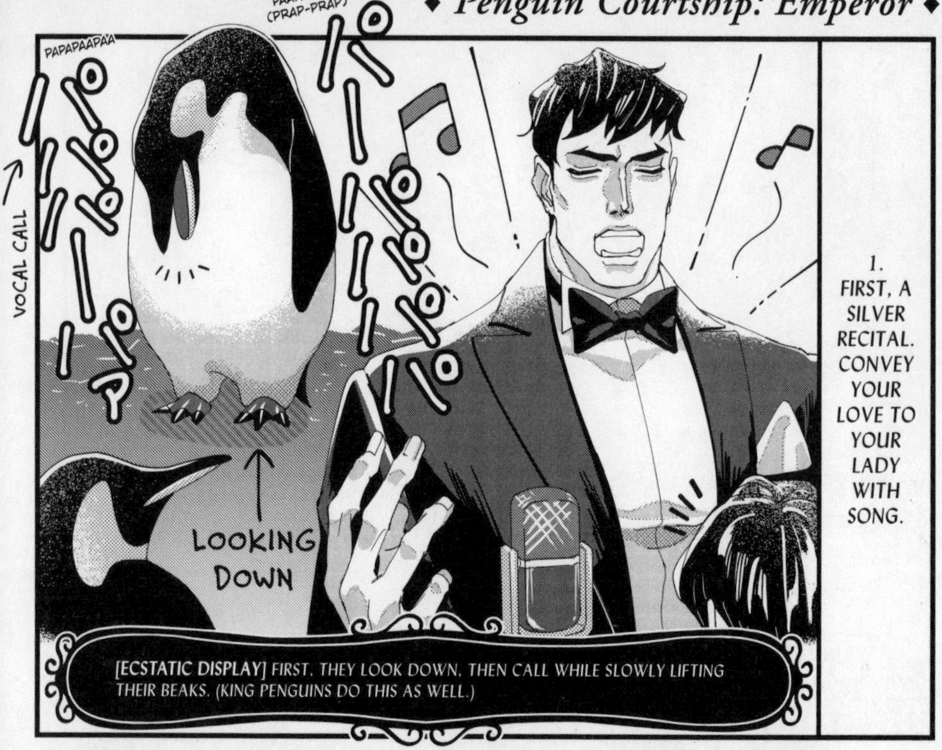
1. FIRST, A SILVER RECITAL. CONVEY YOUR LOVE TO YOUR LADY WITH SONG.
PAAPAPAPA (PRAP-PRAP)
PAPAPAAPAA
VOCAL CALL
LOOKING DOWN
[ECSTATIC DISPLAY] FIRST, THEY LOOK DOWN, THEN CALL WHILE SLOWLY LIFTING THEIR BEAKS. (KING PENGUINS DO THIS AS WELL.)

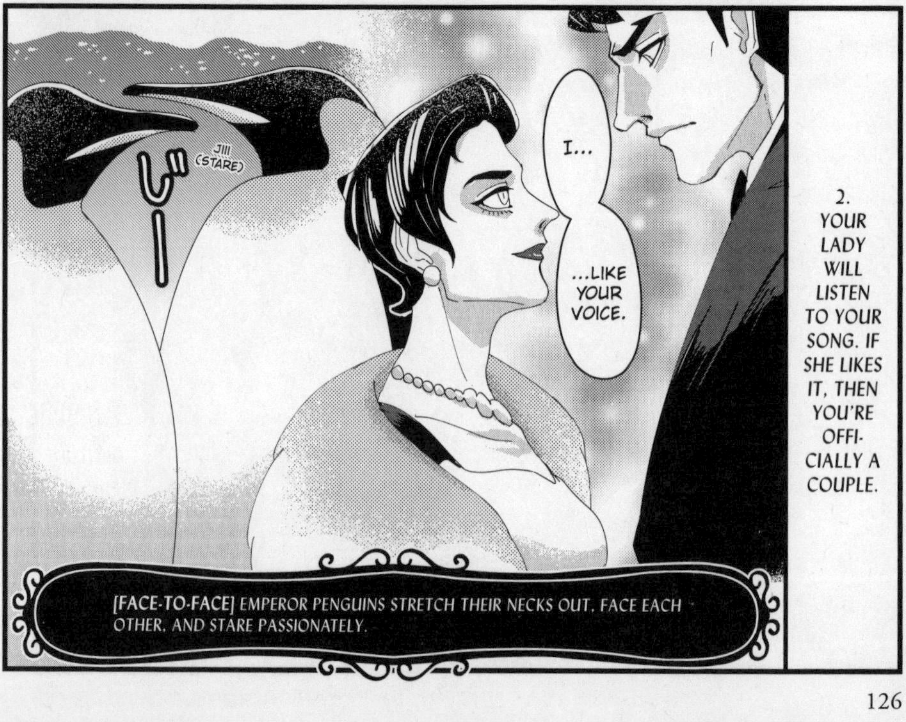
2. YOUR LADY WILL LISTEN TO YOUR SONG. IF SHE LIKES IT, THEN YOU'RE OFFI-CIALLY A COUPLE.
I...
...LIKE YOUR VOICE.
JIII (STARE)
[FACE-TO-FACE] EMPEROR PENGUINS STRETCH THEIR NECKS OUT, FACE EACH OTHER, AND STARE PASSIONATELY.

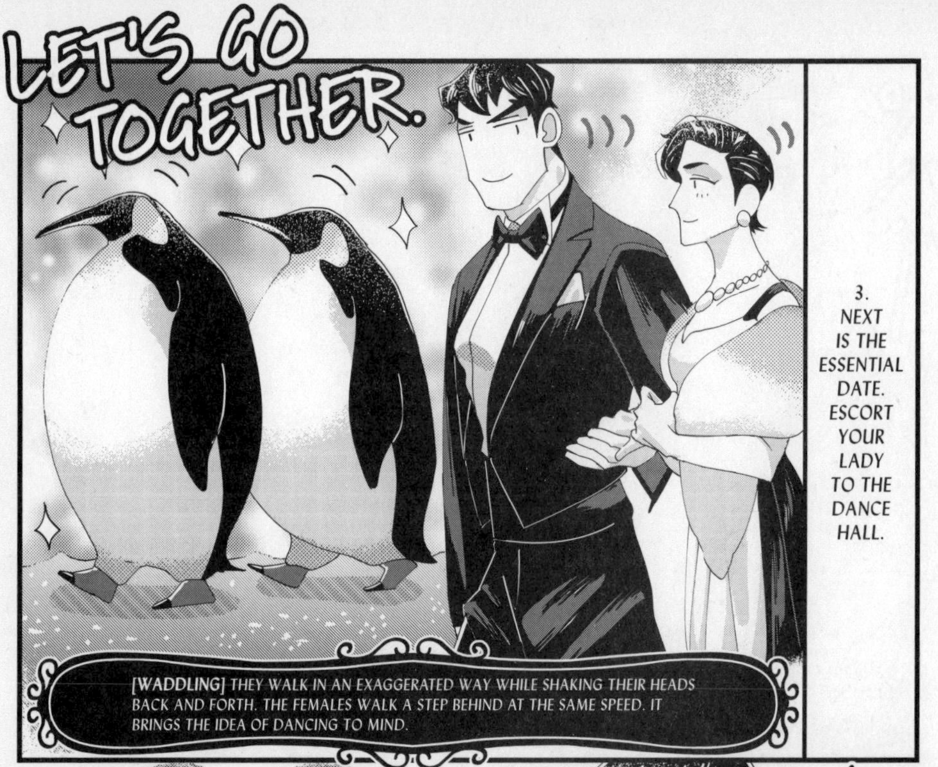
LET'S GO TOGETHER.
3. NEXT IS THE ESSENTIAL DATE. ESCORT YOUR LADY TO THE DANCE HALL.
[WADDLING] THEY WALK IN AN EXAGGERATED WAY WHILE SHAKING THEIR HEADS BACK AND FORTH. THE FEMALES WALK A STEP BEHIND AT THE SAME SPEED. IT BRINGS THE IDEA OF DANCING TO MIND.

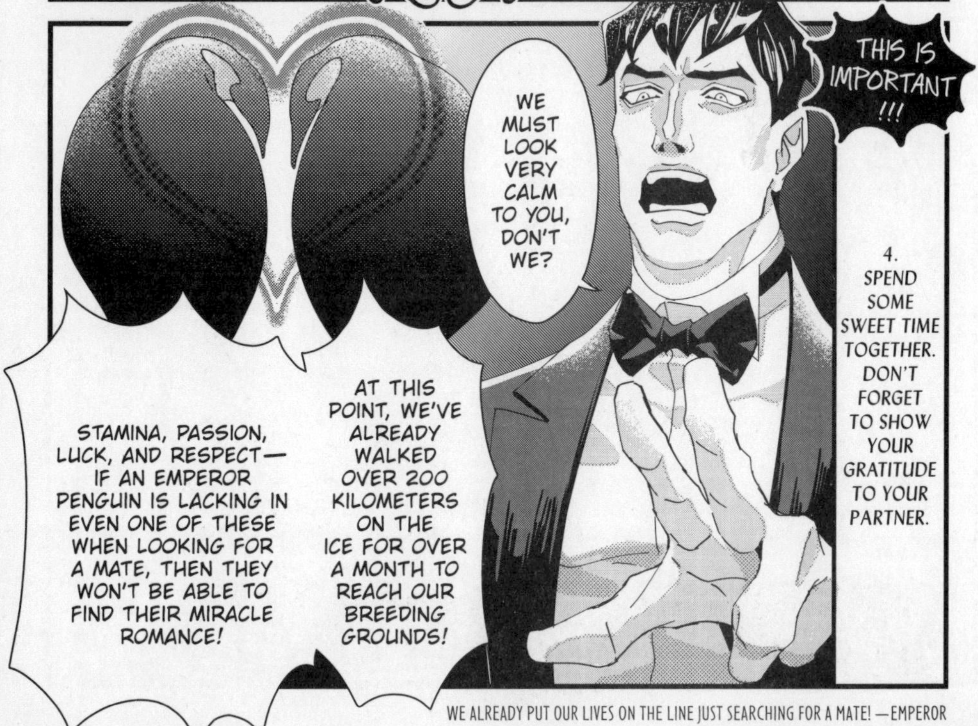
4. SPEND SOME SWEET TIME TOGETHER. DON'T FORGET TO SHOW YOUR GRATITUDE TO YOUR PARTNER.
THIS IS IMPORTANT!!!
WE MUST LOOK VERY CALM TO YOU, DON'T WE?
AT THIS POINT, WE'VE ALREADY WALKED OVER 200 KILOMETERS ON THE ICE FOR OVER A MONTH TO REACH OUR BREEDING GROUNDS!
STAMINA, PASSION, LUCK, AND RESPECT—IF AN EMPEROR PENGUIN IS LACKING IN EVEN ONE OF THESE WHEN LOOKING FOR A MATE, THEN THEY WON'T BE ABLE TO FIND THEIR MIRACLE ROMANCE!

WE ALREADY PUT OUR LIVES ON THE LINE JUST SEARCHING FOR A MATE! —EMPEROR

♦ *Penguin Courtship: King* ♦

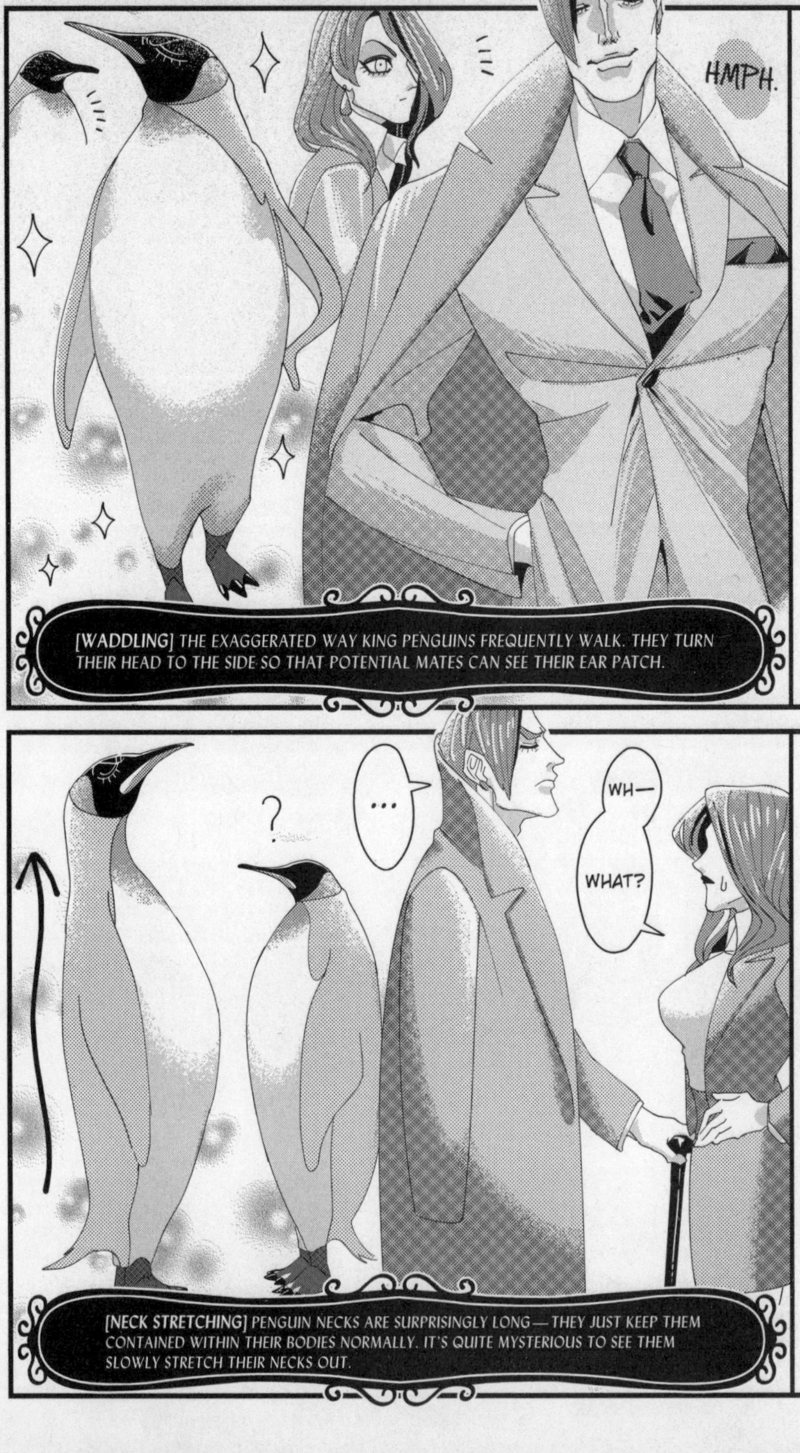
1. YOU NEVER KNOW WHEN YOU'LL MEET A GREAT WOMAN, SO MAKE SURE TO ALWAYS WEAR A DIGNIFIED AIR AND WALK WITH YOUR CHEST PUFFED OUT!
HMPH.
[WADDLING] THE EXAGGERATED WAY KING PENGUINS FREQUENTLY WALK. THEY TURN THEIR HEAD TO THE SIDE SO THAT POTENTIAL MATES CAN SEE THEIR EAR PATCH.
2. WITH YOUR CHEST PUFFED OUT, LOOK DOWN AT HER WITH A SEXY GAZE! SHE'LL BE FROZEN TO THE SPOT!
WH— WHAT?
...
?
[NECK STRETCHING] PENGUIN NECKS ARE SURPRISINGLY LONG—THEY JUST KEEP THEM CONTAINED WITHIN THEIR BODIES NORMALLY. IT'S QUITE MYSTERIOUS TO SEE THEM SLOWLY STRETCH THEIR NECKS OUT.

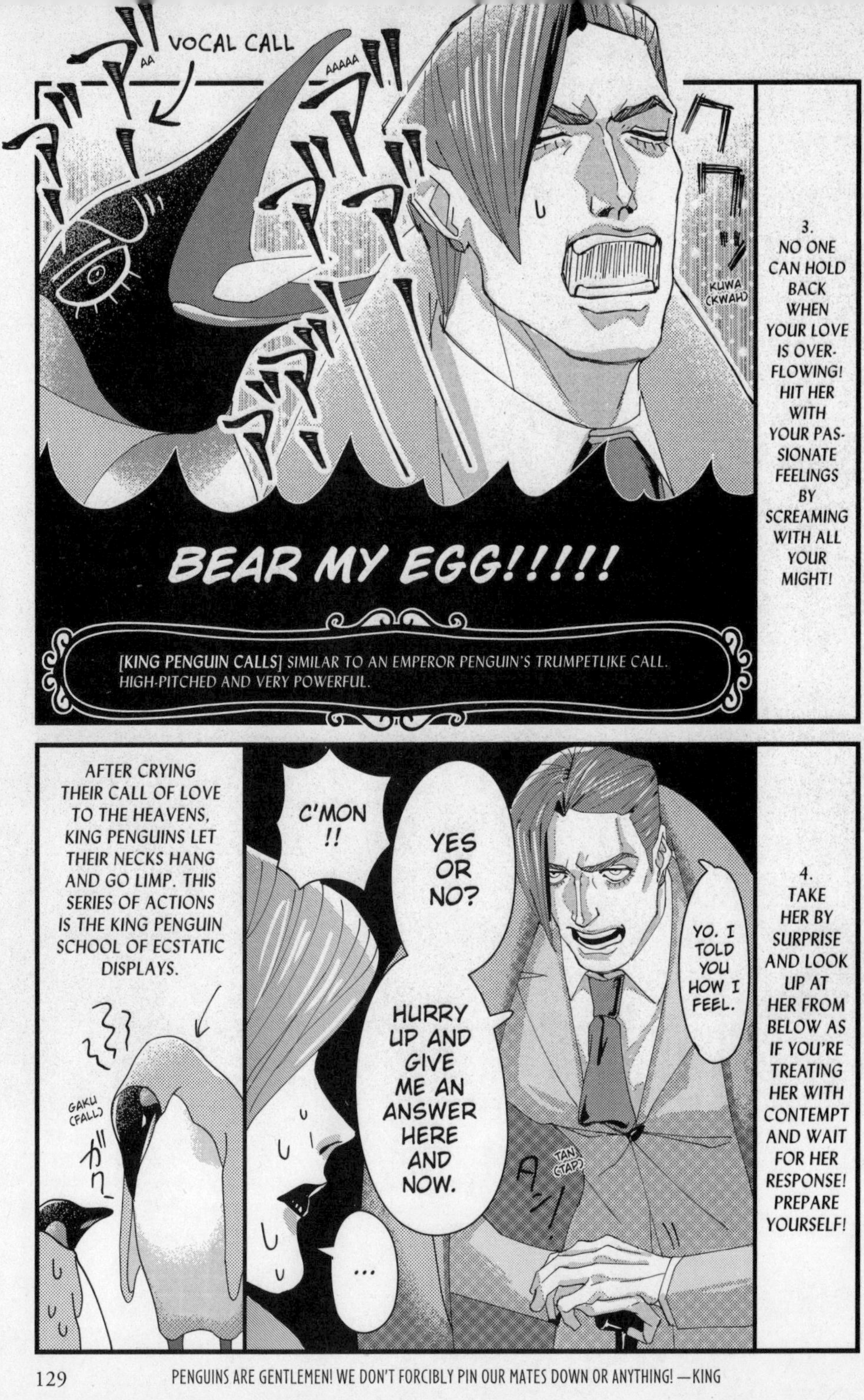
3. NO ONE CAN HOLD BACK WHEN YOUR LOVE IS OVER-FLOWING! HIT HER WITH YOUR PAS-SIONATE FEELINGS BY SCREAMING WITH ALL YOUR MIGHT!
VOCAL CALL
AA
AAAAA
KUWA (KWAH)
BEAR MY EGG!!!!!
[KING PENGUIN CALLS] SIMILAR TO AN EMPEROR PENGUIN'S TRUMPETLIKE CALL. HIGH-PITCHED AND VERY POWERFUL.
4. TAKE HER BY SURPRISE AND LOOK UP AT HER FROM BELOW AS IF YOU'RE TREATING HER WITH CONTEMPT AND WAIT FOR HER RESPONSE! PREPARE YOURSELF!
YO. I TOLD YOU HOW I FEEL.
YES OR NO?
HURRY UP AND GIVE ME AN ANSWER HERE AND NOW.
C'MON !!
TAN (TAP)
...
AFTER CRYING THEIR CALL OF LOVE TO THE HEAVENS, KING PENGUINS LET THEIR NECKS HANG AND GO LIMP. THIS SERIES OF ACTIONS IS THE KING PENGUIN SCHOOL OF ECSTATIC DISPLAYS.
GAKU (FALL)

♦ Penguin Courtship (Strong Habits): Emperor ♦

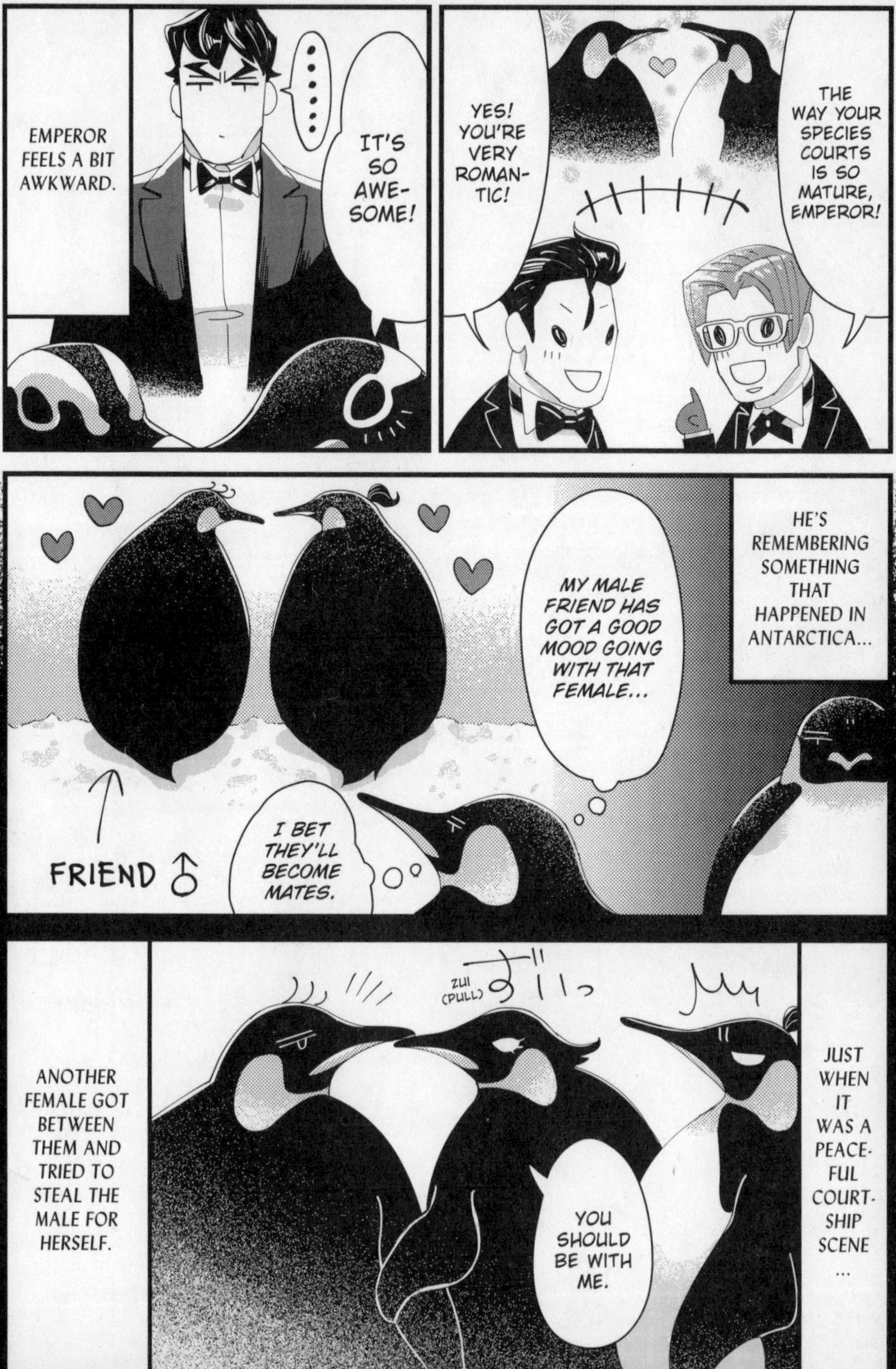

THE WAY YOUR SPECIES COURTS IS SO MATURE, EMPEROR!
YES! YOU'RE VERY ROMAN-TIC!
IT'S SO AWE-SOME!
......
EMPEROR FEELS A BIT AWKWARD.
HE'S REMEMBERING SOMETHING THAT HAPPENED IN ANTARCTICA...
MY MALE FRIEND HAS GOT A GOOD MOOD GOING WITH THAT FEMALE...
I BET THEY'LL BECOME MATES.
FRIEND ♂
JUST WHEN IT WAS A PEACE-FUL COURT-SHIP SCENE...
ZUI (PULL)
YOU SHOULD BE WITH ME.
ANOTHER FEMALE GOT BETWEEN THEM AND TRIED TO STEAL THE MALE FOR HERSELF.

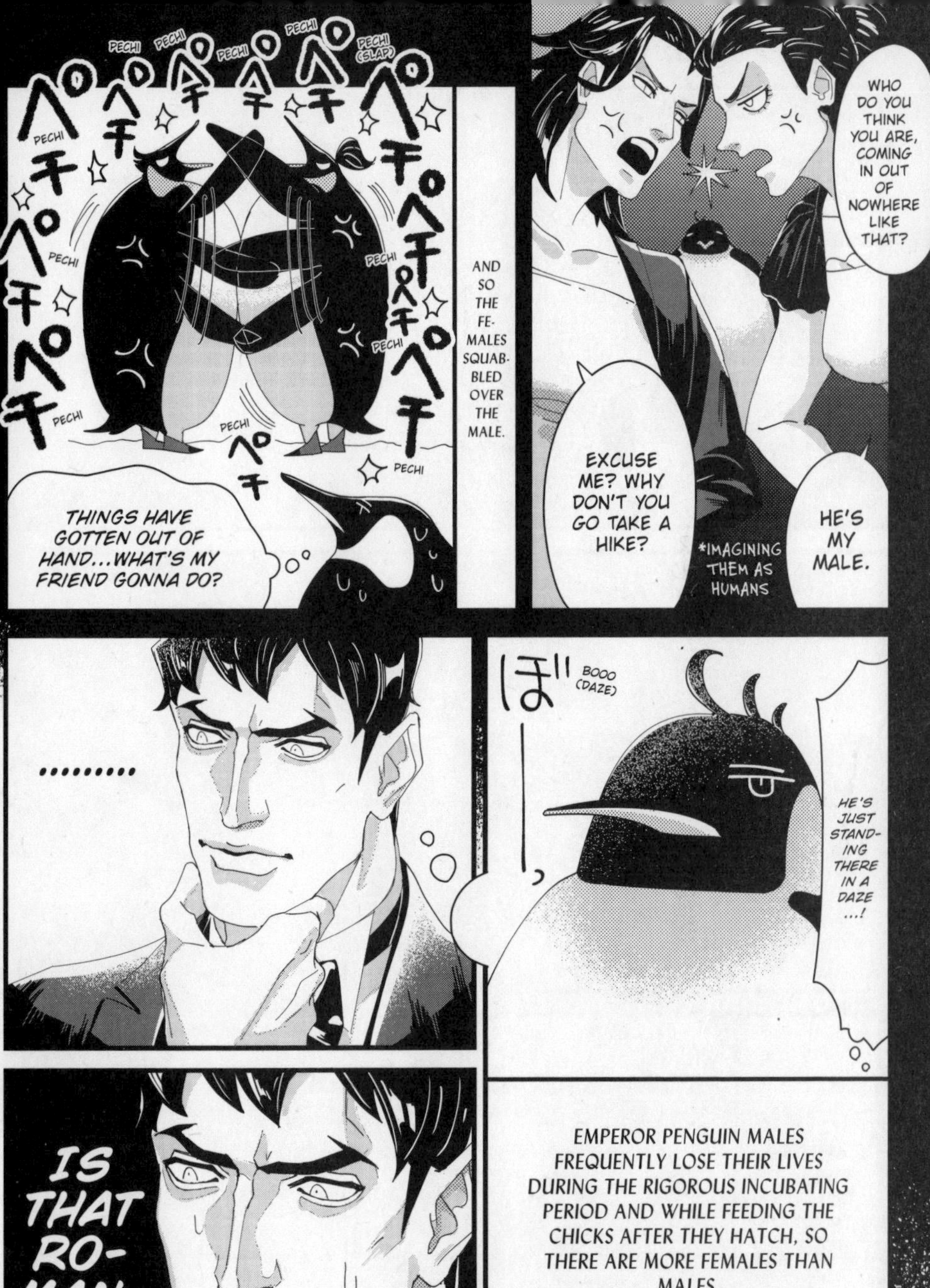
WHO DO YOU THINK YOU ARE, COMING IN OUT OF NOWHERE LIKE THAT?
HE'S MY MALE.
EXCUSE ME? WHY DON'T YOU GO TAKE A HIKE?
*IMAGINING THEM AS HUMANS
AND SO THE FEMALES SQUABBLED OVER THE MALE.
ペチペチペチペチペチペチ
PECHI PECHI PECHI PECHI PECHI (SLAP)
PECHI PECHI PECHI PECHI PECHI PECHI
THINGS HAVE GOTTEN OUT OF HAND...WHAT'S MY FRIEND GONNA DO?
ぼー
BOOO (DAZE)
HE'S JUST STANDING THERE IN A DAZE...!
....
EMPEROR PENGUIN MALES FREQUENTLY LOSE THEIR LIVES DURING THE RIGOROUS INCUBATING PERIOD AND WHILE FEEDING THE CHICKS AFTER THEY HATCH, SO THERE ARE MORE FEMALES THAN MALES.
AS A RESULT, FEMALES ARE FREQUENTLY SEEN FIGHTING OVER MALES AT THEIR BREEDING GROUNDS.
IS THAT ROMANTIC?

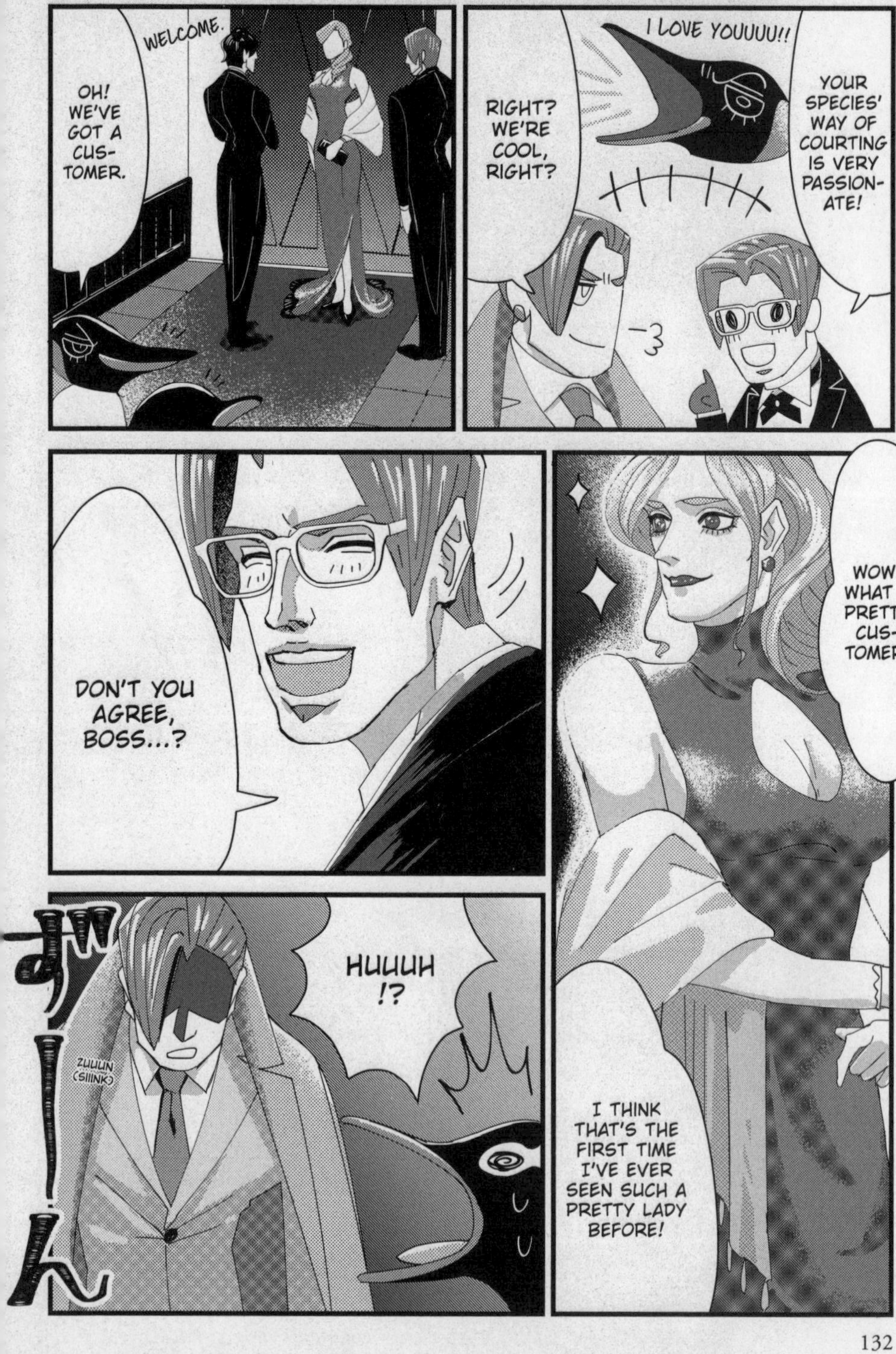
YOUR SPECIES' WAY OF COURTING IS VERY PASSIONATE!
I LOVE YOUUUU!!
RIGHT? WE'RE COOL, RIGHT?
WELCOME.
OH! WE'VE GOT A CUS-TOMER.
WOW! WHAT A PRETTY CUS-TOMER!
I THINK THAT'S THE FIRST TIME I'VE EVER SEEN SUCH A PRETTY LADY BEFORE!
DON'T YOU AGREE, BOSS...?
HUUUH !?
ZUUUN (SIIINK)

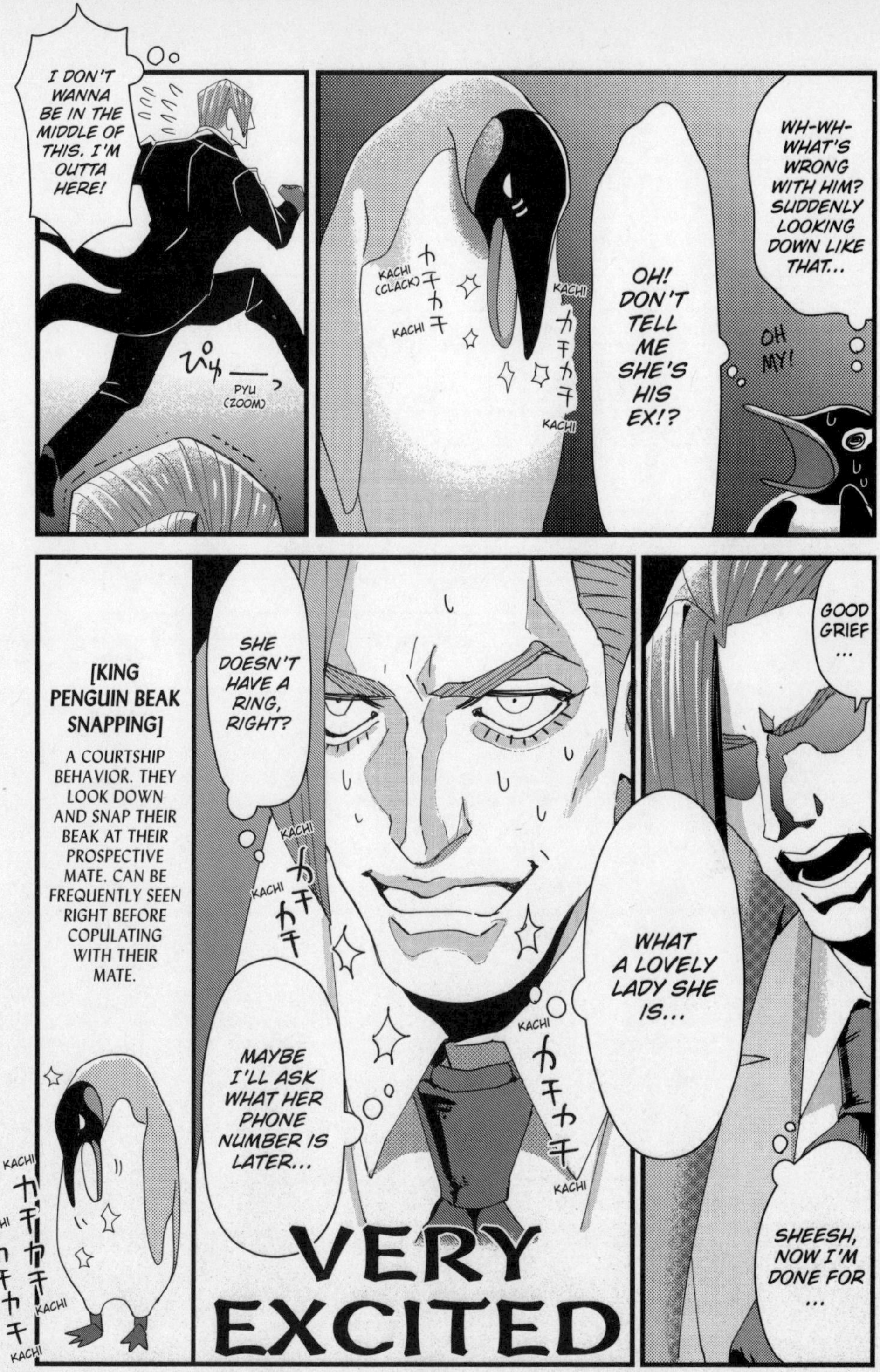

WH-WH-WHAT'S WRONG WITH HIM? SUDDENLY LOOKING DOWN LIKE THAT...
OH MY!
OH! DON'T TELL ME SHE'S HIS EX!?
カチカチ KACHI (CLACK) KACHI
カチカチ KACHI KACHI
I DON'T WANNA BE IN THE MIDDLE OF THIS. I'M OUTTA HERE!
ぴゅ— PYU (ZOOM)
GOOD GRIEF...
SHEESH, NOW I'M DONE FOR...
WHAT A LOVELY LADY SHE IS...
SHE DOESN'T HAVE A RING, RIGHT?
カチカチ KACHI KACHI
カチカチ KACHI KACHI
MAYBE I'LL ASK WHAT HER PHONE NUMBER IS LATER...
VERY EXCITED
[KING PENGUIN BEAK SNAPPING]
A COURTSHIP BEHAVIOR. THEY LOOK DOWN AND SNAP THEIR BEAK AT THEIR PROSPECTIVE MATE. CAN BE FREQUENTLY SEEN RIGHT BEFORE COPULATING WITH THEIR MATE.
カチカチ KACHI KACHI
カチカチ KACHI KACHI

I'M NOT ACTUALLY GOING TO ASK HER! I HAVE A RULE ABOUT NOT HITTING ON CUSTOMERS! —KING

◆ *Translation Notes* ◆

GENERAL
This book uses metric measurements for height and weight, as well as Celsius for temperatures. Approximate conversions to imperial units and Fahrenheit temperatures have been provided below.

1 kilogram (kg)	2.2 pounds (lb)
1 centimeter (cm)	0.39 inches (in)
1 meter (m) or 100 centimeters (cm)	3 feet (ft) 3.37 inches (in)
1 kilometer (km)	0.62 miles (mi)
-75 degrees Celsius (°C)	-103 degrees Fahrenheit (°F)
-50 degrees Celsius (°C)	-58 degrees Fahrenheit (°F)
-25 degrees Celsius (°C)	-13 degrees Fahrenheit (°F)
0 degrees Celsius (°C)	32 degrees Fahrenheit (°F)
25 degrees Celsius (°C)	77 degrees Fahrenheit (°F)
50 degrees Celsius (°C)	122 degrees Fahrenheit (°F)
100 degrees Celsius (°C)	212 degrees Fahrenheit (°F)

PAGE 41
IC Card is a reference to the Suica card, a rechargeable contactless smart card in Japan that people use to pay for train fare, among other things.

PAGE 47
The **wall-slam** (*kabedon*) is a popular romance trope in manga in which someone puts their hand on a wall to corner someone else. Its Japanese name is a combination of the word for wall (*kabe*) and the sound of something slamming against a surface (*don*).

PAGE 52
Convenience stores frequently have in-store promotions in which you can draw a ticket out of a box based on how much yen you spend. These **lottery draw** tickets include a range of prizes, such as free chips or drinks.

PAGE 99
The **mixed sticky rice** is *okowa*, which is a glutinous rice prepared with red adzuki beans. It is also known as *sekihan*.

Chapter 5
Chicks and Raising Children

◆ *Carrying Their Chicks* ◆

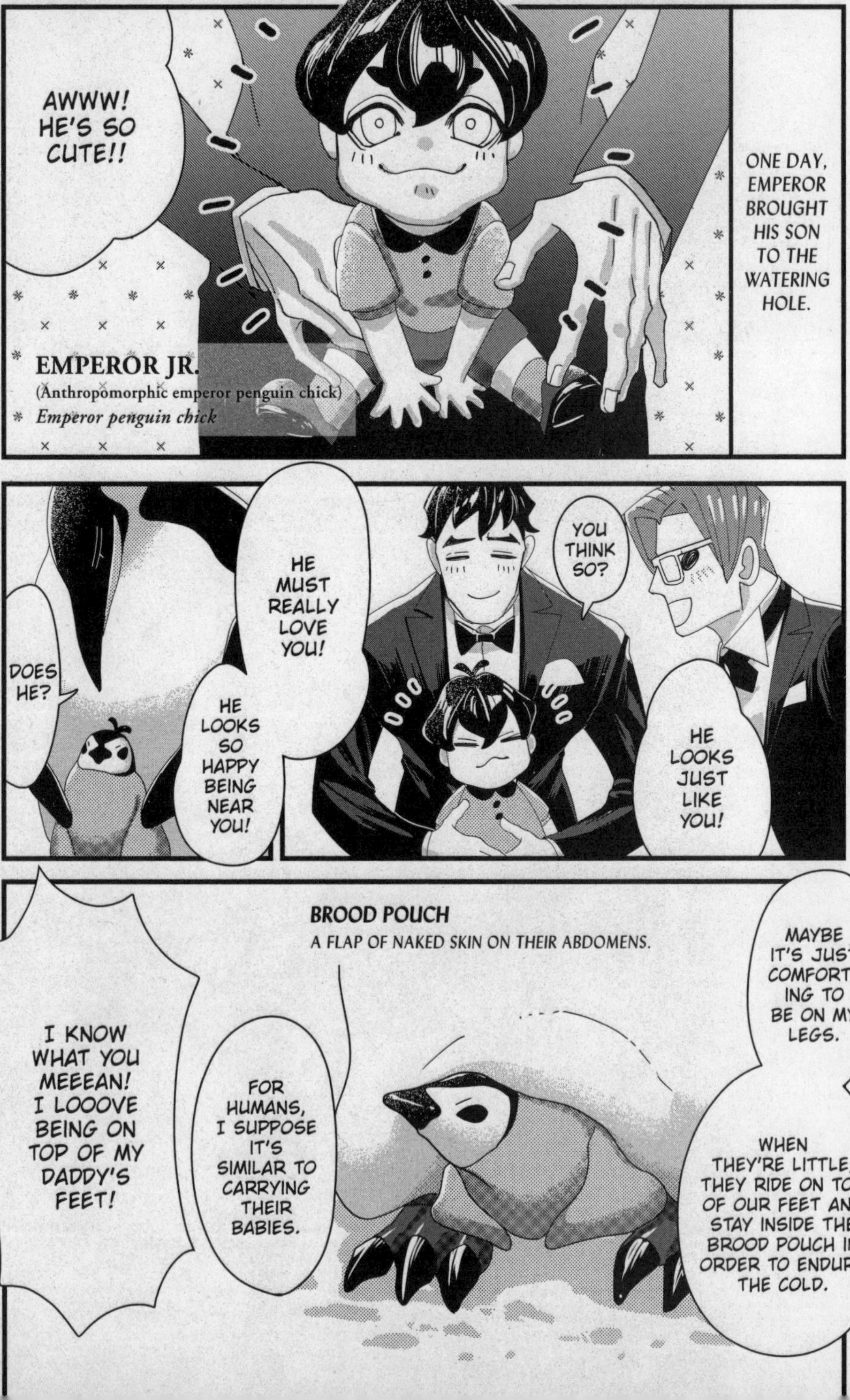
ONE DAY, EMPEROR BROUGHT HIS SON TO THE WATERING HOLE.
AWWW! HE'S SO CUTE!!
EMPEROR JR.
(Anthropomorphic emperor penguin chick)
Emperor penguin chick
YOU THINK SO?
HE MUST REALLY LOVE YOU!
HE LOOKS JUST LIKE YOU!
HE LOOKS SO HAPPY BEING NEAR YOU!
DOES HE?
MAYBE IT'S JUST COMFORTING TO BE ON MY LEGS.
BROOD POUCH
A FLAP OF NAKED SKIN ON THEIR ABDOMENS.
WHEN THEY'RE LITTLE, THEY RIDE ON TOP OF OUR FEET AND STAY INSIDE THE BROOD POUCH IN ORDER TO ENDURE THE COLD.
FOR HUMANS, I SUPPOSE IT'S SIMILAR TO CARRYING THEIR BABIES.
I KNOW WHAT YOU MEEEAN! I LOOOVE BEING ON TOP OF MY DADDY'S FEET!

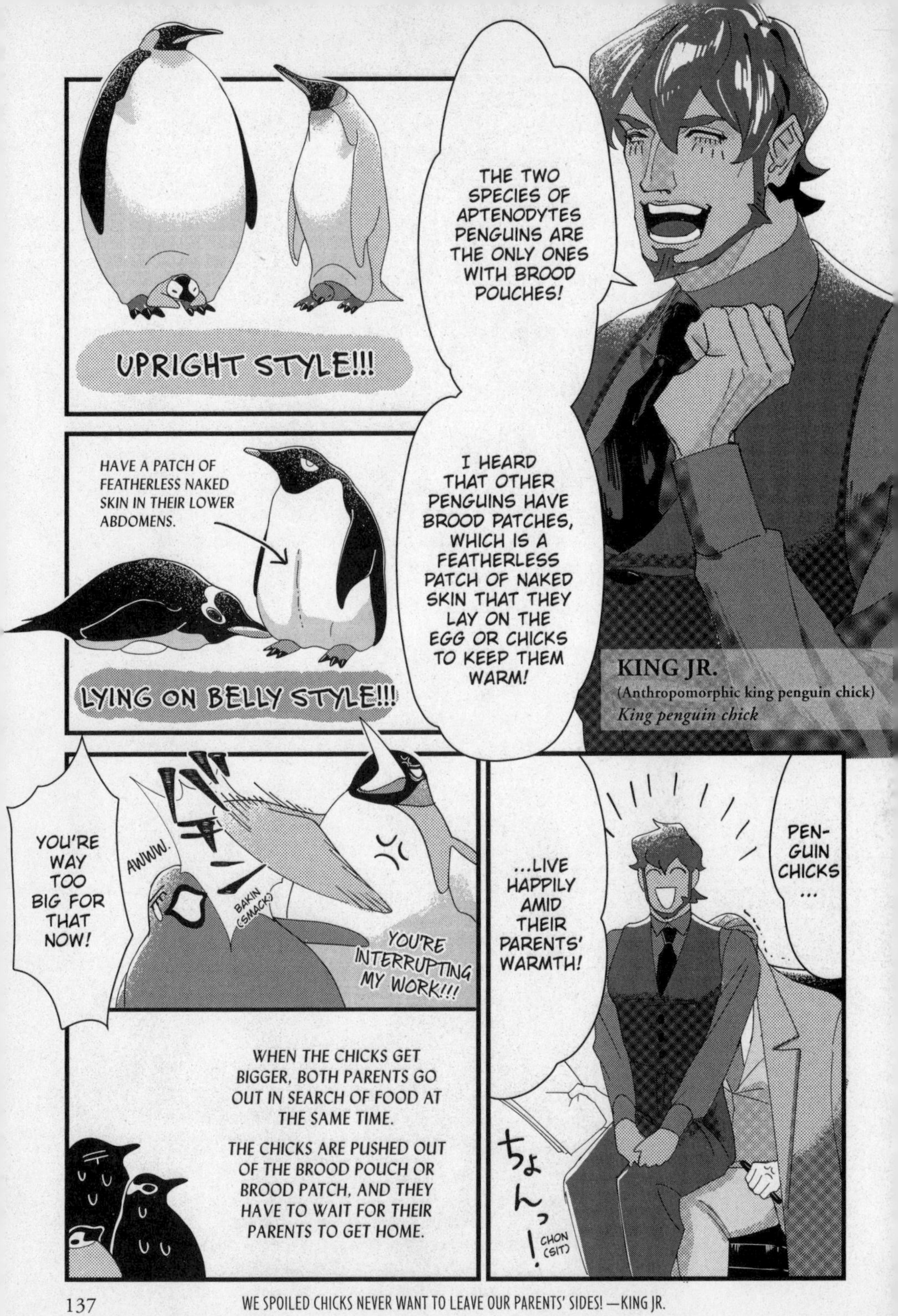
THE TWO SPECIES OF APTENODYTES PENGUINS ARE THE ONLY ONES WITH BROOD POUCHES!
I HEARD THAT OTHER PENGUINS HAVE BROOD PATCHES, WHICH IS A FEATHERLESS PATCH OF NAKED SKIN THAT THEY LAY ON THE EGG OR CHICKS TO KEEP THEM WARM!
KING JR.
(Anthropomorphic king penguin chick)
King penguin chick
UPRIGHT STYLE!!!
HAVE A PATCH OF FEATHERLESS NAKED SKIN IN THEIR LOWER ABDOMENS.
LYING ON BELLY STYLE!!!
PEN-GUIN CHICKS ...
...LIVE HAPPILY AMID THEIR PARENTS' WARMTH!
ちょんっ!
CHON (SIT)
AWWW.
BAKIN (SMACK)
YOU'RE WAY TOO BIG FOR THAT NOW!
YOU'RE INTERRUPTING MY WORK!!!
WHEN THE CHICKS GET BIGGER, BOTH PARENTS GO OUT IN SEARCH OF FOOD AT THE SAME TIME.
THE CHICKS ARE PUSHED OUT OF THE BROOD POUCH OR BROOD PATCH, AND THEY HAVE TO WAIT FOR THEIR PARENTS TO GET HOME.

WE SPOILED CHICKS NEVER WANT TO LEAVE OUR PARENTS' SIDES! —KING JR.

♦ A Chick's Growth ♦

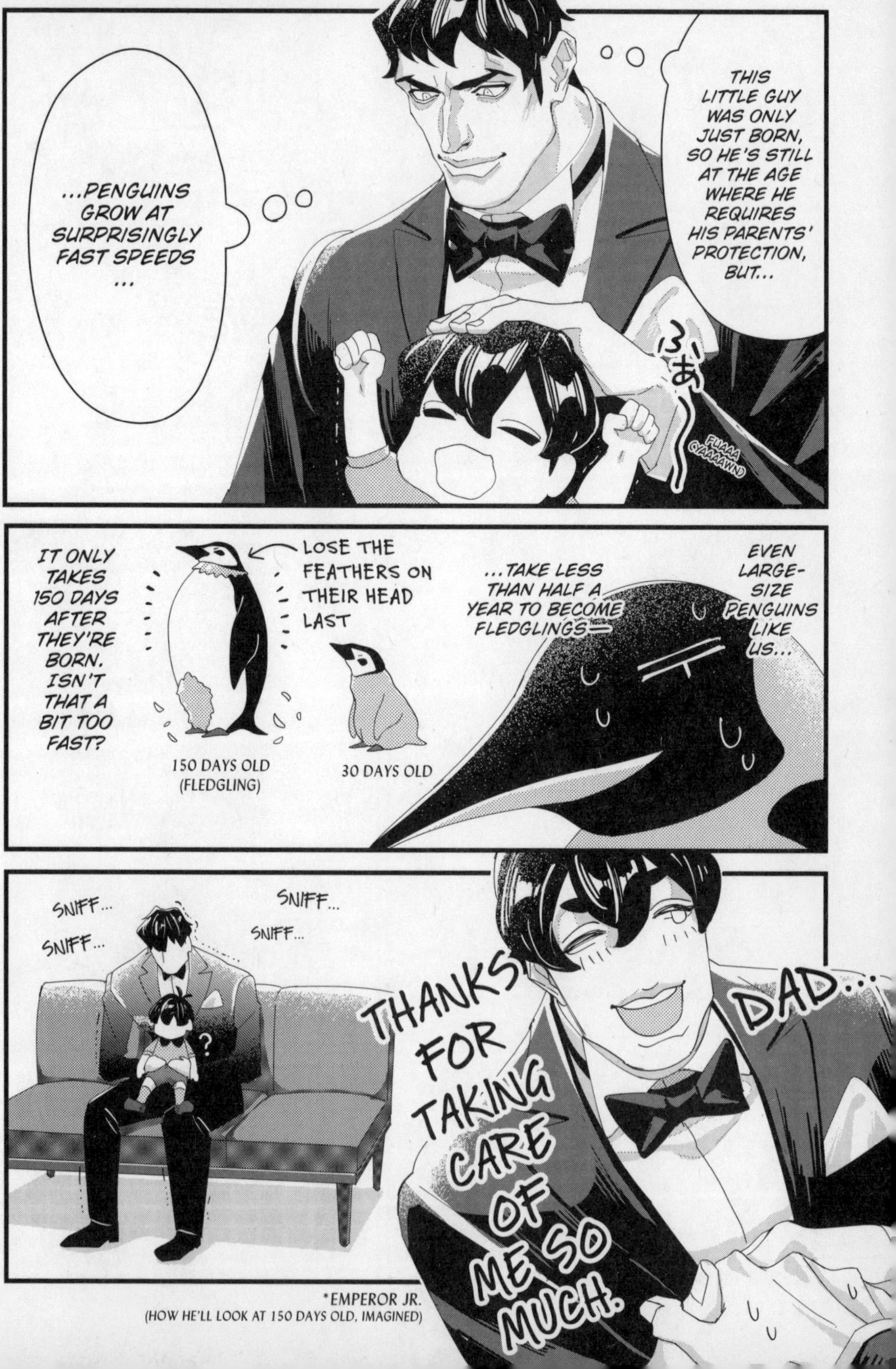
THIS LITTLE GUY WAS ONLY JUST BORN, SO HE'S STILL AT THE AGE WHERE HE REQUIRES HIS PARENTS' PROTECTION, BUT...
...PENGUINS GROW AT SURPRISINGLY FAST SPEEDS ...
ふぁ〜
FLIAAA GYAAAAWN
EVEN LARGE-SIZE PENGUINS LIKE US...
...TAKE LESS THAN HALF A YEAR TO BECOME FLEDGLINGS—
LOSE THE FEATHERS ON THEIR HEAD LAST
IT ONLY TAKES 150 DAYS AFTER THEY'RE BORN. ISN'T THAT A BIT TOO FAST?
30 DAYS OLD
150 DAYS OLD (FLEDGLING)
DAD...
THANKS FOR TAKING CARE OF ME SO MUCH.
SNIFF...
SNIFF...
SNIFF...
SNIFF...
?

*EMPEROR JR.
(HOW HE'LL LOOK AT 150 DAYS OLD, IMAGINED)

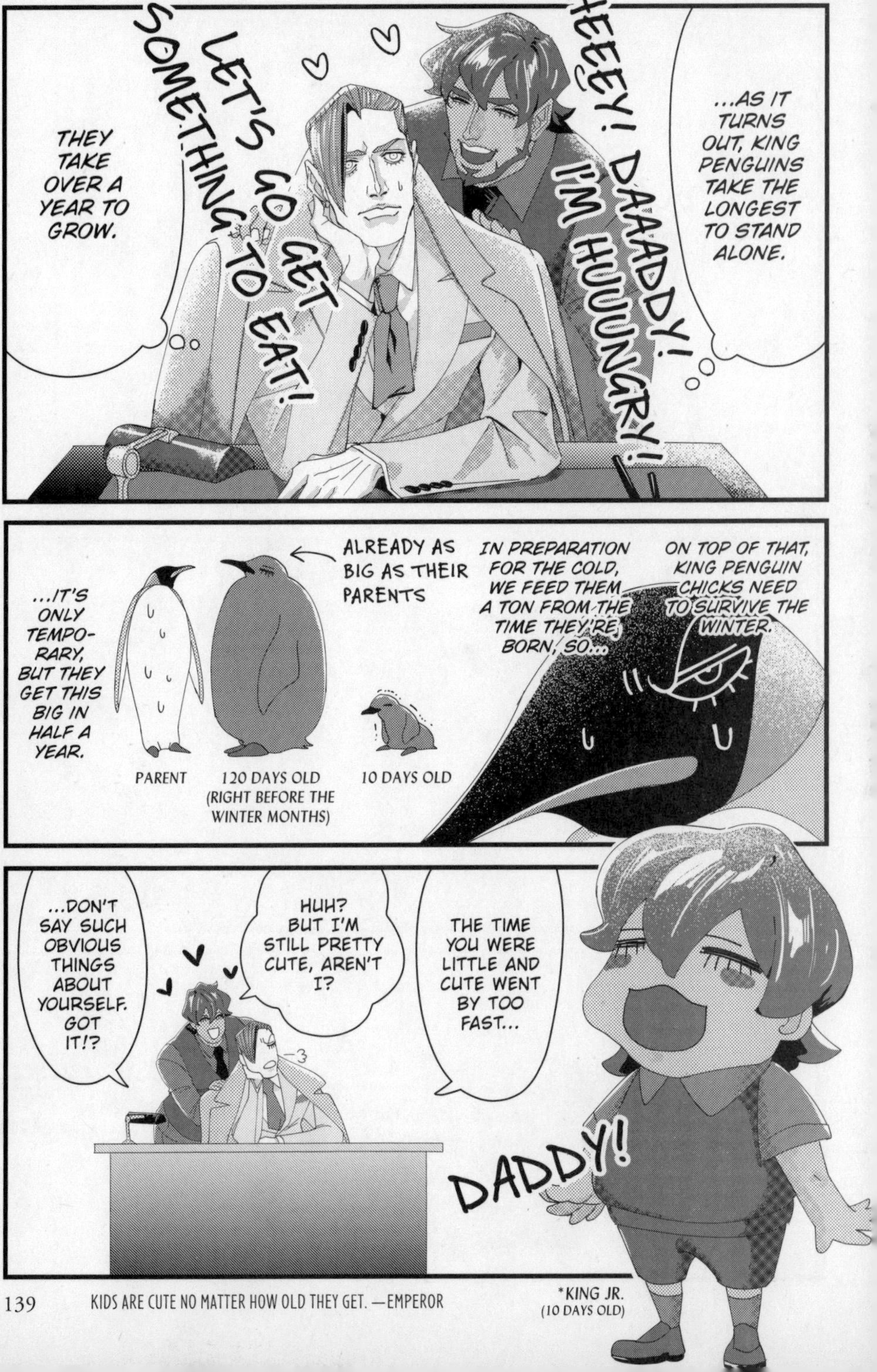
...AS IT TURNS OUT, KING PENGUINS TAKE THE LONGEST TO STAND ALONE.
HEEEY! DAAADDY! I'M HUUUNGRY!
LET'S GO GET SOMETHING TO EAT!
THEY TAKE OVER A YEAR TO GROW.
ON TOP OF THAT, KING PENGUIN CHICKS NEED TO SURVIVE THE WINTER.
IN PREPARATION FOR THE COLD, WE FEED THEM A TON FROM THE TIME THEY'RE BORN, SO...
ALREADY AS BIG AS THEIR PARENTS
...IT'S ONLY TEMPORARY, BUT THEY GET THIS BIG IN HALF A YEAR.
PARENT
120 DAYS OLD (RIGHT BEFORE THE WINTER MONTHS)
10 DAYS OLD
DADDY!
THE TIME YOU WERE LITTLE AND CUTE WENT BY TOO FAST...
HUH? BUT I'M STILL PRETTY CUTE, AREN'T I?
...DON'T SAY SUCH OBVIOUS THINGS ABOUT YOURSELF. GOT IT!?
*KING JR. (10 DAYS OLD)

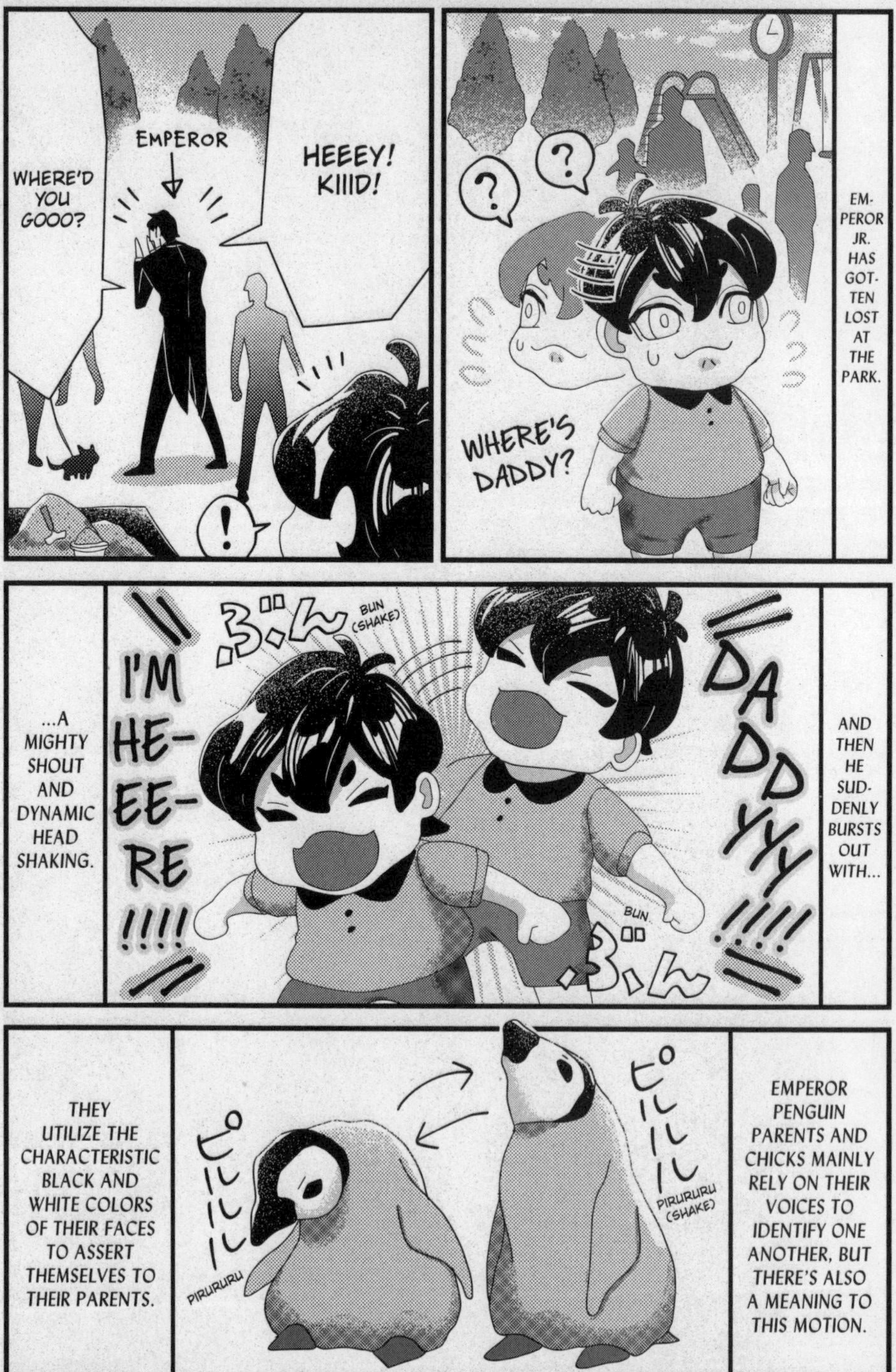
EMPEROR JR. HAS GOTTEN LOST AT THE PARK.
WHERE'S DADDY?
HEEEY! KIIID!
EMPEROR
WHERE'D YOU GOOO?
AND THEN HE SUDDENLY BURSTS OUT WITH...
DADDYYY!!!!
ぶん
BUN
ぶん
BUN (SHAKE)
I'M HE-EE-RE!!!!
...A MIGHTY SHOUT AND DYNAMIC HEAD SHAKING.
EMPEROR PENGUIN PARENTS AND CHICKS MAINLY RELY ON THEIR VOICES TO IDENTIFY ONE ANOTHER, BUT THERE'S ALSO A MEANING TO THIS MOTION.
ピルルル
PIRURURU (SHAKE)
ピルルル
PIRURURU
THEY UTILIZE THE CHARACTERISTIC BLACK AND WHITE COLORS OF THEIR FACES TO ASSERT THEMSELVES TO THEIR PARENTS.

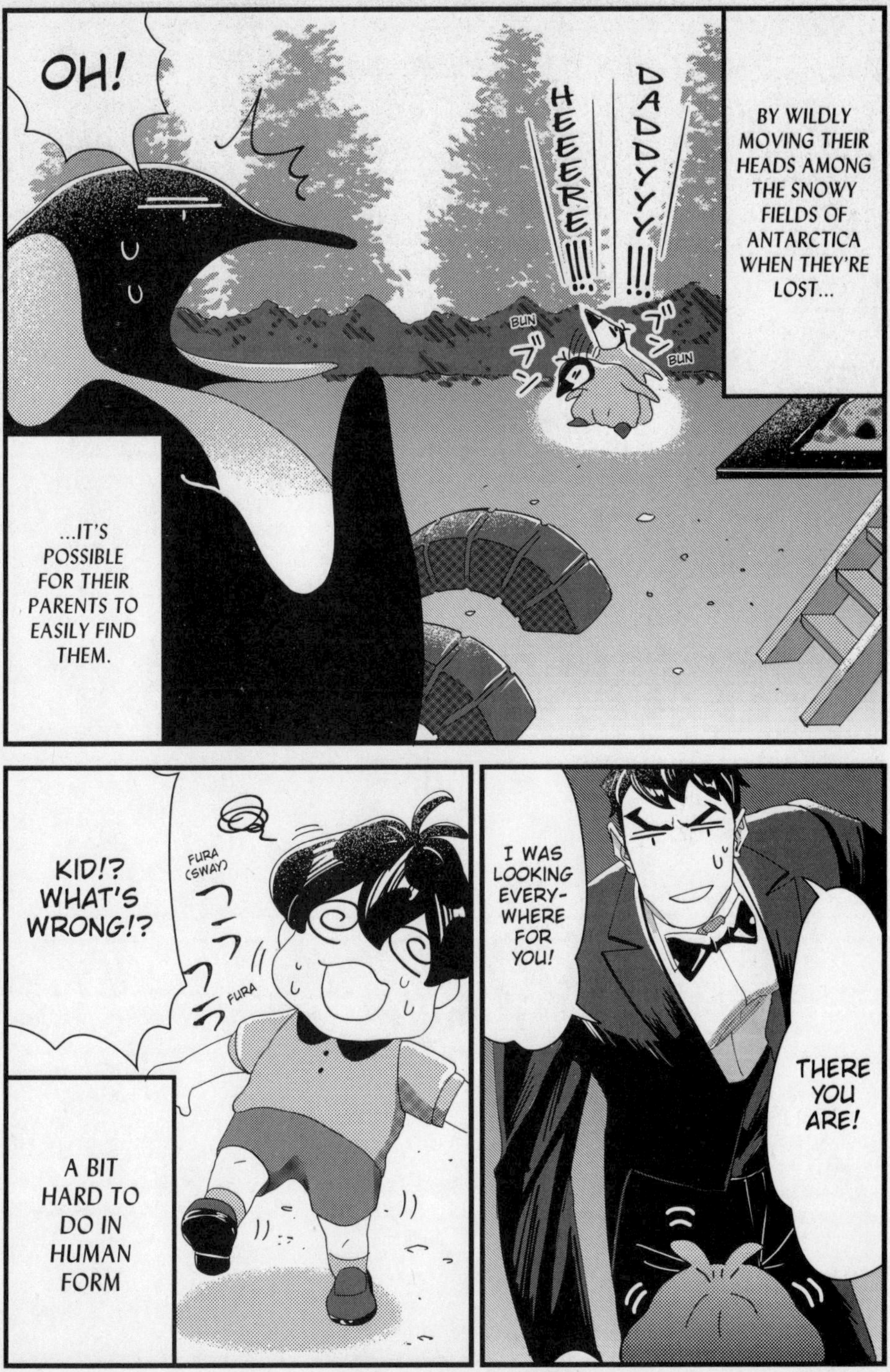
BY WILDLY MOVING THEIR HEADS AMONG THE SNOWY FIELDS OF ANTARCTICA WHEN THEY'RE LOST...
DADDYYY!!!
HEEEERE!!!
BUN
BUN
OH!
...IT'S POSSIBLE FOR THEIR PARENTS TO EASILY FIND THEM.
I WAS LOOKING EVERY-WHERE FOR YOU!
THERE YOU ARE!
KID!? WHAT'S WRONG!?
FURA (SWAY)
FURA
A BIT HARD TO DO IN HUMAN FORM

THEY ALSO DO THIS MOTION WHEN THEY'RE HUNGRY. —ADÉLIE

♦ Nursery School ① ♦

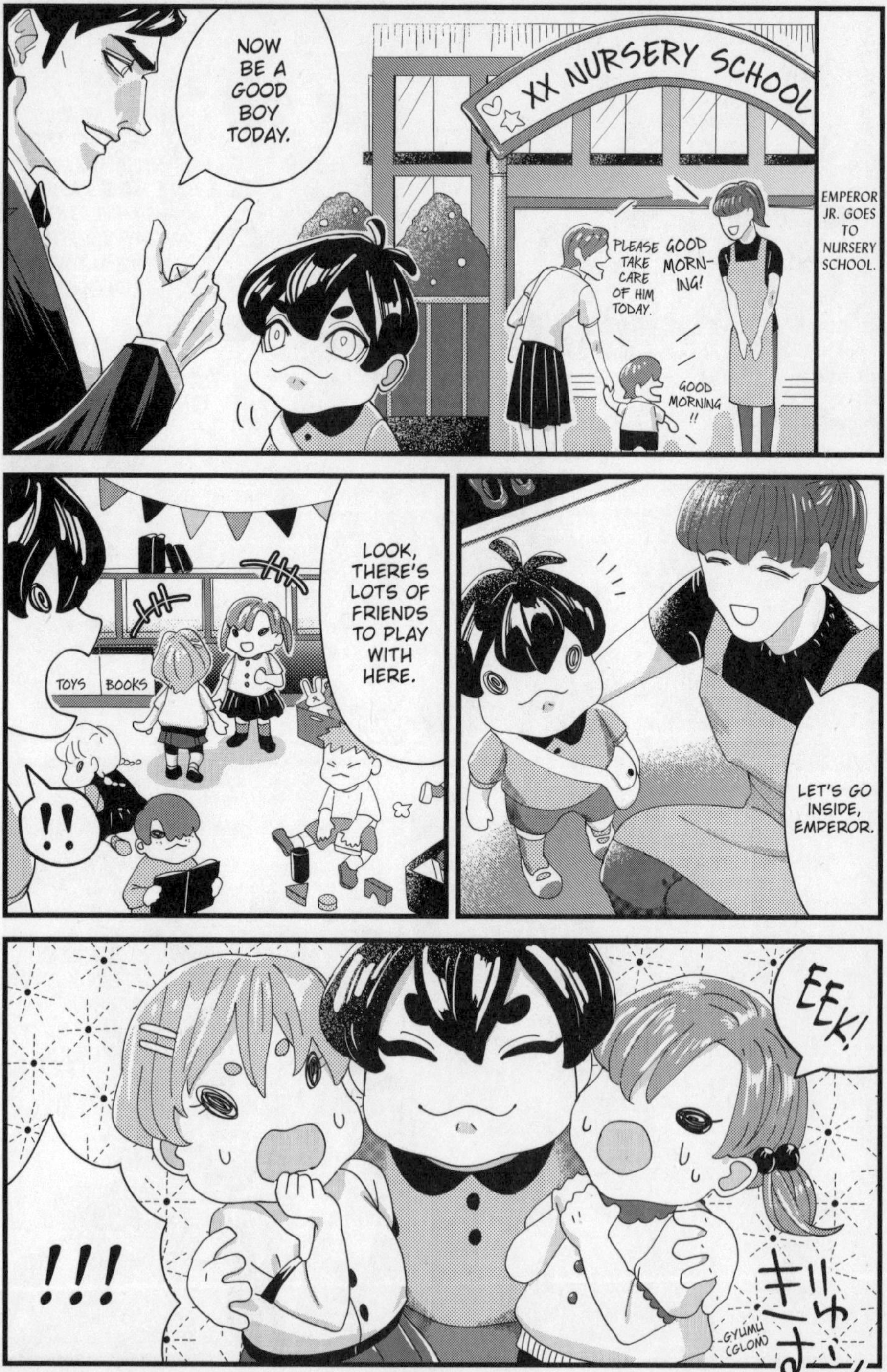

EMPEROR JR. GOES TO NURSERY SCHOOL.
XX NURSERY SCHOOL
GOOD MORNING!
PLEASE TAKE CARE OF HIM TODAY.
GOOD MORNING !!
NOW BE A GOOD BOY TODAY.
LET'S GO INSIDE, EMPEROR.
LOOK, THERE'S LOTS OF FRIENDS TO PLAY WITH HERE.
TOYS
BOOKS
!!
EEK!
GYUMU (GLOMP)
!!!

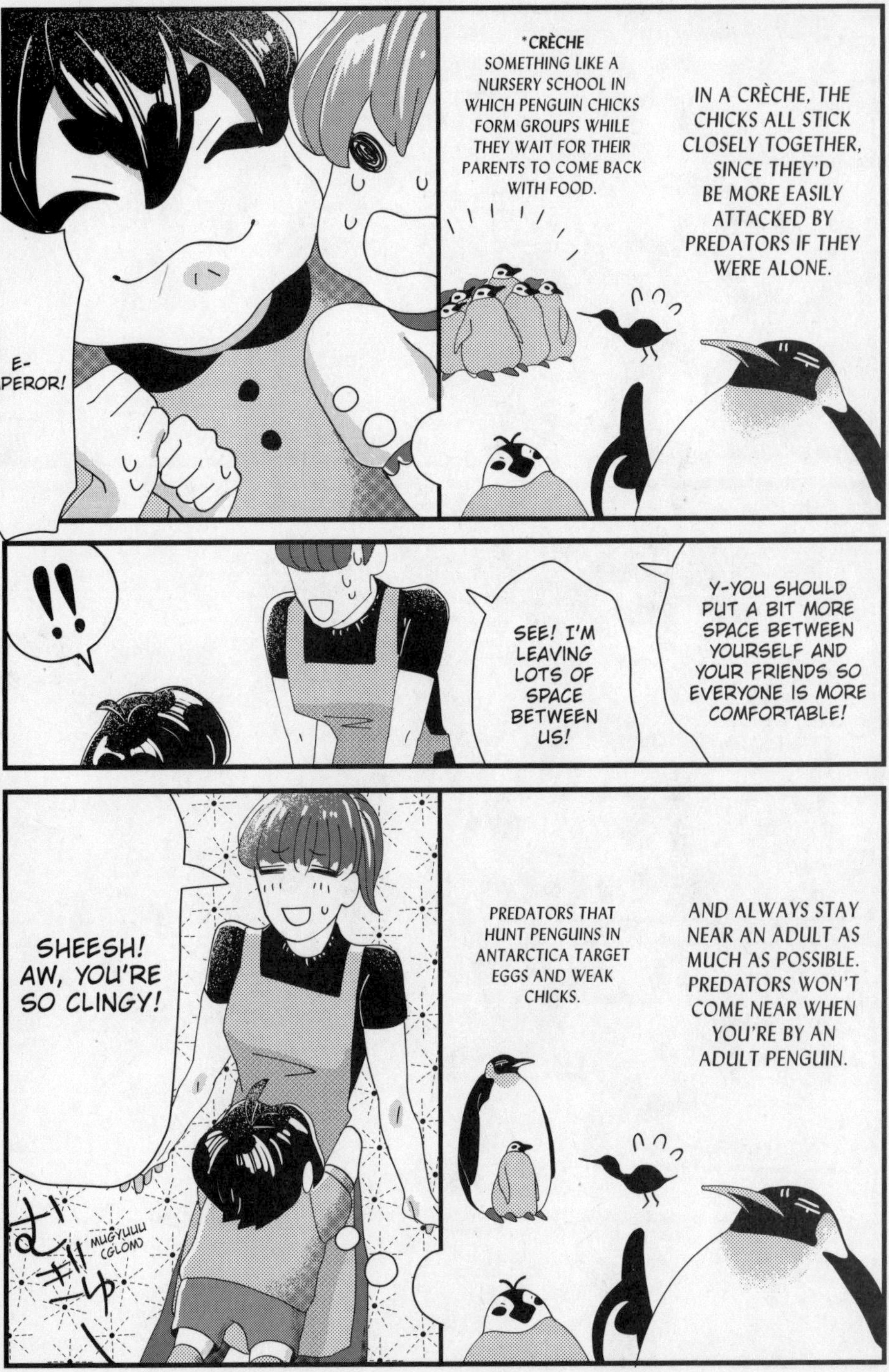
*CRÈCHE
SOMETHING LIKE A NURSERY SCHOOL IN WHICH PENGUIN CHICKS FORM GROUPS WHILE THEY WAIT FOR THEIR PARENTS TO COME BACK WITH FOOD.
IN A CRÈCHE, THE CHICKS ALL STICK CLOSELY TOGETHER, SINCE THEY'D BE MORE EASILY ATTACKED BY PREDATORS IF THEY WERE ALONE.
E-EMPEROR!
Y-YOU SHOULD PUT A BIT MORE SPACE BETWEEN YOURSELF AND YOUR FRIENDS SO EVERYONE IS MORE COMFORTABLE!
SEE! I'M LEAVING LOTS OF SPACE BETWEEN US!
!!
AND ALWAYS STAY NEAR AN ADULT AS MUCH AS POSSIBLE. PREDATORS WON'T COME NEAR WHEN YOU'RE BY AN ADULT PENGUIN.
PREDATORS THAT HUNT PENGUINS IN ANTARCTICA TARGET EGGS AND WEAK CHICKS.
SHEESH! AW, YOU'RE SO CLINGY!
むぎゅ
MUGYUUU (GLOM)

"CRÈCHE" COMES FROM THE FRENCH WORD FOR NURSERY. —EMPEROR

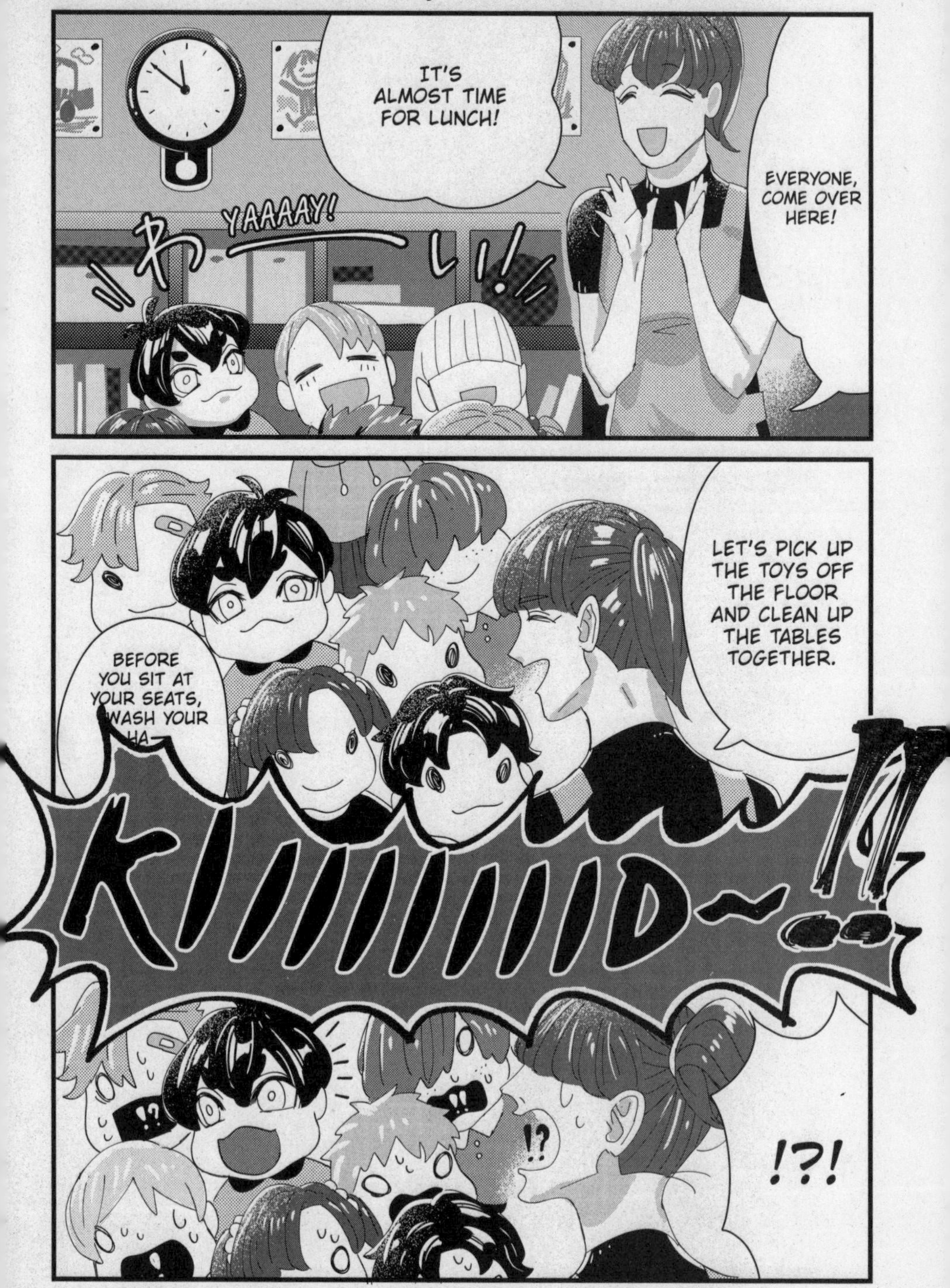
EVERYONE, COME OVER HERE!
IT'S ALMOST TIME FOR LUNCH!
YAAAAY!
LET'S PICK UP THE TOYS OFF THE FLOOR AND CLEAN UP THE TABLES TOGETHER.
BEFORE YOU SIT AT YOUR SEATS, WASH YOUR HA—
KIIIIIIIID~!!
!?!
!?
!?

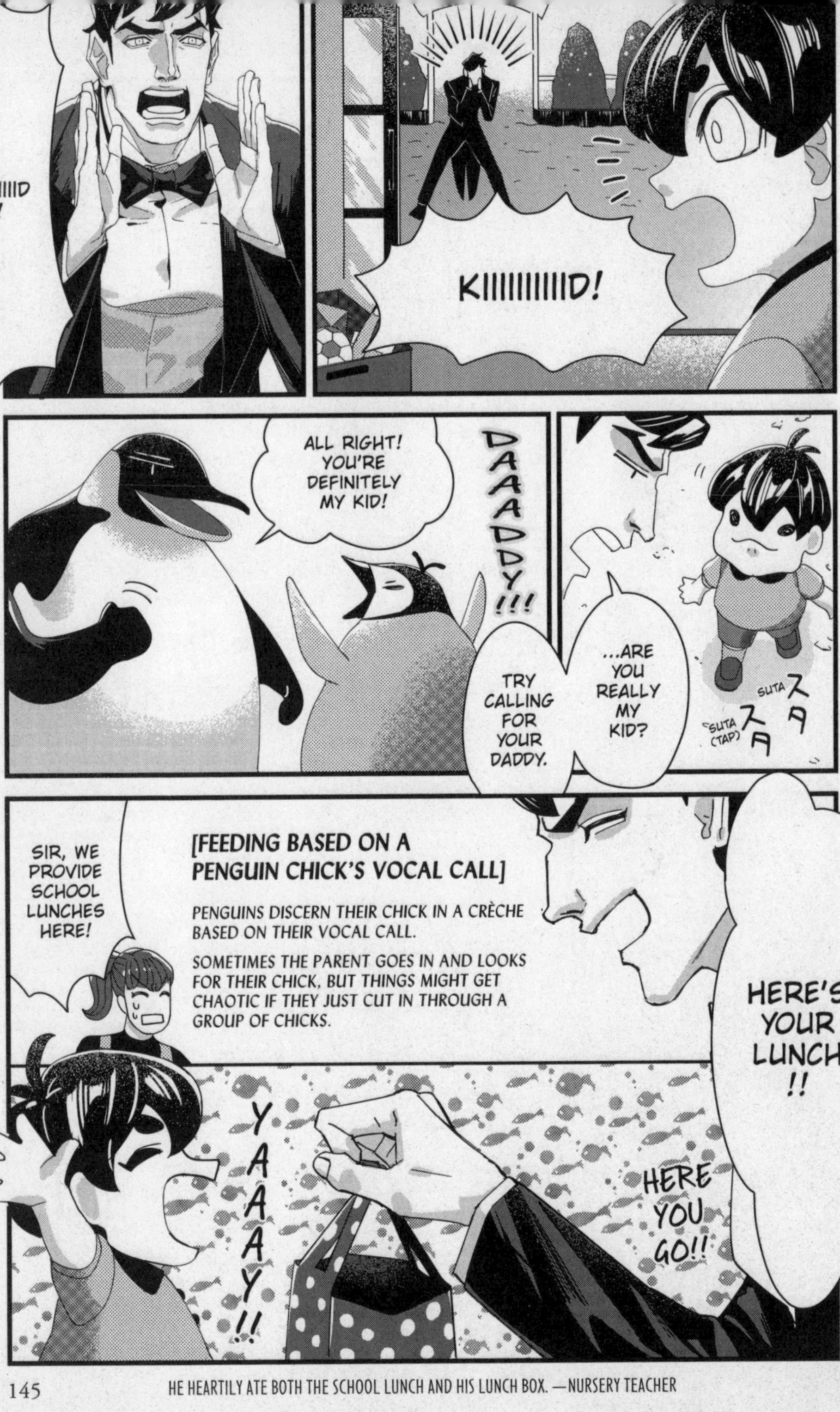
KIIIIIIIIIID!
KIIIIIID !
...ARE YOU REALLY MY KID?
TRY CALLING FOR YOUR DADDY.
SUTA スタ
SUTA スタ (TAP)
DAAAADDY!!!
ALL RIGHT! YOU'RE DEFINITELY MY KID!
HERE'S YOUR LUNCH!!
[FEEDING BASED ON A PENGUIN CHICK'S VOCAL CALL]
PENGUINS DISCERN THEIR CHICK IN A CRÈCHE BASED ON THEIR VOCAL CALL.
SOMETIMES THE PARENT GOES IN AND LOOKS FOR THEIR CHICK, BUT THINGS MIGHT GET CHAOTIC IF THEY JUST CUT IN THROUGH A GROUP OF CHICKS.
SIR, WE PROVIDE SCHOOL LUNCHES HERE!
HERE YOU GO!!
YAAAAY!!

HE HEARTILY ATE BOTH THE SCHOOL LUNCH AND HIS LUNCH BOX. —NURSERY TEACHER

♦ Signs of Becoming a Fledgling ♦

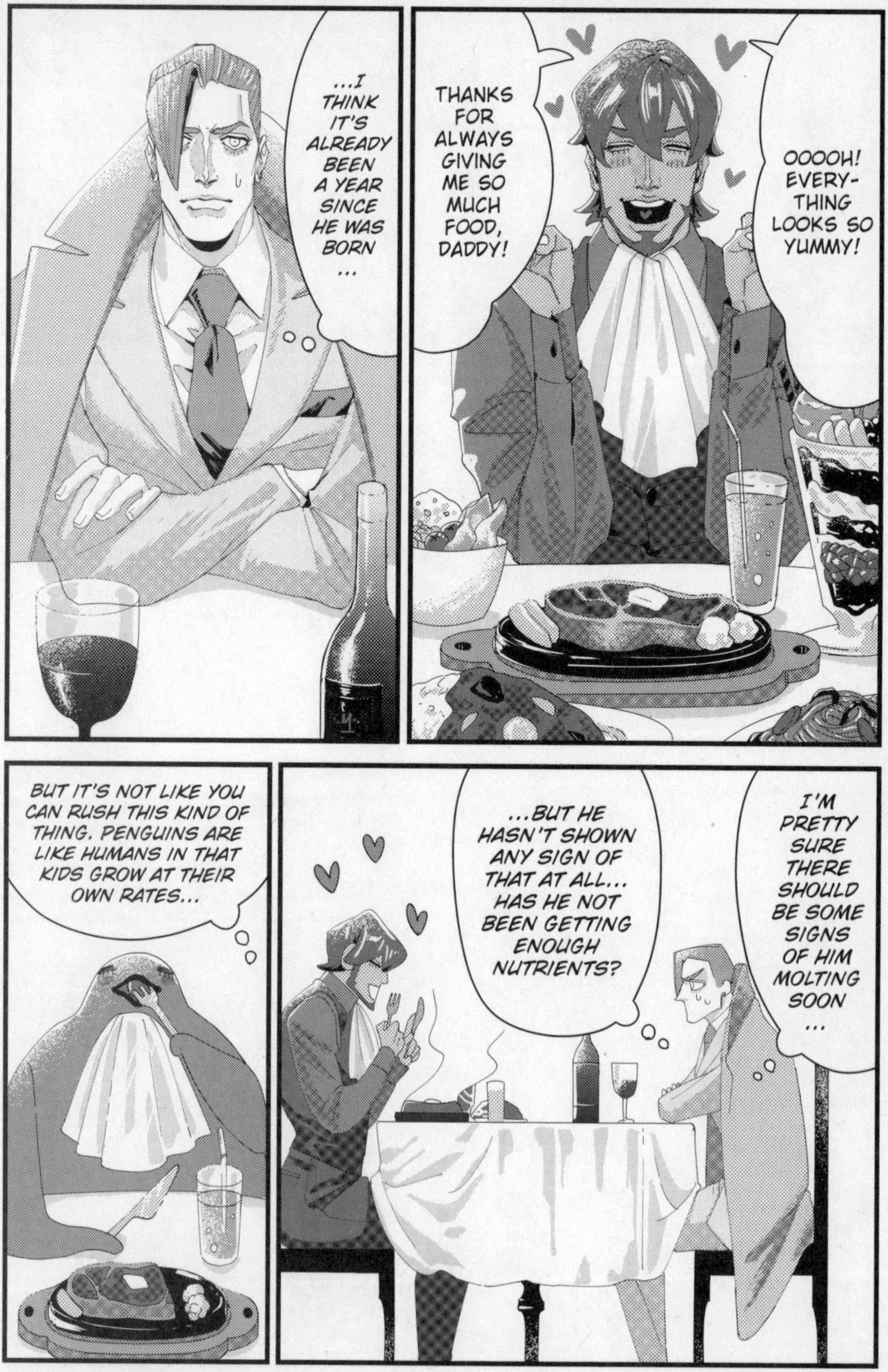
OOOOH! EVERY-THING LOOKS SO YUMMY!
THANKS FOR ALWAYS GIVING ME SO MUCH FOOD, DADDY!
...I THINK IT'S ALREADY BEEN A YEAR SINCE HE WAS BORN...
I'M PRETTY SURE THERE SHOULD BE SOME SIGNS OF HIM MOLTING SOON...
...BUT HE HASN'T SHOWN ANY SIGN OF THAT AT ALL... HAS HE NOT BEEN GETTING ENOUGH NUTRIENTS?
BUT IT'S NOT LIKE YOU CAN RUSH THIS KIND OF THING. PENGUINS ARE LIKE HUMANS IN THAT KIDS GROW AT THEIR OWN RATES...

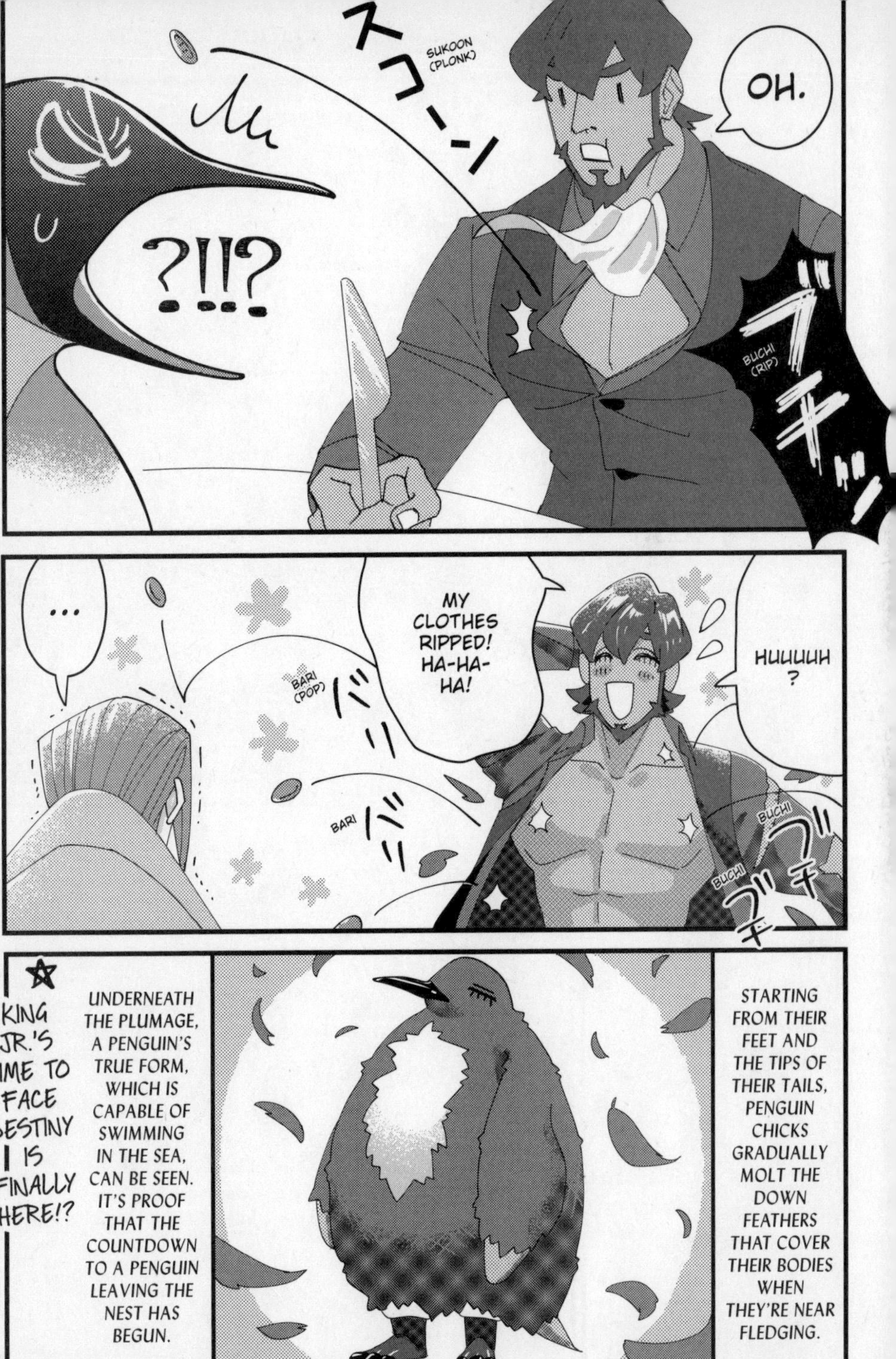

SUKOON (PLONK)
OH.
?!!?
BUCHI (RIP)
HUUUUH?
MY CLOTHES RIPPED! HA-HA-HA!
...
BARI (POP)
BARI
BUCHI
BUCHI
STARTING FROM THEIR FEET AND THE TIPS OF THEIR TAILS, PENGUIN CHICKS GRADUALLY MOLT THE DOWN FEATHERS THAT COVER THEIR BODIES WHEN THEY'RE NEAR FLEDGING.
UNDERNEATH THE PLUMAGE, A PENGUIN'S TRUE FORM, WHICH IS CAPABLE OF SWIMMING IN THE SEA, CAN BE SEEN. IT'S PROOF THAT THE COUNTDOWN TO A PENGUIN LEAVING THE NEST HAS BEGUN.
KING JR.'S TIME TO FACE DESTINY IS FINALLY HERE!?

NAH...IT'S AN EXAGGERATION TO CALL IT DESTINY. —KING

♦ All Grown Up ♦

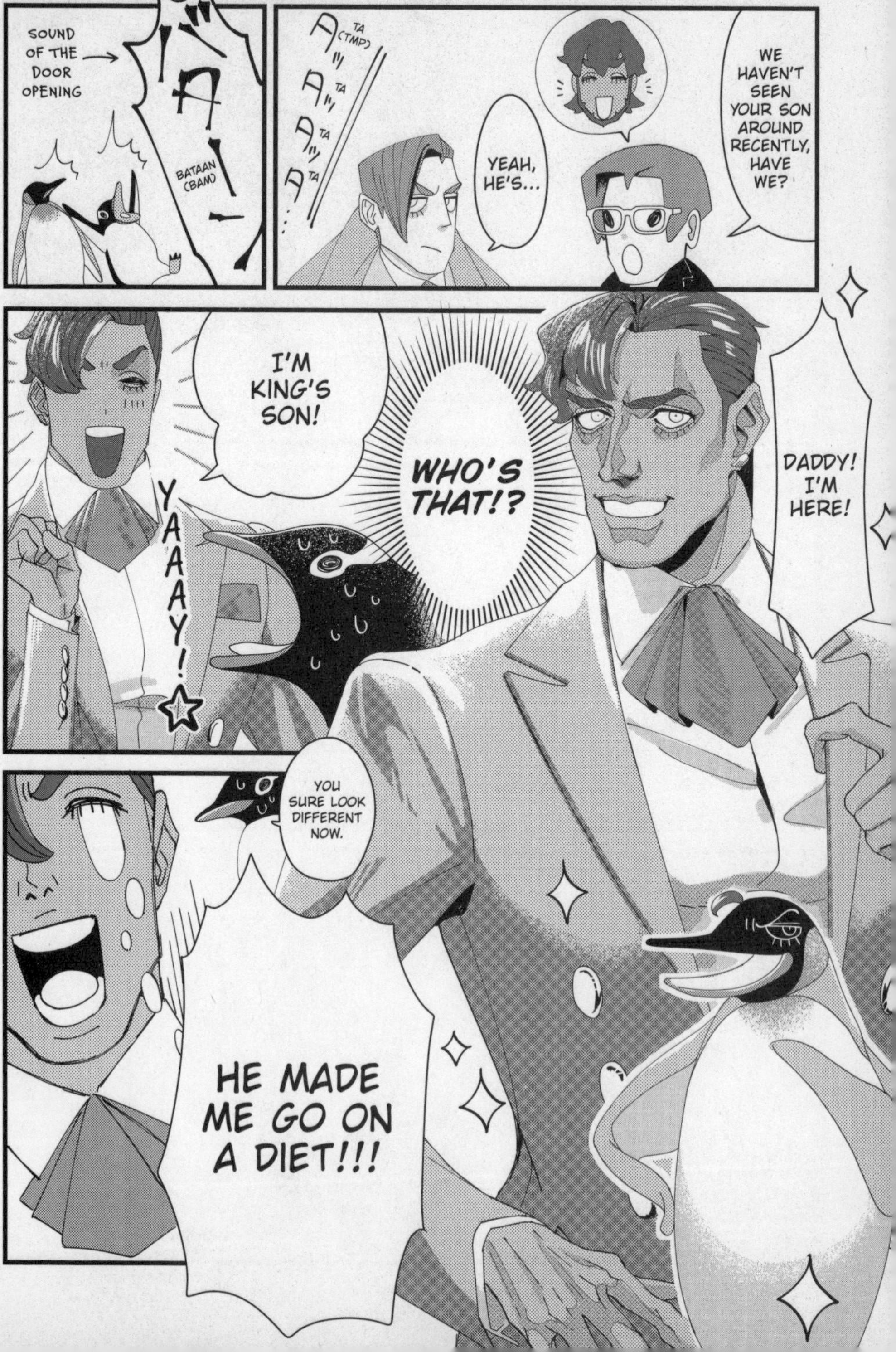

WE HAVEN'T SEEN YOUR SON AROUND RECENTLY, HAVE WE?
YEAH, HE'S...
TA (TMP) TA TA TA TA
SOUND OF THE DOOR OPENING
BATAAN (BAM)
DADDY! I'M HERE!
WHO'S THAT!?
I'M KING'S SON!
YAAAY!
YOU SURE LOOK DIFFERENT NOW.
HE MADE ME GO ON A DIET!!!

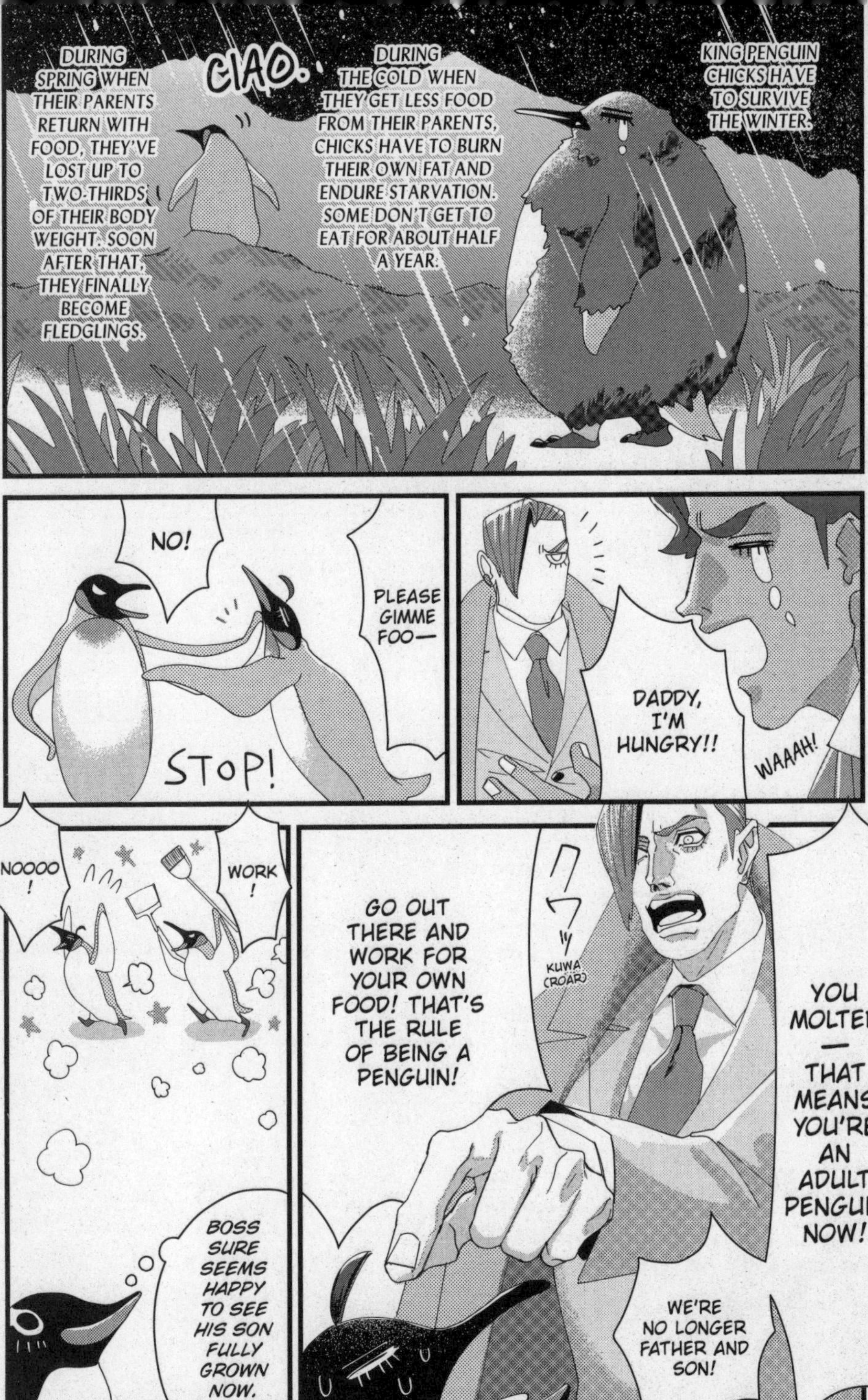

KING PENGUIN CHICKS HAVE TO SURVIVE THE WINTER.
DURING THE COLD WHEN THEY GET LESS FOOD FROM THEIR PARENTS, CHICKS HAVE TO BURN THEIR OWN FAT AND ENDURE STARVATION. SOME DON'T GET TO EAT FOR ABOUT HALF A YEAR.
CIAO.
DURING SPRING WHEN THEIR PARENTS RETURN WITH FOOD, THEY'VE LOST UP TO TWO-THIRDS OF THEIR BODY WEIGHT. SOON AFTER THAT, THEY FINALLY BECOME FLEDGLINGS.
DADDY, I'M HUNGRY!!
WAAAH!
PLEASE GIMME FOO—
NO!
STOP!
YOU MOLTED — THAT MEANS YOU'RE AN ADULT PENGUIN NOW!
GO OUT THERE AND WORK FOR YOUR OWN FOOD! THAT'S THE RULE OF BEING A PENGUIN!
KUWA (ROAR)
WE'RE NO LONGER FATHER AND SON!
WORK!
NOOOO!
BOSS SURE SEEMS HAPPY TO SEE HIS SON FULLY GROWN NOW.

BUT RIGHTFULLY SPEAKING, I'M NOT AN ADULT BIRD YET! (MORE INFO IN THE NEXT CHAPTER) —KING JR.

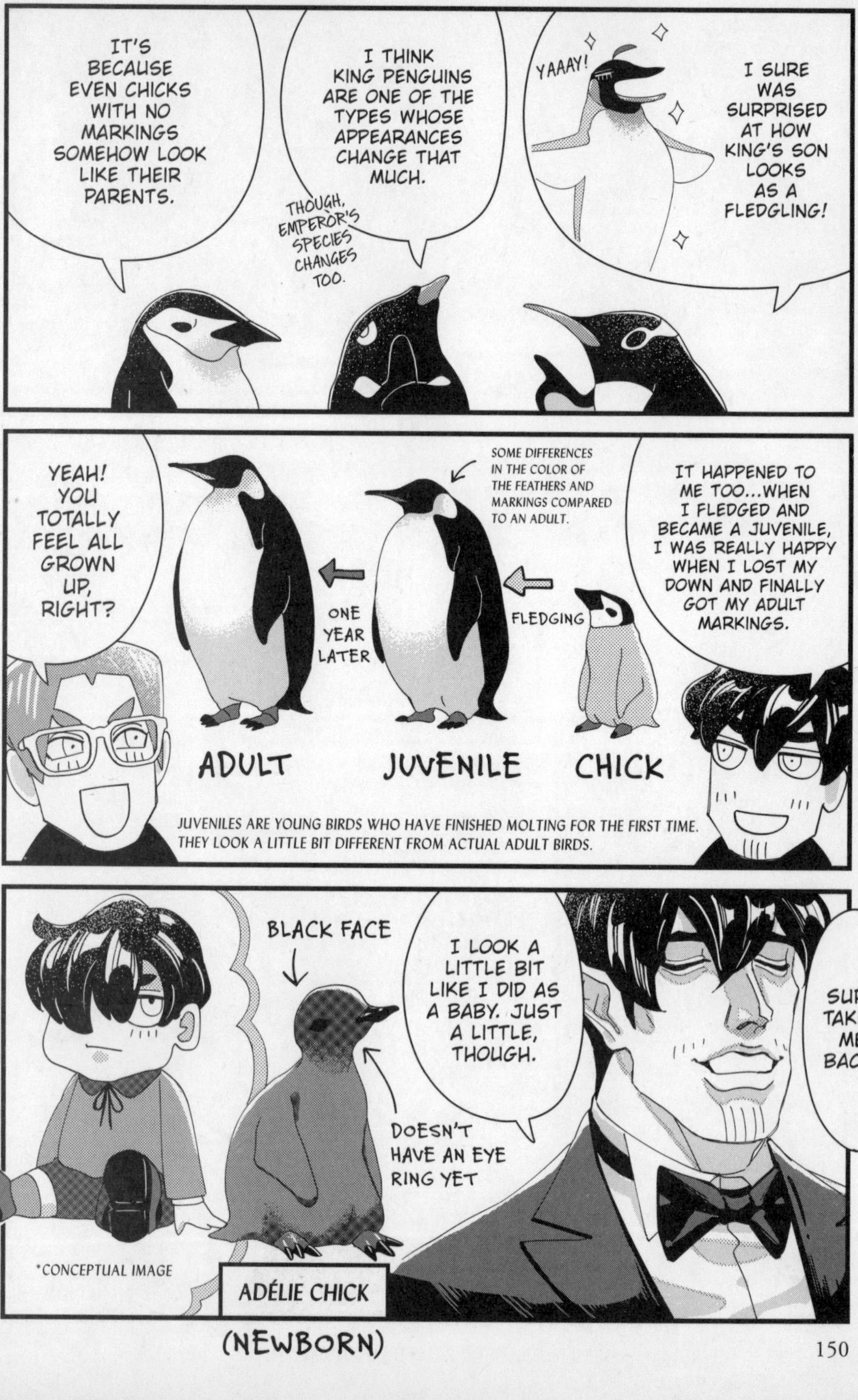
I SURE WAS SURPRISED AT HOW KING'S SON LOOKS AS A FLEDGLING!
YAAAY!
I THINK KING PENGUINS ARE ONE OF THE TYPES WHOSE APPEARANCES CHANGE THAT MUCH.
THOUGH, EMPEROR'S SPECIES CHANGES TOO.
IT'S BECAUSE EVEN CHICKS WITH NO MARKINGS SOMEHOW LOOK LIKE THEIR PARENTS.
IT HAPPENED TO ME TOO...WHEN I FLEDGED AND BECAME A JUVENILE, I WAS REALLY HAPPY WHEN I LOST MY DOWN AND FINALLY GOT MY ADULT MARKINGS.
SOME DIFFERENCES IN THE COLOR OF THE FEATHERS AND MARKINGS COMPARED TO AN ADULT.
FLEDGING
ONE YEAR LATER
ADULT
JUVENILE
CHICK
YEAH! YOU TOTALLY FEEL ALL GROWN UP, RIGHT?
JUVENILES ARE YOUNG BIRDS WHO HAVE FINISHED MOLTING FOR THE FIRST TIME. THEY LOOK A LITTLE BIT DIFFERENT FROM ACTUAL ADULT BIRDS.
SURE TAKES ME BACK.
I LOOK A LITTLE BIT LIKE I DID AS A BABY. JUST A LITTLE, THOUGH.
BLACK FACE
DOESN'T HAVE AN EYE RING YET
*CONCEPTUAL IMAGE
ADÉLIE CHICK
(NEWBORN)

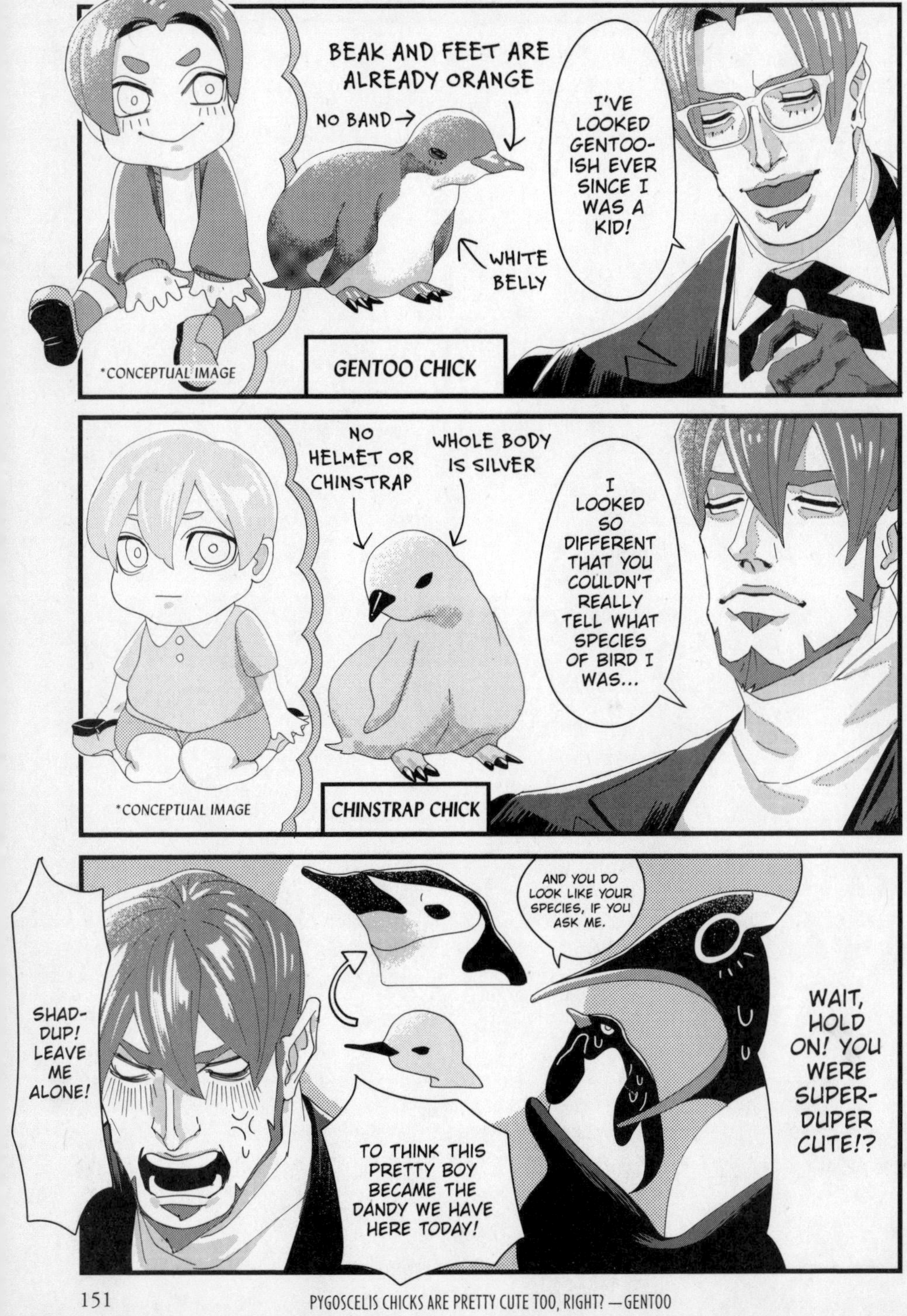
I'VE LOOKED GENTOO-ISH EVER SINCE I WAS A KID!
BEAK AND FEET ARE ALREADY ORANGE
NO BAND →
WHITE BELLY
GENTOO CHICK
*CONCEPTUAL IMAGE
I LOOKED SO DIFFERENT THAT YOU COULDN'T REALLY TELL WHAT SPECIES OF BIRD I WAS...
WHOLE BODY IS SILVER
NO HELMET OR CHINSTRAP
CHINSTRAP CHICK
*CONCEPTUAL IMAGE
WAIT, HOLD ON! YOU WERE SUPER-DUPER CUTE!?
AND YOU DO LOOK LIKE YOUR SPECIES, IF YOU ASK ME.
TO THINK THIS PRETTY BOY BECAME THE DANDY WE HAVE HERE TODAY!
SHAD-DUP! LEAVE ME ALONE!

PYGOSCELIS CHICKS ARE PRETTY CUTE TOO, RIGHT? —GENTOO

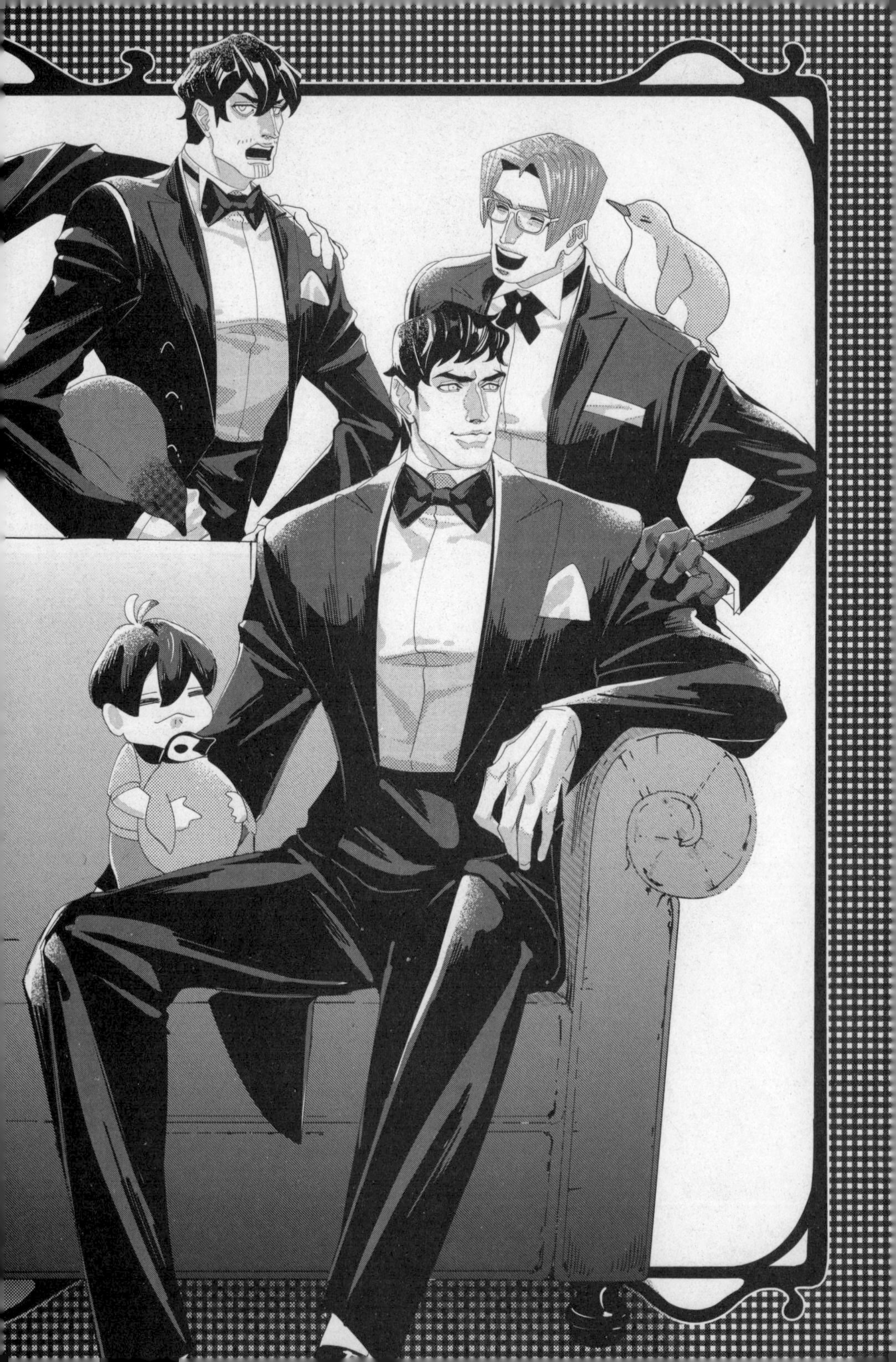

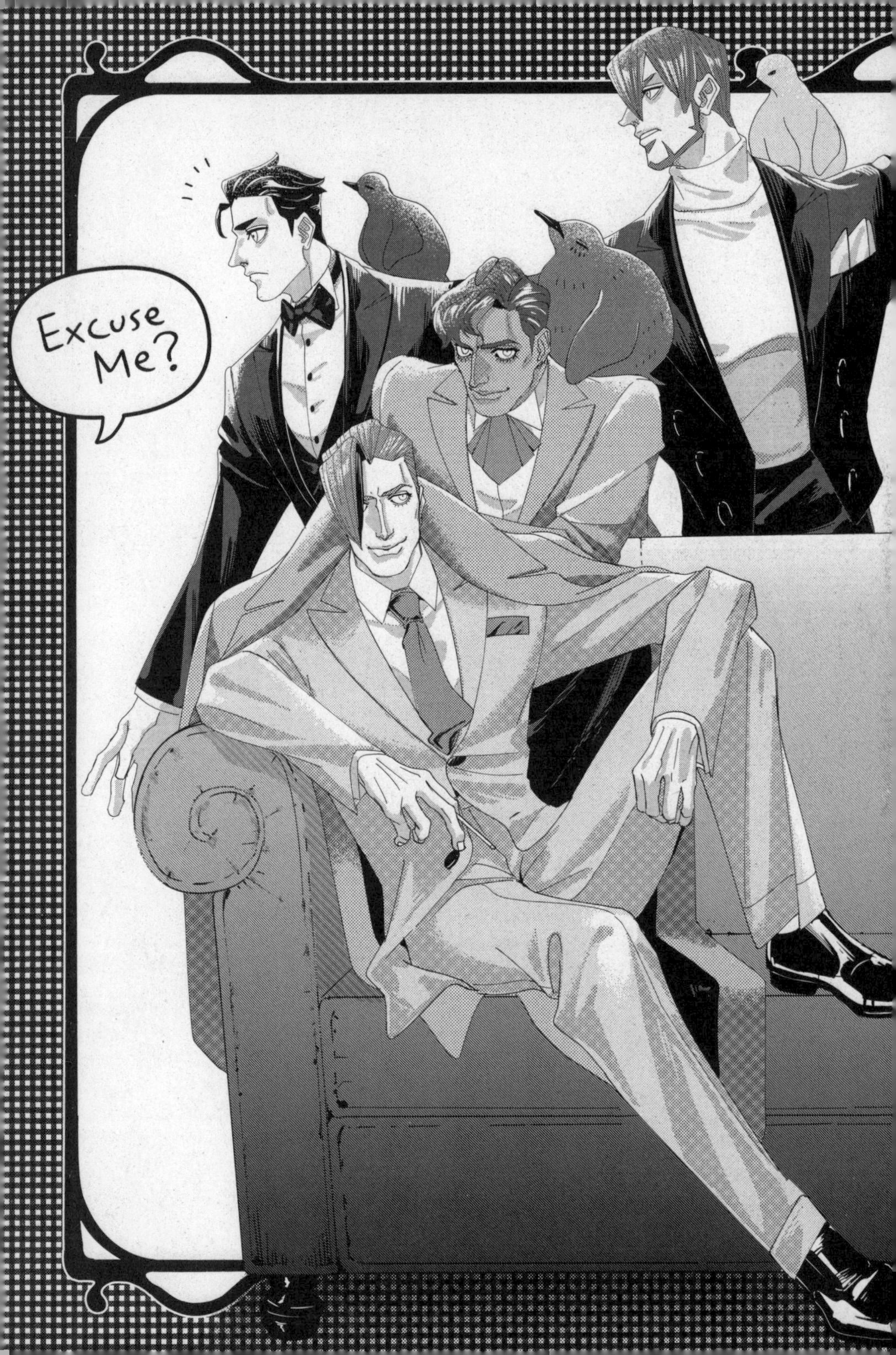
Excuse Me?

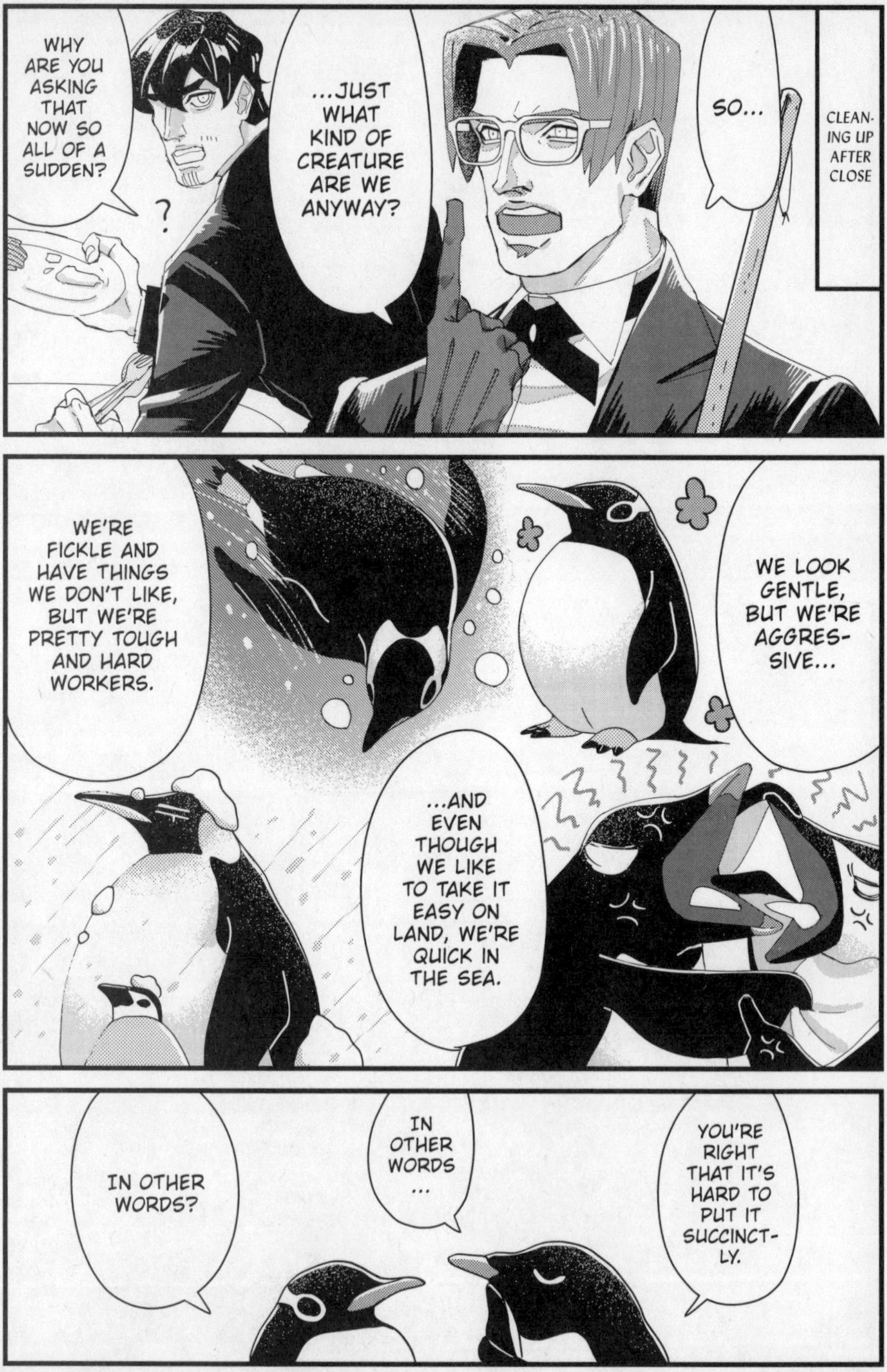
CLEANING UP AFTER CLOSE
SO...
...JUST WHAT KIND OF CREATURE ARE WE ANYWAY?
WHY ARE YOU ASKING THAT NOW SO ALL OF A SUDDEN?
?
WE LOOK GENTLE, BUT WE'RE AGGRESSIVE...
WE'RE FICKLE AND HAVE THINGS WE DON'T LIKE, BUT WE'RE PRETTY TOUGH AND HARD WORKERS.
...AND EVEN THOUGH WE LIKE TO TAKE IT EASY ON LAND, WE'RE QUICK IN THE SEA.
YOU'RE RIGHT THAT IT'S HARD TO PUT IT SUCCINCTLY.
IN OTHER WORDS...
IN OTHER WORDS?

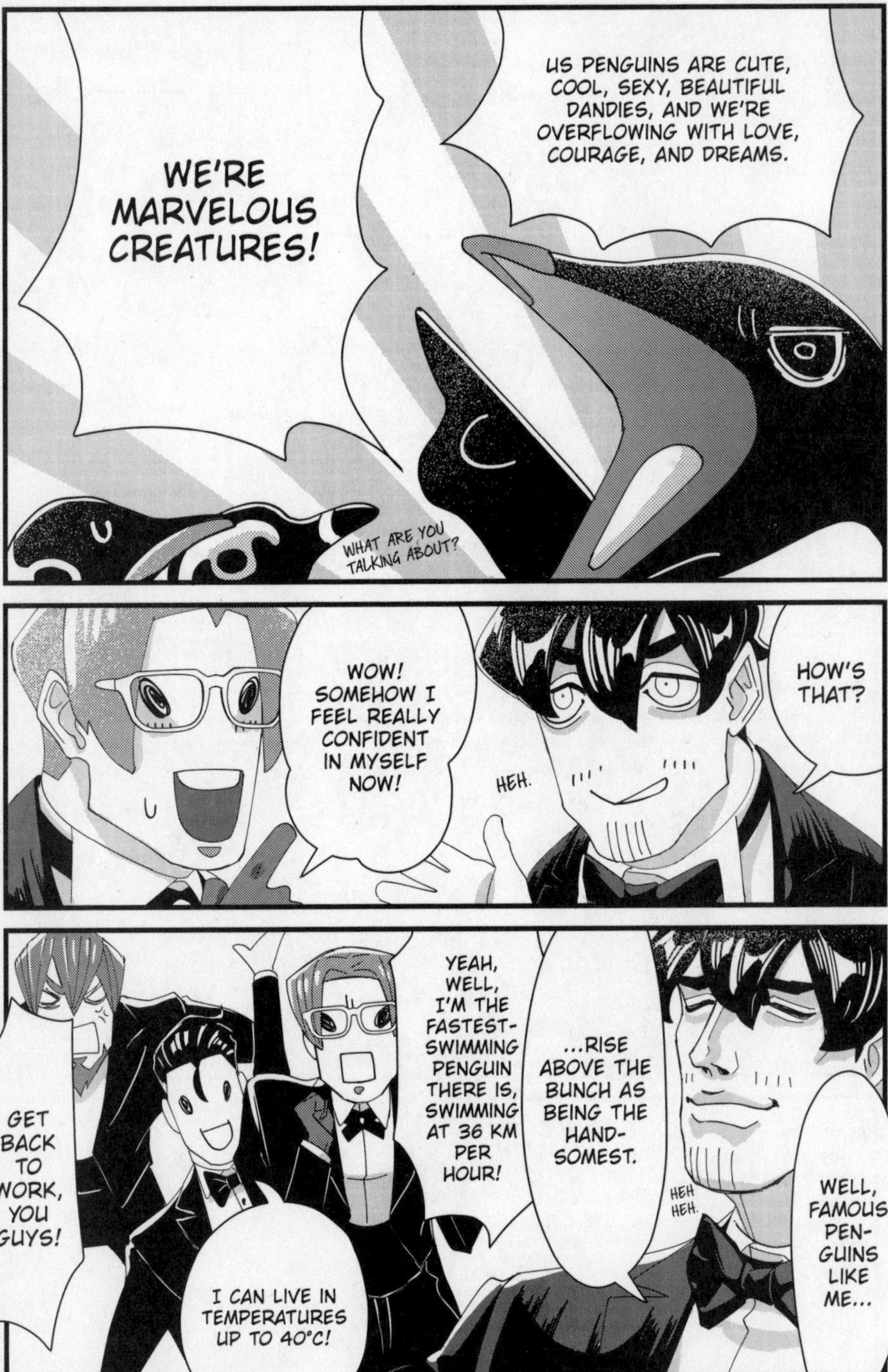
US PENGUINS ARE CUTE, COOL, SEXY, BEAUTIFUL DANDIES, AND WE'RE OVERFLOWING WITH LOVE, COURAGE, AND DREAMS.
WE'RE MARVELOUS CREATURES!
WHAT ARE YOU TALKING ABOUT?
HOW'S THAT?
HEH.
WOW! SOMEHOW I FEEL REALLY CONFIDENT IN MYSELF NOW!
WELL, FAMOUS PEN-GUINS LIKE ME...
HEH HEH.
...RISE ABOVE THE BUNCH AS BEING THE HAND-SOMEST.
YEAH, WELL, I'M THE FASTEST-SWIMMING PENGUIN THERE IS, SWIMMING AT 36 KM PER HOUR!
I CAN LIVE IN TEMPERATURES UP TO 40°C!
GET BACK TO WORK, YOU GUYS!

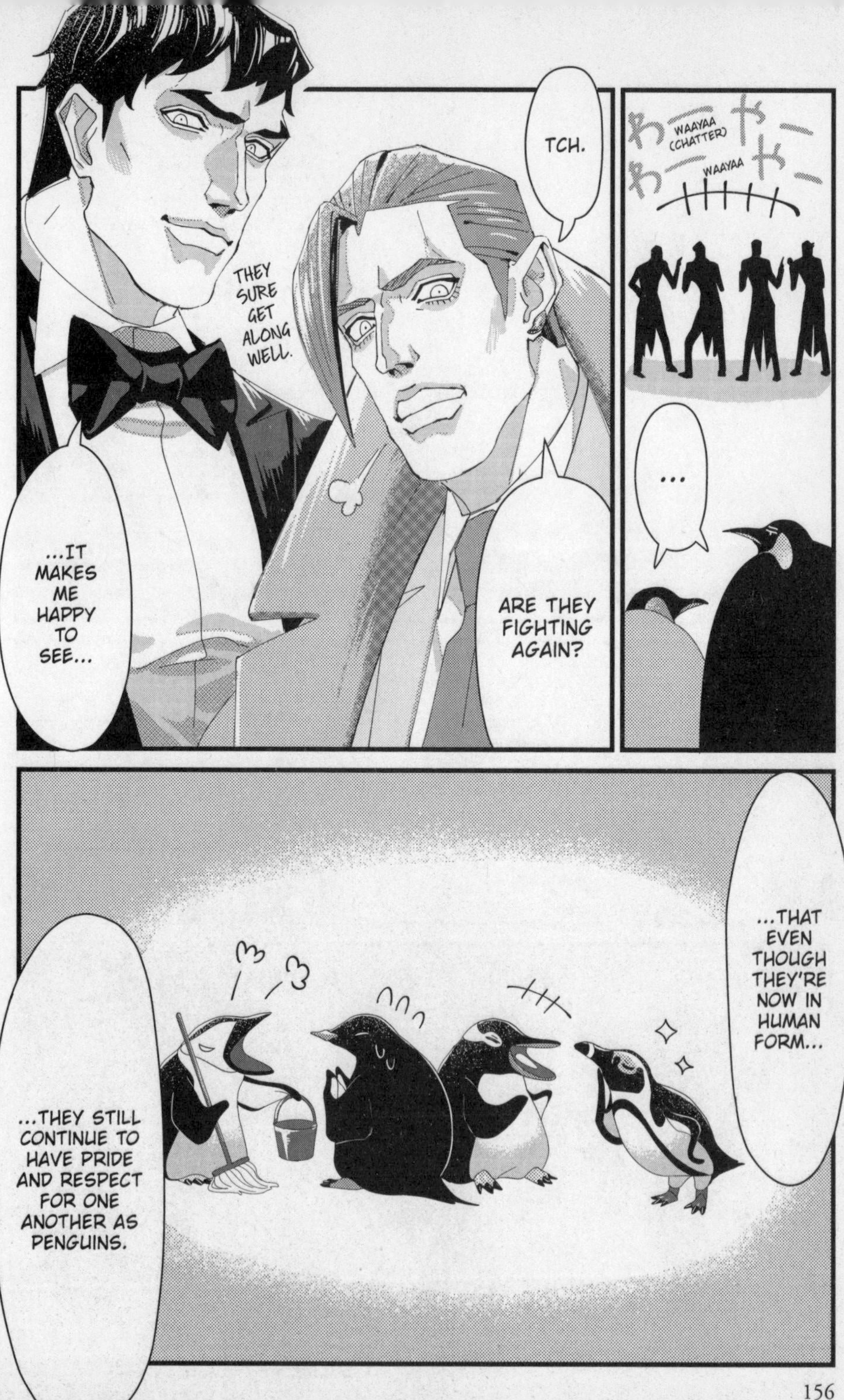

WAAYAA (CHATTER)
WAAYAA
...
TCH.
THEY SURE GET ALONG WELL.
ARE THEY FIGHTING AGAIN?
...IT MAKES ME HAPPY TO SEE...
...THAT EVEN THOUGH THEY'RE NOW IN HUMAN FORM...
...THEY STILL CONTINUE TO HAVE PRIDE AND RESPECT FOR ONE ANOTHER AS PENGUINS.

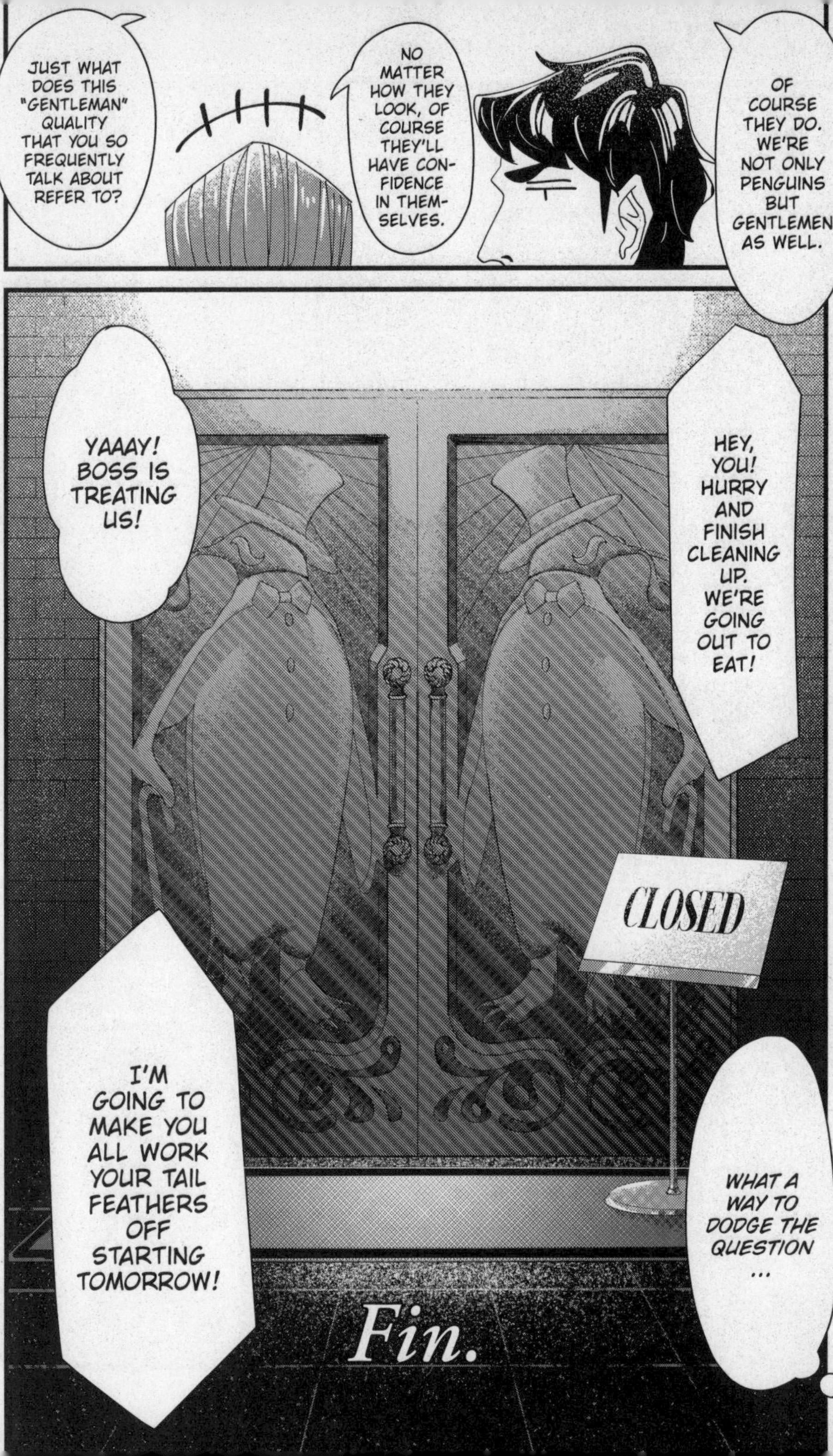
OF COURSE THEY DO. WE'RE NOT ONLY PENGUINS BUT GENTLEMEN AS WELL.
NO MATTER HOW THEY LOOK, OF COURSE THEY'LL HAVE CON-FIDENCE IN THEM-SELVES.
JUST WHAT DOES THIS "GENTLEMAN" QUALITY THAT YOU SO FREQUENTLY TALK ABOUT REFER TO?
HEY, YOU! HURRY AND FINISH CLEANING UP. WE'RE GOING OUT TO EAT!
YAAAY! BOSS IS TREATING US!
CLOSED
WHAT A WAY TO DODGE THE QUESTION ...
I'M GOING TO MAKE YOU ALL WORK YOUR TAIL FEATHERS OFF STARTING TOMORROW!
Fin.

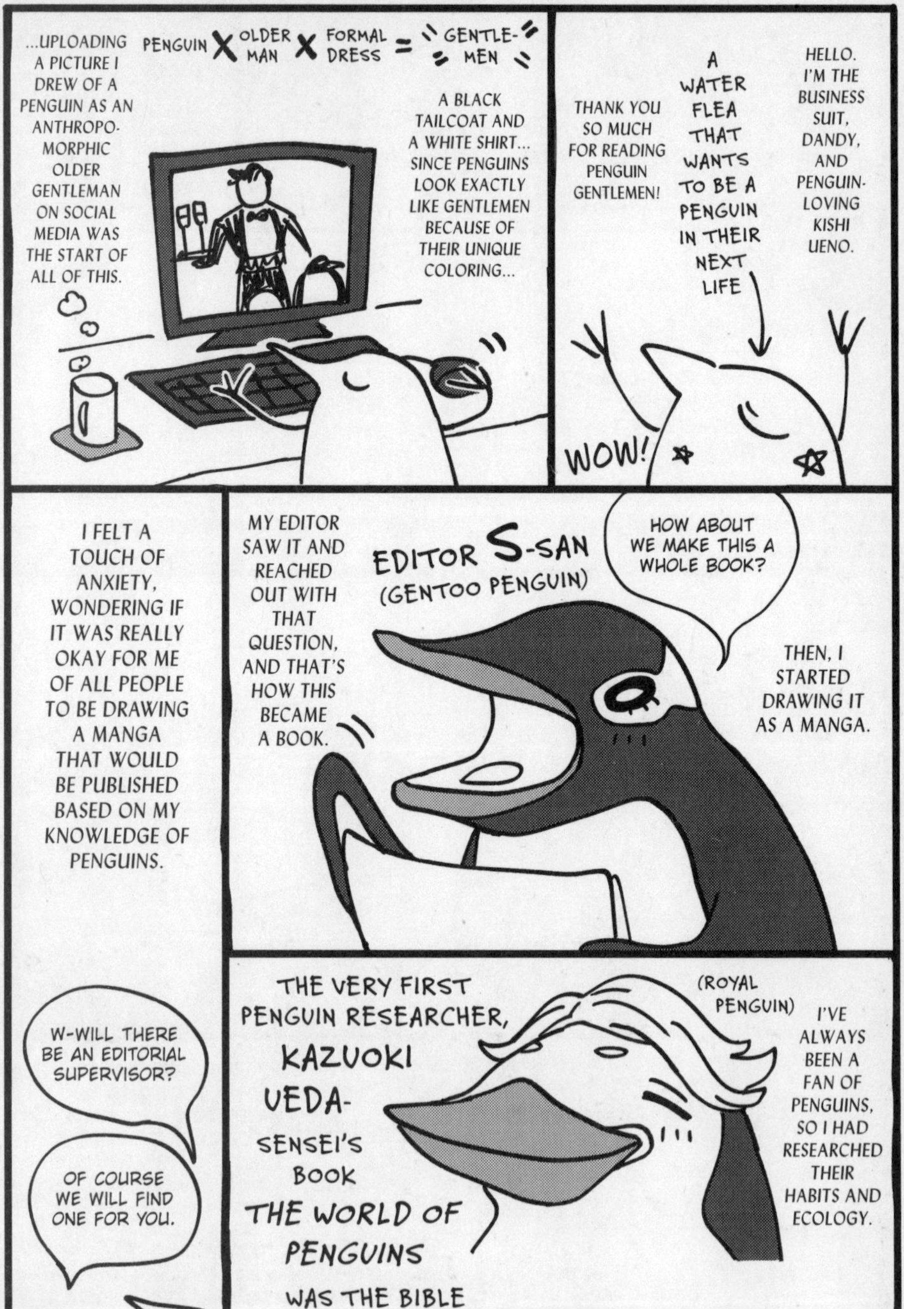
HELLO. I'M THE BUSINESS SUIT, DANDY, AND PENGUIN-LOVING KISHI UENO.
A WATER FLEA THAT WANTS TO BE A PENGUIN IN THEIR NEXT LIFE
THANK YOU SO MUCH FOR READING PENGUIN GENTLEMEN!
WOW!
PENGUIN X OLDER MAN X FORMAL DRESS = "GENTLEMEN"
A BLACK TAILCOAT AND A WHITE SHIRT... SINCE PENGUINS LOOK EXACTLY LIKE GENTLEMEN BECAUSE OF THEIR UNIQUE COLORING...
...UPLOADING A PICTURE I DREW OF A PENGUIN AS AN ANTHROPOMORPHIC OLDER GENTLEMAN ON SOCIAL MEDIA WAS THE START OF ALL OF THIS.
HOW ABOUT WE MAKE THIS A WHOLE BOOK?
THEN, I STARTED DRAWING IT AS A MANGA.
EDITOR S-SAN (GENTOO PENGUIN)
MY EDITOR SAW IT AND REACHED OUT WITH THAT QUESTION, AND THAT'S HOW THIS BECAME A BOOK.
(ROYAL PENGUIN)
I'VE ALWAYS BEEN A FAN OF PENGUINS, SO I HAD RESEARCHED THEIR HABITS AND ECOLOGY.
THE VERY FIRST PENGUIN RESEARCHER, KAZUOKI UEDA-SENSEI'S BOOK THE WORLD OF PENGUINS WAS THE BIBLE THAT LED ME DOWN THE ROAD TO BECOMING A PENGUIN FAN!!!
I FELT A TOUCH OF ANXIETY, WONDERING IF IT WAS REALLY OKAY FOR ME OF ALL PEOPLE TO BE DRAWING A MANGA THAT WOULD BE PUBLISHED BASED ON MY KNOWLEDGE OF PENGUINS.
W-WILL THERE BE AN EDITORIAL SUPERVISOR?
OF COURSE WE WILL FIND ONE FOR YOU.

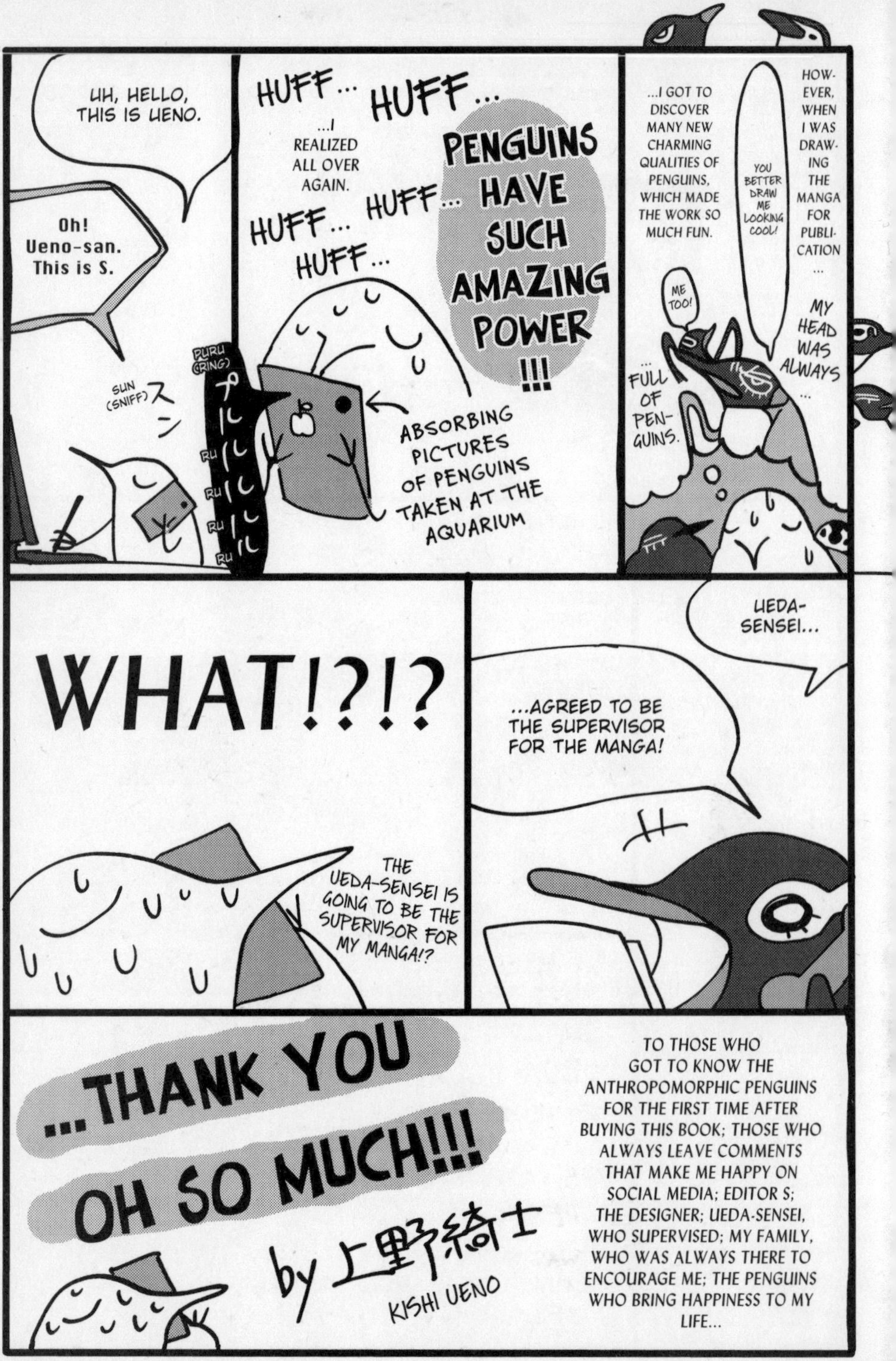
HOW-EVER, WHEN I WAS DRAW-ING THE MANGA FOR PUBLI-CATION...
...I GOT TO DISCOVER MANY NEW CHARMING QUALITIES OF PENGUINS, WHICH MADE THE WORK SO MUCH FUN.
YOU BETTER DRAW ME LOOKING COOL!
ME TOO!
MY HEAD WAS ALWAYS...
...FULL OF PEN-GUINS.
HUFF... HUFF...
...I REALIZED ALL OVER AGAIN.
HUFF... HUFF... HUFF...
HUFF...
PENGUINS HAVE SUCH AMAZING POWER!!!
ABSORBING PICTURES OF PENGUINS TAKEN AT THE AQUARIUM
PURU (RING) プルルルル RU RU RU RU
UH, HELLO, THIS IS UENO.
Oh! Ueno-san. This is S.
SUN (SNIFF) スン
UEDA-SENSEI...
...AGREED TO BE THE SUPERVISOR FOR THE MANGA!
WHAT!?!?
THE UEDA-SENSEI IS GOING TO BE THE SUPERVISOR FOR MY MANGA!?
TO THOSE WHO GOT TO KNOW THE ANTHROPOMORPHIC PENGUINS FOR THE FIRST TIME AFTER BUYING THIS BOOK; THOSE WHO ALWAYS LEAVE COMMENTS THAT MAKE ME HAPPY ON SOCIAL MEDIA; EDITOR S; THE DESIGNER; UEDA-SENSEI, WHO SUPERVISED; MY FAMILY, WHO WAS ALWAYS THERE TO ENCOURAGE ME; THE PENGUINS WHO BRING HAPPINESS TO MY LIFE...
...THANK YOU OH SO MUCH!!!
by 上野綺士
KISHI UENO

Penguin Gentlemen

Kishi Ueno

Translation: JULIE GONIWICH ✦ Lettering: BIANCA PISTILLO

This book is a work of fiction. Names, characters, places, and incidents are the product of the author's imagination or are used fictitiously. Any resemblance to actual events, locales, or persons, living or dead, is coincidental.

PENGIN SHINSHI.
© Kishi Ueno 2020
First published in Japan in 2020 by KADOKAWA CORPORATION, Tokyo.
English translation rights arranged with KADOKAWA CORPORATION, Tokyo through TUTTLE-MORI AGENCY, INC., Tokyo.

English translation © 2021 by Yen Press, LLC

Yen Press, LLC supports the right to free expression and the value of copyright. The purpose of copyright is to encourage writers and artists to produce the creative works that enrich our culture.

The scanning, uploading, and distribution of this book without permission is a theft of the author's intellectual property. If you would like permission to use material from the book (other than for review purposes), please contact the publisher. Thank you for your support of the author's rights.

Yen Press
150 West 30th Street, 19th Floor
New York, NY 10001

Visit us at yenpress.com ✦ facebook.com/yenpress ✦ twitter.com/yenpress
yenpress.tumblr.com ✦ instagram.com/yenpress

First Yen Press Edition: February 2021

Yen Press is an imprint of Yen Press, LLC.
The Yen Press name and logo are trademarks of Yen Press, LLC.

The publisher is not responsible for websites (or their content) that are not owned by the publisher.

Library of Congress Control Number: 2020950223

ISBNs: 978-1-9753-2068-3 (hardcover)
       978-1-9753-2069-0 (ebook)

10 9 8 7 6 5 4 3 2 1

WOR

Printed in the United States of America

KISHI UENO

Manga artist and illustrator. Likes business suits, dandies, and penguins. Has always had a special fondness for penguins ever since they were little and got to know them better at the aquarium and the zoo.

Twitter: @reisei_zero

APR 2021